The State and Labor
in Modern Japan

The State and Labor in Modern Japan

Sheldon Garon

UNIVERSITY OF CALIFORNIA PRESS
Berkeley · *Los Angeles* · *London*

University of California Press
Berkeley and Los Angeles, California

University of California Press, Ltd.
London, England

Parts of the epilogue of this book appeared in an article entitled "The Imperial Bureaucracy and Labor Policy in Postwar Japan," in *Journal of Asian Studies* 43
(May 1984): 441–57. © Association for Asian Studies. Printed by permission.

Library of Congress Cataloging-in-Publication Data

Garon, Sheldon M.
    The state and labor in modern Japan.

    Bibliography: p.
    Includes index.
    1. Industrial relations—Japan—History.
2. Industrial relations—Government policy—Japan
History.   I. Title.
HD8726.G37   1988   331′.0952   86-30890
ISBN 0-520-05983-2 (alk. paper)
ISBN 0-520-06838-6 (ppk.)

Printed in the United States of America

1 2 3 4 5 6 7 8 9

Contents

Tables

Note on Japanese Names

I have followed the practice of rendering Japanese names in accordance with Japanese custom, the family name preceding the personal name. The names of Americans of Japanese ancestry and of Japanese who have authored English-language works have been cited with the personal name first. Macrons in Japanese words have been omitted in the case of the well-known place names—Tōkyō, Ōsaka, Kyōto, Kōbe, Kyūshū, and Hokkaidō—when they appear in the text, in translations of Japanese titles and organizations, or as places of publication.

Acknowledgments

This book owes much to the assistance of several individuals and institutions. I am particularly grateful to James Crowley, who has profoundly influenced my approach to Japanese history since his days as my dissertation advisor. I cannot begin to thank my friend Andrew Gordon for graciously sharing his extensive knowledge of Japanese labor history in the course of the last ten years. Gary Allinson, Marius Jansen, Chalmers Johnson, and Byron Marshall have been invaluable critics throughout the process of revising the manuscript. This work has additionally benefited from the comments of Martin Collcutt, John W. Hall, Thomas Havens, Richard Smethurst, Stanley Stein, Robert Tignor, Gordon Berger, Manfred Boemeke, Kent Calder, Miles Fletcher, Howell J. Harris, Sharon Minichiello, Mike Mochizuki, T. J. Pempel, Arthur Rosenbaum, and Frank M. Turner. My undergraduate assistant, Daniel Fuchs, put in long hours in the preparation of the manuscript, and his own research stimulated my thinking on recent developments in Japanese labor. Barbara Metcalf, Susan Stone, and their colleagues at The University of California Press are to be commended for their diligence in publishing this book.

I would also like to express my gratitude to the many people who assisted my research activities in Japan from 1977 to 1979. Special thanks go to Professor Itō Takashi of Tokyo University, whose insights significantly shaped the ideas in this book. I am equally indebted to my colleague Mikuriya Takashi of Tokyo Metropolitan University. Professor Mitani Taichirō assumed responsibility for securing my affiliation with the Faculty of Law at Tokyo University. Professor Yui Masaomi kindly permitted me to participate in his seminar at Waseda University, where Utsumi Takashi and Fujino Yutaka introduced me to new approaches and documentation. Professor Nimura Kazuo guided me through the rich archives of the Ōhara Institute for Social Research, and Professor Nakamura Masanori of Hitotsubashi University recommended the evocative illustration found on the cover. Lastly, I wish to thank Kitaoka Shin'ichi, Mizuno Reiko, and her father Kurokōchi Tōru for arranging interviews with a number of retired Home Ministry officials, whose recollections of prewar politics and policy were indispensable to my understanding of the role of the bureaucracy.

Research in Japan would not have been possible without generous grants from the Japan Foundation, the Social Science Research Council, and the Inter-University Center for Japanese Studies in Tokyo. Princeton University's award of a Mellon Preceptorship funded the leave devoted to completing this study.

If any one person deserves credit for the publication of this book, it is my wife and fellow historian, Sherrill Cohen. She did more than sustain my spirits over the past five years. The dialectic is no stranger to our home, as many an evening was spent attempting to refute, but in the end incorporating, her incisive editorial comments. I, of course, am solely responsible for the contents and conclusions of this study.

Introduction

Japan entered the 1980s with a new confidence in its institutions and culture. In the present age of MITI and microchips, the Japanese have clearly laid to rest their former reputation as mere imitators of the West. Indeed, Americans now speak of the singular success of Japanese institutions in coping with the problems of modern industrial society, and many point to specific aspects as models for our own country.[1]

This has been particularly true in the case of Japan's famed labor-management relations. The worker's "lifetime" commitment to his company and the preponderance of cooperative enterprise unions are the envy of many a Western manager. Japanese businessmen, and a number of Western observers, term this system "Japanese-style management," and several assume that present-day industrial harmony naturally flowed from the country's traditional social relations.[2] In their view, industrial relations in Europe and the United States evolved from a different tradition of horizontal competition between distinct classes represented by trade unionists, on one side, and employers, on the other. In Japan, the argument continues, employers evaded crippling labor unrest by relying on age-old vertical bonds between the paternalistic master and his loyal subordinate—whether they be the feudal lord and his retainer, or the modern manager and his employee.[3]

This study suggests that confidence in Japan's distinctive industrial relations did not originate under the mythical Emperor Jimmu, or even the prewar Emperors Meiji (1868–1912) and Taishō (1912–26). When

1

the Japanese first faced the problems of modern factory labor during the 1880s, they were far from united on a "Japanese" solution. Their lack of consensus became all the more apparent by the 1920s and 1930s. The nation had just emerged from World War I, and the wartime industrial boom had given rise to a shocking new phenomenon: the massive outbreak of strikes and the widespread formation of assertive labor unions. In search of a higher position in a deeply hierarchical society, the young labor movement confronted the ruling classes with demands for universal suffrage, the legal recognition of labor unions, and the right to strike. As the industrial nations of Europe had earlier discovered, labor unrest constituted a genuine "social question" which governmental officials and party politicians could no longer simply proscribe or leave to the "paternalism" of employers. The question of how the state should deal with the rising unions divided Japan's governing elites and became bound up with a fundamental debate over the desired organization of society.

This is the story of the Japanese leadership's consideration of a series of often conflicting social policies vis-à-vis industrial labor. Throughout the period preceding World War II, there were those in business and government who regarded any organization of workers into economic interest groups as deleterious to prosperity and antithetical to the nation's traditions of social harmony. One of the two major political parties, the Seiyūkai, strenuously opposed the legal recognition of labor unions. Senior officials within the conservative Justice Ministry similarly directed campaigns against "dangerous thoughts," striking workers, and alleged Communist organizers. More remarkable, however, were those interwar civil servants and party leaders who welcomed the development of workers' organizations as essential to sound labor-management relations and social peace. During the 1920s, the Ministry of Home Affairs and the rival party, the Kenseikai (later the Minseitō), came forward with a set of liberal labor policies premised on the right of workers to advance their interests through labor unions. Kenseikai and Minseitō governments enfranchised adult workmen and repealed antistrike regulations. They also repeatedly sponsored (but could not enact) labor union legislation that would have legally protected the right to organize unions.

Nevertheless, in the wake of the Great Depression and Japan's seizure of Manchuria in 1931–32, labor policy took a decidedly authoritarian turn. Between 1938 and 1940, the government maneuvered the nation's labor unions into dissolution, and it reorganized workers into

the Greater Japan Industrial Patriotic Association. Although few scholars discuss the continuities between this drive and the liberal labor
programs of the 1920s, the Industrial Patriotic movement was spearheaded not by Japanese conservatives and industrialists but, ironically,
by many of the former proponents of trade unionism within the bureaucracy. Nor did the continuities end there. Strangely enough, several of
the same elite bureaucrats again switched gears after World War II to
advance democratic labor policies under the American Occupation
(1945–52).

This is also the story of interaction between the labor union movement
and the state. Much like the first generation of social historians in the
West, Japanese scholars have generally written labor history from below
(or from the middle, considering how many studies concern sectarian
divisions among labor leaders). Defiant strikes and radical working-class
consciousness figure prominently in these accounts. When "the state"
appears, it invariably takes the form of a faceless, outside oppressor.[4]
However, as historians of Europe and America have recently argued,
such theories of "social control" exaggerate the unity and self-confidence
of the ruling elites while virtually ignoring initiative on the part of "the
controlled"—that is, the workers.[5] In Japan, as well, the relationship
between organized labor and political authority was much more of a two-
way process. In their struggle against employers, labor activists often
worked closely with sympathetic allies within the bureaucracy and established parties. The partnership was rarely an equal one, to be sure. Yet the
Japanese labor movement shaped state initiatives, just as bureaucrats and
politicians helped shape the economically oriented union movement we
see in Japan today.

By focusing on the relationship among organized labor, bureaucratic
cliques, and party governments, this study offers a new perspective from
which to judge the seemingly abrupt shifts in Japanese politics during
the first four decades of the twentieth century. Historians have long
puzzled over the meaning of the era of "Taishō democracy" or the
"liberal twenties," an extended decade sandwiched between the pre-
1918 oligarchic regime and the authoritarian 1930s. Why did a broad-
based movement for the democratization of Japan's political and social
institutions develop after World War I? Moreover, why did it so totally
collapse after 1931, and how should one describe the repressive system
that replaced it? Some historians have addressed these questions by
examining the brief ascendancy of the political parties and party cabinets during the 1920s. They have generally concluded that politicians

were unable or unwilling to build a mass following and a firm constitutional base against military and bureaucratic rivals.[6] Others analyze the thought of such progressive intellectuals as Yoshino Sakuzō to reveal a disturbingly elitist and idealistic understanding of democracy, which prevented even the champions of Taishō democracy from fully supporting the formation of mass organizations and the rough-and-tumble world of parliamentary politics.[7] In the words of one recent synthesis, "The more [scholars] examine the nature of Taishō democracy, the more shallow they find it to be."[8]

Rather than dwell on the failure of Japanese democracy, I prefer to examine the social foundations of politics and policy before 1945. How the parties and bureaucracy confronted the complex problems of domestic division and social inequities tells us much more about the life and death of Taishō democracy than either the several accounts of the rise and fall of the parties per se or the attempts to measure the Japanese commitment to democracy as an abstract ideal. Looking back on the experience of Western European nations in the late-nineteenth and early-twentieth centuries, one might better describe democratization as a process by which segments of the upper classes broadened the franchise and enacted social reforms in response to assertive working-class movements. What similarly distinguishes the 1920s in Japan as an era of liberalization were the legislative and administrative efforts of the Kenseikai/Minseitō and its bureaucratic allies to offer the laboring classes an institutional role in socioeconomic relations and the political process. An idealistic commitment to egalitarian democracy may have inspired some Japanese reformers, but, as in the Western cases, we must not overlook powerful pragmatic motivations—including economic interest, political advantage, and the maintenance of social order. This study accordingly explains why upper-class Kenseikai leaders and Home Ministry officials sought to encourage the autonomous organization of the working class as a practical solution to popular discontent and work stoppages in the 1920s and early 1930s, and it suggests how a related desire for efficient wartime production lay behind the government's statist reorganization of labor in the face of new circumstances during the 1930s.

It has also become clear that we lack an adequate understanding of the role played by career bureaucrats in the politics of modern Japan. Despite the unquestioned importance of bureaucratic innovation in the postwar period, historians of the pre-1945 era have concentrated on the political parties while generally dismissing the higher civil service as a bastion of conservative opposition to democratic reform.[9] This is unfortunate, for a number of reasons. Whereas the two established parties frequently alternated cabinets during their brief rule in the 1920s, elite bureaucrats and their protégés dealt with labor matters and social movements on a continuous basis from the 1880s to 1945, and indeed well into the postwar era. Second, because they directly confronted problems of social unrest based on their respective ministries' definition of the state's interests, professional administrators often divided more sharply than party politicians over concrete solutions. One has only to look at the widely divergent labor policies pursued by the staunchly antisocialist Justice Ministry, the business-oriented Ministry of Agriculture and Commerce (later Commerce and Industry), and the relatively reformist Home Ministry—the last of which held responsibility for maintaining public order and improving social welfare. Third, bureaucratic proposals took on a political dimension during the era of party cabinets as the two major parties relied heavily on the expertise of like-minded civil servants to formulate and promote their policies. Progressive officials within the Home Ministry, particularly in its Social Bureau, supplied the major initiative behind the labor legislation of the Kenseikai and Minseitō governments, just as the Seiyūkai drew upon the forceful recommendations of conservative or promanagement bureaucrats in the Justice Ministry, the Ministry of Agriculture and Commerce, and other cliques in the Home Ministry.

Any analysis of bureaucracy necessarily examines the complex relationship between state and society. Theda Skocpol has recently argued that states often enjoy considerable "autonomy" from the preferences of the dominant classes, particularly in times of crisis. Such autonomous initiatives structurally derive from (1) officials' greater access to "international flows of communication," (2) the state's basic need to maintain order, and (3) the organizational cohesiveness and insulation of career bureaucrats.[10] Empirical studies of the active role of civil servants in the development of labor and welfare policies in Germany, Britain, and Sweden similarly suggest that the state and its officials constitute more than Marx's "committee for managing the common affairs of the whole bourgeoisie."[11] And yet, how much more?

The Home Ministry's approach to labor policy in Japan presents much the same problem. Of all the governmental agencies, bureaucrats in the prestigious Home Ministry were the most vocal in their claims to be impartial "officials of the Emperor," above selfish class interests and partisan politics. During the 1920s, they were frequently praised by labor leaders and denounced by employers for seeking to elevate the position of workers in society and politics. In the wartime atmosphere of the 1930s and early 1940s, many of these men became known as the "new bureaucrats" or "renovationist bureaucrats" in recognition of their drive to ameliorate socioeconomic problems by imposing stringent controls over all interests—capital as well as labor. Their motivations and programs provide a key measure of the degree of autonomy of the Japanese state vis-à-vis the capitalist classes prior to 1945.

While this analysis underscores the importance of the interwar bureaucracy to social policy, it also highlights the role of the two major political parties, the Seiyūkai and the Kenseikai/Minseitō. Few of the several accounts of the prewar parties have dealt seriously with the relationship of parties to policy, or in any sense with the political economy of the parties. In an effort to refute the early postwar belief that the parties had been the defenders of liberal democracy, historians have more recently emphasized that prewar politicians were fundamentally seekers after power and representatives of local interests.[12] Even those who acknowledge the relatively progressive positions of the Kenseikai/Minseitō conclude that much of this was rhetoric which failed to result in significantly more liberal programs than those of the rival Seiyūkai.[13] Ironically, scholarly treatment of the prewar parties and the bureaucracy has come full circle in Japan. Where once the parties were characterized as liberal and the bureaucracy as conservative, historians increasingly accept the assertions of retired civil servants that it was the bureaucrats who initiated, and the politicians who obstructed, the reformist legislation of the era.[14]

Notwithstanding their shortcomings as a democratic force, it is highly misleading to divorce the parties from discussions of interwar social policy or any other programmatic area. They, too, formed a part of the state structure. Presiding over most cabinets between 1918 and 1932, leaders of the Kenseikai/Minseitō and Seiyūkai successively held responsibility for handling the pressing social and economic questions of the age. Whether liberal or conservative, the parties' ministers of state, like their bureaucratic subordinates, formulated strategies on how to respond to domestic ferment. Although often depicted as provincial hacks, many were former higher civil servants themselves, well qualified to advance policy initiatives or champion the recommendations of their old ministries. Moreover, it was party-led cabinets that ultimately determined which bureaucratic proposals would reach the Imperial Diet and which would perish in the minefield of sectional rivalries. Nor should we ignore the role of the major parties as representatives of the various economic interests concerned with the labor issue. Although many have assumed that strong ties to big business prevented both parties from undertaking meaningful labor reform, the Kenseikai took up the cause of labor union legislation, in part because the issue appealed to a broad range of its constituents. The party not only sought new support among the working class, but also represented an influential segment of the business community which believed that the legal recognition of unions would improve, not impair, industrial relations.

Politicians and bureaucrats sought solutions to social problems based on their nation's economic reality and indigenous ideas of state and society, but Japanese politics and policy did not evolve in isolation. Throughout the interwar decades, Western models of industrial relations influenced Japanese labor policy to an extent seldom recognized in current historiography. In an effort to give Japanese creativity its rightful due, American scholars have tended, during the last two decades, to minimize the impact of foreign influences on Japanese society. Japanese leaders, it is now argued, did not slavishly imitate; rather, they engaged in "selective borrowing," whereby they selected what was necessary from various Western models and then skillfully adapted it to their native culture. As welcome as this new look is in many respects, it reduces the recurrent phenomenon of emulation to nearly tautological insignificance—in other words, the Japanese adopted "Japanese" solutions and nothing else because they themselves were Japanese. In actuality, borrowing between industrial nations has been an important factor in the development of social and economic policies over the last century and a half. Nineteenth-century German reformers studied British factory laws; early twentieth-century British politicians and civil servants, in turn, emulated Bismarckian social insurance; and European industrialists enthusiastically took up American-style scientific management in the 1920s.[15] The time has clearly come to examine the process of Japanese emulation from a comparative perspective without, of course, denying the existence of indigenous innovation and adaptation.[16]

Whereas the Seiyūkai, conservative bureaucrats, and many employers professed to find solutions to labor unrest in Japan's "beautiful customs" of paternalistic social relations, most leaders recognized that there was little of substance in their traditions to prepare them for the modern industrial problems of strikes and unionization. In the 1920s, Home Ministry officials and Kenseikai strategists carefully studied the labor policies of Britain and other European nations before proposing a comprehensive set of reforms designed to encourage the development of labor unions within an English-style framework of universal manhood suffrage, a union law, and a labor disputes conciliation law. Even the Seiyūkai and its conservative and business allies often found themselves opposing the Kenseikai's English model with other Western precedents, most notably the anti-union and antisubversive policies favored by industrialists and federal and state governments in the United States. During the 1930s, many Home Ministry officials and younger politicians turned to newer Nazi and Italian Fascist models of a state-organized labor federation, claiming that the liberal English system of autonomous trade unions and freely competing interest groups was incapable of meeting the nation's needs for economic recovery and military-industrial mobilization. Each of the models carried with it a complex set of assumptions about social organization. Selected by different elites as the inspiration for competing domestic strategies, these models often propelled Japanese labor policies in a more systematic direction than would otherwise have been the case.

Finally, a word of explanation is in order about this study's use of such categories as "liberal," "national socialist," and "corporatist" to describe Japanese policies. Fraught with ambiguity and ethnocentrism, European labels have largely gone out of fashion in recent discussions of prewar Japanese politics.[17] This may be for the better if liberalism is simplistically defined as individualism, or national socialism as charismatic dictatorship. With a proper appreciation of the complexities of these phenomena in Western nations, however, the comparative approach adds a whole new dimension to an analysis of competing Japanese visions of social stabilization. Indeed, in their open emulation of foreign models, Japanese at the time often linked their own policy alternatives to ideological debates then raging in the West. To progressive Japanese politicians and officials in the 1920s, liberalism was no longer identified with the laissez-faire principles of J. S. Mill and Gladstone. Rather, it conjured up the more contemporary "New Liberalism" of Britain's Liberal Party governments (1906–14), which had committed the state to providing social welfare, guaranteeing the workers' right to organize, and mediating in industrial disputes.[18] German National Socialism and, to a lesser extent, Italian Fascism were similarly attractive a decade later because of their proposed socioeconomic solutions, which aimed at restructuring the free-market system into compulsory corporate organizations.

By charting these changing conceptions of social policy, we gain a more subtle understanding of the twists and turns of twentieth-century

Japanese politics—from oligarchic repression before 1918 to the liberal attempts to accommodate popular movements during the 1920s, and from the wartime reorganization of autonomous associations to the fuller, yet still managed, pluralism of the present postwar era. Although the focus is Japan, the challenges and responses presented here were hardly peculiar to that nation. An appreciation of how the Japanese resolved these questions should enhance the comparative study of state and society in the industrial world.

CHAPTER I

The Origins of Japanese Social Policy, 1868–1918

During the Meiji era [1868–1912] and particularly the few years after 1907, people would erroneously equate social welfare and social policy with socialism. It was an era when the very word "social policy" was unfamiliar. . . . In the spring of 1911, I took an examination to become a police sergeant in the Tokyo Metropolitan Police. For the first time [after nearly four years as a patrolman], I was asked the question: "How would you distinguish between socialism and social policy?" I hadn't the slightest idea. Things were that ridiculous.

—*Takahashi Yūsai, former Home Ministry official*[1]

In 1868, a league of domains (*han*) from southwestern Japan overthrew the Tokugawa shogunate and proceeded to establish a modern centralized state in the name of the Meiji emperor. Japan was at the time a predominantly agrarian society with some 80 percent of the working population engaged in agriculture and at most 5 percent in manufacturing. Over the next four decades, Japanese society experienced a pace of industrialization rarely seen in the nineteenth-century world. Mechanized factories first appeared on a widespread basis in the late 1880s, but an astounding 84 percent of the nation's 8,612 companies as of 1902 were founded in the few years following the Sino-Japanese War (1894–95). Remarked one pioneer labor specialist with some exaggeration: "Whereas the Industrial Revolution occurred in Great Britain over the latter half of the eighteenth century, the process worked itself out in Japan between 1895 and 1897."[2] As in Britain, the transition to industrial wage labor created major problems. Faced with escalating demands for manpower, employers found themselves competing for scarce labor and struggling to impose discipline over artisans, day labor-

ers, and peasants. To the first generation of workers, factory life introduced a whole new set of working conditions, often unpleasant, from
which some developed a collective consciousness while others voted
with their feet.

Moreover, as in England, the divergent aspirations of labor and capital invited intervention by the state in the realm of labor policy. But in
whose interest would the Japanese government intervene? The business
community formed a strong lobby after 1880. Although workers remained largely unorganized before World War I, they, too, had their
defenders among the labor leaders, journalists, scholars, politicians, and
higher civil servants who joined together to call for a social policy to
protect labor. By "social policy," these reformers meant that the state
should deal with labor not simply as an element of production, but as a
valuable national resource, whose abuse hindered the state's responsibilities to maintain public health, domestic order, and a strong military.
In 1911, the Diet enacted the Factory Law, modern Japan's first major
social legislation.

Despite this advance, one should not exaggerate the social activism
of the Japanese state during the Meiji era (1868–1912). The argument
has been advanced more than once that Japanese officials lacked the
laissez-faire traditions of their British counterparts and were therefore
more inclined to protect workers and society from unrestrained industrialization. As early as 1902, a former prime minister, Ōkuma Shigenobu,
declared his nation's modern social policies to be firmly grounded in the
Confucian ruling ideology of Japan's preindustrial past. Insisting that
"from ancient times, our statesmen have espoused ideas of state socialism," Ōkuma explained how the Tokugawa shogun and daimyo (lords)
had safeguarded the welfare of the people: they banned the sale of land,
fixed the wages of labor, and frequently ordered landlords to waive
rents during hard times.[3] In a more recent discussion of Japanese factory
legislation in the 1890s, Ronald Dore similarly argued: "The *real* traditionalists [those who called for a return to Confucian morality] . . . were
antipathetic to modern industry as a whole and rather in favor of state
regulation of working conditions."[4] Whether Japanese authorities had
been so benevolent before 1868 is open to question. Much clearer was
the Meiji state's reluctance to intervene decisively on behalf of the nation's workers. This chapter explores the complex process by which
labor only gradually became the leading social question.

THE WORKERS

Although the Japanese often discussed "the labor question" (rōdō mondai) after 1895, there were, in reality, three distinct labor problems, related to (1) the supply of labor, (2) the conditions of workers, and (3) strikes and organized labor. How the state and business responded to labor questions before 1945 was closely bound up with the nature of Japan's industrial revolution and the formation of its working class.

Skilled workers in heavy industry constituted the most self-conscious element of the early working class. Modern heavy industry in Japan dated back to the late 1860s and 1870s, when the new Meiji leadership (and the preceding shogunate and individual domains) sought to develop communications and defense-related industries. Government enterprises were established in mining, armaments, shipyards, machinery works, and railway construction. Compared with other workers, employees in heavy industry possessed the most tenuous links to the traditional rural economy. The first generation were commonly artisans. At the government-run Yokosuka Shipyards, for example, French advisors retrained carpenters and casting craftsmen to become ironworkers and woodworkers after 1864. These enterprises also drew upon an urban labor pool consisting of the sons of craftsmen, former samurai, and peasants who had previously migrated from the countryside.[5] From the start, males constituted the overwhelming majority in heavy industry.

Japan's involvement in the Sino-Japanese War, the Russo-Japanese War (1904–05), and World War I (1914–18) resulted in a major expansion of the nation's industrial work force, in general. This was accompanied by relatively large increases in the number of workers in the war-related machinery and tool-making industries (see table 1). Yet workers in the machinery industry represented only 8 percent of the nation's industrial labor force in 1909. Table 1 shows that the vast majority of Japanese factory workers were employed in textiles before World War I. Silk and cotton products accounted for three-fifths of Japanese exports in 1913.[6] Beginning in the 1870s, the government encouraged private investment in silk-reeling and cotton-spinning, both to reverse the unfavorable balance of payments and to compete with the inexpensive cotton yarns flooding into Japan from the West. The Japanese mills also took advantage of abundant supplies of low-wage labor. Although silk-reeling was rapidly mechanized, the industry remained small-scale and rural, with close ties to the early modern putting-out system. By contrast, cotton-spinning mills, which required more capital, appeared after 1883 in the

TABLE I   INDUSTRIAL WORKERS
BY INDUSTRY, 1902–19
(in thousands)

Industry	1902	1907	1914	1919
Textile	269	355	536	794
Machine and tool	34	62	88	226
Chemical	82	65	84	162
Food and drink	30	48	58	76
Miscellaneous	32	53	79	110
Electrical, metal refining, mining	51	60	9	22
Total	499	643	854	1,391

SOURCE: NRUS, 10:104–7. The figures are based on surveys of factories employing 10 or more workers. The 1914 and 1919 entries exclude miners.

form of large enterprises. These were generally concentrated in the metropolitan areas of Osaka–Kobe–Kyoto and Tokyo–Yokohama.[7]

The most distinctive feature of Japanese textile labor before World War II was the predominance of young, single female operatives, who typically came from rural areas and worked for less than two years. From 1889 to 1930, women formed approximately 80 percent of the cotton-textile labor force.[8] Most were in their teens or early twenties, although some 15 percent were younger than fourteen in 1897.[9] The pattern is a familiar one in the early stages of industrialization. In the cotton-textile mills of Lowell, Massachusetts, as many as 85 percent of the operatives in 1836 were females. Most were likewise young country women who worked for short periods before marrying.[10] Yet the labor force in the Japanese mills differed in at least one major respect:

> Lowell girls (young girls living in company dormitories with no permanent commitment to the industry) were resurrected in Osaka, not as a short episode in the life of one geographic area in a still-young national industry, but rather as the integral force in the fifty-year drive of the Japanese cotton textile industry to world dominance.[11]

Given the central position of textiles in the Japanese economy, women constituted 62 percent of the entire factory work force in 1909. Their proportion stood at 52.6 percent as late as 1930—a rather high figure when compared with other late industrializers, such as France, Italy, and India.[12] This preponderance of female workers aroused a particular set of concerns among Meiji-era social commentators and policymakers.

The rapid rise of mechanized industry from an agrarian base naturally created an enormous demand for labor by the mid-1890s. Japanese employers today boast of the traditional roots of their "lifetime employment system," in which workers develop a long-term commitment to the firm. Factory owners at the turn of the century, however, were preoccupied with the problem of workers leaving their jobs at will. Skilled workmen were especially notorious. The early industrial worker inherited many of the traits of the Tokugawa-era artisan. Among these was the tendency of many journeymen to wander from master to master, seeking the most pay for the fewest hours.[13] With the expansion of industry after 1868, the skills of retrained artisans became all the more prized. Shipyards and arsenals would train workers, only to see them bolt for a higher bidder. As Andrew Gordon has recently shown, contemporary accounts of the early workers hardly convey the image of diligence and loyalty. One newspaper in 1897 reported that workers at an Osaka shipyard "seem free to work or play as they please." The journal of the nascent labor movement was no less critical that same year, when it described the typical worker, in Gordon's paraphrase, as "a hard-drinking, fighting, gambling type with no care for saving or for the future."[14]

The demand for labor was even more intense in the generally low-skilled textile industry. The Japanese victory over the Chinese in 1895 opened up a vast new market for the nation's cotton and silk products on the Asian mainland. Although the Japanese countryside contained abundant supplies of labor, this did not translate into an especially willing or disciplined work force in the initial stages of industrialization. As early as 1884, employers in the silk-reeling industry were forced to search beyond their locales for prospective mill girls. By the late 1880s, big-city cotton-spinning mills and large silk filatures regularly used brokers to recruit young women from faraway villages.[15] Agents sought out impoverished farm families, who were eager to receive any supplementary income and be spared one more mouth to feed. The abuses of the recruiting system are legendary. The government's first comprehensive survey, *Shokkō jijō* (The condition of factory workers), of 1903, had this to say about brokers in the cotton-spinning industry:

> Their method is to approach a girl or her parents at the cake shop where the country people gather for leisurely talk, and persuade them by picturing the "easy life" of a mill worker. Occasionally they simply ask the girl to come to the factory and see for herself, with no obligation to remain. . . . Once they [the girls] arrive at the mills, they find that every-

thing is quite different from what they were led to expect, but they have no alternative but to stay and resign themselves to hard labor.[16]

In actuality, many did not stay. A government survey of an unnamed cotton mill in Hyōgo disclosed that in 1900, 83 percent of the women workers (4,846 in number) who left their jobs "escaped"—in other words, departed without giving notice. Officials recorded their amazement at the turnover among the firm's male and female workers: "Of the 11,721 operatives [working or newly hired during 1900], 7,701 left the company [that same year]. That amounts to a turnover of over 60 percent."[17] Such instability was neither unusual nor short-term. Some of the large cotton mills, such as Kanebō (Kanegafuchi Spinning Company), undertook much-publicized efforts after 1900 to keep workers by improving conditions and establishing welfare facilities. Yet despite a slight decline between 1903 and 1914 in the percentage of workers leaving the company's Hyōgo mill during their first six months, the proportion was still higher in 1914 than 1897. Some of the women were hired away or even kidnapped by agents of other factories, but most simply ran away.[18]

Why textile workers fled was related to the second major labor problem: working conditions. Theirs were by no means the worst. Miners, who constituted 22 percent of the industrial labor force around 1900, worked in a more dangerous environment, subject to beatings by guards and thievery by subcontracting labor bosses.[19] Nonetheless, most surveys and exposés after 1895 highlighted the plight of respectable farm girls in the mills, not that of the rough and marginal male miners. How bad *was* life in the textile factories? The horror stories have received considerable attention from Japanese historians: stories of runaway girls who were caught, stripped, and beaten, or of women workers burned to death because the owners locked the dormitories every night.[20] On the other hand, historians have also shown that many women preferred a few years in the mills to the pain and drudgery of farm life. The operatives achieved some independence, enjoyed the amenities of the cities, and often found the food better.[21]

Whatever the case, this much is clear, based on the official surveys of conditions: even at the most enlightened mills, factory work involved a wrenching set of adjustments. It may have been easier than farming, but mechanized production entailed longer hours and a year-round work schedule. Beginning in 1883, most major cotton-spinning mills instituted "all-night operations" to make full use of expensive imported machinery. As a result, operatives typically worked at least twelve hours a day with scarcely a break, alternating day and night shifts at weekly intervals. Those in silk filatures and small weaving shops might labor as long as seventeen or eighteen hours. Whereas most male operatives in the large spinning mills lived at home or in the firms' married housing facilities, unmarried females generally lived in supervised company dormitories, which often restricted their time spent outside. Although mill owners presented the dormitory system as a means of protecting the morals of young women, the institutions also served to reduce escapes and absenteeism.[22]

The workers' responses to factory conditions varied considerably according to industry and gender. For women in the silk filatures and cotton-spinning mills, the most common form of protest remained the individual act of running away. From time to time, however, female operatives banded together to mount the earliest strikes in the modern industrial sector. In 1886, owners of the Amemiya Silk Filature in Kōfu attempted to lower piecework rates while extending the work day a half hour (*from* fourteen hours). Over 100 young women fled in protest to a Buddhist temple, where they waited until their demands were met. At least three other strikes broke out that summer in area filatures against similar managerial initiatives. The largest work stoppages before the Sino-Japanese War occurred in the urban cotton mills after 1886. Some 250 male and female workers at the Temma Spinning Mill of Osaka demonstrated in 1889 for higher wages until "persuaded" to disband by military police. In 1894, a collective call for the dismissal of three supervisors at the same factory ended when police arrested six workers. In no case did the textile workers organize a labor union, as well.

Most strikes in the spinning industry took the form of outbursts of frustration because the male operatives, who generally led them, lacked the skills and bargaining position to form viable trade unions.[23] The obstacles to organizing unskilled women operatives loomed even larger, as labor historians of North America and Europe have also observed.[24] At the high point of prewar labor organization in the early 1930s, Japanese women formed less than 6 percent of unionized workers.[25] Their brief tenure in the factories gave them little incentive to struggle for long-term improvements in working conditions. Moreover, companies skillfully used the paternalistic dormitory system to reinforce the traditional deference of young women so prevalent in the family relationships of rural Japan.[26]

A small union movement did, however, develop among skilled male workers in heavy industry after 1895. If its organization suggested an American-style craft-union approach, this was no coincidence. The principal organizers, led by the university graduate Takano Fusatarō, first formed the Shokkō Giyūkai (Knights of Labor) among Japanese workers in San Francisco in 1890. They were aided by the American Federation of Labor. Appointed AFL organizer for Japan by Samuel Gompers himself, Takano and other leaders returned home during the Sino-Japanese War. In 1897, together with bourgeois reformers and Christian socialists, they founded the Association for the Promotion of Labor Unions (Rōdō Kumiai Kiseikai), which in turn sponsored several of the early unions. The strongest affiliate, the Ironworkers' Union (Tekkō Kumiai), in 1900 boasted a membership of 5,400, consisting of workers in the machine and metal trades in the large shipyards, arsenals, and engineering works. The Printers' Union (Kappankō Kumiai) and Japanese Railway Workers' Reform Society (Nihon Tetsudō Kyōseikai) of the Japan Railway Company organized another 2,000 and 1,000 workers, respectively, during the late 1890s.[27]

The leaders of the new unions assiduously avoided confrontations with employers. Although the number of labor disputes rose dramatically between 1897 and 1900, few occurred in large-scale heavy industry, excepting the strikes at the Japan Railway Company (1899) and the Kure Naval Arsenal (1902). In its charter, the Ironworkers' Union undertook the mission of "mediating disputes and maintaining the true interests of fellow tradesmen." The labor movement's journal, *Rōdō sekai* (Labor world), concurred. Its chief editor, Katayama Sen, who years later became an official in the Communist International, declared that the journal's policy was "not to engage in a divisive struggle against capitalists, but rather to perfect true harmony and cooperation (*chōwa*)."[28] As a number of scholars have noted, Japanese workers, between 1890 and 1918, rarely phrased demands in terms of natural rights. Rather, they sought first and foremost to raise their lowly position within society and the workplace. In the big strike against the Japan Railway Company, engineers demanded changes in the job classification system that would make them equal in status to the white-collar staff. The engineers also protested such discriminatory treatment as being required to kneel before assistant stationmasters.[29]

Despite their moderation and promising start, the nascent unions faced enormous difficulties. Most fundamental, Japanese labor organizations lacked a strong craft tradition, in contrast to the trade unions of nineteenth-century England. The Tokugawa-era guild system had virtually collapsed by 1800 as rural craftsmen, who were not covered by guild regulations, decimated the wage rates of urban artisans. The Meiji government furthered the break by prohibiting guilds outright in the early 1870s, and the introduction of Western technologies created entirely new trades. Powerless to impose traditional group control over the footloose first generation of skilled workers, the early craft unions proved unable to regulate apprenticeships and the overall labor market. Most dissolved themselves before the end of 1900, in part because of increased pressures from employers and the government, but also as a result of fluctuating membership and inadequate finances.[30] Organized labor did not yet pose a major challenge to industrial production or public order. Consequently, the Meiji state concentrated on what officials perceived to be more pressing labor problems.

STATE AND BUSINESS: FACTORY LEGISLATION AS INDUSTRIAL POLICY

The new regime took a keen interest in the problems of industrial labor. Officials of the Industrial Bureau (Ministry of Agriculture and Commerce) began studying Western examples of workers' legislation and factory regulations as early as 1882. Their subsequent proposals resulted in Japan's first Factory Law of 1911. The case for state autonomy in labor policy was first presented, appropriately enough, by a former chief of the Industrial Bureau. Looking back in 1917, Oka Minoru described his ministry's thirty-year struggle to enact the Factory Law in the face of a hostile business community. Concluded Oka, in the not so humble tones of the imperial official:

> Our nation's Factory Law was championed almost exclusively by the government and academic experts. It did not result from bargaining with workers or their organizations. Nor did the parties ever deal with it as a political question. It was purely a question of protecting labor.[31]

Most accounts of the Factory Law have accepted Oka's assertions as proof of the enlightened, progressive nature of the Meiji-era bureaucracy, which appears committed to protecting workers from the ills of industrialization.[32] Kenneth Pyle described how many bureaucrats took to German ideas of "social monarchy" and "social policy" during the 1890s, and Robert Scalapino remarked that "Japanese tradition harmonized so well" with the German concept of "an expanding welfare state, which would supplant private benevolence and underwrite state security with social justice."[33]

Such interpretations, however, obscure the true nature of the government's initial labor policies. Factory legislation originated in the 1880s as part of the young regime's drive to industrialize. Indeed, the government officially committed itself to *shokusan kōgyō* or "encouraging industry." The condition of the working class did not yet constitute a "social question" in the sense of a widely perceived threat to public health or order. Whether bureaucrats or businessmen, Japanese leaders discussed early labor legislation in largely economic terms: how could state power be applied to improve industrial productivity? In essence, Meiji labor policy emerged within the confines of industrial policy. Individual entrepreneurs might occasionally complain about their lack of political power vis-à-vis the bureaucrats, but for the most part, the business of Meiji Japan was business.

Nor were the officials of late-nineteenth-century Japan overly autonomous from the business community. Business associations rapidly emerged after the founding of the Tokyo Chamber of Commerce in 1878. Leading mill owners formed the powerful Cotton Spinners' Association in 1882. Although the government subsidized the establishment of the early chambers of commerce, business groups evinced no shyness when it came to advancing their interests. Furthermore, their preferences carried considerable weight within the regime, thanks to leadership by several former officials. The Tokyo Chamber was directed by the influential entrepreneurs Shibusawa Eiichi and Mitsui's Matsuda Takashi, both of whom had left the Finance Ministry in the early 1870s. Inoue Kaoru was perhaps the best-known example of a retired official who moved between the two worlds with ease. Frequently a minister of state, he headed several governmental agencies between 1878 and 1898, while serving as director of some of the nation's biggest companies.[34] By the 1890s, the interests of certain cabinet ministers had become so closely intertwined with those of the mine owner Furukawa Ichibei that it took years before the government ordered his company to cease dumping highly toxic wastes at the Ashio Copper Mine.[35]

In a structural sense, as well, Japanese bureaucrats before 1900 generally lacked the cohesiveness and insulation from business interests necessary to champion aggressively protectionist labor policies. In fact, few could be considered modern bureaucrats. The government did not require prospective officials to pass the higher civil-service examination until 1893. The great majority were lower-ranking samurai who obtained posts on the basis of ties to the victorious domains of the Meiji Restoration. Moreover, the administrative context of policy-making strengthened the influence of industrialists. It was the Industrial Bureau of the Ministry of Agriculture and Commerce that handled most questions of labor policy and factory legislation following the ministry's establishment in 1881. Industrial Bureau officials were neither inclined to curb the employer's power over labor nor strong enough to do so had they wished. Their industrial policy did not appear overly interventionist by nineteenth-century standards. Ministry officials concentrated on simply fostering a favorable environment for private entrepreneurial activity. The small staff of the Industrial Bureau (and the Commercial Bureau, with which it was often combined before 1925) spent most of its time disseminating foreign technology, enforcing standards for commercial products, and supervising the insurance industry.[36] In drafting their factory legislation between 1882 and 1911, the bureaucrats closely consulted the nation's business associations but never the labor groups.

In their quest to increase production, Industrial Bureau officials initially proposed factory legislation that strongly reflected the demands of employers. To the bureaucrats, no less than to factory owners, the most pressing problem was the persistence of high labor turnover amid the chronic labor shortage. Far from opposing state intervention, business associations largely favored a factory law that regulated labor mobility. The Tokyo Chamber of Commerce first petitioned the government for a law to bind apprentices and factory operatives to employment contracts as early as 1880.[37] The Cotton Spinners' Association, for its part, attempted to restrain ruinous competition for labor by requiring members to cross-reference the hiring of each new worker and to obtain the consent of the previous employer.[38] Few employers offered the laissez-faire argument that the laws of the market would by themselves solve the problem of high turnover.[39] Although business associations generally opposed the labor-protection features of factory legislation throughout the 1890s, a substantial number looked to the state to regulate workers.[40]

Indeed, for a time the Industrial Bureau's proposed factory legislation aimed more at regulating workers than employers. The bureau's first draft in 1883 contained few safeguards for women and children, whereas it stipulated tough penalties against a worker who broke a contract or "stopped work on his own volition or engaged in a conspiracy to do so."[41] In an effort to prevent workers from abandoning one employer for another while under contract, the proposal also required laborers to carry work permits. During the 1880s and 1890s, drafts by the Ministry of Agriculture and Commerce added stronger protective provisions, such as limitations on working hours for women and children. Nonetheless, the ministry's 1898 draft prominently retained the requirement of work permits and introduced prohibitions against employers who "poached" workers from rival mills with promises of higher wages. Rather than recognizing labor mobility as a characteristic of the marketplace, ministry officials sought to restrict workers' freedom of movement on the grounds that frequent turnover discouraged factory owners from developing a skilled work force.[42]

In the face of economic expansion following the Sino-Japanese War, officials contemplated a more protective factory law that would move beyond the original objective of creating a disciplined work force. In 1896 and again in 1898, the government submitted draft factory legislation to the First and Third Higher Councils on Agriculture, Commerce, and Industry. Established to advise the minister of agriculture and commerce, the Higher Councils consisted largely of representatives from bureaucracy, business, and the academic community. In the course of deliberations, most entrepreneurial delegates rejected the need for a protective factory law for one, or all, of the following reasons: (1) it was premature inasmuch as Japan did not yet experience Western-style industrial abuses; (2) Japanese employers were innately more benevolent toward workers than their Western counterparts; and (3) restrictions on working hours and child labor would raise production costs and ruin Japan's competitive position in world markets.[43]

Defenders of labor protection within the government refuted such charges with economic and productivist arguments of their own. Most represented agencies responsible for promoting economic growth—the Ministry of Finance and governmental banks, as well as the Ministry of Agriculture and Commerce. Though hardly hostile to the business community, these officials defined the state's interests in national industrial development as independent from those of individual entrepreneurs. Invoking the long-term interests of industry, they argued that a factory law would create a cooperative, healthy, and skilled work force. Good workers in turn meant increased productivity and "the healthy development of industry."[44]

This new breed of economic bureaucrats was particularly forceful in rejecting the claims of business that the Japanese tradition of familialism obviated the need for a law regulating relations between employer and employee. As students of economic policy and theory, they possessed firsthand knowledge of industrial development in the Western nations, and they were well aware that traditions changed. The response of

Andō Tarō, chief of the Commercial and Industrial Bureau (Ministry of Agriculture and Commerce), was typical:

> It is true that moral fellowship (*tokugiteki jōgi*) between employers and employees existed in the household industries of the past. Nor can one doubt that these relations resembled those between master and disciple, or lord and retainer. However, of the factories which [today] employ hundreds, even thousands of workers, how many actually possess such harmonious, tranquil relations? . . . it is extremely dangerous to leave matters alone, assuming the existence of moral relations in all of the newly established factories where [employers] pursue only short-term profits.[45]

Insisting that Japan would not escape the problems earlier faced by the industrializing nations of the West, these officials promoted factory regulations as an effective means of "preventing disputes before they occur."[46]

Although the Higher Councils were the scene of heated debates between business leaders and reformist bureaucrats, discussion also revealed a serious lack of consensus within the government over the economic benefits of protective labor policy. For every Andō Tarō, there were many more civil servants who perceived little conflict between the state and the short-term profits of employers. The Ministry of Agriculture and Commerce itself remained divided over the need for a factory law before 1905. In 1897, for example, Ariga Nagafumi publicly opposed protective labor regulations as premature. Ariga, it should be noted, served as a high-ranking official in the Industrial Bureau at the time.[47] His views must not have offended his superiors, for he was promoted the next year to chief of the bureau, which was then promoting its factory bill before the Third Higher Council on Agriculture, Commerce, and Industry. In keeping with the principles of political economy, Ariga began his attack by asserting that workers' problems should be considered solely in terms of the nation's economy, not from the peripheral perspectives of education and public health. If Japan were to survive the perils of international commercial competition, he continued, the nation must rapidly accumulate capital, unimpeded by the costs of protecting labor. Dismissing the charges of unhealthy factory conditions, Ariga joined many other officials in presenting industrialization as the nation's best welfare policy: "If one recalls what life used to be like for these workers, no one could say that they're worse off now. . . . life in the villages meant subsisting on boiled rice and barley, pickled vegetables, and occasionally salted fish. Once they go to work in the factories, however, fish and meat become the daily fare."[48] Ariga concluded that a national policy of workers' protection was unnecessary because the rising demand for labor would by itself improve factory conditions.

Ariga was not alone. Representing the Home Ministry within the Third Higher Council, Vice-Minister Suzuki Jūbi supported the efforts of certain business delegates to table the draft factory bill. Suzuki vigorously opposed the proposed ban on employing children under ten, alleging that a child labor law would conversely hinder the Home Ministry's efforts to improve popular welfare. "Don't lecture me on damage to their health," he chided the bill's supporters. If a factory law barred children from working, predicted Suzuki, "Let's face it, they'd more likely starve."[49] But it was a former Home Ministry bureau chief and council member, Murata Tamotsu, who pushed the boundaries of economism to macabre limits. What was wrong, he asked, with children of five and six working in the match factories of Kobe; the work was really play to them, and, unlike machines, children "don't rust." According to Murata, conditions in the cotton-spinning mills could not be all that bad: "If workers were truly becoming ill in large numbers, by the laws of nature would so many continue to work in those places?"[50]

In October 1898, the Higher Council on Agriculture, Commerce, and Industry approved a draft factory bill by a narrow margin, but only after powerful entrepreneurs diluted the Industrial Bureau's already mild protective features in subcommittee.[51] The council's endorsement notwithstanding, successive governments refrained during the next decade from introducing factory legislation to the Diet, ostensibly because of cabinet changes and resistance from major segments in the business community. In reality, the legislation was as much delayed by officials who thought like businessmen as by businessmen themselves.

THE "SOCIAL QUESTION" AND SOCIAL POLICY

The government might have further postponed factory legislation had it not been for the growing recognition that the problems of Japan's expanding working class constituted more than an economic issue. Whereas most officials and entrepreneurs continued to emphasize the remedial powers of self-help and industrialization, members of the urban intelligentsia increasingly warned of an impending "social question" after 1890. Their conception of social problems combined a vision of Japan's future with observations of actual conditions. Western-style industrialization, they argued, would inevitably produce strikes, trade unions, and a socialist movement of the type seen in contemporary Europe and America. In 1891, one German-educated authority acknowledged that such a social question did not yet exist in Japan, but he predicted it soon would as workers became aware of the growing gap between rich and poor.[52] Other critics linked the plight of factory workers to the already pervasive problem of urban poverty. Writing in 1901, Abe Isoo, a Christian socialist, commented that Western scholars applied the term "social problems" to a variety of issues, including labor:

> However, . . . they all boil down to the question of how to end poverty among mankind and eradicate the gulf separating rich and poor. . . . It is this problem which truly endangers society. Rather than discuss "social problems," I believe it best to speak of "The Social Problem," which eight or nine times out of ten should be considered as distinct from economic questions.[53]

It was the slum, the most visible sign of inequality, that provoked the first public discussion of the social question in Japan. At the height of the Matsukata deflation (1881–86), destitute farmers streamed into Tokyo, Osaka, and other big cities after losing land or livelihood. There they joined artisans and day laborers to form a new class of urban poor. According to a government survey in 1883, a sizable number of rural migrants arrived diseased, spreading epidemics throughout crowded, unsanitary neighborhoods.[54] In 1886, the daily Chōya shimbun uncovered the existence of the "three great slums" of Tokyo in a series on the city's poor.

Exposé followed exposé, but no one publicized the plight of the nation's destitute as forcefully as Yokoyama Gennosuke, an investigative reporter for the liberal Mainichi shimbun. Inspired by Charles Booth's Life and Labour of the People of London (1889 and 1891), Yokoyama published in 1899 his own empirical observations in the influential study, Nihon no kasō shakai (Japan's lower strata of society). The survey graphically described the struggle for survival among tenant farmers, urban paupers, ironworkers, and especially women and children who labored in the textile and match factories. Along with the general public, officials had condescendingly described the poor as the "lean people" (saimin) or "lowly people" (kasō min) since Tokugawa times. Yokoyama, on the other hand, popularized the term "lower strata of society" to denote a condition into which unfortunate members of the rest of society might fall through no fault of their own.[55]

Critics were, of course, better at identifying the social question than at offering concrete solutions. If one looks beyond the sensational exposés, the number of dedicated social reformers remained small in the 1890s. One set concentrated on social amelioration from below. Proponents ranged from philanthropic individuals and left-liberal politicians to socialists and labor organizers. Japan's pioneer socialists had much in common with bourgeois radicals and humanitarians prior to 1900. Christians predominated among both groups, many having first approached social problems from the perspective of the social gospel. Committed to helping workers and the poor to help themselves, Christian socialists and bourgeois reformers occasionally cooperated to found urban settlement houses. They also jointly sponsored the formation of several of the first trade unions during the late 1890s.[56]

Other reformers placed greater faith in the state and its ability to provide beneficial social policies. Their position was most forcefully advanced by Professor Kanai Noburu, an economist at Tokyo Imperial University, and his student, Kuwata Kumazō. Upon returning from four years of surveying social legislation in Germany and England in 1890, Kanai popularized the concept of the "social question" (*shakai mondai*). He also introduced the term "social policy" (*shakai seisaku*), derived from the German idea of Sozialpolitik. Kanai quickly emerged as an early champion of protective factory legislation. In 1897, he joined Kuwata and like-minded political economists to form the Japanese Social Policy Association (Nihon Shakai Seisaku Gakkai). Spearheading the movement for a factory law and other social legislation, this scholarly association expanded to include several higher civil servants and respected businessmen by the time of its first national conference in 1907.

The new interest in social policy reflected larger changes in European and Japanese economic theory during the late nineteenth century. Well into the 1890s, Japanese students of English political economy steadfastly asserted that labor problems were fundamentally a question of economic laws; if left alone, competition would "naturally" bring about harmony between labor and capital.[57] In opposition stood Kanai and a growing group of economists, who espoused the doctrines of Germany's Younger Historical School. German scholars of the Younger Historical School pointedly rejected the Manchester school's equating of economic self-interest with social harmony. Instead, they infused the state with the ethical mission of protecting the weak from the ravages of industrialization in the interests of social order and national greatness. Toward this end, in 1872, German academics had founded the Verein für Sozialpolitik, the model for Japan's later Social Policy Association.[58] Kanai similarly defined Japanese social policy in terms of the Japanese state's obligation to protect and elevate the working class vis-à-vis capitalists. Taking aim at traditionalist arguments of Confucian paternalism, Kanai insisted that social policy was not based on "Tory philanthropy," but rather on the higher interests of the "social state," which transcended those of any one class. Accordingly, the labor issue constituted a major challenge to the state because the widening gap between rich and poor was liable to "destroy the social order and damage the public peace."[59]

Although most higher civil servants adhered to the doctrines of English political economy throughout the 1890s, bureaucratic proponents of factory legislation increasingly supplemented their productivist arguments with considerations of social policy. Professor Kanai reinforced these tendencies as a delegate to the Third Higher Council on Agriculture, Commerce, and Industry in 1898. For the first time, key officials spoke of the state's responsibility to remedy the broader social consequences of hazardous working conditions. As chief of the Commercial and Industrial Bureau, Andō Tarō demonstrated that long hours of factory work not only diminished efficiency but also crippled young workers for life and weakened the offspring of sickly female operatives. Concluded Andō: "If these trends continue, they will affect the development of national strength."[60] The government's leading spokesman for social policy was unquestionably Soeda Juichi, a high-ranking official in the Ministry of Finance and an early advocate of protective factory legislation. Like Kanai, Soeda drew upon his extensive experience in Europe to warn:

> If the state does not intervene to some extent in relations between employers and employees, there will be no way to safeguard the interests of employees. . . . If we leave things as they are today, we will soon witness the onset of a virulent social disease of the type which befell England at the beginning of this century. . . . I fear that our country, too, will inevitably experience the problems associated with such social questions and social ills as strikes. . . . I sincerely hope we can solve these problems before they develop and save ourselves from the disease afflicting the advanced nations of Europe.[61]

While the debate over factory legislation raged at the higher levels of government, an administrative locus for social policy was quietly developing in the Home Ministry. Responsible for disease control, the Bureau of Health and Sanitation led an anomalous existence within the Home Ministry, whose primary functions initially consisted of supervising local government and promoting grass-roots economic development.[62] In 1892, Gotō Shimpei, a physician by training, became bureau chief after returning from a study of German social insurance. Gotō stands out as one of the most visionary and politically ambitious higher civil servants in prewar Japan. He was to sponsor several innovative social policies over the next three decades. Gotō came to his post an outspoken admirer of Bismarck's "state socialism," by which the state recognized its duty to improve the living standards of the nation's workers. Under Gotō's leadership, the Bureau of Health and Sanitation energetically investigated the advanced social policies of Europe. He and his staff drafted Japan's first proposal for a workers' sickness insurance law in 1898. Years ahead of its time, the plan failed to gain the approval of a Home Ministry advisory panel. Bureau officials thereupon directed their energies toward implementing a factory law that would protect the health of workers.[63]

Support from the Home Ministry and its public health officials emboldened the more cautious Ministry of Agriculture and Commerce in its efforts to enact factory legislation. In 1900, the government established a temporary Factory Survey Office (Kōjō Chōsakakari) within the Ministry of Agriculture and Commerce. Headed by Gotō Shimpei's chief assistant from the Bureau of Health and Sanitation, the Survey Office united social policy experts from the two ministries. The agency also recruited such prominent outside reformers as Professor Kuwata Kumazō of the Social Policy Association and the muckraking journalist, Yokoyama Gennosuke.[64] In 1903, the office released the government's authoritative labor survey, Shokkō jijō.

The Shokkō jijō and subsequent surveys demonstrated the social evils of unrestrained industrialization as never before. Conditions in textile manufacturing and other light industries shocked a great many officials and social reformers, who resented the exploitation of defenseless young women. The reports also highlighted the social problem of child labor. Middle-class reformers regarded education as the principal avenue of escape for children of the urban poor. Moreover, the government was committed to creating an educated citizenry, and in 1907 it extended compulsory education to six years.[65] Yet surveys disclosed the widespread employment of slum children, some as young as six and seven, in tapestry and match factories. These findings reinforced the frustrations already voiced by Yokoyama Gennosuke: "While most of the nation's children are in school struggling to master the Japanese syllabary, urchins in the match factories find themselves jammed between spindles."[66]

What ultimately transformed the problems of workers into a pressing social question was the perceived threat to the health of the nation as a whole. The Home Ministry's Bureau of Health and Sanitation took the lead in both pinpointing the dangers and strengthening the protective features of proposed factory legislation. The bureau's position was bolstered by the Central Health and Sanitation Council (Chūō Eiseikai), an advisory board of physicians and health officials chaired by the army's surgeon-general. Council members had long warned the government of the detrimental effects of factory work on the nation's military strength. Crippled children and sickly mothers meant weak, unhealthy soldiers. Evidence had been mounting since 1894, when Osaka's prefectural health council observed that "there is an inverse relation between the number of qualified conscripts and the development of commerce and industry." Such concern became widespread following the Japanese victory over the Russians in 1905. Determined to maintain their newly won hegemony in northeast Asia, Japanese military leaders called for higher standards in public health as a matter of national defense.[67]

The public health issue proved decisive in uniting the government behind a tougher factory bill. In 1909, the second Katsura cabinet (1908–11) introduced the long-awaited factory legislation to the Diet, only to withdraw it in the face of strong opposition from business associations and their supporters in the Lower House. Criticism of the bill centered on the provision that would phase out all night work by women and children over a ten-year period. Into this stalemate stepped the Bureau of Health and Sanitation, which revealed the enormity of the health problem in the textile mills. In a series of surveys on women workers and disease, bureau officials demonstrated how alternating night and day shifts at weekly intervals produced irrecoverable weight loss. Packed into unsanitary dormitories, the weakened factory girls contracted tuberculosis and other contagious diseases in tragically high numbers. Most dramatic, the surveys established that tubercular victims were sent home by the thousands to villages throughout Japan, where they infected others.[68] Factory conditions could no longer be represented as simply an element of industrial production. Armed with new medical evidence, the government overcame the opposition of employers, and the Diet finally enacted the Factory Law in 1911.

The passage of the Factory Law marked a critical first step in the Japanese state's efforts to protect workers. The law imposed minimum health and safety standards in factories employing fifteen or more workers, as well as in any other enterprise engaged in dangerous or unhealthy work. It also established a special factory inspectorate within the Ministry of Agriculture and Commerce. One important provision made employers liable in the case of job-related injuries. The minimum age of employment was set at twelve. With regard to women and youths under fifteen, the law generally established a twelve-hour day, in addition to prohibiting night work.[69]

It would be a mistake, however, to regard the Factory Law as a triumph of the state's social needs—public health, education, and domestic order—over industrial interests. In the final analysis, protective labor legislation succeeded only when state officials and employers agreed that some degree of labor protection would improve, or at least not impair, productivity. By 1909, large cotton-spinning companies accepted the concept of modest limitations on working hours because most had already reduced the number of hours and improved other aspects of work in an effort to conserve manpower. But when it came to proposed restrictions on the still widespread practice of night work for women and children, the big factories forced the government to adopt a full fifteen-year delay in enforcement, despite the proven acuteness of the health problem. Moreover, the more vulnerable smaller firms successfully lobbied to postpone the implementation of the entire Factory Law until 1916.[70] Japanese social policy was still very much in its infancy.

POLICIES TOWARD ORGANIZED LABOR

In addition to the demands of public health and productivity, early social policy was based on a highly conservative view of the social order. Although officials gradually came to recognize the need to establish labor standards for women and children, the Meiji regime remained intolerant of the efforts of workers to organize themselves to advance their own interests. Prior to 1918, reformist bureaucrats expressed confidence that the state could remedy the worst abuses of factory labor from above. Most conceived of protective social policy as a genuine substitute for workers' associations. When the Home Ministry's Gotō Shimpei first proposed Bismarckian social insurance in 1895, he did so in terms of a "One-Hundred-Year State Plan" to prevent the rise of a socialist party—the very idea of which he found "abhorrent."[71] No one, it will be recalled, argued for the autonomous nature of Japanese social policy more vigorously than Oka Minoru, the Industrial Bureau chief responsible for framing the 1911 Factory Law. Oka further boasted that the farsighted Japanese government had enacted the Factory Law without being forced to do so by "the voice of the workers." Lest his point be missed, Oka likened the legislation to "our Imperially bestowed Constitution [of 1889], which was granted to, rather than demanded by, the people."[72]

In contrast to the state's autonomy from labor interests, the government unabashedly sided with employers in matters of industrial relations. During the 1890s, supporters of factory legislation had commonly ridiculed the claims of employers to maintain traditional familialism within large, modern enterprises. By 1911, most officials were singing a different tune, affirming that factory legislation was fully compatible with paternalistic management. According to Oka, Japan's contemporary industrial relations evolved from its "beautiful customs" (bifū) of hierarchical "relations between master and retainer" (shūjū kankei).[73] The Factory Law, he predicted, would further strengthen the nation's distinctive "harmony between people" (jinwa) by eliminating the sources of labor dissatisfaction:

> In the future, our capitalists . . . will be steeped in the generous spirit of kindness and benevolence, guided by thoughts of fairness and strength. The factory will become one big family: the factory chief as the eldest brother and the foreman as the next oldest. The factory owner himself will act as parent. Strikes will become unthinkable, and we can look forward to the increased productivity of capital—the basis for advances in the nation's wealth and power.[74]

In the meantime, the authorities were taking no chances. Several thousand workers took part in a series of largely successful strikes during the late 1890s (see appendix 1). The government responded with a heavy dose of repression. Symbolic of this policy was Article 17 of the Police Regulations (Chian Keisatsuhō), which police officials in the Home Ministry formulated and the Diet enacted in 1900. The roots of Article 17 lay in the numerous antistrike regulations issued by prefectural governments and employers' associations after 1895.[75] The article not only outlawed the use of violence, intimidation, and public slander in strikes; it went further, prohibiting the act of "instigating" (yūwaku) or "inciting" (sendō) others to strike, join unions, or engage in collective bargaining. The law banned neither strikes nor unions per se, but, as contemporary labor leaders protested, how could anyone organize a strike or trade union without somehow persuading fellow workers to join in? Not until the last years of World War I did police extensively apply Article 17 against striking workers. Nonetheless, the mere existence of the regulation constituted a formidable obstacle to the nascent labor movement over the next two decades. Article 17 also inspired other antilabor laws by which the police commonly placed strike leaders under preventive detention for "incitement." The passage of the Police Regulations in 1900 pressured several unions, already weakened by internal disunity and managerial counteroffensives, to dissolve themselves.[76]

The government's measures against organized labor arose within a larger campaign to stamp out the small socialist movement. In 1901, a group of labor leaders and intellectuals founded the Social Democratic Party, whose reformist platform was influenced by its German counterpart and the American social gospel. The party survived a mere half day before the first Katsura cabinet (1901–06) ordered its dissolution. The more tolerant Saionji cabinet permitted the formation of the Japanese Socialist Party in 1906, but it, too, dissolved the party the next year because of the socialists' flirtation with ideas of direct action and anarchism.

The state simultaneously confronted new militancy from workers in the growing heavy-industrial sector after the Russo-Japanese War. More Japanese workers took part in strikes during 1907 than in any previous year. Although the strikes were partly a response to the postwar price inflation, they also stemmed from dissatisfaction with efforts to impose direct management over employees. Arsenals, shipyards, and the big mines were at the time phasing out the system of semi-independent labor contractors. Frustrated by legal impediments to unionization, workers often resorted to loosely organized protests. Two of the most violent incidents occurred in the Ashio and Besshi Copper Mines, where thousands of miners rioted before troops dispersed them.[77]

The worst was yet to come for Japanese labor. The second Katsura cabinet (1908–11) arrested Kōtoku Shūsui and several other anarchists in 1910, on the charge of plotting to kill the emperor. The ensuing Great Treason Trial represented Prime Minister Katsura Tarō's most dramatic effort to eradicate what officials termed "dangerous thoughts." His government executed Kōtoku and eleven others the following year, despite the fact that an actual attempt on the emperor's life had not occurred. Moreover, Kōtoku himself had apparently withdrawn from the conspiracy prior to its discovery.[78] After police arrested the organizers of the Tokyo streetcar strike in early 1912, little remained of the Meiji labor and socialist movement. To prevent its resurgence, the Home Ministry established Special Higher Police (Tokkō Keisatsu) sections in Tokyo and Osaka with a mandate to investigate and control social movements.[79]

The state's obsession with socialism ironically lent new legitimacy to positive social policy. The same Katsura cabinet that hanged Kōtoku sponsored the Factory Law of 1911. Like his communications minister, Gotō Shimpei, the German-trained General Katsura favored the carrot-and-stick policies of Chancellor Bismarck. Upon taking office in 1908, Katsura committed his government to controlling socialist publications and meetings "as we concurrently prevent the sources of calamity with so-called social policy."[80] At about the same time, the Home Ministry embarked on a poor-relief campaign (*kanka kyūsai jigyō*) in the cities to remove the potential for socialism among workers and the impoverished. Officials encouraged local elites to establish charity hospitals, orphanages, and labor exchanges. Katsura personally established the semigovernmental charitable foundation, the Saiseikai (Society to Assist Livelihood), in direct response to the Great Treason Incident. Supported by lavish contributions from the emperor, businessmen, and officials, the Saiseikai funded free medical care for the poor.[81]

Although Katsura's social policy followed the Bismarckian model in many respects, there remained one essential difference. The Japanese government refused to deal with workers as a corporate entity. German social insurance was predicated on the workers' right to a secure livelihood and the state's obligation to institutionalize measures toward that end. Katsura and Home Ministry officials, on the other hand, harkened back to Confucian notions of private philanthropy, firmly rejecting the right of the propertyless to public assistance.[82] Moreover, Japanese bureaucrats made little attempt to encourage the formation of nonsocialist workers' associations.[83] Their indifference ran counter to the bureaucracy's overall strategy of organizing and mobilizing occupational groups behind state policies after the Russo-Japanese War.[84]

Whereas the Cooperative Law (Sangyō Kumiaihō) of 1899 aimed at incorporating the nation's small farmers and other independent producers into cooperatives, the law pointedly denied laborers permission to form producers' cooperatives, in which workers might join together to manage their own shops. This exclusion was all the more striking in view of the fact that conservative governments and philanthropists in nineteenth-century Europe often encouraged producers' cooperatives as an alternative to socialist associations. The Meiji regime, observed one prewar scholar, apparently feared that any "such working-class organization might lead to the spreading of the socialist ideal in Japan."[85]

In contrast, the academic proponents of social policy displayed a much more lively interest in labor organizations. The Japanese Social

Policy Association shared the government's commitment to maintaining the capitalist order and preventing the rise of class struggle and socialism. But from the start, Professor Kanai Noburu and other leaders favored the growth of a reformist labor movement, which, like the German Social Democratic Party, would assist the state in advancing social policies. Throughout the 1890s, Kanai urged officials to consult labor groups, as well as business associations, in deliberations over factory legislation.[86] Support for trade unionism gained new strength within the Social Policy Association in the wake of the government's suppression of the Tokyo streetcar strike in early 1912. Led by cofounder Kuwata Kumazō, the majority opinion defended labor's right to strike and demanded the repeal of the "instigation" and "incitement" clauses in Article 17 of the 1900 Police Regulations.[87] A long-time champion of state-sponsored social reform and philanthropic activity, Kuwata committed the forces of social policy to the equally urgent task of encouraging the formation of labor unions, consumer cooperatives, and mutual-aid societies. Workers must be able to advance their own interests, he believed.[88]

The Social Policy Association went on to play a leading role in the development of the most successful of the early labor organizations, the Yūaikai (Friendly Society). The Yūaikai was founded in 1912 by an association member, Suzuki Bunji, a Christian social reformer who had studied with Professor Kuwata at Tokyo Imperial University. In addition to Kuwata, the organization's advisors and counselors included such prominent figures in the Social Policy Association as Takano Iwasaburō and the economic bureaucrat, Soeda Juichi. Suzuki modeled the Yūaikai after the British friendly societies, which had similarly served that nation's workers when unions were illegal in the early nineteenth century. By dedicating themselves to "harmony and cooperation between Labor and Capital," Yūaikai leaders adroitly evaded legal repression. By April 1917, the federation claimed a membership of over twenty thousand. Suzuki strove throughout to persuade the public of the social and economic benefits of labor unions. Unions, he asserted, promoted productivity by regulating labor markets, furnishing new skills, offering mutual aid, and raising the "moral character of workers."[89] The Yūaikai's moderation impressed a number of employers, who permitted the formation of local branches within their enterprises. Nevertheless, the question remained: how would the government and capital respond to the rise of a much larger, more assertive labor union movement?

PARTIES AND SOCIAL POLICY

No history of factory legislation in nineteenth-century Britain would fail to mention the central role of members of Parliament. In Meiji Japan, on the other hand, higher civil servants took the lead in formulating labor policy in an era of weak political parties. Governmental officials first proposed factory legislation nearly a decade before the establishment of the Imperial Diet in 1890. In alliance with bureaucratic protégés, the samurai oligarchs of the early Meiji state held the reins of executive power well into the twentieth century. Except for a brief party-led government in 1898, the young parliamentary parties were unable to form cabinets of their own until 1918. It was in view of these circumstances that the Industrial Bureau's Oka Minoru could claim that the parties never dealt with the Factory Law "as a political question."[90] Like many prewar civil servants, Oka cavalierly equated bureaucratic initiative with the final implementation of policy. Subsequent accounts have similarly emphasized the role of dynamic officials while scarcely mentioning the social policies of the political parties. Although the parties rarely had a direct hand in framing labor measures before 1918, their positions unquestionably affected the legislative outcomes.

Despite frequent changes in names and memberships, two major political groupings dominated the Diet subsequent to its establishment. In 1900, one group collaborated with the oligarchs, Marquis Itō Hirobumi and Marquis Saionji Kimmochi, to found the Rikken Seiyūkai (Constitutional Association of Political Friends). In exchange for parliamentary support, Seiyūkai leaders were given seats in cabinets headed by party president Saionji (1906–08, 1911–12). The anti-Seiyūkai forces remained fragmented among the Rikken Kokumintō (Constitutional People's Party), the Chūō (Central) Club, and smaller parties. Gradually these politicians coalesced around Saionji's oligarchic rival, General Katsura Tarō. In 1913, Katsura persuaded most members of the Kokumintō and minor parties to join his newly orₜ nized Rikken Dōshikai (Constitutional Association of Friends). Although the decimated Kokumintō continued under the leadership of Inukai Tsuyoshi, the pattern of political competition had shifted to two-party rivalry between the Seiyūkai and Dōshikai. After absorbing another small party in 1916, the Dōshikai was renamed the Kenseikai (Association for Constitutional Government).[91]

In terms of their respective social bases, little seemed to distinguish the Seiyūkai and Dōshikai/Kenseikai before 1918. Property qualifications limited the franchise to a mere three percent of the population, effectively excluding workers, tenant farmers, and the urban middle classes. Landlords, merchants, and manufacturers dominated the electorate, and they constituted the core of both parties, together with a number of lawyers, journalists, and former bureaucrats. Although a few politicians favored expanded poor relief and legalized labor unions, the parties as a whole shared the bureaucracy's aversion to public assistance, organized labor, and tenant-farmer movements.[92] In 1900, the Lower House of the Diet overwhelmingly approved the repressive Police Regulations, with scarcely any debate over Article 17.[93] Neither party attempted to revise the controversial clause until 1919.

Yet beneath this apparent consensus lurked a fundamental disagreement over factory legislation and other social policies. According to the contemporary social policy expert, Professor Kuwata Kumazō, Seiyūkai-supported cabinets tended to be "extremely cool" toward the Factory Law even after it passed in 1911. Kuwata singled out Seiyūkai president Saionji Kimmochi for failing to understand the nature of factory legislation. When a Diet member demanded an explanation of his cabinet's social policy in 1912, Prime Minister Saionji simply replied: "Social policy has been the national policy of our Empire since its origins." If that was so, editorialized Kuwata, "why is everyone now clamoring for the Factory Law?"[94] Indeed, the Seiyūkai possessed a consistent record of opposition to factory legislation. As the majority party in the Lower House in 1910, the Seiyūkai blocked the Katsura cabinet's first factory bill. Seiyūkai spokesmen charged that such a law would "bring about a depression in industry."[95]

Before the government reintroduced the measure the next year, it grudgingly agreed to postpone implementation of the ban on night work by women and minors for fifteen years, once the law took effect. Yet the Seiyūkai remained uncompromising. A Lower House committee, chaired by Seiyūkai leader Ōoka Ikuzō, weakened the revised bill further by limiting coverage to factories employing a minimum of fifteen workers, an increase from ten in the government's draft. After the Diet enacted the Factory Law in 1911, the Seiyūkai again lobbied on behalf of irate textile manufacturers to prevent implementation of the legislation. Ostensibly for budgetary reasons, the second Saionji cabinet (1911–12) and the first Yamamoto Gonnohyōe cabinet (1913–14) delayed enforcement of the entire Factory Law. In reality, the two governments deferred to the continued opposition of the Seiyūkai, which held important seats in both cabinets.[96] (See appendix 2 for a list of cabinets and ministers related to labor policy between 1908 and 1932.)

Seiyūkai actions reflected the top leadership's longstanding denial of the state's responsibility for ameliorating social problems. The party's dynamic president, Hara Takashi (Kei), had been strongly influenced by nineteenth-century English political economy. As a young newspaper editor in 1880, he wrote that the burden of poor relief lay with individuals.[97] True to his laissez-faire philosophy, Hara, as home minister in the first Saionji cabinet, permitted the formation of the Japanese Socialist Party in 1906. He similarly condemned Prime Minister Katsura's heavy-handed suppression of socialism and anarchism at the time of the Great Treason Trial.[98] Seiyūkai leaders were unwilling, however, to reduce the sources of working-class discontent by regulating the actions of employers. Takahashi Korekiyo, former president of the Bank of Japan and finance minister in the Yamamoto cabinet, bore the ultimate responsibility for not funding the Factory Law in 1913. This same Takahashi had categorically opposed factory legislation while serving on the Third Higher Conference on Agriculture, Commerce, and Industry in 1898.[99] The familiar arguments of the era's industrialists were most closely echoed by the Seiyūkai's Ōoka Ikuzō, who continued to speak out against enforcing the Factory Law as late as 1916:

> Relations between factory owner and employee in our country are quite different from those prevailing in the West. We have no laws now, yet isn't it true that relations here are conducted in the spirit of friend-ship? . . . Particularly in the large factories with their ample facilities, owners have demonstrated a deep concern for the treatment of their employees because it is in their interests. Is it wise to enforce an unneces-sary law and thereby destroy these beautiful friendly relations by using legal language to guide relations between employee and employer in a forcible and explicit fashion?[100]

The rival Dōshikai, by contrast, supported a noticeably more positive social policy. The Dōshikai's forerunner, the Kokumintō, had vigorously defended Katsura's original factory bill in 1910. When the government subsequently diluted the measure, party members criticized the new bill for in fact protecting capitalists, not women and children.[101] Soon after the formation of the Dōshikai in 1913, party leaders were invited to fill most of the key posts in the Ōkuma cabinet (1914–16). In his opening instructions to prefectural governors, Prime Minister Ōkuma Shigenobu stressed the importance of social policy to improve the plight of the poor. In 1916, Dōshikai ministers authorized funds to enforce the long-postponed Factory Law after overcoming resistance from manufacturing groups and the Privy Council.[102] In the words of the party's secretary-general, those such as the Seiyūkai's Ōoka Ikuzō who persisted in their opposition were hopelessly out of touch with "the trends of the times."[103]

The Dōshikai's greater commitment to labor reform was based on a coalition of two distinct leadership groups. The first consisted of veteran liberal politicians who had been associated with the old Kokumintō. Several had played a leading role in the 1880s movement to force the Meiji oligarchy to institute a parliamentary system. With the establishment of the Diet in 1890, these politicians redirected the fight for constitutional government toward expanding the franchise and improving the conditions of the poorer classes. The parties' best-known social reformer was Shimada Saburō. As president of the *Mainichi shimbun,* Shimada published Yokoyama Gennosuke's influential revelations about Japan's lower strata in 1899. A socially minded Christian, Shimada cooperated with the era's Christian socialists and labor leaders to found the Association for the Promotion of Labor Unions in 1897. So great was his dedication to organized labor that two years later he accepted the presidency of the Printers' Union. Shimada also supported the efforts of the young Christian liberals, Nagai Ryūtarō and Uchigasaki Sakusaburō, who would lead the Kenseikai's drive for labor legislation during the 1920s.[104]

The Dōshikai and later the Kenseikai were also led by a group of reformist ex-bureaucrats who had earlier promoted the Factory Law from within Katsura's governments. At Katsura's request, several trusted officials entered the Dōshikai in 1913. They included the Home Ministry's social policy activist, Gotō Shimpei. Although the press branded the Dōshikai the "bureaucratic party," administrative experience had its pluses. Drawing on their expertise and bureaucratic ties, the former officialsgavetheDōshikai/Kenseikaiamuchfirmerprogrammaticbasethanwas commoninthepartiesofthetime. TheDōshikai'sŌkumacabinetinherited not only the personnel but also the social policies of the second Katsura cabinet. As minister of agriculture and commerce in both cabinets, Ōura Kanetake fought for the passage of the Factory Law in 1911 and then lobbied for its enforcement in 1914.[105] Finance Minister Wakatsuki Reijirō, who took charge of funding the Factory Law, had similarly developed an interest in health care for the poor in 1911 when, as vice-minister, he arranged financing for Katsura's Society to Assist Livelihood.[106]

Association with liberal politicians and parliamentary politics gradually tempered the harsh statist elements of the Katsura legacy among the

Dōshikai's younger former officials. Katsura himself died in 1913, and most of the older former bureaucrats who had served him, notably Gotō Shimpei, left the Dōshikai soon afterward. Leadership of the Dōshikai's bureaucratic wing passed to Gotō's rival, Katō Takaaki (Kōmei). A career diplomat and three-time foreign minister, Katō became party president following Katsura's death. In contrast to the Bismarckian Gotō Shimpei, Katō was a self-proclaimed Anglophile. He preferred the more English blend of social legislation and the accommodation of working-class organizations.[107]

One must not, however, exaggerate the degree of social reformism within the Dōshikai/Kenseikai before 1918. Dōshikai politicians were hardly insensitive to the demands of the business community. In 1916, for example, the Dōshikai's minister of agriculture and commerce reluctantly granted the cotton-weaving industry a special two-hour extension to the Factory Law's stipulated twelve-hour day for women and minors, despite the hazardous working conditions prevailing in the industry. This he did to quell a major party revolt led by prominent members who had interceded on behalf of the manufacturers.[108] Moreover, the Kenseikai's opening platform on social policy in 1916 emphasized relief for indebted farmers with little mention of labor and urban problems.[109] Party leaders, no less than the bureaucratic proponents of social policy, remained convinced that mildly protective factory legislation would be sufficient to prevent labor unions and strikes. Oka Minoru, author of the Factory Law, put it best when he wrote in 1917:

> What makes us proudest is that we have no labor problems on the order of the Western nations. This condition results from the true tranquillity and peace of our society. . . . Conflict currently plagues the societies of the West to a degree unimaginable to us. Take the workers of England. In an effort to increase wages, they have launched widespread strikes, oblivious to the Great War and the precarious fate of their nation. Or Germany and France, where socialist parties, based on workers, dare to engage in conduct and speech harmful to the unity and tranquillity of their nations. American workers have also organized to resist capitalists, thereby precluding harmonious relations between the two groups. Lastly, the recent revolution in Russia rests on an alliance of workers and soldiers. . . . Social policy in the West looks for cures to the "labor disease" (if I may call it that) which has already broken out. Social policy in our own country aims at preventing the outbreak of this disease.[110]

Or so thought Japan's elites.

CHAPTER II

A Crisis in Relations between Labor and Capital, 1918–22

Japan has been blessed with the time-honored relations between master and retainer, or what could be called paternalistic (*onjōteki*) employment relations. If we ably utilize these beautiful customs, there will be no need to ape the ways of the West.

—*Home Minister Tokonami Takejirō (Seiyūkai),*
February 1919[1]

Our nation [recently] approved the fundamental principles of international labor at the [Paris] Peace Conference. We must immediately undertake a series of reforms to make these principles a reality. . . . When we persist in the pretense that conditions in our industry are different [from those of other nations], are we not arguing against the times? Such arguments not only impede the development of our country's fortunes, they reduce Japan to a straggler among the world's civilized nations.

—*Katō Takaaki (Kenseikai president),*
July 1919[2]

THE LABOR QUESTION

Political and economic changes associated with World War I forced a reexamination of Japan's alleged harmony between workers and owners. In September 1918, the Home Ministry sent a rising young police officer to survey conditions in the aftermath of the rice riots. His influential report described a widespread "crisis in relations between Labor and Capital."[3] From ordinary workers to cabinet ministers, Japanese questioned fundamental assumptions about the nation's labor-management relations more in the months following the Armistice of November 1918 than during years of debate over factory legislation. According to one survey by the police, the number of titles published on "the labor question" and socialist and democratic thought increased dramatically from 21 in 1917 to 190 in 1919.[4] The new awareness reflected, first and foremost, the rapid rise of Japanese labor-management tensions toward the end of World War I.

Although Japan played a limited role in the war, its industries profited tremendously, thanks to increased orders from both the Allied powers and the former Asian markets of the belligerents. Industrial expansion nearly doubled the number of workers in privately owned factories, from 950,000 (1914) to 1,612,000 (1919). A disproportionate amount of the growth occurred within heavy industry, government-owned enterprises, transportation, and other sectors that employed large numbers of skilled male workers.[5] Amid wartime inflation and the new demand for skills, more and more workmen turned to strikes to win higher wages. Whereas fewer than 9,000 workers engaged in work stoppages in any of the years between 1914 and 1916, the number soared to 57,000 in 1917 alone. The strike wave continued during 1918 and 1919, involving 66,457 and 63,137 workers, respectively. The public found itself increasingly affected as strikes in large and vital enterprises became commonplace during the latter half of 1919 (see table 2). In the Tokyo printers' strike of July and August, striking engravers forced sixteen of the city's newspapers to suspend publication for five days. Other walkouts shut down the Tokyo Arsenal and the Osaka streetcar system. By 1919, industrial relations could no longer be persuasively represented as a private matter between paternalistic employers and grateful workers.

The rise in labor assertiveness coincided with another unparalleled exhibition of popular unrest—the rice riots of 1918. Spurred by growing urban demand and speculation, rice prices doubled between early 1917 and June 1918, increasing another 50 percent during the first ten days of August alone. The first disturbances broke out in late July in a Toyama fishing village, where women resisted the shipment of scarce rice to Osaka. Spreading like a modern-day Great Fear, rioting erupted during the next fifty-three days throughout Japan, from metropolitan centers to remote farming villages. Angry consumers looted the shops of rice merchants and clashed with police. A staggering one to two million Japanese took part in the protests. They included more than 34,000 factory workers and miners who mounted strikes for better pay during

TABLE II   INDUSTRIAL STRIKES,
JULY 1918–DECEMBER 1919

	Incidents	Participants	Rice prices (yen/koku)
1918			
July	42	2,529	30.39
August	108	26,458	38.70
September	47	8,478	38.23
October	34	3,017	43.91
November	12	852	39.77
December	9	491	40.58
Subtotal	252	41,825	
1919			
January	15	1,935	40.94
February	19	2,637	40.86
March	15	1,118	37.30
April	15	728	39.19
May	16	2,335	42.40
June	44	3,238	44.10
July	106	16,889	47.85
August	115	12,487	49.56
September	38	6,152	51.26
October	38	7,716	51.06
November	46	6,294	52.20
December	30	1,608	53.87
Subtotal	497	63,137	

SOURCE: Watanabe Tōru, "Nihon ni okeru rōdō kumiai hōan," pt. 1, p. 4.

August and September. Although the popular demonstrations seldom articulated demands for political change, they sent shock waves throughout the bureaucratic elites. The oligarchic government of Field Marshal Terauchi Masatake (1916–18) dispatched 92,000 troops to put down the disorders. The liberal press and the political parties seized upon the weakness of Japan's unrepresentative political structure to call for a cabinet responsible to the popularly elected Lower House of the Diet. To restore public confidence, the worried elder statesmen (*genrō*) appointed Hara Takashi, leader of the majority Seiyūkai party, to be prime minister.[6]

What most distinguished the labor disputes of 1917–19 from previous strike waves was the accompanying widespread formation of labor unions. The number of unions quadrupled between 1918 and 1923 (from 108 to 432). Although Suzuki Bunji had committed his Yūaikai to a cautious policy of "harmony and cooperation between Labor and Capital," local branches of the embryonic labor federation spearheaded many of the major strikes during 1917 and early 1918. Industrialists retaliated by dismissing Yūaikai members and smashing several locals. The conservative Terauchi government joined in, arresting striking workers in record numbers under Article 17 of the 1900 Police Regulations and other repressive laws (see appendix 3).[7]

Employers and officials, however, were fighting a losing battle against a seller's market. Despite massive dismissals and dissolutions, the Yūaikai attracted thousands of new members from among skilled workmen. The Yūaikai's growth also owed much to its shift to industrial unionism (organization by industry), beginning in 1918–19. Although Yūaikai leaders had originally organized craft unions, they quickly found, as had their predecessors in the 1890s, that in the absence of strong craft traditions, such unions lacked control over apprenticeships and the labor supply. By the end of 1919, the federation boasted a membership of thirty thousand, organized in branches throughout Japan. Symbolic of the Yūaikai's transformation into a genuine labor union federation, delegates to the 1919 convention pledged to "rid the world of the evils of capitalism." The Yūaikai was renamed the Greater Japan General Federation of Labor and the Friendly Society (Dai Nihon Rōdō Sōdōmei-Yūaikai). It became simply the Japan General Federation of Labor (Sōdōmei) in 1921.[8]

The new labor unions constituted a political as well as an economic challenge to the established elites. Firsthand experience with repression convinced many labor leaders that they must turn to political activity to remove the obstacles to organizing labor. To Yūaikai locals in the Kansai area (Osaka, Kobe, Kyoto), this meant, above all, the repeal of Article 17 of the Police Regulations and the enactment of a labor union law. On 16 January 1919, the Yūaikai's Osaka and Kobe federations sponsored the first "Rally to Promote the Official Recognition of Labor Unions." Speakers explained how legal recognition promised more than the basic freedom to organize. It meant acceptance by society at large. In an effort to break out of their isolation, the Kansai federations joined with the urban intelligentsia in the burgeoning campaign for universal suffrage.[9] As one activist argued, the capitalist-dominated Diet would never enact labor reforms until the working class elected its own representatives.[10]

International developments also focused Japanese attention on the expanding strength of organized labor. Ever since the Meiji Restoration, Japanese leaders had read their nation's future in the contemporary events of the West. Officials were quick to note the coincidence of domestic unrest and the 1917 Bolshevik Revolution. As the rice riots flared, Terauchi's communications minister, Den Kenjirō, recorded in his diary that "superficial democratic thought and radical Communist ideology are little by little eating away at the brains of the lower classes."[11] Recent scholarship has shown that the Russian Revolution was not a major influence in the new militancy of rank-and-file workers. Nevertheless, Bolshevism did inspire a rising generation of student activists, such as Asō Hisashi and Nosaka Sanzō, who aimed at transforming the Yūaikai into a vehicle for radical change.[12] The end of the World War confirmed labor's growing strength abroad. Working-class movements played prominent roles in overthrowing monarchic regimes not only in Austria-Hungary but also, more significantly, in Germany, which had served as the role model for oligarchic rule in Japan. Although the threat of revolution remained remote in Great Britain, France, and the United States, Japanese leaders noted that these nations, too, were shaken by waves of large-scale industrial strikes during 1919.

More than any other international influence, the Paris Peace Conference shaped the discussion of labor problems in Japan. The Japanese attended the conference as the only non-Western nation to be admitted to the ranks of the victorious Big Five. But with status came responsibilities. By signing the Treaty of Versailles in June 1919, Japan pledged to guarantee the right to organize trade unions. The treaty also rejected the view of labor as a commodity, and it authorized the creation of the International Labor Organization (ILO). The first annual International Labor Conference was scheduled to meet in Washington in October 1919. The agenda prominently featured draft conventions for an eight-hour day and the prohibition of night work for women and minors.[13] ILO members agreed to send a representative of the nation's workers, in addition to one delegate each from the business community and the government. The Yūaikai and other Japanese unions wholeheartedly supported the ILO, for they believed that Japan's participation represented the first step toward the official recognition of labor unions.[14]

The Seiyūkai's Hara cabinet, on the other hand, found itself in a quandary. Government leaders welcomed Japan's new respectability, but they adamantly refused to guarantee labor's right to organize. The first test occurred in September 1919 over the selection of the Japanese workers' delegate to the ILO conference. Led by the Yūaikai's Suzuki Bunji, union chiefs insisted that the unions alone elect the workers' delegate in their capacity as the sole representative of Japanese labor. To their extreme disappointment, the authorities totally rejected the demand, fearing that it would imply official recognition of labor unions. By permitting unorganized workers as well as union members to vote, officials essentially negated the influence of the small union movement. The way was paved for the strange election of a representative of management, the chief engineer Masumoto Uhei, as the workers' delegate. At the International Labor Conference that October, labor representatives from other nations joined Japanese unions and the liberal press in protesting the government's perversion of the ILO's principles.[15] Added to domestic developments, the international embarrassment persuaded many Japanese that the time had come to reformulate the labor policies of the past.

CAPITALISTS PROPOSE REFORMS

The upsurge in labor unrest placed once-confident employers on the defensive. They, too, felt a sense of crisis in the face of the singularly successful postwar strikes. Despite previous resistance to factory legislation by individual trade associations and local chambers of commerce, Japanese capital lacked a strong central organization to unite businessmen from different industries on specific issues. In this respect, the new strength of organized labor proved a critical element in the emergence of several employers' associations during and after World War I.

The most prominent employers' association, the Japan Industrial Club (Nihon Kōgyō Kurabu), firmly opposed any legislation that would recognize labor unions, just as its predecessors had denied the need for state intervention to protect factory workers. Dominated by the newer heavy industries and the major *zaibatsu,* the Industrial Club represented those companies best able to thwart unionization within their plants.[16] During World War I, several large shipyards and steel mills began offering seniority bonuses and other benefits to reward workers held up as models of good conduct. Amid the strike wave of 1917–21, these firms attempted to mollify disgruntled workers by extending bonuses to the strikers. Another innovation was the personnel or labor section, which *zaibatsu* concerns and some independent shipyards established during this period. To wean workers from outside labor unions, the sections sponsored various company welfare programs.[17]

Although highly creative and often cosmopolitan in their responses to the changing labor situation, the entrepreneurs of the Japan Industrial Club adroitly couched their hostility to governmental labor reforms in the traditionalistic language so popular with conservatives at the time. In a report to the home minister, the club's special committee on labor problems summarily explained the ongoing strike wave in terms of the influx of "foreign thought which assumes antagonistic relations between Labor and Capital." The panel's solution was a familiar one: make workers and owners "one in harmony and cooperation" (*wachū kyōdō ippon*), based on Japan's "time-honored beautiful customs."[18] With respect to other areas of labor legislation, the Japan Industrial Club rejected compulsory unemployment insurance as "premature" for Japan. Employing the usual arguments of profits and paternalism, club leaders asserted that such a system would "weaken the factory owner's view of his responsibility to his workers. The workers, on the other hand, are liable to get used to this protection, and the results, on the contrary, will encourage labor turnover and mobility."[19]

Whereas members of the Japan Industrial Club trusted in their own efforts to restore harmonious relations, no such confidence prevailed within other segments of the business community. Many employers reluctantly acknowledged that Japan's supposed traditions of paternalism and master-retainer relations were of little avail against the quite modern problems of strikes and unions, and they embarked on a search for new methods of industrial relations.[20] In June 1919, 120 of 161 large factories surveyed in the Osaka area replied that they would permit the formation of workers' unions (*shokkō kumiai*); another 12 expressed conditional acceptance depending on who led the unions.[21] Postwar instability in labor relations convinced many managers that it was far easier to negotiate with disciplined labor unions than with the existing bands of loosely organized strikers.

Most remarkable, several employers' associations actively campaigned during 1919 for the prompt enactment of a labor union law. The Osaka Industrial Association (Ōsaka Kōgyōkai), the largest federation of industrialists in the Osaka-Kobe-Kyoto area, petitioned the Hara cabinet in June for a law that would recognize craft unions.[22] In marked contrast to the Japan Industrial Club, the association also favored the adoption of comprehensive state-sponsored labor insurance covering unemployment, accidents, sickness, and disability, and leaders contemplated a British-style labor ministry and arbitration courts to mediate industrial disputes.[23] The Osaka Industrial Association's greater interest in labor reform reflected the labor movement's higher level of organization in the industrialized Kansai region than in Tokyo. The association, moreover, contained a much larger proportion of small and medium companies, whose owners were in a less powerful position to resist unions.[24] Six months later, the Tokyo Federation of Business Associations (Tōkyō Jitsugyō Kumiai Rengōkai) similarly called on the government to sponsor union legislation:

> The organization of labor unions in the Western nations has long been recognized as in the interests of industry. In our nation, on the other hand, the absence of such organizations is truly unfortunate. The enactment of a union law is especially necessary in view of the boisterous advent of the labor question. A union law will elevate the position of the worker and assure him stability in his livelihood through mutual assistance [within the union]. By furnishing proper guidance, the law will bring about the smooth development [of unions] in a manner appropriate to the nation.[25]

Both the Osaka Industrial Association and the Tokyo Federation of Business Associations envisioned labor union legislation as a means of isolating militant unions. Neither countenanced the legal recognition of industrial unions, which employers believed to be more prone to syndicalist ideals of workers' control over an entire industry. The Osaka Industrial Association further insisted that the recognized craft unions be restricted to prefectural boundaries under strict governmental control (although the Tokyo Federation's draft permitted national federations of craft unions). Moreover, the Tokyo Federation proposed the prohibition of acts to "inhibit work"—strikes and slowdowns.[26] Nevertheless, these business groups recognized the indispensability of horizontally based unions to viable industrial relations. The Osaka Industrial Association recommended opening union leadership to "learned men" (gakushiki keikensha) and workers from outside the workplace, but forbidding capitalists to join.[27] When Home Minister Tokonami Takejirō of the Hara cabinet sought instead to restrict labor organizations to company unions or councils of workers and managers within each enterprise, the Osaka Industrial Association vigorously protested. Tokonami's approach, countered these executives, failed to consider the sentiments of the worker, who, psychologically speaking, cannot possibly remain satisfied with his past dependence on the paternalism and patronage of his employer. He wishes to undertake his daily work on the basis of a certain self-reliance, as is his reasonable demand and natural right. These spiritual demands of the times, however, will not be satisfied by a vertical union within a single factory. A vertical union within a single factory is essentially under the supervision and patronage of capitalists. It therefore greatly damages the characteristics of impartiality, independence, and freedom, which are the life blood of any union. The state's official recognition of the formation of unions in similar trades will relieve the worker's inner discontent, as well as satisfy his psychological needs. It will particularly encourage the development of self-respect, heretofore lacking in our nation's workers, and it will foster the virtues of responsibility for oneself.[28]

Labor and Capital were by no means united on a concrete solution to labor problems in 1919, but many on both sides looked to the state to help define a new system of industrial relations.

THE SEIYŪKAI GOVERNMENT AND THE MODERNIZATION OF "HARMONY"

The state that confronted the new labor problems was itself undergoing a major transformation. After fifty years of rule by virtue of their proximity to the emperor, the aging Meiji oligarchs resigned themselves to placing the regime on a firmer parliamentary base. In September 1918, they delegated the Seiyūkai's Hara Takashi to organize his own cabinet. Except for the short-lived cabinet of Ōkuma Shigenobu and Itagaki Taisuke in 1898, the Hara government (1918–21) became the nation's first party cabinet in the sense that the head of a parliamentary party and his party's ministers of state held ultimate responsibility for governmental policy. The essentially bourgeois Seiyūkai, which had once battled the oligarchy as a "popular party," thenceforth itself faced challenges from below.

As a party, the Seiyūkai remained hostile to labor organizations and labor union legislation, just as it had earlier opposed the protective Factory Law. This opposition was based, in part, on the Seiyūkai's increasingly close ties to the Japan Industrial Club and the major *zaibatsu*. Two of the party's leading businessmen, Yamamoto Teijirō and Wakao Shōhachi, actively participated in the Japan Industrial Club's committee on labor problems, which lobbied against unemployment insurance and the legal recognition of unions. Yamamoto, the president of the Taiwan Sugar Corporation, also used his influence in urging the Hara government to petition the ILO to exempt Japanese firms in Taiwan from proposed international regulations for the protection of labor.[29] Miyashima Seijirō, another Industrial Club activist and managing director of the giant Nisshin Spinning Company, later ran for the Lower House as a Seiyūkai candidate. In 1919, Miyashima called for a "law to prevent labor disputes."[30] In addition, club members influenced the Seiyūkai's antilabor stance from the outside. Dan Takuma, head of Mitsui's holding company (Mitsui Gōmei), generously contributed to the Seiyūkai. As chairman of the governing board of the Japan Industrial Club, Dan led the drive against labor union legislation throughout the next decade.[31]

The Seiyūkai's leadership numbered several other major industrialists. Of the sixteen members of the Seiyūkai's executive council between 1914 and 1921, eight were businessmen. Most represented large-scale heavy industries of the type resisting organized labor at the time.[32] The growing importance of industrialists within the Seiyūkai dated back to 1912, when party president Hara Takashi began recruiting nationally prominent businessmen into the Seiyūkai. Many businessmen eagerly joined, in an effort to gain greater influence over economic policymaking from within the powerful party. By 1920, Seiyūkai candidates for the Lower House included a number of well-known industrialists, especially those from the Mitsui *zaibatsu*.[33] Few favored the more conciliatory approach toward organized labor advocated by the Osaka Industrial Association.

The Seiyūkai's rural-oriented electoral strategy also contributed to the party's lack of interest in the generally urban issues of labor legislation and universal manhood suffrage. Because of tax qualifications, less than 3 percent of the population held the right to vote in 1917. Moreover, a disproportionate number of voters lived in the countryside, where over half of the nation's working population was still engaged in agriculture and forestry. The Seiyūkai had thrived under the system of limited suffrage, achieving large pluralities in all but one election for the Lower House since 1902. During that period, Hara Takashi successfully attracted large numbers of landlords and local businessmen to the Seiyūkai. As a three-time home minister before 1918, Hara instructed Home Ministry officials to construct railroads, highways, and riparian works in contested districts to gain support for the Seiyūkai. One historian contrasted Hara with the infamous Hoshi Tōru, leader of the

Seiyūkai's predecessor: "Hoshi bribed individual members of the Diet; Hara bribed the electoral district itself."[34]

Although Seiyūkai leaders continued to respond to the needs of the provincial elites after 1918, they faced no significant electoral pressures to protect the rights of labor or to enact a universal suffrage law that would enfranchise the working and middle classes of the cities. Prime Minister Hara made his preference for the countryside clear when his party revised the electoral system in 1919 so as to enfranchise those who paid a minimum of three yen (formerly ten) in direct national taxes. He also gerrymandered election districts in favor of the Seiyūkai's rural strongholds. Inasmuch as the chief beneficiaries of the reform were small landholders, the proportional increase of voters in rural districts was much greater than in the cities. Hara sponsored his electoral reform to strengthen those whom he termed "moderate, middle-of-the-road" Seiyūkai candidates, against "those who win elections by instigating workers and other poor people."[35] The latter category referred to the rival Kenseikai and the rump Kokumintō, both of which advocated universal manhood suffrage and labor union legislation. Hara, on the other hand, vehemently opposed the immediate enactment of universal manhood suffrage, and he dissolved the Diet in February 1920 specifically to prevent the Kenseikai and the Kokumintō from introducing a unified manhood suffrage bill. Hara's election law contributed directly to the Seiyūkai's impressive victory in the May elections. With the Seiyūkai holding a decisive majority of 278 seats in the Lower House (of the total 464), the party had less reason than ever to appeal to workers and the urban disenfranchised.

Although Seiyūkai leaders remained opposed or indifferent to labor reform, the Hara cabinet as the new government in 1918 found itself directly confronting popular dissatisfaction and industrial unrest. Scholars commonly portray Prime Minister Hara as a cautious political boss, whose dedication to unobstructed economic growth made his cabinet insensitive to the postwar need for social reform.[36] In fact, the Hara government embarked on a fundamental reexamination of social policies following the rice riots in 1918. During his three years in office, Hara convened an unprecedented number of governmental commissions to consider relief measures, labor union legislation, a farm-tenancy law, and other innovative programs. Hara had roundly condemned the preceding Terauchi cabinet for relying on suppression against popular movements.[37] Japan's first "commoner" prime minister self-consciously worked to relax censorship and expand civil liberties during his first year.[38] Hara also prized Japan's seat on the eight-nation governing board of the International Labor Organization, and he was determined to distance his government from the union-busting and strike-breaking activities of past regimes, in an effort to avoid international criticism of Japanese labor practices during 1919.

The chief architect of the cabinet's revised labor policy was the Seiyūkai's controversial home minister, Tokonami Takejirō. In most accounts, Tokonami appears as an old-fashioned, rather slippery politician, who jumped from party to party during the 1920s in a vain attempt to become prime minister. Far more important for our purposes was Tokonami as bureaucratic activist and visionary. Tokonami entered the Seiyūkai in 1913 after a distinguished career in the Home Ministry. He had established himself as chief of the Local Affairs Bureau, subsequently rising to the highest administrative post of vice-minister.

A nativist in many respects, Tokonami was nonetheless well acquainted with Western administrative practices relating to local government, poor relief, and policies toward religious organizations. In the course of service, he developed a distinctive approach toward dealing with economic dislocation and social problems. The state, he believed, must actively integrate society by patronizing local organizations that served to harmonize the often conflicting interests of their members. Tokonami vigorously supported the formation of cooperatives among farmers during the Local Improvement Movement (1906–12). As vice-minister in 1912, he similarly sponsored the "Assembly of the Three Religions" (Sankyō Kaidō), an attempt to mobilize Buddhist, Shinto, and Christian clergy behind social-work projects and a national campaign against political radicalism.[39] Upon becoming home minister in 1918, Tokonami fashioned a like-minded clique among such senior Home Ministry officials as Kobashi Ichita (vice-minister), Kawamura Takeji (chief, Police Bureau), and Soeda Keiichirō (chief, Local Affairs Bureau). All three later joined the Seiyūkai.[40]

Home Minister Tokonami reacted to the eruption of labor disputes toward the end of World War I by similarly seeking to bring the disputants together. Drawing on his subordinates' reports of a crisis in labor-management relations, Tokonami proposed the following approach:

> we should not thoughtlessly imitate the examples of foreign nations. We have special ideals based on the conditions of our country. For example, in the labor relations of the West, the boundary between capitalist and worker is a broad line, drawn horizontally to separate the higher and lower

strata. In our country, on the other hand, I believe it best to solve these problems with a policy based on the spirit of harmony and cooperation (kyōdō chōwa), which pervades the unit of work in a vertical fashion.[41]

With those words, Tokonami presented "harmony" as Japan's alternative to Western-style unions. He totally dismissed the need for a labor union law, which by its nature was premised on the Western notion of "antagonism between capitalist and worker."[42] The rhetoric of Japanese harmony and vertical relations was not new, but Tokonami energetically pursued several policies to adapt Japanese ideals to the changing industrial conditions of the postwar era.

Tokonami and his staff began by reinterpreting the "instigation or incitement" clause in Article 17 of the 1900 Police Regulations, which the Terauchi government had frequently invoked against unions and striking workers. Top officials of the Home Ministry reaffirmed their opposition both to repealing the controversial clause and legally recognizing labor unions. However, in a departure from previous policy, the chief of the Police Bureau, Kawamura Takeji, declared that workers were free to organize labor unions. In his judgment, Article 17 barred only "instigation or incitement" in a strike or in the formation of a union, not the strike itself nor the organization of a union by "peaceful means."[43] To be precise, as Home Minister Tokonami explained, his ministry's police force would encourage enterprise-based "vertical unions" (jūdanteki kumiai) while continuing to check the growth of horizontally organized trade unions: "I believe we should enforce Article 17 in cases in which those outside the factory attempt to instigate and incite employees. We should not apply it against those within the factory who advance their position through mutual discussion with the object of bringing harmony to relations between employer and workers."[44] The new policy of selective enforcement resulted in a marked reduction of strike-related arrests under Article 17 and other laws during 1919 (see appendix 3).[45]

Yet Tokonami was not one to await patiently the development of vertical unions, and he concurrently sponsored the creation of the semigovernmental Kyōchōkai for the purpose of promoting harmony between labor and management. Inaugurated in December 1919, the Kyōchōkai (Harmonization Society) consisted primarily of senior officials, prominent businessmen, and academic specialists. After initial reluctance on the part of many executives, the business community agreed to fund a substantial endowment of 6.8 million yen. Tokonami and Home Ministry leaders hoped the Kyōchōkai would preclude the need for horizontal trade unions.[46] While the Kyōchōkai was still in the planning stages, Vice-Minister Kobashi Ichita presented the organization as a body that would combat "incitement" by "radicals"; the Harmonization Society would educate workers in the "spirit of cooperation and self-restraint," besides urging employers to take better care of their workers.[47] In December 1918, Police Chief Kawamura Takeji advised Suzuki Bunji of the Yūaikai labor federation that the foundation would serve as the government's central coordinating agency in a hierarchical system of "Labor-Capital harmonization bodies," designed to supplant the labor unions at every level.[48] During the first half of 1919, Tokonami and his subordinates engaged in discussions on the structure of the projected Kyōchōkai with a group of business and political leaders headed by Baron Shibusawa Eiichi, one of modern Japan's pioneer businessmen.

Contrary to the fears of Yūaikai leaders, the establishment of the Kyōchōkai did not prove particularly threatening to organized labor. As cofounder, Shibusawa shared Tokonami's desire to restore labor-management harmony, but he categorically rejected the home minister's plans to organize a government-directed surrogate for genuine unions. Shibusawa envisioned the Kyōchōkai as a strictly private foundation that would study social problems and provide informal conciliation by instilling cooperative attitudes in workers and capitalists before strikes could occur.[49] Shibusawa had been one of the Yūaikai's original advisors, and he remained a strong supporter of Chairman Suzuki Bunji in 1919.[50] Like many other businessmen in the immediate postwar era, Shibusawa believed in the constructive role of labor unions. In his mind, the Kyōchōkai would simply supplement the efforts of unions and managers to reach compromises. Calling for the recognition of labor unions and the abolition of Article 17, Shibusawa branded Tokonami's "so-called principle of Labor-Capital verticalism" a relic of the "era of cottage industries."[51]

In its final form, the Kyōchōkai approached Shibusawa's vision of a neutral body and marked a clear defeat for Tokonami's scheme to create vertical unions. The society's charter limited its activities to research on social problems, coordination of employment offices and social work, and the arbitration and conciliation of industrial disputes. Kyōchōkai officials further assured worried employers that the foundation would not, as a rule, intervene to mediate disputes.[52] Because the modest role of the Kyōchōkai was clear by the autumn of 1919,

Tokonami and senior Home Ministry officials considered more direct methods of establishing vertical unions and staving off the development of horizontal labor unions.

In response to a new wave of strikes after July, Tokonami and his staff offered legislation that would establish works councils (rōdō iinkai), which grouped workers and managers, in all enterprises employing a minimum of fifty workers. After announcing the outlines of the works council bill in October, the Home Ministry released a detailed draft two months later on the eve of the Forty-second Diet. According to an unnamed ministry official, the legislation was designed to "create unions in each factory while severing contact with those in other factories."[53] Tokonami evidently hoped to seize the political initiative from the opposition Kenseikai, which was preparing legislation that would recognize genuine labor unions.[54] The Home Ministry's draft bill gave factory owners the right to select the council president, and it stipulated that new employees (that is, potential union organizers) could neither elect nor serve as workers' representatives to the councils.

Tokonami's works councils bill drew sharp criticism not only from organized labor and business groups but also from his own government and party. Officials within the sponsoring Home Ministry itself worried that the legislation would provoke greater disorder and problems of enforcement by denying any legality to existing horizontal unions. By mid-October, Prime Minister Hara publicly shelved his home minister's works councils proposal, citing similar fears.[55] To demonstrate the viability of vertical unions, however, Tokonami set up works councils within the National Railways in May 1920, and he inspired other governmental employers, as well as several large zaibatsu concerns in heavy industry, to set up similar councils or company unions over the next few years. Nevertheless, Tokonami did not succeed in legislating the formation of works councils on a nationwide basis.[56]

Despite the failure to mandate vertical unions by means of the Kyōchōkai and works councils legislation, Home Minister Tokonami adopted a much more flexible approach than that of previous Japanese governments, which had discouraged almost all workers' organizations. Tokonami's nativist rhetoric notwithstanding, his bureaucratic subordinates frequently drew upon American innovations to remold labor policy. To justify the enforcement of Article 17 against those outside the workplace, one influential official cited the Sherman Antitrust Act and various judicial decisions by which the United States government restricted "incitement" of workers by union organizers from other states.[57] Moreover, Police Bureau Chief Kawamura Takeji claimed to pattern the proposed works councils after American shop committees, Britain's Whitley Councils, and Germany's works councils. In the postwar world's new "era of harmony and cooperation," he insisted, factory councils—not divisive horizontal unions—had come to the fore as workers recognized the folly of their previous attitudes of "class struggle."[58] Not exactly, countered critics. The works councils resembled neither the British nor the German institutions, and they likened the home minister's vertical unions instead to the company unions of the United States.[59] As the Yūaikai's Suzuki Bunji rightly noted, workers sat on the labor-management Whitley Councils as trade union members, whereas Japanese authorities proposed works councils as substitutes for genuine unions.[60]

Whatever their source of inspiration, Home Ministry leaders continued to regard trade unions and strikes as fundamentally illegitimate. As one member of the rival Kenseikai party observed, the government might not apply Article 17 against workers within an enterprise, yet the prohibition of "instigation or incitement" by outsiders effectively banned trade unions, which necessarily organized workers in different firms.[61] Senior Home Ministry officials often equated the very formation of horizontal unions with the "propagation of radical ideas" by the Soviet Union. Police Bureau Chief Kawamura maintained that Japan's labor problems were not domestic in origin, but stemmed from the incendiary activities of a "few outsiders" who sought to ruin the nation's traditionally harmonious relations between labor and management. Kawamura considered Article 17 essential to protecting Japanese workers from these radical ideas.[62] Nor did the head of the Police Bureau accept strikes as an inevitable aspect of industrial relations. After Takano Iwasaburō, a liberal professor, recommended the elimination of "instigation or incitement" from Article 17 on the grounds that strikes were an illness that would heal naturally if unhindered, Kawamura retorted, "just as you can't call an illness a right, you can't call the strike a right. If one believes illness in a person is undesirable, the bacillus should be driven out. It is just as proper to root out incitement, the bacillus of the strike.[63] To the Home Ministry's senior officials, no less than to Seiyūkai leaders, true labor-management harmony rested on hierarchy and paternalism. There was little room for equal relations between management and legally recognized trade unions.

THE KENSEIKAI AND THE SOCIAL
FOUNDATIONS OF INTERWAR REFORM

Whereas the Hara government sought a labor policy based on tradi-tional values, many political figures questioned the efficacy of applying Japan's "beautiful customs" to the postwar problems of social instabil-ity. As the largest opposition party in the Lower House during 1919, the Kenseikai offered a radically new approach. Historians have long em-phasized the Kenseikai's endorsement of universal manhood suffrage in early 1920. But Kenseikai leaders at the time regarded labor reform as equally central to their ambitious plans for the postwar "reconstruc-tion" (kaizō) of Japanese society. In contrast to the Seiyūkai cabinet, the opposition party not only attempted to repeal Article 17 of the Police Regulations, but also proposed a labor union bill that would recognize the fundamental right of workers to organize unions.

The reformism of the Kenseikai remains a largely unexplained phe-nomenon. Japanese scholars commonly discuss the immediate postwar years in terms of "Taishō democracy," by which they refer to the new assertiveness of the masses. The Kenseikai appears progressive only in so far as it responded to popular demands for reform.[64] Some American scholars add the explanatory factor of partisan rivalry. They maintain that "before 1918, the Kenseikai and the Seiyūkai seemed cut from the same mold, both born out of tactical considerations and hence devoid of any strong ideological coloring or any pronounced difference in pro-grams." In their view, the Kenseikai's subsequent espousal of demo-cratic reform stemmed, in part, from Katō Takaaki's character as a political leader, "but it sprang as well from the fact that the Seiyūkai was in power and the Kenseikai was not."[65]

Yet Taishō democracy was more than a movement from below. Nor did it simply result from the Kenseikai's oppositional position or the idealism of party president Katō. In a study of social policies in Europe, Hugh Heclo cogently argued that political parties must be seen as more than "strictly electoral devices—passive petitioners to and executors of a defined electoral will."[66] Kenseikai leaders were not so much political "outs" trying to get in, as one group of social elites proposing a more flexible means of staying in, amid popular discontent and new interna-tional trends. Their plans to liberalize the political and economic order rested on much firmer historical and social foundations than scholars have generally recognized.

To begin with, the Kenseikai's program of labor reform did not burst forth suddenly in late 1918, but rather evolved from the Dōshikai's earlier support of the Factory Law of 1911 and other social policies. The Factory Law established that employers were liable in the case of job-related injuries. Extending the principle of state intervention in industrial relations, Kenseikai leaders called for a comprehensive labor insurance law and introduced a resolution to that effect to the Fortieth Diet in early 1918. The rice riots and heightened labor unrest, later that year, significantly deepened the party's commitment to reform. On 16 September 1918, the chairman of the Kenseikai's policy affairs research committee explained: "Our party unveiled several policies prior to the Fortieth Diet. However, in view of the tremendous changes which have occurred since then in both the trends of the world and circumstances within Japan, we have deemed it necessary to devise new programs."[67]

The committee thereupon recommended a labor insurance law, the expansion of suffrage, the creation of an agency for unemployment relief, and a survey of "equitable methods of distributing profits between Capital and Labor in industrial and other firms." The panel also explored policies to protect children and the elderly, to reform the farm-tenancy system, and to provide greater relief.[68] Egi Tasuku, the Kenseikai leader who framed the party's labor-union and workers' sickness insurance bills the next year, explained that the party's social legislation embodied "the fundamental view that society as a whole is obligated to help those living in poverty."[69]

Egi Tasuku's efforts highlight a key element in the Kenseikai's promotion of social policy: the active role of the reformist ex-bureaucrats who had led the Dōshikai and the Kenseikai since 1913. The Seiyūkai, too, had its share of former officials, but they never formed a cohesive leadership faction. Nor, with the exception of the Home Ministry's Tokonami Takejirō and Mizuno Rentarō, had they promoted social legislation before 1918. In addition to Egi and President Katō Takaaki, the Kenseikai's inner circle included Wakatsuki Reijirō and Hamaguchi Osachi, both of whom had originally risen within the Finance Ministry. Even though out of power, these highly trained bureaucratic politicians repeatedly managed to put the Hara government on the defensive with detailed and carefully researched proposals. Few party members could match their skills, and Wakatsuki and Hamaguchi later became presidents of the Kenseikai and Minseitō, respectively, after Katō's death in 1926.

Egi Tasuku ranked as the Kenseikai's undisputed authority on labor questions. He entered the Dōshikai at the relatively young age of thirty-nine after distinguishing himself in the Home Ministry, in the Colonial Bureau, and as chief cabinet secretary in the third Katsura government. Egi never became prime minister, but his varied expertise made him a central figure within the unusually active policy affairs research committee of the Kenseikai and later the Minseitō. Between 1918 and 1921, Egi singlehandedly drafted or co-authored every bill in the Kenseikai's impressive package of labor legislation, which covered the recognition of labor unions, revision of Article 17 of the Police Regulations, workers' sickness insurance, unemployment insurance, and amendments to the Factory Law and Mining Law. He also directed the party's work on electoral reform and emerged an ardent proponent of European-style proportional representation. In all these endeavors, Egi did what interwar Japanese bureaucrats did best. He painstakingly studied various Western laws and policies as models for Japanese legislation.[70] Although higher civil servants often asserted that the parties lacked the expertise to formulate policy, the Kenseikai's introduction of Egi's sickness insurance bill, for example, forced the government to draw up and enact Japan's first Health Insurance Law in 1922.[71]

Progressive businessmen in the Kenseikai constituted a second major source of support for a labor union law and related measures. As in earlier years, the Kenseikai depended heavily on campaign contributions from the business community. In this respect, the Kenseikai was not very different from the Seiyūkai. In 1920, company presidents, managers, and corporate-board members constituted well over half of the parliamentary delegation of each party (see appendix 4). Historians have accordingly assumed that ties to employers doomed the Kenseikai's labor reforms, or conversely that the former officials and liberal politicians somehow overcame resistance from the representatives of capital. In actuality, the party's labor legislation mirrored the demands of those employers who in 1919 favored union legislation and a new role for the state in industrial relations. To Uemura Kōsaku, an insurance company president and Kenseikai member, workers had understandably became radicalized during the wartime industrial boom as capitalists grew richer and the workers poorer. As a corrective, he proposed a system of labor insurance patterned after schemes that existed in Western nations. Social insurance, he reasoned, brought "soundness and steadiness" to the thoughts of the working class and, by relieving workers of their everyday anxieties, greatly contributed to productivity.[72]

Most striking were the close relations between the Kenseikai and the enlightened employers of the Osaka Industrial Association. Kataoka

Naoharu, a Kyoto entrepreneur and Kenseikai leader, personified the association's influence on the party's labor program. Kataoka's younger brother served as president of the Osaka Industrial Association until 1922, when he was succeeded by Kataoka's adopted son.[73] In February 1919, Kataoka Naoharu resigned the presidency of the Japan Life Insurance Company, declaring that he would devote his fortune to the study of labor problems. Echoing the Osaka Industrial Association, he proclaimed governmental recognition of labor unions to be the pressing issue of the times: "The protection of workers in unions under strict supervision [by their own officials and the state] will, in all respects, benefit the nation. However, we must not allow them to become arrogant. This will be to their benefit, as well as to the nation's."[74] And like the Osaka Industrial Association, Kataoka ridiculed the campaign by Hara's home minister, Tokonami Takejirō, to perpetuate the ideology of "relations between master and retainer."[75]

On some issues, however, the Kenseikai businessman adopted a much more tolerant line toward organized labor than that of his fellow entrepreneurs. No major employers' association came forward to advocate labor's right to strike, yet Kataoka in March 1919 cosponsored the Kenseikai's first attempt to eliminate the prohibition against "instigation or incitement" from Article 17 of the Police Regulations.[76] Drawing on his experience in insurance matters, Kataoka also proposed a workers' insurance system to be underwritten by employers, employees, and the government. In early 1920, he joined Egi Tasuku in drafting the Kenseikai's sickness insurance bill.[77]

Although the Kenseikai reflected the mood of many employers, the party was less receptive than the Seiyūkai to the uncompromising stand on labor questions taken by the Japan Industrial Club and heavy industry, in general. The Kenseikai, it is true, relied on contributions from big business, especially the Mitsubishi *zaibatsu*. Party president Katō Takaaki was in fact a former Mitsubishi employee and a son-in-law of the *zaibatsu*'s founder, Iwasaki Yatarō.[78] However, in contrast to the Seiyūkai, the captains of large-scale industry rarely reached positions of top leadership within the Kenseikai. Kataoka Naoharu, the Kenseikai's leading spokesman for business, for example, represented the older world of commerce and light industry in Kyoto and Osaka.[79] Another Kenseikai executive, Machida Chūji, was an Osaka banker who had founded the liberal newspaper, the *Tōyō keizai shimpō*, the most consistent advocate of labor's rights during the 1910s.[80] Even in the case of Katō Takaaki, Mitsubishi money did not necessarily dictate his approach to labor issues. After the spring of 1919, Katō repeatedly urged the legal recognition of labor unions. When his brother-in-law, Iwasaki Hisaya, refused to meet with striking workers at Kobe's Mitsubishi Shipyards in 1921, Katō publicly blamed greedy capitalists, as well as undisciplined workers, for the strikes.[81] Katō and other Kenseikai leaders were, of course, not hostile to the interests of business. Rather, they faced an array of conflicting recommendations from the economic community on how best to handle the crisis in industrial relations. In the end, they were persuaded by sound business reasons for rationalizing labor-management relations around a system of labor union legislation.

In addition to reformist ex-bureaucrats and progressive businessmen, the existence of a highly vocal band of veteran liberals and younger party members helps explain the Kenseikai's enthusiasm for labor legislation in 1919. The press commonly termed this group the party's "radical wing" (*kyūshin-ha*) in pointed reference to the Radicals of the Liberal Party in late-nineteenth-century Britain.[82] Like the British Radicals, these Kenseikai politicians generally hailed from the free professions—journalism, law, and education—and they tended to distance themselves from the interests of industrial employers. Moreover, they resembled their Western counterparts in the pursuit of social reform and in their efforts to create an electoral base among the working and middle classes of the big cities. Although some in the Seiyūkai similarly favored mass enfranchisement and labor legislation, their numbers were much smaller and their influence on party leadership far weaker. In February 1919, thirty-five members (or 30 percent) of the Kenseikai's Lower House delegation urged their more cautious leaders to take up the cause of universal manhood suffrage. Nearly half of these Radicals represented the six largest cities or such industrial centers as Yawata and Yokosuka.[83] Younger Radicals were particularly caught up in the euphoria for social and political "reconstruction" following the victory of the Allied democracies in 1918. One of their leaders, Nagai Ryūtarō, a professor of social policy, quickly emerged as a forceful proponent of labor's right to organize after his election to the Diet in 1920.[84]

The Radicals were not content to stop at legislative reform. Remarkably enough, many Kenseikai politicians took part in actively organizing trade unions. Their efforts contributed to the mushrooming of some 211 new labor unions in 1919 alone.[85] Younger Radicals in the Kenseikai's support group, the Constitutional Young Men's Party (Rikken Seinentō), directed the campaign. Together with the staff of an affiliated journal, the *Rōdō sekai,* they assisted the formation of several unions. Some unions, notably the Rōdōkai at the mammoth Tokyo (Koishi-kawa) Arsenal, repaid the favor by closely cooperating with the Kensei-kai in support of universal manhood suffrage during 1920.[86] Although some Kenseikai members undoubtedly wished to restrain the trade unionist aspects of the labor organizations, others acknowledged the need for aggressive bargaining to advance the interests of workers. A dramatic case in point involved Yokoyama Katsutarō, a distinguished Tokyo lawyer and Kenseikai executive. In June 1919, Yokoyama be-came president of the Tokyo engravers' union, the Kakushinkai (Reno-vation Society). Later that summer, he personally led the Tokyo print-ers' strike, one of the period's most crippling work stoppages.[87]

Recent studies demonstrate the depth of the Kenseikai's drive to cul-tivate a labor base at the local level. At the height of the universal suffrage movement in October 1919, the party branch in the city of Kure helped found the Kure Labor Union among workers in the city's huge naval arsenal. The first president of the Yūaikai-affiliated union was a Kensei-kai prefectural assemblyman who had earlier served as legal advisor to the Yūaikai's local in neighboring Hiroshima. His successor, an influen-tial businessman, was a frequent Kenseikai candidate in Lower House elections. Through the Kure Labor Union, the Kenseikai made sizable inroads among the arsenal's 35,000 employees, who constituted one-half of Kure's work force. The Kenseikai and later the Minseitō subsequently reduced the Seiyūkai to a minor party in Kure in local and general elec-tions during the 1920s.[88] Despite the limited franchise operative in the general election of 1920, the Kenseikai also benefited from the support of pockets of enfranchised skilled workers in certain districts. In the indus-trial city of Yawata, where workers of the Yawata Steel Works reportedly accounted for 75 percent of the electorate, the Kenseikai's branch sum-marily deputized leaders of the Yūaikai and two other unions as local party officials shortly before the election. The strategy paid off when the district encompassing Yawata elected the Kenseikai candidate.[89]

The city-based Radical politicians provide a key to understanding why the Kenseikai/Minseitō promoted the rights of labor unions after 1918 whereas the Seiyūkai did not. Previous studies have tended to dismiss the existence of an urban-rural split between the two parties, citing electoral statistics to assert that both parties drew most of their votes from the countryside.[90] Yet statistics also show that the Dōshikai/Kenseikai emerged as the leading party of the metropolitan centers and provincial cities as early as 1915 (see table 3). Furthermore, relative to the Seiyūkai,

TABLE III   MAJOR PARTIES' ELECTORAL PERFORMANCE
IN URBAN DISTRICTS, GENERAL ELECTIONS, 1915–24
(seats won)

Election year and party	Total seats won	Six largest cities[a]	Major provincial cities[b]	Total urban seats won[c]	Urban/ total seats won
1915					
Dōshikai	153 (40%)[d]	11 (42%)	4 (36%)	29 (38%)	19%
Seiyūkai	108 (28)	1 (4)	2 (18)	8 (11)	7
Kokumintō	27 (7)	6 (23)	0 (0)	7 (11)	26
Total[e]	381	26	11	76	20
1917					
Kenseikai	121 (32%)	9 (35%)	3 (27%)	20 (26%)	17%
Seiyūkai	165 (43)	4 (15)	4 (36)	25 (33)	15
Kokumintō	35 (9)	7 (27)	1 (9)	9 (12)	26
Total	381	26	11	76	20
1920					
Kenseikai	110 (24%)	14 (35%)	6 (46%)	36 (32%)	33%
Seiyūkai	278 (60)	10 (25)	3 (23)	39 (35)	14
Kokumintō	29 (6)	9 (23)	1 (8)	15 (14)	52
Total	464	40	13	111	24
1924					
Kenseikai	152 (33%)	14 (35%)	5 (38%)	37 (33%)	24%
Seiyūkai	102 (22)	5 (13)	2 (15)	19 (17)	19
Seiyūhontō	111 (24)	5 (13)	1 (8)	15 (14)	14
Kakushin Club	30 (6)	8 (20)	1 (8)	13 (12)	43
Total	464	40	13	111	24

SOURCE: Tōyama Shigeki and Adachi Yoshiko, pp. 194–207.
[a]Tokyo, Osaka, Kyoto, Nagoya, Yokohama, and Kobe (excluding environs).
[b]Cities over 100,000 population—Hiroshima, Nagasaki, Hakodate, Kanazawa, Kumamoto, Fukuoka, Sapporo, Sendai, Kagoshima, Otaru, Okayama, Yawata, and Kure (1915 and 1917 figures do not include Yawata and Kure).
[c]Urban seats include all districts designated as *shi* (city) or special districts (Hokkaido).
[d]As a percentage of each column's total.
[e]The totals include seats won by minor parties and independents.

urban representatives constituted a much greater proportion of the Kenseikai's parliamentary delegation between 1915 and 1924.

The Seiyūkai's landslide victory in the general election of 1920 paradoxically strengthened the influence of the urban Radicals within the Kenseikai. Kenseikai candidates made significant gains in the cities, but suffered disastrous defeats in the countryside. As a result, fully one-third of the party's diminished contingent in the Lower House, many of them Radicals, represented urban districts in the early 1920s. Only the much smaller Kokumintō (later the Kakushin Kurabu) relied more heavily on urban seats, and that party, too, championed labor legislation, suffrage reform, and other urban concerns.

On the basis of its greater identification with urban problems, the Kenseikai explicitly linked the issues of labor reform and suffrage expansion. In December 1919, the party's special committee on labor problems favored the enactment of their labor union bill *first* as "a precondition for universal suffrage." If the franchise were extended before unions received legal protection, worried the committeemen, the political demands of workers would remain fragmented, and presumably the Kenseikai would fail to gain the labor vote.[91] In January 1920, party leaders shifted priorities slightly in agreeing to the concurrent implementation of the union law and universal manhood suffrage. Their suffrage measure would enfranchise all adult males not receiving substantial assistance from their families or the state. Kenseikai strategists looked forward to attracting grateful new voters in both the countryside and their existing urban strongholds.

Their hopes of winning over the working class seem to have been well founded. Japanese unions had organized at most 100,000 workers by the end of 1919.[92] Few union officials seriously expected the development of a strong labor party in the near future. Many Yūaikai leaders accordingly sought the cooperation of the opposition Kenseikai and Kokumintō parties to promote the rights of workers. During the early months of 1920, Kenseikai Radicals, for their part, worked closely with the Yūaikai and other unions throughout the nation in a concerted drive to enact the party's universal suffrage bill.[93] To the Kenseikai's radical wing, sponsorship of labor legislation fitted within a grander scheme of transforming the party into a "Lib-lab" coalition.

THE LIBERAL VISION

Historians increasingly argue that the reforms of the 1920s did not result from "grand Democratic ideals."[94] The influence of liberal thought on the Kenseikai, however, should not be dismissed so easily. In the years that followed World War I, Kenseikai members offered an articulate liberal alternative to the programs pursued by the Seiyūkai. This vision, as we have seen, was firmly grounded in pragmatic business considerations, a belief in state-sponsored social policy, and a greater attentiveness to urban problems.

To be sure, few Kenseikai politicians subscribed to the classically liberal aversion to state intervention. But then, neither did most members of the British Liberal Party by the end of the nineteenth century, as several studies have shown. Britain's "New Liberalism" pragmatically justified governmental regulation in cases when the individual rights of the powerful conflicted with those of the community. Although remaining committed to the primacy of market forces in determining wages, Liberal Party governments (1906–14) sought to lessen the insecurity in workers' lives through tougher factory legislation, health and unemployment insurance, and other measures. Moreover, their dedication to a "balanced and harmonious society" led British Liberals to defend the basic rights of trade unions against aggressive challenges from employers. Liberal Party governments not only eliminated old prohibitions against workers' combinations during the 1870s; they also enacted the landmark Trade Disputes Act of 1906, which prevented owners from suing unions for losses incurred in industrial disputes.[95]

It was this socially minded variety of British liberalism that most interested Kenseikai leaders after World War I. Egi Tasuku incorporated several features of the Trade Disputes Act into the Kenseikai's labor union bill.[96] Party president Katō Takaaki, in particular, admired the social conscience of Britain's upper-class politicians, having spent several years in London. While serving as ambassador to the Court of St. James in 1912, Katō made the following observations to a Japanese correspondent:

> As the franchise broadened [in Britain], the representatives of the lower classes of society quickly attained a position of strength in the Parliament. In response, the Liberal Party rushed forward with a series of social reforms in an effort to appeal to the desires of the lower classes and endeavor, directly or indirectly, to advance their happiness. The Liberal Party has recently created labor exchanges, inaugurated a system of old-age pensions, and introduced labor insurance and other measures.[97]

Despite his anxieties over the British parties' tendencies to "curry favor with the lower classes," Katō shared their conviction that the extension of political, social, and civil rights to the working class served to stabilize the social order. Impressed with the nearly total freedom of expression accorded socialists and trade unionists, Katō praised the resulting moderation of the labor movement and the "spirit of compromise" that prevailed in British labor-management relations. Violence and disorder, he noted, rarely marred British disputes; negotiating sessions between labor and management "seem no different from meetings between fellow gentlemen."[98]

The conclusion of World War I strengthened the Kenseikai's desire to reform Japanese industrial relations and political institutions in accordance with what party spokesmen termed the democratic "trends of the world." Shimada Saburō, the party's pioneer social reformer, represented the war as a triumph over the "militaristic" forces of Germany and Austria-Hungary by the forces of "liberty and equality"—Great Britain, France, the United States, and by extension, Japan.[99] In January 1919, the Paris Peace Conference began deliberations on international labor legislation. At the time, the Japanese government was attempting to insert a racial-equality clause into the Covenant of the League of Nations as confirmation of the country's newly acquired great-power status. To its dismay, many Western delegates ridiculed Japanese employment practices as antiquated, casting doubt on the nation's claim to be a true equal.

Responding in part to these criticisms, the Kenseikai introduced an unprecedented bill to the Diet on 13 March that would broaden workers' rights to strike and form unions by eliminating the crimes of "instigation or incitement" from Article 17 of the Police Regulations. Koyama Shojū, the bill's chief sponsor and one of the party's leading Radicals, had recently called on the government to revise Article 17 and recognize labor unions in keeping with the country's newly acquired position among the Big Five powers.[100] The proposed revision failed, and so did Japan's racial-equality clause. The Kenseikai Radical, Nagai Ryūtarō, subsequently blamed the Japanese delegation for its stubborn defense of old-fashioned industrial relations. The Hara government's gray-haired delegates, quipped Nagai, so totally lacked the ideals of democratic reconstruction that they seemed more like envoys who had set out for the Congress of Vienna and taken a wrong turn to Versailles.[101]

The Kenseikai's growing interest in liberal labor policy represented more than a desire for international status or mere mimicry of the West. Kenseikai politicians looked to European models of social amelioration because they genuinely believed that Japan was beginning to face a

European-style crisis in social relations. Party leaders related the recent rice riots in Japan and rising class conflict in the Western nations to common economic dislocations caused by World War I. Taketomi Tokitoshi, a former finance minister in the Ōkuma cabinet, predicted in November 1918 that demobilization would lead to acute unemployment and exacerbate labor-management tensions in Germany, Britain, France, and the United States. Concluded Taketomi: "Accordingly, if revolutionary changes do occur [in the West], they will almost certainly result from the clash of Labor and Capital." Japan's distance from the European conflict notwithstanding, Taketomi charged that his country would not escape the postwar readjustments confronting the Western nations.[102] As large-scale strikes became commonplace at home during the latter half of 1919, Kenseikai leaders became all the more convinced that Japanese society was moving with "the trends of the world." Moreover, they drew lessons from daily news reports of strikes in the British railways and American coal mines. Liberal politicians and the Japanese press were quick to discern an English alternative to the American model of labor policy often cited by the Seiyūkai government. Whereas editorials praised the constructive role played by the mediation committee of the British Trades Union Congress, they condemned the United States government for provoking strikes by denying the legality of labor unions.[103]

What made English liberalism so appealing to bourgeois politicians in the Kenseikai was its historical record of successfully minimizing social conflict without fundamentally altering the social hierarchy. Party spokesmen called for universal manhood suffrage, less as a natural right and more as a "safety valve" for popular discontent.[104] They presented the specter of a radicalized Japan if capitalists and the Hara government persisted in indiscriminately repressing moderate socialists and denying the rights of workers and the poor to a stable livelihood.[105] Katō Takaaki touted his party's new social and labor policies as the most effective way "to check the rampancy of extremist socialism."[106] Seeking support from Nagoya businessmen, Katō quoted David Lloyd George's speech on behalf of his "People's Budget" of 1909:

> I shall be little troubled at being called a Socialist if I be given that title because I take measures to make the majority of the nation happy. As a matter of fact there is no way to check the swelling tide of the people's power, and my social policy is intended as a palliative, and may serve in the end the purpose of preventing a revolutionary movement. Therefore this policy is, on one side, in accordance with the interests of capitalists.[107]

Kenseikai liberals and the more conservative Seiyūkai government both extolled the value of harmony in social relations, but they differed in significant ways over the means to that end. Whereas Home Minister Tokonami insisted that the nation's "paternalistic" employment practices removed the need for horizontal unions and strikes, Kenseikai parliamentarians acknowledged the inevitability of conflict between workers and managers, the rich and the poor. They therefore called upon the state to establish a more orderly framework for conflict resolution between the concerned parties. Labor unions would attain a recognized role within the capitalist order, and the newly enfranchised would work within the parliamentary system. Turning the tables on such traditionalists as Tokonami, Kenseikai leaders declared the natural development of unions essential to maintaining "harmony between capitalists and workers."[108] In the words of the liberal Ōsaka asahi shimbun, workers without unions tend to form "disorderly mobs."[109]

This actively liberal approach to social harmony played a key role in the Kenseikai's decision to draft an integrated program of labor legislation at the end of 1919. The party introduced the measures to the Forty-fourth Diet in March 1921. The first set of bills consisted of Egi Tasuku's sickness-insurance bill for workers, as well as amendments to the Factory and Mining Laws. Following the legislative session of 1921, the party added Egi's unemployment insurance bill, the first of its kind in Japan. These measures stemmed from the Kenseikai's longstanding belief in the state's responsibility to maintain the health and productivity of the labor force, but they were also designed to reduce the sources of radical thought among workers. Second, as they had in February 1919, Kenseikai policy-makers again submitted legislation to remove the crime of "instigation or incitement" from Article 17 of the Police Regulations. Explaining that strikes were "inevitable in today's times," Egi criticized Article 17 for unnecessarily antagonizing the working class. Like most liberals, Egi looked upon strikes as regrettable occurrences, and he favored the retention of Article 17's penalties against the use of "violence" and "intimidation" by striking workers. Nonetheless, the cosmopolitan ex-bureaucrat incorporated the distinctions made by the British Trade Disputes Act of 1906, which legalized the act of picketing so long as it did not involve violence. Egi concluded: "Even in a strike, if its object is to secure just increases in wages, these means [nonviolent instigation and incitement] must be held to be legal."[110]

Egi's labor union bill was the final and most important element of the

Kenseikai's legislative package. A labor union law, argued Kenseikai leaders, was necessary to mold a system of industrial relations in which unionized workers negotiated with management in an orderly fashion. Egi vehemently contested the charge that the formation of unions would lead to more strikes. The recognition of labor unions, he countered, would create a legally responsible group of union officials, who would instead curb their members' tendencies toward reckless strikes. Egi further emphasized the constructive role played by unions in providing mutual assistance in cases of unemployment, accidents, sickness, old age, and death.[111] In its final form, the Kenseikai's labor union bill of 1921 exempted unions from taxes on profit-making activities with the express purpose of encouraging worker-financed insurance programs and other forms of mutual aid. The bill legally recognized labor unions as corporate bodies and granted organized labor its most important protection in Article 10, which read: "An employer may not dismiss an employee for reasons relating to the employee's membership in a labor union."[112] The measure recognized all types of unions, whether craft or industrial, and it permitted national labor federations.

At the same time, Kenseikai drafters gave the state considerable powers to shape the emerging labor movement. Unions would be compelled to go through the often-cumbersome and costly process of incorporation, and governmental authorities were empowered to approve or reject a new union on the basis of those articles of incorporation. The bill further granted officials the authority to dissolve a union, if its acts and decisions violated either the law or its own articles of incorporation, or if they endangered the "public interest." Moreover, the legislation neither guaranteed the right of unions to represent members in collective bargaining nor imposed penalties against employers who violated the prohibition against dismissing union members. Despite these constraints, the Kenseikai's labor union bill, in tandem with the proposed revision of Article 17 of the Police Regulations, were clearly liberal measures within the context of Japan's two major political parties.[113] In view of the Kenseikai's ties to the business community, it is noteworthy that the party was far more willing to guarantee labor's rights to strike and organize than were the relatively progressive industrialists of the Osaka Industrial Association. Only Inukai Tsuyoshi's small Kokumintō party sponsored a more progressive union bill (1922), which imposed fines on union-busting employers, limited governmental suppression, and exempted labor unions from liability for damages suffered by employers during industrial disputes (see appendix 5).[114] The Seiyūkai, on the other hand, never once introduced or supported a labor union bill during the interwar era.

In a ringing endorsement of trade unionism, the Kenseikai explained the rationale behind its labor union bill in 1922:

> A labor union is, of course, a unit of association by which workers combine with the object of the self-defense and protection of their common interests. It is the purpose of this bill to direct such units, which may further amalgamate to form federations, so that they may manage their own relief services for members. The key to the development of industry based on the national economy is naturally the harmony and unity of Capital and Labor. With social progress and in reaction to the omnipotence of Capital, workers have recently become more aware of their rights and position. The rapid growth of the so-called labor movement by which workers organize themselves to assert their interests is, in fact, a natural economic trend. Some capitalists, however, feel that unions will work against their interests, but organizations of capitalists are presently recognized. Surely there is no reason to deny workers the right to form unions for the purposes of protecting their interests against these strong organizations. Rather, capitalists will benefit from the unification of the workers' group consciousness and activities, as well as from the tendencies of unions to avoid futile clashes and to strive for mutual understanding.[115]

The Kenseikai had wedded the foreign idea of rights to existing beliefs in social harmony and political economy, producing a powerful liberal vision for post-World War I Japan.

LABOR ESTRANGED, 1920–22

When the year 1920 began, Prime Minister Hara's labor policy was under fire from a number of sources. The ineffectual Kyōchōkai had scarcely "harmonized" industrial relations, and Hara himself discouraged Home Minister Tokonami's works council proposal. Although unionization and strikes continued unabated, the cabinet's only substantial labor policy remained Tokonami's selective enforcement of Article 17. From within the bureaucracy itself, pressures mounted for the enactment of a labor union law. Officials of the Ministry of Agriculture and Commerce unveiled the working draft of a trade union bill toward the end of January. Some within Hara's own Seiyūkai joined the call for recognizing craft unions in the interest of restoring industrial harmony.[116] In the meantime, the Kenseikai was busily preparing Egi

Tasuku's union bill and other labor legislation for introduction to the current Diet.

To ward off further criticism, Prime Minister Hara created the Extraordinary Commission to Investigate Industry (Rinji Sangyō Chōsakai) in late January, with instructions to reconcile basic disagreements between the Home Ministry and the Ministry of Agriculture and Commerce over labor legislation and policy. At one point, the commission even considered a Home Ministry proposal for labor union legislation more favorable to unions than that of either the Ministry of Agriculture and Commerce or the Kenseikai (see next chapter). Yet it was clear by June that Prime Minister Hara rejected both draft union bills. During the rest of 1920 and 1921, Home Minister Tokonami and senior ministry officials reasserted that the existing freedom to organize unions made a special labor union law totally unnecessary.[117] Their position remained unchanged under the Seiyūkai's succeeding Takahashi Korekiyo cabinet (1921–22), in which Tokonami continued as home minister.

Hara's rejection of his bureaucracy's labor union bills marked the end of the Seiyūkai's serious examination of labor reform. Politically, the party was at the time moving sharply toward the conservatism that would characterize the Seiyūkai throughout the 1920s. Hara, it must be remembered, dissolved the Diet on 26 February to prevent the Kenseikai and Kokumintō from jointly introducing a universal manhood suffrage bill. The ensuing election became a referendum over the further democratization of Japan. The Seiyūkai took the offensive, portraying the Kenseikai and the Kokumintō as allies of organized labor and socialists. Labor policy itself took on political overtones as the Hara government launched a new offensive against strikes and politicized unions. The conservative elder statesman, Prince Yamagata Aritomo, and military authorities had become alarmed at the wave of large-scale work stoppages in governmental and municipal enterprises in the wake of the Tokyo Arsenal strike in August 1919.

Hara shared their concern. When similar strikes broke out against the Yawata Steel Works and the Tokyo Streetcar Company in January and February 1920, respectively, the prime minister concluded that the strike organizers were in league with the advocates of universal suffrage from the Kenseikai and the Kokumintō. This cabal, wrote Hara in his diary, threatened to "impair the present organization of society."[118] Perceiving a combined political and economic challenge, Hara aban-

doned Tokonami's policy of generally avoiding governmental intervention in labor disputes, and he personally directed the harsh suppression
of the two strikes. On the political front, the Seiyūkai's landslide victory
in the May 1920 election discredited his reformist foes. Shortly thereafter, a confident Hara shelved his government's proposed labor union
bills.[119]

International developments gave the Seiyūkai added ammunition
with which to refute the Kenseikai's contention that the failure to reform labor policy would "reduce Japan to a straggler among the world's
civilized nations." The cabinet anxiously awaited the first meeting of
the International Labor Conference in October 1919. Many predicted
that the International Labor Organization would censure the Japanese
for sending a manager as the workers' delegate. Contrary to their fears,
the ILO conference neither denied the credentials of Japan's bogus workers' delegate nor called upon the Japanese government to recognize
labor unions. The conference even exempted Japan from the full provisions of a convention establishing an eight-hour day, citing probable
damage to Japan's many small industries.[120] Spokesmen for the Hara
cabinet were also quick to note that Western businessmen and governments paid little attention to the decisions of the ILO. When the Kenseikai's Egi Tasuku demanded the immediate enactment into law of the
ILO's labor conventions, Foreign Minister Uchida Yasuya retorted that
only one nation had ratified all of the conventions within the required
time.[121] Between 1920 and 1922, Seiyūkai cabinets ratified only one
major convention adopted by the first ILO conference—the Employment Offices Law of 1921.[122]

Lastly, the Seiyūkai's increasingly antilabor position was, in large
part, related to the shifting balance between labor and management
during the early 1920s. Under the immediate postwar conditions of
prosperity and inflation, employers had generally acceded to the workers' demands for higher wages and shorter hours. Industrial disputes
had been limited in scale and duration, and many companies had
deemed it in their interests to deal directly with disciplined labor
unions. In the spring of 1920, however, the Japanese economy began
to experience a postwar recession and growing unemployment. As the
bargaining position of organized labor weakened, industrialists initiated widespread dismissals and wage reductions. The number of
strikes and striking workers sharply decreased during the latter half of
1920 and throughout the early 1920s. Yet the strikes themselves became longer, larger, and more violent as workers defensively strove to

resist wage cuts and layoffs (see appendix 1). At the same time, many union officials grew skeptical of alliances with the bourgeois parties following Prime Minister Hara's open opposition to manhood suffrage. Syndicalist labor organizers seized the opportunity to denounce parliamentary tactics in favor of strikes and other forms of direct action.[123]

In the summer of 1921, these trends culminated in Japan's largest labor dispute before 1945, the coordinated work stoppages at Kobe's Kawasaki and Mitsubishi Shipyards. Led by the Sōdōmei (the renamed Yūaikai), strike organizers demanded the rights to organize unions and to bargain collectively. An estimated thirty-five thousand marched through Kobe to protest Kawasaki's use of strikebreaking thugs. After strikers announced plans to take over production at the Kawasaki Shipyard, the Hara government dispatched soldiers and extra police to ban further rallies. Several hundred strike leaders were arrested, and violent clashes resulted in at least one death and many injuries. Worn down by employers and the authorities, organizers called an end to the month-and-a-half-long strike on 9 August.[124] The Kawasaki-Mitsubishi Shipyards strike had a profound impact on labor policy. It forced many in business and government to reassess their previous interest in recognizing labor unions, which they increasingly viewed as uncooperative and politically radical. The government's response, in turn, reflected a growing tendency to enforce the "instigation or incitement" clause of Article 17 and other repressive laws in the large union-related strikes of 1920 and 1921.[125]

Although the Seiyūkai cabinets of Hara and Takahashi maintained a policy of basic opposition to labor unions and a union law, the rival Kenseikai reaffirmed its commitment to progressive labor legislation. Between 1921 and 1923, the party annually introduced its labor union bill, accompanied by the sickness insurance bill and revisions to the Police Regulations and Factory and Mining Laws. The unemployment insurance bill was added in 1922. As men of property, Kenseikai members naturally shared the government's concern about the new belligerency displayed by organized labor in the Kawasaki-Mitsubishi Shipyards strike and other large disputes.[126] The Kenseikai's president, Katō Takaaki, worried about the inflationary effects of the unions' demands for higher wages in a period of economic stagnation.[127] Many Kenseikai politicians also questioned the political wisdom of appealing to "revolutionary" factory workers, who constituted a mere 10 percent of the working population and who had, moreover, withdrawn support from the Kenseikai's drive for universal manhood suffrage and labor legislation.[128]

On balance, however, growing labor militancy served to strengthen the Kenseikai's faith in a union law and protective legislation as the best means of reducing the sources of radicalism among workers.[129] During the Kawasaki-Mitsubishi strike, the Kenseikai charged the Hara cabinet with responsibility for the outbreak of violence because the government had refused to enact the Kenseikai's remedial legislation.[130] One Kenseikai elder, who as minister of agriculture and commerce had directed the implementation of the Factory Law in 1916, similarly condemned the succeeding Takahashi cabinet for ignoring the social causes in its preoccupation with the criminal manifestation of extremist ideologies. The government, he argued, had done nothing to alleviate the plight of workers, for it "is cowed by the capitalist class." Home Minister Tokonami, he sneered, preferred such "makeshift antiquated methods" as sponsoring wandering storytellers (*naniwabushi*), who left the populace with little more than moral platitudes.[131]

The different approaches of the two major parties to industrial peace and social harmony were even clearer in 1922 than they had been in 1919. Nonetheless, neither party's position substantially altered the nature of labor-management relations in the short term. Home Minister Tokonami had failed to convince most employers and fellow Seiyūkai leaders of the need to establish vertical labor organizations. The Kenseikai, for its part, introduced labor legislation year after year with no hopes of passage, given the Seiyūkai majority in the Lower House. Moreover, the Kenseikai's plans to incorporate workers into the existing order remained unworkable so long as labor leaders espoused political ideologies opposed to parliamentary solutions and compromise with capitalists.

Yet the debate over labor policy in 1919–20 was important, less for immediate results than for the diversity of innovative proposals for the reform of industrial relations. Whether they couched their recommendations in terms of conforming to "the trends of the world" or building upon Japan's "beautiful customs," most politicians, employers, and bureaucrats favored significant changes in past labor practices and the role of the state to cope with the emerging crisis in labor-management relations. While the Kenseikai and representatives of the Seiyūkai government clashed within the Diet over the best approach to social stabilization, higher civil servants plunged into a less spectacular, yet far-reaching, bureaucratic debate over the reconstruction of Japanese society.

CHAPTER III

The Social Bureaucrats and the Integration of Labor, 1918–27

There are essentially two competing views of the nature of the state. Marxist thinkers portray the state as class-based. That is, the state is simply an institution by which the ruling class oppresses the ruled.... On the other side are those who view the state as capable of occupying a neutral position vis-à-vis the capitalist and working classes.... For the state to maintain such a neutral position, it must totally eliminate those laws that oppress the workers. Growing numbers within the working class accept the class-based view of the state, and they increasingly see governmental officials as the teeth and claws of the capitalists. As a result, those who recognize the state's transcendent position above the classes firmly believe that, before all else, laws like Article 17 of the Police Regulations must be stricken without delay.... If we are to maintain that the state has the duty and ability to uphold social justice, then it is the natural responsibility of the state to enact legislation to protect labor unions.

—*Yasui Eiji, Social Bureau (Home Ministry),*
1923[1]

History has not dealt kindly with the bureaucracy of interwar Japan. In most accounts, elite bureaucrats, when they are mentioned at all, appear as the conservative opponents of "Taishō democracy." They harass progressive intellectuals, break up labor rallies, and attack the legitimacy of party rule. Although the image is not entirely false, it does not explain a central paradox of "Taishō democracy." The initiative behind many of the most important democratizing reforms of the 1920s came not so much from the bourgeois parties—and certainly not from the weak social democratic movement—but rather from activist cliques of higher civil servants. The drive to establish legal rights for tenant farmers is a case in point. In 1920, before tenant unions constituted a nationally organized interest, high-ranking officials in the Ministry of Agriculture and Commerce began formulating, and in the course of the next decade vigorously promoted, protective tenancy legislation in the face of opposition from Japanese landlords.[2]

Ironically, the most comprehensive bureaucratic proposals for change originated from within the powerful Home Ministry, whose police agencies had been associated with the suppression of socialist and labor movements before 1919. In the realm of labor administration and social welfare, a new center of reform emerged with the establishment of the Social Bureau within the Home Ministry—in addition to the semiofficial Kyōchōkai, which retained close ties to the Home Ministry. Rising officials such as Yasui Eiji, quoted above, called on the government to abolish the antistrike Article 17 of the Police Regulations, and in its place, they drafted and championed the decade's most progressive labor union legislation. Whereas the "economic bureaucrats" of other ministries primarily worked to further industrial development, the "social bureaucrats" of the Home Ministry sought to reduce the sources of social unrest that arose from unrestrained economic relations and inadequate living and working conditions.

Any meaningful definition of the social bureaucrats must also include a cohesive group of somewhat higher-ranking Home Ministry officials which concurrently promoted a wide array of political and social reforms in the wake of World War I. Known as the "new men" (shinjin) by their colleagues, these middle-level bureaucrats collectively served as councilors (sanjikan). The strategically placed councilors reviewed draft proposals of the ministry's bureaus and, in effect, set priorities.[3] In the words of Nagaoka Ryūichirō, a particularly progressive councilor who later headed the Social Bureau:

> When I think back, the Councilors' Room of the Home Ministry in those days [1919–22] was an awfully curious phenomenon. Argumentative and bright, our group drew on the likes of Tsugita Daisaburō and Maeda Tamon. . . . The bunch in the Councilors' Room would lock horns with the individual bureaus by unabashedly advocating the abolition of Article 17 of the Police Regulations, the official recognition of labor unions, and the immediate enactment of universal [manhood] suffrage. These positions are no longer debated today [1939], but under the Hara cabinet, such opinions were considered heretical. . . . Ensconced in the Councilors' Room, we fought to change the stagnant air of the Home Ministry,

strangely enough beyond the control of either the home minister [Toko-nami Takejirō] or the vice-minister.[4]

Besides working to broaden the franchise and workers' rights, the "new men" went far beyond either major party in a campaign to liberalize the censorship provisions of the Meiji-era Newspaper and Publication Laws.[5] In all these endeavors, the social bureaucrats justified the protection of workers' rights in terms of the autonomous needs of the state versus the parochial interests of capital.

Scholars have generally been skeptical of bureaucratic claims to have protected the workers and advanced democracy. There is, of course, the basic Marxist view of the state as an instrument of the ruling class. Even the neo-Marxist theorist Nicos Poulantzas, who granted states "relative autonomy" from the dictates of individual capitalists, nevertheless concluded that capitalist states can go only so far, because they are committed to reproducing "the conditions of production of a system that itself determines the domination of one class over the others."[6]

Other scholars have pointed to the historically autocratic nature of Japanese bureaucratic reformers. After assisting in the reform of Tokyo municipal government in 1922 and 1923, the American historian Charles Beard described Japanese officials as follows: "They are often ardent advocates of enlightened policies, but they are not as a rule zealous to promote the rapid growth of a public sentiment which might endanger their prerogatives."[7] Kenneth Pyle has more recently examined the role of "social-minded bureaucrats" during the 1920s. Yet he, too, maintains that these officials were "trained during the previous generation," and thus their approach to social problems was firmly grounded in the collectivism and thought guidance emphasized by the Meiji era's proponents of social policy. Ultimately, he concluded, "in the 1930s, a totalitarian solution to the social problem was devised by the so-called 'revisionist bureaucrats'—who came originally from the social policy tradition that [Professors] Kanai and Kuwata pioneered."[8]

One should not, however, overemphasize the theme of bureaucratic conservatism at the expense of disregarding major changes. The social bureaucrats of the 1920s represented a new generation that went far beyond the limited objectives of the advocates of early factory legislation. To begin with, the interwar officials viewed most independent workers' organizations as a positive, not a radical, force. They also proved much bolder in insisting that the state's highest interests comprised more than unrestrained industrial growth. Recent studies in the social sciences suggest that although there are clear limits to the autonomy of the state, governments have historically asserted relatively autonomous positions on behalf of subordinate classes under certain conditions.[9] It is noteworthy that Home Ministry officials developed their new labor policy between 1918 and 1924, despite the generally antilabor stance of the period's Seiyūkai and nonparty cabinets. This chapter explores the conditions under which Japanese higher civil servants took the initiative in reformulating labor policy after 1918. The sources of their actions lay, first and foremost, in the new crisis in labor-management relations, but also in a qualitative transformation of the Japanese bureaucracy.

FROM ECONOMIC TO SOCIAL BUREAUCRATS

The rise of the social bureaucrats had its roots in the trend toward specialization within the Home Ministry after the Russo-Japanese War of 1904–5. Prior to that, it will be recalled, labor matters tended to be treated as problems of industrial production by economic bureaucrats within the Industrial Bureau of the Ministry of Agriculture and Commerce. The Home Ministry's few social policy experts, who did call attention to the larger social implications of poor working conditions, generally remained isolated in the Bureau of Health and Sanitation. Bureau chief Gotō Shimpei later held several influential posts in the higher civil service and the cabinet, but he was the exception that proved the rule. Indeed, little differentiated the Home Ministry official from his counterparts in the economic ministries. The Home Ministry's prefectural governors regularly consulted local businessmen on how to further economic development, and the ministry's police frequently intervened against striking workers, who were thought to impede the nation's industrial progress. The Home Ministry also lacked a distinct identity in terms of personnel. According to one survey of eighty prefectural governors between 1884 and 1900, nearly 40 percent had served or would serve in at least one other ministry.[10]

Furthermore, the early Home Ministry was not an overly hospitable place for those with specialized training. In the wake of the Meiji Restoration of 1868, the first generation of governmental officials largely consisted of former samurai from Satsuma and Chōshū, the two strongest victorious domains. The aforementioned survey of governors between 1884 and 1900 also indicated that 98.5 percent had not received a university education and that nearly all had been recruited on the basis of participation in the Meiji Restoration (74 percent) or because of exposure (brief as it usually was) to Western education (23 percent).[11] More rigorously trained individuals entered the bureaucracy following the establishment of Tokyo Imperial University as the first imperial university in 1886. In 1887, the government instituted an examination system for the higher and lower levels of the civil service, and in 1893, it required almost all candidates for the higher civil service to pass the extremely competitive examination. With the exception of candidates for diplomatic and judicial service, prospective higher civil servants sat for the annual examination in administration.

These reforms notwithstanding, graduates of Tokyo Imperial University did not begin to fill the Home Ministry's influential positions of bureau chief and prefectural governor until the time of the Russo-Japanese War. Even the university-educated officials, most of whom were trained in law, tended to avoid technical fields such as social policy, priding themselves on general self-cultivation as the key to ruling the people.[12] Moreover, the prefectural police, which was nominally responsible for public health and factory safety, remained the preserve of an old guard of veteran policemen, retired military men, and reinstated civil functionaries. Existing regulations allowed the home minister to appoint the prefectural police chief and his key assistants from outside of the higher civil service. As late as 1913, the top leaders of most prefectural police departments were in their fifties, and a disproportionate number hailed from the Satsuma clique of the early Meiji period.[13]

Yet the new problems of industrialization and urbanization called for a new type of bureaucrat. In contrast to their generalist predecessors, the higher civil servants who entered the Home Ministry after 1908 increasingly concentrated on labor questions, urban affairs, and relations between tenant farmers and landlords. Year by year, the Japanese government expanded its social agencies. With the implementation of the Factory Law in 1916, the Ministry of Agriculture and Commerce created a central factory inspectorate and assigned factory inspectors and assistant inspectors to prefectural police departments. In August 1917, the reformist Gotō Shimpei, then home minister, established a Relief Section (Kyūgoka) within the ministry's Local Affairs Bureau for the purpose of coordinating prefectural efforts to relieve unemployment and poverty. Gotō had intended to name the agency the "Social Section," but "social" sounded too much like "socialism" to the conservative prime minister, Terauchi Masatake. Complained Terauchi: "For an official to work in a section defined by the word 'social' is simply outrageous."[14]

The Relief Section provided the core for the Home Ministry's first Bureau of Social Affairs (1920), which dealt with unemployment, poor relief, veterans' assistance, and children's welfare. In the meantime, the Home Ministry added building inspectors (1919) and an entire City Planning Bureau (1922). To mediate labor disputes, the posts of conciliation officer and assistant conciliation officer were instituted within prefectural police departments in 1926. At the local level, the city of Tokyo set up its own Bureau of Social Affairs in 1919.[15] Most important, in 1922 the Home Ministry united its labor and welfare functions and those of the Ministry of Agriculture and Commerce into a superagency, also called the Bureau of Social Affairs or Social Bureau (Shakaikyoku). The new Social Bureau assumed primary responsibility for dealing with labor unions and industrial relations. One authority on Japanese bureaucracy has termed the creation of the enlarged Social Bureau the most significant structural change in the Home Ministry since its separation from the Ministry of Agriculture and Commerce in 1881.[16]

With each new office grew a vested bureaucratic interest in labor and social policies. Several characteristics, summarized below, distinguished the Home Ministry's social bureaucrats from other officials and contributed to their increasingly progressive position on labor reform.

RELATIVE AUTONOMY FROM EMPLOYERS' INTERESTS

Interwar officials prided themselves on their distinctiveness from the rest of society, including the business community. Their feelings of autonomy were partly based on social origins. As would be expected in a meritocratic system of civil-service and school-entrance examinations, nearly all of the most prominent pre-1947 bureaucrats were the sons of former samurai, prosperous landowners, and others of strong educational background (see table 4). What was striking, however, was the relatively low proportion from business families and, conversely, the large number whose fathers had themselves been governmental officials—and often high-ranking officials, at that. The proportion of the latter rises if one adds those from military households. Marital ties further solidified one's identification with officialdom. Powerful bureaucrats routinely married daughters off to young officials who had distin-

TABLE IV   SOCIAL BACKGROUNDS OF PROMINENT
HIGHER CIVIL SERVANTS, CA. 1896–1947

Father's occupation	Number of bureaucrats	Percentage of total
Gov't officials and public employees:		
Top gov't officials	49	8.7%
Other gov't officials	31	5.5
Judges and procurators	17	3.0
Professors in gov't universities, higher schools	25	4.4
Public employees	28	5.0
Subtotal	150	26.7
Military men	25	4.4
Agriculture and forestry	134	23.8
Brewing	16	2.8
Commerce	55	9.8
Industrialists	26	4.6
Company staff	14	2.5
Diet members	20	3.6
Doctors and lawyers	36	6.4
Teachers	18	3.2
Shinto and Buddhist priests	10	1.8
Nobles	12	2.1
Artisans and workers	15	2.7
Others	31	5.5
Total	562	100.0

SOURCE: Hata Ikuhiko, *Kanryō no kenkyū*, p. 14. The sample is confined to those born after 1871 whose fathers' occupations are clearly known.

guished themselves at Tokyo Imperial University and in their higher-civil-service examinations. One historian has shown that 350 of 1,373 prominent pre-1947 bureaucrats had at least one close relative in that same prestigious group.[17] Although the prewar Japanese bureaucracy never became a closed caste, top officials by the interwar era could look forward to reproducing their influence within the higher civil service via sons, sons-in-law, and younger brothers.

No agency projected a stronger image of autonomy from economic interests than did the Home Ministry. Unlike the preexamination officials of the nineteenth century, the university graduates remained in the Home Ministry or related offices for most of their bureaucratic careers.[18] According to later interviews and memoirs, many of the brightest graduates of Tokyo Imperial University's Faculty of Law chose to enter the Home Ministry after 1905 because, in the words of one, "I had little attachment to money."[19] Although as many (or more) Faculty of Law students entered the business world as entered government after 1908, Home Ministry veterans commonly recalled that the best graduates selected official careers.[20] Attitudes toward business also influenced which ministry a successful examination candidate chose. Yasui Eiji, who joined the Home Ministry in 1916 and went on to draft the Social Bureau's labor union bill, remembered differences in expectations. Among his friends at Tokyo Imperial University, several opted for the economic bureaucracy—Finance Ministry and Ministry of Agriculture and Commerce—because they wished to work for companies and banks after retirement. The Home Ministry, on the other hand, appealed to candidates like Yasui who sought the chance to exercise power or, in the tradition-based parlance of the time, to "govern the people" (bokumin).[21] Social policy occupied a central place within the art of governing.

Table 5 confirms Yasui's distinctions concerning the postretirement careers of top Home Ministry officials versus those of the economic bureaucrats of the Ministry of Agriculture and Commerce (reorganized as the Ministry of Commerce and Industry in 1925). After retiring in their early fifties, Industrial Bureau chiefs and the administrative vice-ministers of Agriculture and Commerce often drew on contacts with business clientele to become company presidents or directors of major corporations. The practice survives in present-day Japan under the name of amakudari or "descent from heaven."[22] One notable example was Shijō Takafusa, who served continuously as Industrial Bureau chief and then vice-minister from 1919 to 1929. Shijō steadfastly opposed the Home Ministry's proposed labor union legislation throughout the 1920s. Upon leaving the Ministry of Commerce and Industry, he became president of an insurance company and sat on the board of directors of the vehemently antiunion Japan Industrial Club.[23] By contrast, nearly all of the Home Ministry's vice-ministers and Social Bureau directors remained within the government in higher posts or joined the political parties, which often appointed the former bureaucrats to cabinet-level positions.

TABLE V   CAREERS AFTER RETIREMENT FROM THE
HIGHER CIVIL SERVICE: HOME MINISTRY VS. MINISTRY
OF AGRICULTURE AND COMMERCE / COMMERCE AND
INDUSTRY, 1918–31

Career	Agriculture and Commerce/Commerce and Industry (vice-ministers, Industrial Bureau chiefs)	Home Ministry (vice-ministers, Social Bureau directors)
Big business	5 (50%)	—
Higher administrative posts[a]	4 (40%)	6 (50%)
Party activists	1 (10%)[b]	5 (42%)
House of Peers (main activity)	—	1 (8%)
Total	10 (100%)	12 (100%)
Average age at retirement	52.0[c]	50.3

SOURCE: Senzenki kanryōsei kenkyūkai, ed., *Senzenki Nihon kanryōsei no seido, soshiki, jinji,* pp. 11–261, 327, 330, 371, 376–77.

[a]Home Ministry retirees typically became colonial administrators or ministers in non-party cabinets. Former vice-ministers of agriculture and commerce occasionally headed government-sponsored associations of agricultural cooperatives or fishermen.

[b]Two, if one includes Tanaka Ryūzō, who was also managing director of Fujita Mining.

[c]Excludes Tanaka Ryūzō, who initially retired at the level of bureau chief (aged 41). He became an industrialist and Seiyūkai politician before serving as vice-minister (1920–22) under two Seiyūkai cabinets.

Finally, a highly cultivated sense of elitism and activism emboldened the social bureaucrats against employers. One official summed up the self-image of his colleagues in the Social Bureau in these terms: "In Japan, if His Majesty's bureaucrats weren't progressive, they wouldn't amount to much."[24] The "new men" who first championed the rights of labor in 1919–20 consisted of the best and brightest amongst their entering cohort. Almost all had placed among the top group of candidates in the general administrative examination, thereby ensuring rapid advancement to the highest posts in the Home Ministry.[25] Granted substantial authority in their twenties and thirties, these officials possessed extraordinary confidence in their abilities to engineer social change.

Gotō Fumio (1884–1980) was one such man. Gotō (no relation to Gotō Shimpei) is best known as the "new bureaucrat" who served as minister of agriculture and commerce and home minister during the crisis-filled 1930s. His earlier career merits attention as well.[26] The son of a low-ranking samurai and prefectural official from the Kyushu castle town of Ōita, the academically able Gotō gained entrée to Tokyo Imperial University's Faculty of Law and then to the Home Ministry's elite track. In 1908, he placed first among 130 successful candidates in the administrative higher-civil-service examination. As Gotō later recalled, he and several other future social bureaucrats entered the Home Ministry amidst a "major transition between old and new bureaucrats."[27] In 1913, Home Ministry leaders retired some ten veteran chiefs of prefectural police departments, and for the first time, replaced them with younger civil servants, who averaged only four or five years of administrative experience. The twenty-nine-year-old Gotō found himself commanding the police force of Aomori prefecture, where he rapidly developed skills in supervising relief measures following a bad rice harvest and an influenza epidemic. Around the same time, the Home Ministry began appointing entering elite bureaucrats to the post of county head (gunchō), a position previously staffed by older, low-ranking functionaries. After a mere one-year training period, explained Gotō, many of his peers were given responsibility for a county's law-enforcement, welfare, and educational systems. Some quickly earned their spurs in budgetary battles with local notables in the county assembly. Whether police chiefs or county heads, these officials possessed an élan which Gotō traced back to his days in higher school:

> Most in our group [at higher school] considered themselves a kind of elite, filled with an almost indescribable desire to work for "country and realm." We'd read the biographies of the great men of ancient times [both Japanese and Chinese] and discuss their administrative accomplishments. . . . We were captivated by politics, administration, the thoughts of the people, and the statecraft practiced by the ancients.[28]

Every bit the "governor of the people," Gotō returned to the Home Ministry's central Police Bureau in 1914. He concurrently headed the two sections most concerned with policing leftist and labor movements—the Public Security Section (Hōanka) and the Publications Section (Toshoka). In 1922, he assumed control of the entire Police Bureau at the unusually young age of thirty-eight.

STUDY IN THE WEST

Kenseikai politicians called for the legalization of trade unions in the name of the post-World War I "trends of the world," but most learned about these trends through newspapers and books. The emerging social bureaucrats, on the other hand, were profoundly influenced by first-hand observations of the changing labor situation in Europe and the United States. Although Home Ministry officials had previously toured the West on an occasional basis, the cosmopolitan Home Minister Gotō Shimpei institutionalized a study-abroad program toward the end of World War I. Believing ministry and prefectural officials to be appallingly dilettantish, Gotō began sending rising young bureaucrats to the West for a period of two years (often shortened to one). To encourage creativity, the Home Minister instructed those selected to study any issue they considered important. Amid the social and political dislocations of war-torn Europe, the visiting bureaucrats gravitated toward surveying labor unions, social welfare, electoral reform, and police tactics toward labor movements and leftist political organizations.[29]

For many, the long stay abroad utterly transformed their thinking about social issues and democratization. The first wave of Home Ministry officials returned in 1919–20. These were the "new men" who spearheaded reform efforts in their capacity as councilors. Convinced that industrializing Japan would similarly experience Western-style labor militancy and class tensions, they proposed to emulate many of the democratic countermeasures seen abroad. Gotō Fumio spent much of his two-and-a-half-year tour in London. He observed the passage of women's suffrage in 1918, as well as British efforts to implement proportional representation. Equally intrigued by the unprecedented strength of European labor in the immediate postwar months, he recognized that most workers simply wished to raise their own position, rather than overthrow the existing order in favor of socialism.[30] If England offered a possible model for Japan, Czarist Russia was its antithesis. En route to Western Europe during the early summer of 1917, Gotō Fumio stopped in Petrograd just as Alexander Kerensky's hold was slipping away to the Bolsheviks. He vividly remembered feeling: "If Japan dillydallies, we'll face the same chaos. . . . We can't continue the approaches of the past. We'll have to make some changes."[31]

Other touring "new men" drew similar conclusions. Horikiri Zenjirō, a police official who was later appointed mayor of Tokyo, visited postwar Germany in 1919. He surveyed the workings of the newly adopted Weimar Constitution and accompanying election laws that introduced proportional representation and equal, universal suffrage. Upon returning home later that year, he joined Gotō Fumio and other returning councilors in lobbying senior ministry officials for the immediate enactment of universal manhood suffrage.[32] Another young police bureaucrat, Nagaoka Ryūichirō, had already developed a familiarity with social issues as the Health Section chief of the ministry's Bureau of Health and Sanitation. According to one colleague, he came back from an investigation of wartime police administration in Europe with "liberal ideas" and began calling for the abolition of the antilabor Article 17 of the Police Regulations. After becoming the director of the Social Bureau in 1924, Nagaoka succeeded in revising Article 17 and revamping the entire structure of labor legislation. Even the rather conservative Maruyama Tsurukichi, a long-time officer in the Tokyo Metropolitan Police, was so impressed by the level of social work in America and Europe that he embarked on a crusade for improved welfare services in Japan. Hardly off the boat in 1918, he was appointed chief of the Home Ministry's new Relief Section.[33]

Foreign study did more than inspire Japanese officials to reexamine their nation's institutions. Experience abroad provided comprehensive models for new programs and legislation. Following the creation of the Social Bureau in 1922, bureau leaders routinely sent promising officials to Europe and the United States. In contrast to earlier tours that surveyed broad political and social trends, Social Bureau officials concentrated on more technical aspects of labor policy. They appeared most attracted to highly codified models, which were easiest to emulate. Ōno Rokuichirō researched labor exchanges and unemployment insurance in Britain and Weimar Germany between 1923 and 1924 before returning to draft an unemployment insurance law. He met with such British experts as Sir William Beveridge. But he found German models of welfare more appropriate to Japan because of their systematic nature, unlike the general Anglo-American "emphasis on charity."[34]

Industrialists and conservative politicians frequently accused the Social Bureau of attempting to impose translated versions of the labor laws of advanced industrial societies without appreciating Japanese conditions. One might further question how well the social bureaucrats understood the actual workings of their legislative models. While in Germany, Paris, and London, the bookish Yasui Eiji gathered extensive materials pertaining to collective agreements in preparation for authoring Japan's first detailed proposal for a labor agreements law. Yet, by his own admission, he spoke so little German and English (and no French) that he would usually walk into a union headquarters and hand over a note requesting relevant publications.[35]

In defense of his reliance on Western models, Yasui cited the Fabian socialist, G. D. H. Cole, who stated that while the United States labor movement was essentially "American," and his own, "English," one helped one's people most by comparative study. And Yasui concluded: "The comprehensive solution to the labor problems in our country calls for forms that are most closely based on our nation's special conditions. If we ignore these [special conditions], we will pay a useless sacrifice. Nonetheless, the labor movements of today run through all contemporary civilized nations. We cannot overlook the fact that they have a common ideological background."[36] Whatever its limitations, firsthand knowledge of the West greatly enhanced the authority of the young social bureaucrats vis-à-vis employers, politicians, and senior officials, who generally lacked such access. As a direct result, several of the Social Bureau's experts eventually rose to the esteemed positions of administrative vice-minister and even minister of state. The progressive Yasui himself later served as education minister (1937–38) and home minister (1940).[37]

DEMOCRATIC INFLUENCES

The social bureaucrats who entered the Home Ministry around 1909 could be considered neither democratic nor liberal. At one time responsible for censoring the nation's publications, Gotō Fumio was inclined to perceive postwar social change in terms of unwelcome and dangerous "convulsions in people's thought."[38] Together with Maruyama Tsurukichi and Nagaoka Ryūichirō, he never fully accepted the legitimacy of rule by political parties.[39] Nevertheless, Gotō maintained that the emerging young officials were not impervious to the democratic and socialist ideas sweeping Japan at the end of World War I. They did not simply criticize the parties, but talked of the need for "comprehensive reform" in social and political institutions.[40] Gotō himself took the unprecedented step of studying the essentials of Marxism. While visiting New York in 1919, he met with a small band of Japanese Communists led by the exiled Meiji-era socialist, Katayama Sen. One aide to Katayama informed a rather skeptical comrade that Gotō "is truly a progressive bureaucrat" and "well versed in the theory of Communism."[41] Home Minister

Tokonami Takejirō later chastised Gotō, terming it outrageous for an official of the Home Ministry to study Marxism. The confident young bureaucrat replied that Marx was not the source of social problems; the world would have changed in any event.[42]

The second generation of social bureaucrats, which graduated from Tokyo Imperial University during World War I, received a stronger dose of "Taishō democracy" and internationalism. Yasui Eiji recalled his Faculty of Law course with Professor Yoshino Sakuzō, the well-known advocate of party cabinets, universal suffrage, and legalized labor unions.[43] Whereas the pre-1914 Home Ministry had been a bastion of conservative influence from Imperial Germany, wartime and postwar officials avidly read the more liberal British social treatises, particularly those by the Webbs and other Fabian socialists.[44] The new emphasis on England may also have resulted from the closure of wartime Germany, then an enemy of Japan, to the first generation of touring Home Ministry bureaucrats.

At least one Social Bureau member, Kitaoka Juitsu of the Labor Inspection Section, returned enamored of democratic politics in Great Britain. Like other Japanese officials present in London during 1924, Kitaoka was fascinated by the orderly establishment of the first Labour Party cabinet by Ramsey MacDonald. What made Kitaoka something of an anomaly within the Home Ministry, however, was his eager participation in a summer school sponsored by the Independent Labour Party, the voice of principled socialism within the Labour movement. There, he heard several ministers from the new MacDonald cabinet and became interested in Quaker pacificism.[45] Kitaoka so closely identified with British labor practices that one nationalistic subordinate recalled that he virtually prefaced each policy recommendation by saying, "Now, in my England, we'd . . . ."[46]

Historians often overlook the impact of religion on Japanese policymaking, but it is clear that Christian social reformism inspired several of the most progressive social bureaucrats. Although Christianity is often portrayed as a nonestablishment force, the first two young officials to propose the legal recognition of labor unions were both Christians. Nambara Shigeru, who is best known for his later academic career and chancellorship of Tokyo University, suggested and wrote the Home Ministry's first labor union bill in 1919. As students at the First Higher School, he and a long-time Social Bureau activist, Kawanishi Jitsuzō, had come under the influence of the school's famous liberal Christian principal, Nitobe Inazō. In 1911, both joined a tightly knit Bible-study group with other socially minded Christians led by the Christian reformer, Uchimura Kanzō.[47] Uchimura's church was at the time a principal sponsor of the pioneer labor organization, the Yūaikai.

The other major Christian bureaucrat, Kawai Eijirō, had similarly been drawn to labor reform at Tokyo University by his association with Reverend Uchimura and by the study of Marxism. An exceptional student, Kawai married the daughter of his mentor, the social policy theorist Kanai Noburu. After two years as a specialist in factory inspection within the Ministry of Agriculture and Commerce, he was sent to the United States in 1918 to report on American labor practices. To the dismay of his promanagement superiors in the Industrial Bureau, Kawai returned the next May with bold recommendations for the official recognition of unions, abolition of Article 17, and establishment of binding arbitration in industrial disputes. He resigned later in 1919 over his ministry's refusal to recognize unions, taking the opportunity to lambaste the Hara government's conservative labor policy in the *Tōkyō asahi shimbun*. Kawai thereupon assumed a teaching position at Tokyo Imperial University, from which he wrote numerous tracts on social policy and liberalism before being suspended for his progressive views in 1939.[48]

REEXAMINATION OF POLICE TACTICS

It may seem odd that many of the Home Ministry's social bureaucrats initially proposed the recognition of labor unions and other reforms while serving in the very police agencies that controlled the labor movement. However, police in other nations have occasionally intervened on behalf of labor when they believed that the demands of individual employers, if left unchecked, might so radicalize workers as to conflict with their ultimate responsibility for maintaining social order. During the decade preceding the Russian Revolution of 1905, for example, the Czarist police pressed factory owners to improve conditions and court labor moderates in a campaign to weaken the appeal of radical working-class organizations.[49]

In Japan, too, labor reform was closely related to a fundamental reassessment of law-enforcement policies at the end of World War I. Prior to 1918, the Japanese police had been one of the most interventionist in the world. They not only harassed organized workers and socialists, but also massively intruded in the lives of ordinary subjects, monitoring a stringent system of household registration and requiring numerous special permits for businesses. The Tokyo Metropolitan Police even supervised house cleaning twice a year.[50] Yet the post-World War I surge in labor organization and popular dissatisfaction convinced many Home Ministry officials that continued levels of surveillance would overly tax the undermanned police and serve to antagonize the working classes. In the interests of restabilizing Japanese society, younger bureaucrats proposed a more realistic course of somewhat accommodating popular demands for universal suffrage and legally protected trade union activity.

The result was an internal campaign to "democratize the police" (keisatsu no minshūka) in order to further understanding between the populace and the often arrogant police. Once again, an English model stood out as the direct inspiration during 1919 and 1920. The Home Ministry's returning bureaucrats filled the pages of the Keisatsu kyōkai zasshi (Bulletin of the Police Association) with praise for the London police. Nothing impressed the rising officials more than the ability of the British police to preserve order and maintain popular trust with a minimum of force.[51] One such enthusiast was a young inspector, Maeda Tamon, who later represented Japan on the ILO's board of directors. He resurfaced as the first minister of education after World War II. On the basis of observations made in 1918–19, Maeda marveled at how the bobbies refrained from breaking up strikes and socialist meetings. He witnessed one election rally of thirty thousand workers at which speakers attacked the government and demanded the recognition of the Soviet Union. Recognizing that Japan's own labor and social problems were growing "by leaps and bounds," Maeda urged fellow officers to exercise restraint as a "major key" to solving the nation's "social question."[52]

His and other essays in the Police Association's bulletin reflect the depth of soul-searching within the Home Ministry. After remarking on the freedom of expression accorded British socialists and Bolsheviks, Amanoya Keiji of the Police Bureau caustically reminded colleagues that the Japanese police would never have stood silent at such rallies. Soon to become a Social Bureau official responsible for policy toward unions, he concluded that "respect for expression" was England's strength, whereas its absence in nations like Japan could only be termed a "weak point."[53] Some of the strongest criticism of Japan's existing police practices came from Matsui Shigeru, director of the Police Training School and chief spokesman for the "democratize the police" movement. Matsui argued that Japanese police administration "cannot remain isolated from world trends," including democratic thought and a greater role for labor. He condemned the police of post-1868 Japan as "a kind of militaristic and bureaucratic police," dominated by former Satsuma samurai.[54] And he sounded the oft-heard warning of 1919: "Our Imperial Police have sinned in their excessive role as a political police. This has unquestionably obstructed the progressive development of other police functions [including social policy]. Did not the same thing happen to the police of [Imperial] Russia?"[55] To the younger bureaucrats, the issues and solutions were clear. Toleration and occasional encouragement of peaceful trade union activity and social democratic parties would ultimately convert workers into supporters of the established order.

TOWARD A NEW LABOR POLICY

For all their reformism, the Home Ministry's "new men" and social bureaucrats represented merely one opinion within one ministry in early 1920. Home Minister Tokonami and his senior officials remained opposed to a labor union law, repeal of Article 17, and enactment of universal manhood suffrage. They committed themselves instead to Tokonami's paternalistic vision of harmonious labor-management relations based on vertical unions and a works council law. Just the same, Tokonami seems to have fostered an atmosphere of experimentation within the Home Ministry. The most important product was an unusually progressive draft labor union bill by the Christian bureaucrat, Nambara Shigeru, then a junior official in the Police Bureau.

Sometime around July 1919, Tokonami assembled the ministry's higher civil servants and opened the floor to the younger bureaucrats. Nambara seized the opportunity to urge the government to recognize labor unions and to place them legally on an equal negotiating level with capitalists. Despite his overwhelming preference for a works council law, the flexible Tokonami permitted Nambara to draft a labor union bill as a contingency measure. The twenty-nine-year-old police official then did what social bureaucrats did so well. He recruited three new graduates of Tokyo Imperial University's Faculty of Law. One had studied English law, another, French law, and the third, German law. Together, they researched various foreign labor statutes before concluding that Japan should follow the English model of trade union legislation. They also recommended the creation of an independent labor ministry. Completed in the spring of 1920, the draft union legislation was vigorously promoted within the Home Ministry by the "new men" councilors just back from the West—notably Gotō Fumio, Nagaoka

Ryūichirō, Maeda Tamon, Tsugita Daisaburō, Horikiri Zenjirō, and Yamada Junjirō.[56]

Although the government never introduced Nambara's union bill to the Diet, the author's public explanation indicated the new mood of pragmatic reform and even democratic idealism among the Home Ministry's junior and middle-level officials. Nambara championed the legalization of *all* labor unions and the repeal of Article 17. He did so in terms of advancing social justice and maintaining public order. The legal recognition of unions, he asserted, was simply the "recognition of a social fact which has naturally evolved." Nambara bluntly criticized any legislation that would exclude certain types of unions or federations (industrial or mixed) or that restricted union activities within an "unnatural" framework. This was a thinly veiled reference to Home Minister Tokonami's works council bill, as well as to the trade union bill proposed by the Ministry of Agriculture and Commerce earlier that year. Such constraints, he insisted, would only discriminate against unrecognized unions and cause unnecessary law-enforcement problems. Unrecognized unions would neither be eligible to vote for the workers' delegate to the annual International Labor Conference nor be able to sit on works councils. Recognition of only craft unions would invariably exclude less-skilled workers, as had happened in Britain.

Nambara also challenged his immediate superior, Police Bureau Chief Kawamura Takeji, by declaring the right to strike "an acknowledgment of social justice" and the "last resort to realize a union's objects as clearly endorsed by the workers." Like Kenseikai leaders, he called Article 17 "unreasonable" inasmuch as viable unions, by nature, must be able to assist and propagandize workers from outside a given enterprise.[57] Nambara concluded on a highly philosophical note:

> We must recognize the futility, indeed the destructiveness, of foolishly building a dike against the world currents of the age. We do not let matters take their natural course out of human cowardice or negligence. On the contrary, we see their destination as the Promised Land and therefore deem it essential to enact legislation of love for our coexistence as the human race.[58]

Nambara's non-Christian colleagues within the Home Ministry may not have used the same language, but many agreed that the natural development of most unions was a healthy phenomenon.

To foster the growth of "sound and orderly" labor organization, Nambara's labor union bill granted legitimacy and legal protections to unions with a minimum of governmental supervision.[59] The proposed legislation would recognize any union or federation that simply registered with the authorities, regardless of whether it acquired corporate status. At the same time, Nambara expected his union law to encourage "a sense of duty and responsibility under state regulation." The measure, for example, empowered the authorities to annul or revise union decisions deemed unlawful. Yet the draft denied the government the power to dissolve a union under any circumstance. That power, according to Nambara, would be tantamount to the "death sentence" for a union. Most important, Nambara's bill would protect trade unionists from dismissal or the refusal of employment on the basis of their membership. He also inserted a liberal provision from the 1906 British Trade Disputes Act stipulating that a union could not be held liable for damages sustained by an employer during an industrial dispute.

Although this was not explicit in the bill, Nambara believed his union law would make it possible for Japanese unions to engage in political activities such as funding candidates for public office. In support, he cited Britain's recent Trade Union Amendment Act of 1913, by which the Liberal Party government had revised the 1909 Osborne judgment and legalized political fund-raising, with certain restrictions. Like other social bureaucrats, Nambara viewed rising labor-based parties in Britain and Germany as moderate forces that gave labor movements a stake in the parliamentary order.[60] Although Nambara's union bill lacked a guarantee of collective-bargaining rights, it was more favorable to organized labor than anything yet proposed by either the Kenseikai or the Ministry of Agriculture and Commerce (see appendix 5).

The Nambara draft would have remained an intraministerial proposal had it not been for competition from the Ministry of Agriculture and Commerce. The ministry's Industrial Bureau unveiled its own draft trade union bill (*shokugyō kumiai hōan*) in January 1920, thereby challenging Home Minister Tokonami's much publicized works council bill. Top officials of the Ministry of Agriculture and Commerce had previously shared the Home Ministry leadership's aversion to recognizing existing labor unions. As late as December 1919, ministry spokesmen advised caution concerning union legislation to avoid the "destruction of industry" witnessed in Great Britain.[61] Nevertheless, Agriculture and Commerce leaders soon endorsed the legal recognition of most existing unions because it seemed the only practical solution to the twin problems of domestic labor unrest and international criticism of the selection of a manager to represent Japanese workers at the ILO conference in 1919.[62] The Industrial Bureau's draft incorporated the views of such pragmatic employers' associations as the Osaka Industrial Association, which maintained that industrial peace would best be advanced by the development of responsible and legally recognized craft unions. Indeed, the Osaka Industrial Association heartily supported Agriculture and Commerce's completed trade union bill, while labeling Nambara's draft "quite radical" and "tending toward idealism."[63]

The Ministry of Agriculture and Commerce's union bill clearly reflected the managerial orientation of its sponsors. Officials proposed the legislation to the Hara cabinet as a means of rectifying the evils of "immoderate and disorderly unions" by placing stringent controls on union activities.[64] Unlike the Kenseikai's legislative package, the draft neither prohibited employers from arbitrarily dismissing union members, nor did it revise Article 17 of the Police Regulations. Nevertheless, Agriculture and Commerce's proposal of January 1920 provided an obvious contrast to Home Minister Tokonami's works council measure, which ignored the existing labor movement. Unlike the Home Ministry's "outrageous works council bill," remarked the daily *Kokumin shimbun,* Agriculture and Commerce's draft at least recognized genuine craft unions, allowed outside nonworkers to serve as union leaders, and permitted a certain degree of federation between unions in different prefectures.[65]

A few months later, the Ministry of Agriculture and Commerce included the recognition of industrial unions, as well, in its renamed "labor union bill" (*rōdō kumiai hōan*). In pointed reference to Home Minister Tokonami's preoccupation with Japan's unique social relations, Agriculture and Commerce spokesmen represented their draft union bill as a measure that sought to accommodate Japan's labor union movement, recognizing unions as part of "the trends of the world."[66] Joined by senior Home Ministry officials, Seiyūkai leaders in turn denounced Agriculture and Commerce's trade union bill for failing to appreciate how Japan's "beautiful customs" had forestalled the development of Western-style class antagonisms and the need for a legal structure stipulating rights and duties.[67]

By the end of January 1920, the differences between the Ministry of Agriculture and Commerce's union bill and Home Minister Tokonami's works council bill resulted in an open bureaucratic clash. To defuse the controversy over which ministry represented the government on labor policy, Prime Minister Hara submitted the dispute to the newly created Extraordinary Commission to Investigate Industry. To the complete bewilderment of the press, Home Ministry leaders shifted 180 degrees in the course of the commission's deliberations. Sometime during the first meetings in late March, Home Minister Tokonami backed away from his works council proposal and substituted Nambara's progressive draft as the Home Ministry's own labor union bill.

Historians disagree over the meaning of this act. Many assume that senior Home Ministry officials thenceforth endorsed the legal recognition of all unions and that the Nambara draft became the Home Ministry's official labor union bill.[68] The evidence for such a conclusion, however, is less than convincing. First, Home Ministry leaders abruptly submitted the Nambara draft to the Extraordinary Commission as a mere "discussion proposal" (sankōan). An official proposal would have required the formal approval of both the Police Bureau and the ministry.[69] Second, transcripts of commission discussions reveal acute contradiction and posturing on the part of the ministry's spokesman, Police Bureau Chief Kawamura Takeji. At one meeting, Kawamura initially advocated the enactment of the works council bill before discussing the general recognition of labor unions as stipulated in the Agriculture and Commerce bill: "We should compel capitalists to put their rhetoric [for labor-capital harmony] into practice by having them create unions based on the enterprise unit, in general." Switching to a liberal position, Kawamura then attacked Agriculture and Commerce's union bill for allegedly banning all unions except those restricted to the same craft or enterprise. By contrast, he claimed, the "Home Ministry draft" (Nambara's) realistically recognized all types of unions.[70] Lastly, while Kawamura used Nambara's draft to batter the Agriculture and Commerce proposal, he made little effort to persuade the commission to discuss Nambara's union bill on its own merits. During the latter half of 1920, the Police Bureau chief reaffirmed his opposition to the enactment of a labor union law in the near future.[71] In May 1921, Nambara himself resigned under pressure from Kawamura.[72]

It is more likely that Nambara's draft labor union bill achieved prominence in 1920 only because of a long-standing jurisdictional dispute between the Home Ministry and the Ministry of Agriculture and Commerce over which would determine governmental labor policy. The leaders of the two ministries had been competing for a proposed Labor Bureau since the preceding autumn. The rivalry continued into January, when the announcement by the Ministry of Agriculture and Commerce of its trade union bill put the Home Ministry's widely criticized works council bill on the defensive. Tokonami apparently publicized Nambara's liberal draft during the spring to convince skeptics that the Home

Ministry, not the Ministry of Agriculture and Commerce, deserved the Labor Bureau by reason of its more realistic policy toward labor unions.[73]

Although the two union bills both died in the Extraordinary Commission in June, the interministerial debate had implications for future labor policy. The Ministry of Agriculture and Commerce would never again offer labor union legislation. It would instead seek to weaken union bills later sponsored by the Home Ministry and the Kenseikai/ Minseitō cabinets. In August 1920, the ministry's Industrial Bureau added a Labor Section, whose staff formulated the 1922 Health Insurance Law, Japan's first labor insurance law. But a labor union law was clearly not on the agenda. The Labor Section's first chief, Zen Keinosuke, soon left government to become managing director of the Japan Industrial Club in its struggle against labor union legislation.[74] In contrast, the Home Ministry's junior and middle-ranking officials of 1920 proceeded to transform their ministry into the leading bureaucratic proponent of liberal labor policy. The establishment of the welfare-oriented first Bureau of Social Affairs in August 1920 simply whetted the Home Ministry's appetite for an independent office responsible for every aspect of labor policy.

The social bureaucrats won an unqualified victory in November 1922, when the cabinet led by Admiral Katō Tomosaburō (1922–23) placed all labor and social administration in the Home Ministry's enlarged Social Bureau. The Ministry of Agriculture and Commerce reluctantly yielded its Labor Section and factory inspectorate, and the Social Bureau absorbed other labor functions from the Foreign Ministry (ILO matters) and the Ministry of Communications (seamen's affairs). Unlike the first Bureau of Social Affairs, the new Social Bureau was granted the lofty status of "external bureau" (*gaikyoku*), which made it directly responsible to the home minister, rather than his vice-minister. Headed by a director (*chōkan*), the Social Bureau ranked above the Home Ministry's internal bureaus, even the Police Bureau. An ILO report described its subsequent annual budget as much larger than that of some ministries.[75] Including administrative officers, technical officers, and other higher civil servants above the rank of *hannin,* the Social Bureau's staff came to 142 in 1925, as compared with 83 and 39 for the central offices of the Police bureaus, and Local Affairs respectively.[76]

The Katō cabinet's decision to establish the Social Bureau highlights the nature of conservative and bureaucratic reform during the early 1920s. Political historians, who have been primarily interested in the advance of party government and liberalism, generally dismiss Admiral Katō Tomosaburō's government and the two succeeding nonparty cabinets as conservative throwbacks to the Meiji oligarchy. To be sure, the Katō cabinet opposed the attempts of the opposition Kenseikai to enact labor union legislation, revise Article 17, and enfranchise all adult males. Yet some of the most important breakthroughs in the realm of labor and social policy occurred between 1922 and 1924 under the nonparty cabinets. Admiral Katō and his home minister, Mizuno Rentarō, did not create the Social Bureau to guarantee the rights of unions. But they keenly felt the need for an authoritative welfare agency that could deal with the growing postwar problems of urban poverty, unemployment, poor health care, and inadequate working and housing conditions. Katō had recently negotiated the Washington Naval Treaty of 1922 in his capacity as naval minister. As prime minister, Katō reportedly sponsored the Social Bureau, in part, to alleviate the expected unemployment resulting from the treaty's substantial limitations on shipbuilding.[77] An organizational chart of the early Social Bureau indicates that policy-making regarding unions and labor relations was only one of several activities:

First Division (Labor Division)
Labor Section (unions, labor relations)
Inspection Section (enforce factory laws)

Second Division (Social Division)
Protection Section (children's welfare, etc.)
Vocational Section (labor exchanges, unemployment relief and prevention)
Relief Section (charity and general relief)

Health Insurance Division (established 1923)

International considerations also played an important role in the cabinet's decision to found the Social Bureau. Officials had long blamed Japan's confusing and often embarrassing policies toward the ILO on the diffusion of jurisdiction over labor matters.[78]

The Katō Tomosaburō cabinet's coolness to the recognition of unions notwithstanding, the unification of labor administration set in motion the liberalization of governmental labor policy. The progressive orientation of the Social Bureau's energetic staff profoundly influenced the Home Ministry's general approach to labor problems. Social Bureau personnel included the Home Ministry's Tsugita Daisaburō, Yasui Eiji,

Amanoya Keiji, and other young labor experts who had earlier promoted Nambara Shigeru's draft labor union bill and the repeal of Article 17. The agency also inherited from the Ministry of Agriculture and Commerce several of its younger specialists on factory inspection and labor insurance. Moreover, the Social Bureau enjoyed the crucial support of the former reformist councilors who had since risen to high-ranking positions in the Home Ministry. Gotō Fumio now headed the Police Bureau, and Nagaoka Ryūichirō was chief of the City Planning Bureau.[79] Thus strengthened, officials of the newly created Social Bureau prevailed upon the government to enforce some of the long-deferred ILO conventions on working conditions.

In early 1923, the Katō cabinet approved the Social Bureau's proposed revision of the Factory Law of 1911, in addition to two bills that established minimum ages and other standards for the employment of industrial workers and seamen. The amendments to the Factory Law substantially expanded the number of factories covered, shortened the maximum hours of employment for women, and completely prohibited night work for women and children under sixteen years of age. The Diet enacted these measures into law in March 1923, only months after the creation of the Social Bureau.[80]

The Social Bureau's specialists next turned to formulating legislation that would recognize labor unions and restructure industrial relations. Yasui Eiji had already developed considerable expertise in the area since he replaced Nambara Shigeru in 1921. In keeping with the outspoken style of the social bureaucrats, Yasui chose to explain the Social Bureau's proposed legislation in a commercially published book released in June 1923.[81] At times highly critical of the government's existing labor policies, the erudite young official announced drafts of a labor union bill, the abolition of Article 17 of the Police Regulations, and a labor disputes conciliation bill (rōdō sōgi chōtei hōan). His draft labor union bill retained the liberal features of Nambara's proposal, but went further to guarantee that no contract of employment could negate the provisions of collective agreements concluded between unions and management. The Social Bureau's growing interest in a labor agreements measure was quite progressive for its time. Whereas the labor movement had made collective-bargaining rights a central demand, most Japanese employers adamantly refused to recognize unions as bargaining agents during the early 1920s.[82] Yasui recalled Home Minister Tokonami Takejirō's outrage when he had earlier dared to suggest that labor's demand for the right to bargain collectively was "perfectly reasonable."[83]

The Social Bureau's draft labor disputes conciliation bill represented a major effort to place industrial relations within a systematic, legal framework. Although Yasui emphatically condemned Article 17's ban on "instigation or incitement" in strikes, he and most other Home Ministry officials believed it a "mistake to overlook [conciliation] systems and stand idly by" in the face of increasing strikes. As stipulated in Yasui's preliminary draft, a conciliation committee would be established if requested by both labor and management in disputes in private enterprises. To be chaired by a governmental official or another third party, the committee would consist of an equal number of representatives from labor and management. At the same time, Home Ministry officials favored more forceful restraints over both workers and managers in work stoppages occurring in public utilities or other enterprises "having a large bearing on the lives of the general public." In the event of public-interest disputes, the government could order conciliation proceedings on its own initiative. The legislation also provided a short cooling-off period in public-sector disputes to coincide with the meeting of the conciliation committee. During this period, the conciliation law would place some restrictions on "instigation or incitement"—lockouts by employers or strikes by workers—thereby removing the need to retain Article 17's more open-ended controls. Despite these temporary limitations, Yasui repeatedly defended workers' rights to strike in all industries: "Strikes must occur as a right with the same basis as the property rights they challenge."[84]

The Home Ministry's interest in labor conciliation may be traced in part to a traditional Japanese penchant for harmony over conflict. Yet Western governments of the time were also avidly engaged in the search for workable conciliation and arbitration mechanisms. Yasui, in fact, based his proposal on up-to-date Western models from nations with sizable labor movements and generally sympathetic liberal governments. Noting the British state's growing commitment to maintaining "the harmony of economic interests between Labor and Capital," he cited the Conciliation Act (1896), the Industrial Council (1911) chaired by a Labour Department official, and the Industrial Courts Act (1919). Like labor reformers throughout the West, Yasui expressed interest in the early-twentieth-century legislation of Australia and New Zealand, where governmental officials could compel conciliation proceedings and tender binding arbitration in many cases. In the end, Social Bureau officials largely emulated Canada's Industrial Disputes Investigation Act (1907), because it combined English-style voluntary conciliation in private-

sector disputes with special rules for compulsory, yet nonbinding, conciliation in the case of public-utility disputes.[85]

Taken together, the Social Bureau's draft labor legislation rested on
an emerging set of remarkably liberal assumptions about the relation of
the state to labor and capital. Older Japanese officials such as Tokonami regarded social conflict as an aberration from a harmonious norm.
Their labor policy had therefore attempted to preempt a class-conscious
labor movement by organizing familial labor-management councils
within individual enterprises. Yasui's generation, on the other hand,
more willingly accepted the clash between workers and employers as
"an inevitable product of the present economic organization, namely
capitalism." Rather than intervene to eliminate class-based competition,
the Home Ministry's new officials placed their faith in "the liberation of
the working class by its own strength."[86]

The problem, as Yasui saw it, was that individual workers could
not at that time deal with the much stronger capitalists on an equal
level. If the state wished to solve the labor question and "maintain the
present economic organization," it must enable the workers "to organize themselves and rival the strength of 'capital' with the strength of
'numbers.'" The Social Bureau's draft legislation, declared Yasui, was
designed "to rationalize the economic organization of capitalism."[87]
Playing the role of referee, the state would indirectly develop a more
rational system of industrial relations by protecting the rights of
unions to represent workers in collective bargaining and on conciliation committees during disputes.

So far as Yasui and other younger officials were concerned, an effective labor disputes conciliation law depended on the concurrent enactment of a union law. To no one's surprise, however, Social Bureau
leaders shelved the union bill and in June 1923 announced plans to
introduce only the conciliation measure and the repeal of Article 17 to
the next Diet in early 1924.[88] Few believed that either the conservative
nonparty cabinets or the Seiyūkai-dominated Diet would approve a
union law in the near future. The fate of Nambara Shigeru's draft labor
union bill in 1920 convinced many of the Home Ministry's reformist
officials that the passage of a progressive union law might require
twenty or thirty years.[89] Nor did the Nambara-Yasui draft union bills
enjoy much support in other ministries, especially the Ministry of Agriculture and Commerce and the Justice Ministry. But one obstacle tow-
ered above the others. As Yasui had warned, leaders of the labor movement itself had seemingly lost all faith in the reformist potential of the
state.[90]

RESHAPING THE LABOR MOVEMENT

The Social Bureau's vision of rational labor relations may seem rather abstract. In the United States during the 1910s and 1920s, Department of Labor specialists similarly compiled impressive surveys of other nations' progressive labor laws, with negligible effects on federal legislation, much less actual industrial relations.[91] Yet by the time Yasui Eiji's provocative book appeared in June 1923, Social Bureau officials were hard at work encouraging the growth of the "sound" labor union movement they envisioned. Japanese scholars commonly describe the government's labor strategy in terms of "the candy and the whip"—a rendition of "carrot-and-stick" with implicit emphasis on the whip.[92] That interpretation, however, is somewhat misleading. What began in 1923 might be better portrayed as a two-way process of trial and error by which the Social Bureau and non-Communist labor leaders joined together to persuade the government and the labor movement, as a whole, that the state and the unions could benefit each other.

Judging by the rhetoric of the labor movement between 1920 and 1923, the prospects for an understanding with the Japanese state were dim. Those years witnessed a notable rise in political radicalism within the unions.[93] The changes were most striking in the largest and most active federation, the Sōdōmei (successor to the Yūaikai). By 1920, anarcho-syndicalist organizers, who held sway in two smaller printers' unions, made significant inroads into the Sōdōmei-Yūaikai's local unions in the Kantō area (Tokyo-Yokohama). Rejecting any accommodation with the existing economic and political order, they launched several ill-fated strikes as a form of "direct action" to overthrow capitalism. In opposition stood the trade-unionist and mildly socialist national leaders of the Sōdōmei-Yūaikai. They instead emphasized collective bargaining and centralized control over the decision to strike.[94] At the federation's annual convention in October 1920, the leadership easily defeated two anarcho-syndicalist resolutions, one to approve general strikes as a tactic and the other to reject collective bargaining and abandon the drive for universal suffrage.

Nonetheless, the anarcho-syndicalist challenge served to weaken the Sōdōmei-Yūaikai's already faltering commitment to parliamentary solutions. Leaders of the national headquarters and Kantō Regional Labor Federation (Kantō Rōdō Dōmeikai) had remained aloof from the universal suffrage campaign of early 1920. The conservative Seiyūkai's overwhelming victory that May simply confirmed their belief in the hopelessness of soon expanding the franchise. Asō Hisashi and other

Bolshevik-inspired university graduates were naturally skeptical of bourgeois politics, but so were such working-class trade unionists as Matsuoka Komakichi, who did not wish to dissipate the unions' energies in political activities. Unions in the Sōdōmei-Yūaikai's Kansai area (Osaka-Kobe-Kyoto), on the other hand, had enthusiastically campaigned for universal suffrage and the legal recognition of labor unions. But even the reformist Kansai Regional Labor Federation dropped universal suffrage from its objectives in February 1922.[95] Sōdōmei-Yūaikai's position on labor legislation further reflected organized labor's distrust of the state. Amid the anarcho-syndicalist onslaught on the use of parliamentary means, delegates to the 1920 convention shelved a proposal to work for the enactment of a union law and a revised factory law. Union legislation did not appear as a stated goal of the federation during the next three years.[96]

Although the anarcho-syndicalist forces declined after the middle of 1922, Communists effectively replaced them as the radical challenge to labor moderates. Aided by the Soviet Union, a group of intellectuals led by Sakai Toshihiko, Yamakawa Hitoshi, and Arahata Kanson organized the clandestine Japanese Communist Party in July 1922. Despite a tiny membership of rarely over fifty, the Communists acquired considerable influence at the upper levels of the Sōdōmei. Nosaka Sanzō, Akamatsu Katsumaro, and other members of the labor federation's intelligentsia joined the party. Working-class Communists were more of a rarity, except for a few like Watanabe Masanosuke, who organized the Nankatsu Labor Society in the small factories of impoverished eastern Tokyo.[97]

The secret of the Communists' success lay in the united front forged with non-Marxist trade unionist leaders against the anarcho-syndicalists. The Communists and trade unionists shared a common commitment to centralized control, avoidance of direct action, and broadening the mass base of the union movement. Putting aside obvious differences, Sōdōmei's moderate leaders adopted a surprisingly pro-Communist line in late 1922. Frustrated by the ILO's reluctance to force the Japanese government to let unions select the workers' delegate, the federation's central committee in August went beyond its previous refusal to participate in the annual selection process; this time, the leadership denied the legitimacy of the ILO itself. Delegates to Sōdōmei's October convention demanded the recognition of the Soviet Union, and they approved the provocative statement that workers and capitalists could not coexist. In January 1923, the central committee dismissed the use of parliamentary means to advance labor's interests as "compromising and reformist."

The committee also criticized the ineffectual nature of the Social Bureau's proposed revision of the Factory Law, further claiming that the bureau's rumored labor union bill (Yasui Eiji's progressive draft) aimed at crushing, not protecting, labor unions.[98]

Although many in government and business were convinced of the revolutionary nature of the labor movement, Social Bureau officials sensed that the unions' mainstream remained politically moderate and trade unionist in orientation. As Director Nagaoka Ryūichirō later remarked, union manifestos might call for an end to the capitalist system, but the actual aims of most organizations centered on improving working conditions within the existing economic order.[99] Writing in September 1922, Yasui Eiji unhesitatingly called the Sōdōmei "realistic" in its cultivation of class consciousness, aversion to "radical means," and belief in coexistence with capitalists. The social bureaucrats smiled with particular benevolence on the "gradualism" of the Kansai Regional Labor Federation, which, they noted, represented the majority of the Sōdōmei's members. According to Social Bureau sources, the abandonment of the universal suffrage campaign by the Kansai Federation and other unions resulted more from depleted treasuries and a reassessment of priorities than from an ideological denial of parliamentarianism.[100]

Most striking, Social Bureau personnel pinned much of the blame for labor's radicalization on the government and employers. Warned Yasui: "Statesmen and capitalists alike should strongly bear in mind that the more the working class is oppressed, the more radical becomes its thought."[101] These officials reasoned that union members would gladly forsake syndicalist and Communist tactics when given the opportunity to advance their position within a system of parliamentary representation and legal safeguards. If most unions displayed indifference toward expanding the franchise, "that is because the gates of the Diet are at present closed to the working class. If universal suffrage were effected in the future and the working class could send representatives to the Diet, would there be any question as to whether [workers] would continue to disavow parliamentary tactics as they do today?"[102]

As a first step toward ending organized labor's isolation, the Social Bureau lobbied to change the government's policy of rejecting the unions' claim to select Japan's workers' delegate to the annual International Labor Conference. After Masumoto Uhei, the nation's first "workers' delegate," survived his credentials challenge in 1919, the Japanese government faced mounting criticism for its continued selection of labor delegates from the ranks of nonworkers. The advisor to the workers' delegate at the 1921 conference greatly embarrassed the government by denying his own credentials as spokesman for Japanese labor. In autumn 1922, the credentials committee of the ILO conference reluctantly accepted the credentials of Tazawa Yoshiharu, a socially minded former Home Ministry bureaucrat, but only after urging the Japanese government to base the future selection of workers' delegates on the nation's labor unions.[103] Determined to avoid further embarrassment, Home Minister Mizuno Rentarō and a few others in Katō Tomosaburō's cabinet endorsed the Social Bureau's proposal for the official recognition of labor unions as the sole representative of workers in the election process. However, officials of the management-oriented Ministry of Agriculture and Commerce flatly rejected this recommendation.[104] In July 1923, the Katō cabinet approved a compromise, which permitted unions with over a thousand members, together with workers in large enterprises, to cast bloc votes for the workers' delegate. The inclusion of unorganized workers fell far short of the Social Bureau's proposal to make unions the exclusive electorate. Disappointed with the cabinet's decision, the major labor unions refused to participate in the new mode of selection.[105]

Undaunted, the social bureaucrats gained new ammunition at the next ILO conference that autumn. Once again, an enlightened but bogus workers' delegate, the personnel expert Uno Riemon, demanded an examination of his own credentials. This time, the credentials committee presented the Japanese government with an ultimatum: consult the labor unions in the future or face certain rejection of the selected workers' delegate. The bankruptcy of Japanese labor policy was most keenly felt by Maeda Tamon, the nation's permanent representative on the ILO's governing board and himself a former "new man" from the Home Ministry. In an angry letter to the home minister, Maeda warned that if the government caused another such spectacle, it might as well not send a workers' delegate at all.[106]

Although the Social Bureau failed in its first attempt to lure the labor movement from radical leadership, the police proved more successful. On orders from the Home Ministry and Justice Ministry, police arrested some fifty members of the newly formed Communist Party on 5 June 1923. The crackdown was not primarily aimed at the labor unions, but the arrested did include Sōdōmei's Nosaka Sanzō and Watanabe Masanosuke.[107] Organized labor was still reeling when a devastating earthquake leveled the Kantō metropolitan area on 1 September 1923. The number of dead and missing came to 105,000, and some 364,000 homes in the cities of Tokyo and Yokohama were destroyed or badly damaged. Amid destruction and disorder, rumors spread that revolutionaries and minority groups were exploiting the chaos. Panic-stricken citizens and vigilante groups murdered more than six thousand hapless Koreans and some two hundred Chinese. Military and civilian police joined in to arrest scores of Communists, anarchists, and labor organizers. In one tragic incident, guards at the Kameido prison bayoneted ten labor activists, eight of whom belonged to the Communist-linked Nankatsu Labor Society. In another, an antisocialist military-police officer and his men strangled the labor movement's leading anarchist intellectual, Ōsugi Sakae, his wife, and his seven-year-old nephew.[108]

Officials of the Social Bureau were not directly responsible for the arrests and harassment of left-wing labor leaders, yet they essentially endorsed the anti-Communist policy pursued by colleagues in the Home Ministry's Police Bureau and Metropolitan Police. Indeed, the creation of the Social Bureau did little to sharpen the distinctions between the social bureaucrat and the police official who restricted radical movements.[109] As chief of the Police Bureau in June 1923, Gotō Fumio directed the first round-up of Communists while supporting the Social Bureau's proposed labor union legislation.[110] Conversely, the relatively liberal Yasui Eiji of the Social Bureau went on to supervise the nation's Special Higher Police in 1929. The Special Higher Police existed to control Communist and other allegedly extremist movements, but Yasui apparently perceived no contradiction between his police work and his reformist labor policies. As he later explained, knowledgeable elite bureaucrats routinely headed Special Higher Police sections because they were capable of dealing with the subtleties of "thought crimes" and presumably could distinguish between moderate trade unionism and revolutionary activity.[111]

Little by little, leaders of the Social Bureau and the Police Bureau jointly developed the Home Ministry's new approach to labor problems. They adopted a conciliatory stance toward the "sound" mainstream of the labor movement. At the same time, they crushed Communists, anarchists, and other groups that sought the overthrow of the government and the existing economic order. Its harsh features notwithstanding, the Home Ministry's dual strategy contrasted with the rival Justice Ministry's indiscriminate campaign against peaceful union activities and the mere propagation of "radical" thought (see next chapter).[112]

As Social Bureau officials astutely predicted, it did not require much to reinforce the "realistic" tendencies of the Sōdōmei and other labor unions. The "whip" had its immediate effects, to be sure. Shocked by the persecution of Communists and labor activists, workers either bolted the unions or sought to purge radical elements. Nishio Suehiro, the Sōdōmei's most prominent working-class leader in the Kansai area, remembered fearing that "although I had nothing to do with the Communist Party, I would be suspected on the grounds of my affiliation with a red labor union."[113] Together with other moderate leaders, he criticized Communist and anarcho-syndicalist elements for provoking suppression and the public's antipathy toward organized labor.

In many respects, however, the government's anti-Communist campaign did not change the direction of the labor movement as much as it assured the hold of such social democratic leaders as Nishio and Suzuki Bunji, chairman of the Sōdōmei. Unlike their Marxist comrades, these activists had never really abandoned hope in the reformist potential of the state. A graduate of Tokyo Imperial University, Suzuki had built the original Yūaikai on the basis of cooperation with progressive officials and establishment scholars from the Social Policy Association. He even accompanied the Japanese delegation to the Paris Peace Conference in 1919. When he later denounced the ILO and the quasi-official Kyōchō-kai, he did so partly because of pressure from his federation's young Marxists, but also out of honest frustration with the government's refusal to recognize him or genuine labor unions as spokesmen for Japanese workers.[114] Even then, he and other social democratic labor leaders often looked to the bureaucracy for solutions. As late as the middle of 1920, when syndicalism was reputedly on the rise, many Sōdōmei-Yūaikai leaders still favored the establishment of a state-administered system of compulsory arbitration.[115] Rather than take pride in the Sōdōmei's new militancy, editors of the federation's journal protested in 1921 that the public was too quick to identify the Sōdōmei with "red, leftist, and pernicious tendencies." Sōdōmei did not reject parliamentary politics, they cautioned, only the Hara government's negative policies toward workers and labor organizations.[116] The message was clear. A meaningful change in official labor policy would moderate the labor movement.

In addition, one must question whether most rank-and-file union members ever subscribed to the radical ideologies of their leaders. Andrew Gordon and Thomas Smith have recently examined the language of organized workers' demands in heavy industry during the late 1910s and early 1920s. Both detect an increasing level of class consciousness and willingness to band together, often quite assertively, to improve their collective position. However, the workers did not glory in their separation. On the contrary, they displayed a fervent desire "to be admitted, first, to *society,* to be treated as humans, with dignity, not as 'slaves' or 'animals.' They also wanted to be admitted to the company, as members and equals, to be dealt with sincerely and accorded respect."[117] Resentful of their lack of status vis-à-vis the white-collar staff, workers often struck for better "treatment" (*taigū*) or benefits similar to those enjoyed by the staff. More research on the rank and file needs to be done, but it seems clear that philosophies of "direct action" and "the dictatorship of the proletariat" frightened away many workers, who remained staunchly assimilationist. Devastated by poorly planned strikes, confrontational tactics, and mass arrests, Sōdōmei suffered declining membership and a sharp drop in dues after 1920. Sōdōmei membership within the city of Tokyo plummeted to a mere 852 in 1922.[118] In 1924, the federation's national membership stood at a mere twenty-eight thousand, roughly equivalent to its peak in 1919.[119]

At the leadership level, the Sōdōmei's Nishio Suehiro (1891–1981) embodied the desire of the working class for integration and "realistic socialism" (*genjitsuteki na shakaishugi*). Amid the internecine battles of the early 1920s, power gradually passed from intellectuals, both social democratic and radical, to Nishio and another moderate worker-leader, Matsuoka Komakichi. Nishio's career is all the more significant, for after World War II he became chief cabinet secretary in Japan's only socialist cabinet (1947–48). In 1959, he led reformist blue-collar unions out of the Socialist Party to form the Democratic Socialist Party, which closely cooperates with today's ruling Liberal Democratic Party.

Although often ridiculed as an ineffectual opportunist, Nishio pursued a lifelong strategy of promoting the fortunes of organized labor within the parliamentary and capitalist order. Stephen Large likened Nishio to the "bourgeoisified" and "ossified" leaders of Weimar Germany's Social Democratic movement.[120] A better analogy might be the German Social Democrats *before* 1914. Excluded from middle-class society and a conservative imperial state, those earlier labor leaders resembled Japanese counterparts in their inner desire to be admitted to both.[121] As a skilled workman in 1916, Nishio founded his first labor union in Osaka to promote workers to higher-status positions while astutely declaring the organization's commitment to contributing to the Meiji-era ideal of "a rich nation and strong army."[122] Above all, Nishio maintained a deep suspicion of intellectuals with radical ideologies. Despite flirtations with anarcho-syndicalism and communism, he concluded that both detracted from the economic needs of workers and unrealistically ignored the might of Japanese capital and the state. Nishio preferred occasional collaboration with sympathetic elites. His autobiography scarcely conceals his delight at accompanying Home Ministry bureaucrats to the ILO conferences and serving in the Diet alongside bourgeois politicians.[123]

The Kantō earthquake of September 1923 provided the unusual setting for a rapprochement between the labor movement's "realists" and the state. By Sōdōmei estimates, the quake left three thousand of its members unemployed.[124] Publicly, the Sōdōmei issued strong denunciations of the government for the Kameido prison massacre. Behind the scenes, however, Suzuki Bunji immediately approached Social Bureau officials and Home Minister Gotō Shimpei, the venerable reformist bureaucrat. The distraught federation chairman urgently requested relief for displaced workers and the protection of labor leaders from roving vigilantes. This was an opportunity long awaited by Kawarada Kakichi, chief of the Social Bureau's Labor Division. Kawarada and Gotō gladly pledged police protection. Moreover, appreciating the organizational capacity of unions, Kawarada appointed Suzuki to the Provisional Office for Earthquake Relief, from which Sōdōmei provided relief work to hundreds of unemployed union members. The government also granted Sōdōmei a huge sum for administering shelters for displaced workers. Suzuki's collaboration with the Home Ministry marked the beginning of close relations between Social Bureau officials and moderate trade unionists. Kawarada subsequently nominated Suzuki to be the first labor representative to serve with businessmen, scholars, and officials on the Social Bureau's advisory council.[125] Sōdōmei leaders declined the invitation, but this did not prevent Suzuki from cleverly playing upon Sōdōmei's new legitimacy in bureaucratic circles to demand official recognition of unions in the selection of the ILO workers' delegate.[126]

In conjunction with the Social Bureau's overtures to organized labor, the newly installed nonparty cabinet of Admiral Yamamoto Gonnohyōe (September 1923–January 1924) announced its intention to sponsor a universal manhood suffrage bill. The measure's chief proponent, Home Minister Gotō Shimpei, echoed the views voiced by his ministry's social bureaucrats since 1919. Expressing alarm at the breakdown of law and order during the earthquake, Gotō argued that social peace required the participation of the people in the political process.[127] Although the cabinet fell before taking any action, the government's public commitment to suffrage expansion greatly enhanced the position of those labor leaders who favored the parliamentary representation of workers' interests.

The dramatic developments on both sides set the stage for the defeat of the labor movement's left-wing fringe by the mainstream's trade unionist officials, the self-styled "realists." Led by Suzuki Bunji and Nishio Suehiro, the social democrats attacked the Communists for "utopian theories." The realists instead desired the public recognition of labor unions as responsible organizations which utilized collective bargaining to minimize, not instigate, damaging strikes.[128] Moderate leaders of Sōdōmei and other workers' organizations welcomed the government's promise of enfranchisement as an opportunity to promote labor's interests in the Diet. Within a month of the Yamamoto cabinet's announcement in October, Sōdōmei's central committee created a panel on parliamentary strategy. Several leaders contemplated the formation of a separate labor party, after an interim period of cooperation with sympathetic established parties.

The appearance of the first Labour Party cabinet in Britain in January 1924 further strengthened the hand of union officials such as Suzuki Bunji who argued for the long-term benefits of cooperating with bourgeois reformers in the Diet on behalf of labor legislation.[129] The high point of Sōdōmei's proclaimed "change of direction" came at its annual convention on 10–12 February 1924. Nishio coauthored a series of resolutions aimed at disassociating Sōdōmei from the Communists. After years of issuing radical statements, the federation once again endorsed the objectives of universal suffrage and parliamentary activism. Delegates also pledged to participate in the selection of the workers' delegate to the next ILO conference, anticipating that the Social Bureau would reform the selection process in the near future. Other large unions similarly declared their support for universal suffrage and the ILO.[130]

Circumstantial evidence suggests the existence of a prior arrangement between Sōdōmei and the Social Bureau. Bolstered by labor's "change of direction," the Home Ministry immediately pressed again for the official recognition of the union movement. The new Kiyoura Keigo cabinet (January–June 1924) was the most conservative of the decade's three nonparty cabinets, dominated as it was by the largest faction of the House of Peers. Yet cabinet members were well aware of both the ILO's recent ultimatum and emerging union moderation. On 15 February, only days after the Sōdōmei convention, the Kiyoura cabinet approved the Social Bureau's year-old proposal to recognize large labor unions (those with over one thousand members) as the sole voting bloc for Japan's workers' delegate to the ILO conferences. As in 1923, the Ministry of Agriculture and Commerce and the major governmental employers—the Army and Navy—led the bureaucratic opposition to the Social Bureau. Official recognition of the labor movement, they charged, would legitimize the essentially undesirable labor unions, which represented only a small fraction of the nation's workers. The majority of the cabinet, however, accepted Home Minister Mizuno Rentarō's contention that Japanese prestige in the ILO dictated a significant change in the government's inflexible position toward unions.[131]

The cabinet's recognition of labor unions represented a turning point in administrative policies toward the labor movement. The Japanese government had, for the first time, accepted the principle that encouragement of social democratic labor unions would inhibit the rise of more militant unions. Kawarada Kakichi of the Social Bureau personified this change. In 1919, as a police administrator under Home Minister Tokonami Takejirō, Kawarada had equated labor-capital "harmony" with the prevention of Western-style labor unions. By 1924, Kawarada sought to send Japanese labor leaders to the International Labor Conference to expose them to the "sound and steady" influence of non-Communist union officials from Western nations.[132] One year later, he explained why a labor union law should aim to encourage political activities by unions: "Even the socialist movement is now relatively moderate (onken) and leans toward the [anti-Communist] Second International."[133] Operating under the new rules in March 1924, the country's large unions chose Suzuki Bunji of Sōdōmei to head Japan's labor delegation to that year's ILO conference. They selected as his advisors Yonekubo Mitsusuke and Kawamura Yasutarō, the respective chairmen of the moderate Japan Seamen's Union (Nihon Kaiin Kumiai) and the Japan General Federation of Workers in Governmental Enterprises (Nihon Kangyō Rōdō Sōdōmei).

Just as labor moderation and governmental initiatives reformulated the relationship between the unions and the state, the labor movement's "change of direction" helped to transform the Kyōchōkai into a bureaucratic ally of organized labor. This may seem highly ironic. Most accounts of the semigovernmental Kyōchōkai dwell upon the anti-union aspects of the "Harmonization Society" during its first year.[134] They stress the conservative views of the cofounder, Home Minister Tokonami Takejirō, and the influence of the several prominent industrialists who served on the board of directors. Having pledged over six million yen in contributions, participating employers severely constrained the foundation's ability to conciliate between labor and managers. When a strike broke out at the Fuji Gas Spinning Company in July 1920, the Kyōchōkai declined the workers' request for mediation and further equivocated on whether workers possessed the right to organize. Adding insult to injury, Kyōchōkai directors insisted that their stand had nothing to do with the opinions of fellow board member, Wada Toyoji, the president of Fuji Gas Spinning.

Unrecognized by most historians, however, the Fuji Gas Spinning strike gave rise to a more open-minded Kyōchōkai.[135] Stung by public criticism of their failure to win the trust of workers, board members in November 1920 appointed three new executive directors—Soeda Keiichirō, Tazawa Yoshiharu, and Nagai Tōru. These men proved more willing to defy the board's anti-union directors. Tazawa, a young Home Ministry official, was placed in charge of labor education programs. In his own words, he approached industrial relations in terms of the "absolute equality of man."[136] Nagai directed the Kyōchōkai's extensive survey of progressive Western labor laws. He had earlier been a personnel expert and social policy reformer in the Ministry of Railways. Soeda Keiichirō, the oldest and most conservative of the three, was closely associated with Tokonami's ideas of "harmony," having served as the Home Minister's chief of the Local Affairs Bureau. But his views on labor would rapidly change. Like their colleagues in the Social Bureau, the three executive directors redefined Tokonami's concept of "harmony" in an opening manifesto. Although they opposed the use of illegal tactics and syndicalist strategies by unions, they directed their harshest criticism at employers who espoused "paternalism" (onjō-shugi). Such an ideology, they asserted, was "all too often tantamount to the rule of the weak by the strong" and "far from the principle of harmony." The Kyōchōkai's new leaders preferred the "sound development and spread" of labor unions as a step toward true industrial harmony.[137]

And much like Social Bureau officials, the Kyōchōkai's staff responded favorably to the labor movement's moderating tendencies. Following the Yamamoto cabinet's announced support of universal suffrage, Nagai Tōru called for the creation of a political party for the proletarian classes, in addition to more labor unions. These organizations, he predicted, would bring about "renovation and recovery in industry and a progressive reconstruction of society."[138] In November 1924, Nagai and Soeda Keiichirō approved the Kyōchōkai's own draft labor union bill, although various pressures prevented its release.[139] Non-Communist union leaders, in turn, increasingly looked to the Kyōchōkai as a trusted ally in a hostile environment. In the wake of the 1923 earthquake, the moderate Japan Seamen's Union offered the Kyōchōkai the hefty sum of twenty thousand yen with which the foundation could assist the activities of the union. The Harmonization Society often hosted such Sōdōmei leaders and social democratic politicians as Nishio Suehiro, Matsuoka Komakichi, Akamatsu Katsumaro, and Abe Isoo. The Kyōchōkai did more than bless the establishment of an anti-Communist social democratic party; several staff members eagerly participated in the preparations. Fujii Tei, chief of the foundation's Survey Section, sat with socialists and Communists on the central committee of the preparatory Society for the Study of Politics (Seiji Kenkyūkai) in 1925. Nagai Tōru himself later gave campaign speeches for Abe Isoo of the Social Democratic Party. Other Kyōchōkai activists were accused of taking the unions' side in the organization's numerous efforts to mediate strikes.[140] Businessmen who had lavishly contributed to the Kyōchōkai now complained that the executive directors and staff had become "puppets of the Left."[141]

THE IMPACT ON LABOR AND MANAGEMENT, 1924–28

The improvement in relations between the government and the labor unions established a pattern that persisted until the late 1930s. Reforms in interwar labor policy generally resulted from administrative changes, rather than new laws enacted by the Diet. In the absence of a labor union law, Social Bureau officials endeavored to protect the right to organize unions throughout the 1920s and first half of the 1930s. But did their efforts make much of a difference in a nation where employers held the upper hand and other parts of the state remained hostile to organized labor? Kitaoka Juitsu, chronicler of the Social Bureau and a former bureau official himself, naturally replied in the affirmative. Under the Social Bureau's enlightened policies, he observed, the total number of labor union members nearly quadrupled from 125,551 (1923) to 420,589 (1936).[142] Kitaoka's assertion raises a number of questions. Was official labor policy responsible for this growth, or did it result primarily from the new strength of workers? Could the bureaucracy have intervened more forcefully to guarantee workers' rights? Or did official intervention instead constrain an otherwise vital labor movement?

It is best to begin with the impact of the new labor policy on employers and labor-management relations. As reformist as the social bureaucrats may appear, they lacked the power to force capitalists to accept labor unions. Pending the passage of a labor union law, the Social Bureau occasionally instructed governors to invalidate any shop regulations that required that an employee "not enter a labor union or that [he or she] leave a union" as a condition of employment.[143] Yet managers easily evaded such directives by simply removing the offending regulations. In practice, they fired or refused to hire large numbers of union members, ostensibly for reasons unrelated to union affiliation.[144] At bottom, unionization depended on the collective strength of workers and the responses by employers.

By the mid-1920s, labor organization appeared closely correlated with factory size. Union organizers did best in small and medium enterprises. Employers in such plants tended to be weaker, and poor working conditions and wages were more likely to cause labor dissatisfaction. Moreover, unions found it easier to control a few hundred workers or less.[145] In contrast, companies with over five hundred employees successfully broke most horizontal unions during the recession of the early 1920s. Large-scale unionization occurred almost exclusively in governmental and public enterprises—notably arsenals and municipal transportation—and among merchant-marine seamen and their officers.

Scholars have offered several explanations for the absence of unions in large private companies. Some cite the greater ability of wealthy firms to weather strikes and lockouts. Big companies could also afford to lure workers away from unions by offering improved benefits, better working conditions, and attentive personnel or labor sections. Others argue that managers routed the horizontal unions by instituting works councils, company unions, and other vertical organizations.[146] Recent studies suggest that blue-collar workers themselves took the initiative to demand equal treatment, job security, seniority-based wages, and other innovations associated with Japan's present-day industrial relations. They abandoned horizontal unions only after managers began to respond.[147] Whatever the reasons, the Social Bureau's extralegal measures were hardly sufficient to reverse organized labor's fundamental inability to penetrate the big companies. Despite steady growth after 1923, unions accounted for a mere 7.9 percent of the industrial work force at their peak in 1931.

There were, however, some areas in which Social Bureau policy significantly influenced employment practices. Effected in 1926, the 1923 revisions to the Factory Law forced companies to pay ill or injured workers 60 percent of their wages for six months and 40 percent thereaf- ter (increased from 50 percent for three months and 33 percent subse- quently). Moreover, the Health Insurance Law of 1922 (fully enforced in 1927) provided a new forum for face-to-face negotiations between worker representatives and employers. By law, companies could accept governmental administration of the health-and-accident-insurance pro- gram or set up their own health insurance associations consisting of an equal number of workers and managers. Most opted for health insur- ance associations to preserve their independence. The Health Insurance Law required firms to contribute at least 50 percent, the remainder coming from workers. Accordingly, some labor unions sought represen- tation in the insurance associations to force owners to bear more of the costs. Several strikes broke out over this issue, and nearly half of the firms surveyed in 1927 ended up paying over 50 percent.[148]

The Home Ministry's most direct form of intervention in industrial relations occurred in the realm of mediating labor disputes. In 1926, the Diet repealed the antistrike Article 17 of the Police Regulations and enacted in its place the Social Bureau's Labor Disputes Concilia- tion Law. As in Yasui Eiji's original draft, the new law established rules for conciliation committees composed of representatives from labor, management, and the public. The committees would be con- vened voluntarily by the concerned parties in private-sector disputes and by state compulsion in public utilities and governmental enter- prises. Although officials invoked the Conciliation Law's compulsory feature only six times between 1926 and 1942, the legislation sparked the growth of extralegal mediation by the police and other officials. In tandem with the operation of the Conciliation Law on 1 July 1926, the government created a supervisory Labor Affairs Section within the Social Bureau. It also assigned eighty specialized conciliation officers and assistant conciliation officers to prefectural police departments. During strike-ridden 1926, official and private conciliation settled an unprecedented 41 percent of all work stoppages and lockouts.

Most labor federations initially opposed the enactment of the Con- ciliation Law in 1926 because it briefly banned "instigation or in- citement" by outside "third parties" during conciliation proceedings in public-sector disputes. Nevertheless, the Sōdōmei and other moderate unions increasingly perceived the police and Kyōchōkai as honest bro- kers and often sympathetic allies. In practice, workers and labor unions more commonly requested outside mediation than did employers, who ordinarily occupied the stronger position.[149] Even before the passage of the Conciliation Law, a lawyer for Sōdōmei argued that the measure would "in a sense" legally recognize unions as the representatives of workers on the conciliation committees.[150] By the 1930s, Sōdōmei leaders so welcomed state arbitration that they proposed amendments to the Conciliation Law granting authorities the power to order conciliation proceedings in *any* dispute, not simply those in public enterprises.[151]

Relative to its impact on employers, the Home Ministry's emerging labor policy stimulated far more profound changes within the labor movement. The new mix of concessions and repression unquestionably encouraged the development of anti-Communist labor unions and social democratic parties. Some would call this strategy one of co-optation. A better term might be "incorporation," for the social bureaucrats consciously sought to give labor unions an institutional role in industrial relations and policy formation. Suzuki Bunji's assistance in post-earthquake relief efforts was simply one of the earliest episodes of growing cooperation between non-Communist unions and the Home Ministry. Shortly before the earthquake, the Social Bureau established another precedent. In drafting important ordinances effecting the 1923 revisions to the Factory Law, officials formally consulted labor unions, as well as employers' associations.

During the 1930s, labor groups requested greater participation. The Social Bureau warmly complied by regularly soliciting their opinions on legislation and executive ordinances.[152] In December 1930, amidst controversy over the government's labor union bill, Home Minister Adachi Kenzō sponsored Japan's first major tripartite meeting between representatives of government, employers, and organized labor. Labor and social democratic leaders enthusiastically attended, but business delegates boycotted the conference (see chapter 5). At the local level, governors and big-city mayors occasionally turned to labor leaders and social democrats. Horikiri Zenjirō, mayor of Tokyo and a former "new man" from the Home Ministry, tapped the Christian labor and tenant movement leader, Kagawa Toyohiko, to be his personal advisor on social problems in 1929.[153] Attendance at meetings of the II O and the Tokyo-based Association for International Labor (Kokusai Rōdō Kyōkai) also spawned lasting friendships between Social Bureau officials such as Kitaoka Juitsu and the labor figures, Nishio Suehiro and Matsuoka Komakichi.[154] The former Sōdōmei leader, Akamatsu Katsumaro, had nothing but praise for the Social Bureau's "liberal bureaucrats." Nishio went further, calling Kitaoka, Yasui Eiji, Yosh:da Shigeru, and other Social Bureau officials "the most progressive in the government." When Nishio sat on a Diet committee deliberating the 1931 labor union bill, he proudly considered himself "one of the government's members" along with the Social Bureau's experts.[155]

The new legitimacy accorded the unions revitalized and reshaped the Japanese labor movement. The government's shift to official recognition in 1924 did much to stimulate the recently stagnant union movement. During 1924 alone, union membership nationwide nearly doubled, from 126,000 to 228,000 (see appendix 6). The rapid increase partly reflected the hurried efforts of governmental officials to forestall a victory by socialist unions in the election of the ILO delegate. Military and civilian authorities intervened to organize labor unions in public transportation and in army and navy arsenals, notably the 47,000-member League of Naval Labor Unions (Kaigun Rōdō Kumiai Remmei). Many of these "unions" began as company-sponsored mutual-aid societies, which the new rules barred from voting in the ILO elections. Whatever their origins, a large number soon became bona fide labor unions dedicated to maintaining and improving working conditions. The Autonomous Association of Tokyo City Streetcar Employees (Tōkyō Shiden Jūgyōin Jichikai) was one such example. Although city officials founded the association as a "friendship" society of *all* employees in the Streetcar Bureau, worker-leaders quickly expelled staff employees and forged a purely workers' organization of 8,000 members. Even the League of Naval Labor Unions, which naval authorities had previously barred from engaging in political activities, eventually affiliated with Sōdōmei and its Social Democratic Party. By 1924, governmental employers and the police considered the trade unionist activities of these "realistic" labor organizations a welcome alternative to the politicized tactics of the radical left-wing unions.[156]

Recognizing the benefits of trade-unionist and social democratic activity, Sōdōmei's "realists" accelerated their drive to isolate Communist elements within the General Federation. They also appreciated the risks of official repression courted by continued association with such known Communist labor leaders as Watanabe Masanosuke, who had recently met with Soviet agents in Shanghai. In May 1925, Akamatsu Katsumaro, Matsuoka Komakichi, and Nishio Suehiro led the central committee in expelling twenty-five unions that backed the Communist group. The purged unions immediately formed the Japan Council of Labor Unions (Nihon Rōdō Kumiai Hyōgikai). In line with Comintern policy, the Hyōgikai organized workers as part of a political class struggle, committing the federation to forming a united proletarian party in anticipation of universal manhood suffrage. During 1926, the Hyōgikai mounted a number of unusually militant and, in most cases, unsuccessful strikes. The most famous was the 105-day strike against the Japan Musical Instruments Company (known today as Yamaha) in Hamamatsu. Launched to improve working conditions, the dispute took on the aspect of an ideological Armageddon. The company portrayed itself as a bulwark against Communism and brought in right-wing strikebreakers. The government arrested well over 200 Hyōgikai organizers and workers after the labor organization threatened a general strike together with other Hamamatsu unions. Soeda Keiichirō, executive director of the Kyōchōkai, finally mediated the dispute. The workers gained little. Some 350 of the 1,380 striking employees were dismissed, albeit with a combined severance pay of thirty thousand yen.[157]

From 1925 to 1928, the Hyōgikai and Sōdōmei battled for the hearts and minds of Japanese workers. By the end of 1925, the Hyōgikai had doubled its membership from an initial 10,778 to 21,110; the rump Sōdōmei grew from approximately 17,000 to 31,801. Governmental policy was probably not decisive in the Sōdōmei's eventual victory over its left-wing rival. The militant federation lost as many members as it gained during 1926 and 1927. The Hyōgikai's membership still stood at 21,000 on the eve of its dissolution by the Tanaka cabinet in April 1928. According to the official history of the Sōdōmei, Hyōgikai organizers dug their own grave by indiscriminately waging politicized and ill-fated strikes against capitalists amid recession.[158] Their tactics and ideology further alienated the Hyōgikai from the rest of the labor movement. At the end of 1925, the Social Bureau pointedly contrasted the small membership of organized labor's Hyōgikai-dominated "left wing" (23,000) with the "social democratic" unions (70,000), led by Sōdōmei, and the cooperative "socially reformist" unions (120,000), such as the League of Naval Labor Unions.[159]

Yet there can be little doubt that the Home Ministry's dual policy of accommodation and control contributed to the triumph of the labor movement's "right wing," as it was then called. Put simply, the Sōdōmei and its moderate allies operated with a far more realistic understanding of which activities officials would tolerate and which would bring down the wrath of the imperial state. For example, aggressive unionization by both the Hyōgikai and the Sōdōmei led to a sharp increase in strikes and strike participants in 1926 (see appendix 1). Whereas the police detained more than five thousand Hyōgikai members, Sōdōmei strikers were generally left alone.[160] Social Bureau officials and Sōdōmei leaders offered similar explanations for this contrast. The non-Communist unions were beginning to impose more centralized control over locals' decisions to wage strikes.[161] Eschewing political and overly risky strikes, Sōdōmei achieved sixty-eight victories, twenty-eight compromises, and only about ten outright defeats during 1926.[162]

Sōdōmei leaders played their new moderate image for all it was worth. Reaffirming the commitment to "realism" and economically based "trade unionism," annual conventions after 1925 not only endorsed stricter controls over strike-making, they further declared their dedication to peaceful settlements, collective agreements with employers, and the enactment of labor legislation. The immediate gains were modest, yet represented real progress compared with the preceding era of stagnation. Whereas employers had totally rejected union demands for the right to bargain collectively during the early 1920s, fear of the Hyōgikai persuaded several companies to conclude collective agreements with Sōdōmei from 1924. The most notable triumph came in 1926, when Sōdōmei formulated a collective agreement with the Tokyo Wire Company, which covered nearly two thousand workers. Although many of these accords later lapsed for various reasons, the federation added new agreements every year. Not until the 1930s would the Social Bureau and the police intervene to forge collective agreements as a matter of policy. But the Social Bureau and Kyōchōkai repeatedly expressed their support for the Sōdōmei's growing emphasis on "sound" trade unionism.[163]

Sōdōmei's focus on cooperation with officials and employers provoked cries from the Left that the federation had sold out the cause of labor and socialist unity. The image of Sōdōmei as "spoiler" appears in many Japanese-language histories and more recently in Stephen Large's study of interwar socialist politics.[164] The leadership's refusal to cooperate with Communist-linked unions and parties resulted, it is true, in two additional schisms of Sōdōmei. In December 1926, the socialist intellectual Asō Hisashi led six thousand workers out of the federation to form the "centrist" Federation of Japanese Labor Unions (Nihon Rōdō Kumiai Dōmei). In August 1929, Sōdōmei's worker-leaders expelled an Osaka-based faction representing five thousand workers for vociferously criticizing both the federation's support of the ILO and its opposition to allying with leftist labor organizations. This third schism cost Sōdōmei much of its stronghold in the Osaka-Kobe area.[165]

What critics of the reformist federation overlook, however, is that Sōdōmei leaders more than made up for their losses to the labor's relatively small left-wing and centrist camps by unifying the much larger "right wing." Following the "change of direction" in 1924, Sōdōmei agreed to combine their votes for the ILO delegate and advisors with two like-minded trade unionist organizations—the Japan General Federation of Workers in Governmental Enterprises and the Japan Seamen's Union. By the end of 1928, the Governmental Workers numbered over 14,000, drawn primarily from transportation and arsenals. With 80,000 members, the Seamen's Union constituted the nation's largest and most effective union. Together with the Japan Maritime Officers' Association (Nihon Kaiin Kyōkai), the Seamen's Union concluded the interwar era's only industry-wide collective agreement with the shipowners' association in 1926, covering 55,000 seamen and officers.[166]

In 1928, Sōdōmei formally allied itself with the Governmental Workers, the Seamen's Union, the Maritime Officers' Association, and the cooperationist League of Naval Labor Unions. The five federations formed the Council to Promote Labor Legislation (Rōdō Rippō Sokushin Iinkai), which represented approximately 190,000 of the nation's 309,000 organized workers. Including smaller unions, the Social Bureau estimated that over 80 percent of all unionists belonged to "right-wing" unions—that is, those concentrating on advancing workers' welfare or which were affiliated with the Council to Promote Labor Legislation and the moderate Social Democratic Party.[167] The Council symbolized the type of institutionalized channels envisioned by the social bureaucrats. Dedicated to enacting labor legislation, it acted as a conduit between member organizations and governmental policy-makers.

The Home Ministry played a particularly direct role in the formation of socialist parties after the passage of the Universal Manhood Suffrage Law in March 1925. Here, too, the alliance with Sōdōmei was pivotal. The Social Bureau and Kyōchōkai, it will be recalled, favored the creation of a British- or German-style labor party oriented toward social democracy. Officials were less sanguine about a party dominated by the Hyōgikai and other organizations associated with the outlawed Communist Party. During the autumn of 1925, Sōdōmei representatives fought in vain to oust the Hyōgikai-led camp from the committee to establish a united "proletarian party." Authorities grew alarmed when Sōdōmei and fellow social democratic groups withdrew two days before the inauguration of the planned socialist party. On 1 December 1925, Home Minister Wakatsuki Reijirō dissolved the Farmer-Labor Party

(Nōmin Rōdōtō) only hours after its formation. Spokesmen for the Home Ministry and Wakatsuki's Kenseikai pointed to the founding role of the Hyōgikai and similarly radical groups as proof that the new party was a front for the Communist Party, hence prejudicial to public order under Article 8 of the Police Regulations of 1900. Hyōgikai representatives had in fact formally withdrawn at the last minute in an effort to prevent dissolution.[168]

Although the state's actions against the Farmer-Labor Party were repressive, to say the least, they did not originate entirely from above. Nishio Suehiro of Sōdōmei publicly supported the government's case. Branding the Hyōgikai's positions those of "the Communist Party itself," Nishio cited Western examples to show why the mainstream of the labor movement should form its own labor party, independent of the Communist Party.[169] Moreover, newspapers printed fairly convincing stories of a secret pact between Sōdōmei and the Home Ministry. It was well known that Chairman Suzuki Bunji had been a university classmate of the Social Bureau's Kawarada Kakichi and Police Bureau Chief Matsumura Giichi, both of whom reportedly sought to cultivate an anti-Communist proletarian party.[170]

Accordingly, Home Ministry leaders looked favorably on the founding of the Sōdōmei-led Labor-Farmer Party (Rōdō Nōmintō) in March 1926. Moderate labor and tenant-farmer groups initially excluded the Hyōgikai and other left-wing bodies. But after the moderates again failed to keep the Communist-linked organizations out, the Sōdōmei bloc and such left-liberal intellectuals as Yoshino Sakuzō withdrew to establish the Social Democratic Party (Shakai Minshūtō) in December. As if to make matters more confusing, Asō Hisashi, who had just been expelled from Sōdōmei, founded a third party—the "centrist" Japan Labor-Farmer Party (Nihon Rōdō Nōmintō). Of the three, the Social Democrats enjoyed by far the strongest labor base, supported by the large "right-wing" unions. The Social Democratic Party also benefited from official sympathy and continued persecution of its left-wing rivals. The Social Democrats would form the core of a united socialist party in the 1930s.

In view of their interventionist role in reshaping the labor movement, how should we evaluate the social bureaucrats of the 1920s? Labels are of little help. Their ideals were often "liberal," for they envisioned the optimal society as one in which interest groups freely and fairly competed before the referee-state. Yet Home Ministry officials hardly eschewed the use of force against those left-wing labor groups that did not conform to their conception of a rational, orderly society.

Nevertheless, we must take care not to judge Japan's social bureaucrats by idealized comparisons with Anglo-American liberals, many of whom similarly favored cracking down on Communists and anarchists. For their time and place, these higher civil servants were remarkably progressive. Officials of the Social Bureau and Kyōchōkai deserve credit for fundamentally reformulating labor policy in a manner that went well beyond the initiatives of other elites in bureaucracy, business, and the major political parties. Most important, they helped to break down the barriers isolating the mainstream of the labor movement from the rest of society. The social bureaucrats took full advantage of the Home Ministry's relatively high level of independence from the business community. But there were limits to their autonomy. They essentially represented one bureau in one ministry in a bureaucracy subject to diverse pressures from political parties, economic elites, and various ideological groups on the Right. The extent to which organized labor secured a legally protected position depended, in large measure, on a shifting balance of power between rival coalitions of party politicians and bureaucrats in the course of the next half decade.

CHAPTER IV

The Politics of Social Policy, 1924–29

MORI KAKU [Seiyūkai member, the Lower House]:	The executives of U.S Steel are sworn to the philosophy of refusing to employ any worker who joins a union. . . . We urge the government to consider putting this practice into the labor law [present labor union bill]. . . .
NAGAOKA RYŪICHIRŌ [Social Bureau director]:	As Mr. Mori well knows, conditions in America are very different from those in Japan. . . . [In Japan], we certainly welcome the welfare programs of enlightened capitalists, . . . but in view of present economic and social conditions, there must also be laws [like the labor union bill] to bring about further improvements [in workers' welfare], and we must, at the same time, recognize the creation of unions by the workers' own efforts.

*—Lower House committee hearings on the 1926
labor union bill.*[1]

Japanese politics experienced its own "change of direction" during 1924. The installation of yet another nonparty government, the Kiyoura cabinet, precipitated a fundamental restructuring of the major parties. Indeed, the majority Seiyūkai split in two over the question of whether to support Kiyoura. The schism brought an end to the Seiyūkai's nearly total domination of the Lower House over the past two decades. Factional cleavages first appeared following the assassination of Seiyūkai president Hara Takashi in 1921. The elder statesmen (*genrō*) added fuel to the fire in 1922 when they selected an admiral to be prime minister, rather than reappoint the Seiyūkai's Takahashi Korekiyo, despite his party's parliamentary majority. When Count Kiyoura Keigo became prime minister in January 1924, Takahashi and other Seiyūkai leaders joined the Kenseikai and Inukai Tsuyoshi's Kakushin Club to oppose the nonparty cabinet in the "movement to protect the Constitution." Tokonami Takejirō and Yamamoto Tatsuo thereupon led pro-Kiyoura forces out of the Seiyūkai to organize the Seiyūhontō (True Party of the Seiyūkai). To distance itself from the oligarchic Kiyoura cabinet, the rump Seiyūkai took up the cause of universal manhood suffrage in alliance with the historically progressive Kenseikai and Kakushin Club.

The fragmentation of the relatively conservative Seiyūkai removed many of the obstacles to reform legislation. In the ensuing election of May 1924, the anti-Kiyoura alliance won a decisive victory. The Kenseikai netted 152 seats, followed by the rump Seiyūkai (102 seats) and the Kakushin Club (30 seats). The pro-government Seiyūhontō garnered only 111 seats. The Kiyoura cabinet resigned, and Prince Saionji Kimmochi, the only surviving elder statesman, chose the Kenseikai's Katō Takaaki to head a three-party coalition government (June 1924–August 1925). After years of advocating universal manhood suffrage and liberal labor policy in the opposition, the Kenseikai was given an opportunity to advance its programs as the principal governing party. In March 1925, Katō's coalition enacted the Universal Manhood Suffrage Law, which enfranchised nearly all males aged twenty-five years or older. The passage of universal manhood suffrage by bourgeois-landlord parties stands out as a remarkable achievement in the democratization of interwar Japan, coming only six and seven years after the enactment of truly equal and universal male enfranchisement in Weimar Germany and Great Britain, respectively.

Equally significant, the political events of 1924 set in motion the alternation of the power between two large parties. Katō's coalition cabinet was followed by the Kenseikai's two minority cabinets (August 1925–April 1927). During this period, the Seiyūkai absorbed the mainstream of the Kakushin Club in 1925, and the Kenseikai merged with Tokonami's Seiyūhontō to form the Minseitō in 1927. Thus strengthened, the Seiyūkai organized the Tanaka Giichi cabinet in April 1927, before yielding power to two successive Minseitō cabinets (July 1929–December 1931). The pattern was not exactly British, but it came close. Speaking for the emperor, the elder statesman Saionji brought in the rival party when he felt the current party cabinet had lost its ability to govern. The new cabinet would then hold elections, which invariably gave the ruling party a workable majority in the Lower House.[2]

What did this dizzying alternation of party cabinets mean in terms of actual policy? Not much, according to most Japanese scholars. To historians of "Taishō democracy," the Kenseikai-led cabinets offered a chance for bourgeois democratic reform, yet in the end they compromised with the entrenched elites, rather than break the power of the bureaucracy, the military, and the House of Peers.[3] The leading historian of Japanese political parties concluded with representative bluntness: "The two major parties were the same in substance when it came to [policies concerning the farming villages, labor, cities, and social problems]. Differences in policies, of course, existed, but the opposing and ruling parties seem to have exaggerated them for rhetorical purposes during the heat of battle."[4] Curiously enough, a younger generation of Japanese historians has taken to criticizing the interwar parties for *not* giving a freer rein to the bureaucracy—especially the "reform bureaucrats" from the Home Ministry. In this view, rivalry between the Seiyūkai and the Minseitō politicized and corrupted bureaucratic specialists, making "the promotion of social reform from a transcendent position extremely difficult."[5]

The above interpretations suffer from two major shortcomings. They all ignore ample evidence that contemporaries perceived clear programmatic differences between the two parties. Many progressive commentators portrayed the Kenseikai/Minseitō as the "liberal party" and the Seiyūkai as the "conservative party." Moreover, Japanese historiography generally fails to appreciate the complex relationship between the parties and higher civil servants. Party cabinets provided the invaluable function of coordinating policy formation and implementation through their ministers of state and parliamentary floor managers. The governing party thus possessed the power to make or break various bureaucratic initiatives. Scholars who focus solely on the reformism of the Social Bureau overlook the fact that meaningful labor legislation would not have emerged from the Home Ministry, much less been introduced to the Diet, had it not been for crucial support by the Kenseikai and Minseitō cabinets. The course of interwar labor policy was very much a tale of two parties.

"A UNIVERSAL SUFFRAGE FOR INDUSTRY": THE LABOR UNION BILLS OF 1926 AND 1927

Katō Takaaki's coalition cabinet offers a unique glimpse into the interaction of partisan politics and bureaucratic policy-making. For the first and only time, the Kenseikai-Seiyūkai debate over political and social democratization moved from the floor of the Lower House to the cabinet room itself. Kenseikai leaders were in a staunchly reformist mood, bolstered by the latest "trends of the world" in early 1924. They appeared almost as excited as Japanese trade unionists by the accession of MacDonald's Labour Party cabinet. And in France, they noted, Édouard Herriot came to power by means of a liberal-socialist coalition. The Kenseikai may not have been a workers' party, but spokesmen viewed the respectable British Labour Party as a fellow progressive party which would "advance reformist tendencies throughout the world."[6] Katō likened the "aristocratic" cabinet of Count Kiyoura to the fallen empires of Russia, Germany, and Austria-Hungary. As he had since 1918, the Kenseikai president urged his countrymen to avoid social chaos by following the Anglo-French "democracies." Programs of social reform and suffrage expansion, he reiterated, offered the best chance of mollifying popular dissatisfaction, because they instilled a sense of "rights and obligations."[7]

With respect to labor policy, the division of cabinet posts among Katō's coalition established a working alliance between the Kenseikai and the Home Ministry's social bureaucrats, as is shown below:

Kenseikai:	Prime Minister (Katō Takaaki), Home Affairs (Wakatsuki Reijirō), Finance (Hamaguchi Osachi), Railways (Sengoku Mitsugu), Foreign Affairs (Shidehara Kijūrō, pro-Kenseikai), chief cabinet secretary (Egi Tasuku)
Seiyūkai:	Agriculture and Commerce (Takahashi Korekiyo), Justice (Yokota Sennosuke)
Kakushin Club:	Communications (Inukai Tsuyoshi)

The Kenseikai's control of the Home Ministry significantly advanced the Social Bureau's progressive voice in the formulation of labor policy.

Home Minister Wakatsuki Reijirō quickly dismissed top Home Ministry officials associated with the Seiyūkai/Seiyūhontō clique of former
Home Minister Tokonami. In their place, he appointed a pro-Kenseikai
group of higher civil servants led by the incoming administrative vice-
minister, Yuasa Kurahei, a veteran reformist official.[8] Kataoka Naoharu, the Kenseikai businessman who had advocated the legal recognition of labor unions since 1919, became parliamentary vice-minister.
Kenseikai leaders also invited the Social Bureau's first director, Tsukamoto Seiji, to head the cabinet's influential Bureau of Legislation. But
Wakatsuki's greatest contribution to labor reform was his appointment
of the outspoken bureaucrat, Nagaoka Ryūichirō, to replace the Social
Bureau's director, Ikeda Hiroshi. Ikeda had consistently stifled his subordinates' recommendations for a labor union law and the repeal of Article 17. Nagaoka, in contrast, came to his post as the most forceful
proponent of those two measures among the Home Ministry's "new
men" of 1920. Over the next four and a half years, he transformed the
Social Bureau into a politically potent lobby for progressive labor and
welfare policies.[9]

Home Minister Wakatsuki, himself a former higher civil servant,
deserves particular credit for coordinating reform efforts between his
Kenseikai and the Home Ministry. Most political historians portray
Wakatsuki as a weak party leader prone to compromise and lacking any
vision of politics.[10] As home minister from 1924 to 1926, however,
Wakatsuki championed the era's democratic legislation with a great
deal of vision. He successfully pushed the Home Ministry's universal
manhood suffrage bill through the Diet, despite substantial resistance
from the conservative House of Peers and Privy Council. One veteran
Social Bureau official praised Wakatsuki for understanding the complexities of social and labor policy far better than any other interwar
home minister of partisan origin.[11] As he repeatedly informed prefectural governors, the solutions to the "social question" lay in raising the
standard of living, opening political participation to the common people, and encouraging the activities of "moderate, legal" labor and tenant organizations.[12] Soon after assuming his duties in mid-1924, Home
Minister Wakatsuki ordered his staff to formulate a legislative package
based on the Social Bureau's draft labor union bill, labor disputes conciliation bill, and proposed repeal of Article 17.[13]

The coalition government did not in fact introduce the three labor
bills to the next Diet in early 1925. This was partly a question of
priorities, given the importance of the universal manhood suffrage bill

and other measures. Yet the postponement was most related to obstruc-tionist tactics by the Kenseikai's coalition partners, particularly Seiyūkai president Takahashi Korekiyo. In his capacity as minister of agriculture and commerce, Takahashi united bureaucratic and business opposition against all three of the Home Ministry's labor bills during the last months of 1924. Whereas the Ministries of Communications, Railways, Army, and Navy were receptive to the Social Bureau's legislation with some revisions, the Ministry of Agriculture and Commerce remained implacably opposed.[14] Agriculture and Commerce officials drew addi-tional strength from the behind-the-scenes protests of such influential employers' organizations as the Greater Japan Association of Cotton Spinners, the National Federation of Chambers of Commerce, and the Japan Industrial Club.[15]

Agriculture and Commerce leaders borrowed the standard manage-rial arguments to attack the Social Bureau's draft proposals. Takahashi charged the Social Bureau with "blindly translating" European laws, inasmuch as its union bill would legally recognize collective agreements and all types of unions. These provisions, he and his staff argued, hardly conformed to Japanese society and the existing state of industrial devel-opment. Selecting their own favorite Western model, they smugly noted that even the advanced United States did not guarantee the results of collective bargaining. While acknowledging the value of labor unions in preventing strikes in times of prosperity, they claimed that unions and a union law served no useful purpose during the current recession. Taka-hashi and ministry officials especially worried that legal recognition would politically "inflame the consciousness of workers" and encour-age the growth of a strong labor party. They also objected to the dis-putes conciliation measure for its tacit recognition of labor's freedom to strike in private enterprises. Agriculture and Commerce leaders further fought to retain the seldom-enforced Article 17 on the grounds that the "existence of an unnecessary law educates society" about the undesir-ability of strikes.[16] Ministers of a single-party cabinet might have united the Home Ministry and Ministry of Agriculture and Commerce behind mutually acceptable labor legislation, but the Seiyūkai's Takahashi dis-played little desire to compromise with the Kenseikai.

The Seiyūkai's withdrawal from the coalition cabinet in July 1925 removed a major political obstacle to the Kenseikai's campaign for a new labor policy. The Kakushin Club's Inukai Tsuyoshi had resigned from the cabinet earlier that year. On 2 August, Katō Takaaki formed a minority Kenseikai cabinet. Labor legislation reportedly became the "number-one policy of the new Katō cabinet" in preparation for the Fifty-first Diet (early 1926). Home Minister Wakatsuki billed the proposed recognition of labor unions and expansion of welfare services as the social analogue to the Kenseikai's extension of electoral rights to the populace. The press concurred, dubbing the government's labor legislation the "universal suffrage for industry."[17]

Katō replaced the Seiyūkai's ministers with the architects of the Kenseikai's original labor policy—Egi Tasuku as justice minister and Kataoka Naoharu as minister of commerce and industry (the Ministry of Agriculture and Commerce had been divided in April into the Ministry of Commerce and Industry and the Ministry of Agriculture and Forestry). Kataoka quickly moved to align his obstructionist ministry behind the programs of the Kenseikai and the Home Ministry.[18] During the autumn of 1925, Home Minister Wakatsuki concentrated on the difficult task of unifying bureaucratic opinion behind the government's labor legislation. Sensitive to past resistance from the Ministry of Agriculture and Commerce, Wakatsuki submitted the Social Bureau's three draft bills to the cabinet's advisory Investigative Commission on Administration (Gyōsei Chōsakai). The commission consisted primarily of administrative vice-ministers and high-ranking bureau chiefs from each ministry.[19]

Bureaucratic representatives to the Investigative Commission were most critical of the Social Bureau's proposed labor union bill. Not until the United States Occupation of Japan in 1945 would a Japanese government or major political party produce a bill as favorable to organized labor (see appendix 5). Based on Yasui Eiji's 1923 draft, the Social Bureau bill would have guaranteed the validity of collective agreements, levied fines against employers who arbitrarily dismissed or refused to hire union members, and exempted unions from liability for dispute-incurred damages.[20] Officials from the Ministry of Agriculture and Commerce and the conservative Justice Ministry led the drive for revisions within the commission. They were occasionally joined by representatives of the ministries employing large numbers of workers—Railways, Communications, Finance, Army, and Navy.[21]

The results were hardly unexpected. The Investigative Commission substantially revised the Social Bureau's draft union bill in December 1925. Legal recognition was confined to craft and industrial unions, thereby eliminating the Social Bureau's proposed coverage of mixed unions and federations. The panel also struck the key article enforcing collective agreements and recommended that anti-union employment practices simply be invalidated without penalizing the guilty employers. The commission's draft further empowered the government to dissolve disruptive labor unions, and it required unions to become incorporated. These recommendations formed the basis of the Kenseikai cabinet's labor union bill, which was introduced to the Diet in February 1926.[22] Influential dailies accused the government of emasculating the Social Bureau's progressive draft. The liberal labor specialist, Professor Suehiro Izutarō of Tokyo Imperial University, bitterly termed the measure a "bill to control labor unions."[23]

Nonetheless, a Japanese government had, for the first time, overcome administrative sectionalism to produce a labor union bill and other industrial relations legislation. The Social Bureau's labor disputes conciliation bill and proposed repeal of Article 17 emerged unscathed. Although the cabinet's official labor union bill of 1926 fell short of the Social Bureau's draft in terms of providing safeguards to organized labor, the measure represented a clear advance over the Kenseikai's labor union bill of 1921 (see appendix 5). The government's labor union bill exempted unions from any liability for damages sustained during disputes. In place of the Kenseikai's earlier requirement that a union obtain governmental authorization to organize, a new union would simply have to report its formation to the authorities. Whereas the Kenseikai's 1921 bill invalidated only the discriminatory dismissal of a union member, the 1926 bill also prohibited "yellow-dog contracts," by which employers forced workers to agree not to join a union. Furthermore, the government's labor union bill contained a proviso that would recognize all currently existing unions and federations, including those not organized by craft and industry. Although they were disappointed with the cabinet's retreat, Social Bureau officials asserted that the government's labor union bill would at least inhibit employers from openly opposing the formation of unions, besides legitimizing organized labor in the eyes of society.[24]

Home Minister Wakatsuki was preparing the cabinet's labor legislation for parliamentary approval in January 1926, when the death of Katō Takaaki elevated him to the post of prime minister (he continued as home minister until June). Given the Kenseikai's minority status in the Lower House and the general hostility of the House of Peers toward the government, leaders of the Wakatsuki cabinet were privately skeptical that the Diet would pass all three measures in their original form.[25] They also confronted a rare instance of "harmony between Labor and Capital." Both sides detested the government's labor union bill. Led by

Sōdōmei and the General Federation of Workers in Governmental Enterprises, moderate labor organizations had eagerly supported the Social
Bureau's draft union bill. Following the cabinet's revisions, however,
the two federations joined with the militant Hyōgikai in a series of
rallies to protest the cabinet's "three pernicious bills"—the union bill,
the labor disputes conciliation bill, and the Justice Ministry's bill to
control violent activities.[26]

Despite the government's dilution of the Social Bureau draft, many
employers' associations attacked the labor union bill almost as vehemently. To be sure, most stopped short of absolutely opposing the
cabinet's labor legislation. Employers' organizations did not vigorously
contest the labor disputes conciliation bill and the proposed repeal of
Article 17. The police had rarely applied Article 17 in recent years, and
governmental representatives reassured businessmen that the Criminal
Code continued to outlaw "violence" and "intimidation" in strikes and
that the new conciliation law would restrict "instigation or incitement"
in public-sector disputes.[27] Moreover, some business groups still endorsed the principle of legally recognizing unions under certain constraints. Even the Japan Industrial Club simply lobbied for revisions
because Chairman Dan Takuma feared that the public would criticize
direct opposition to the union bill as resistance to "the trends of the
world."[28]

Nonetheless, the amendments proposed were for the most part designed to gut the labor union bill. The influential Japan Industrial Club
urged the government to delete key provisions that would prohibit
discriminatory employment practices, safeguard unions from dispute-
related liability, and recognize existing unions of all types.[29] The formation of the politicized Hyōgikai particularly alarmed employers, many
of whom predicted that the legal protection of unions would result in a
labor-based Communist Party with the advent of universal manhood
suffrage.[30]

Bolstered by the business community's generally hard line, the
Seiyūkai adopted a position of total opposition to the labor union bill
within the Lower House. Having absorbed the Kakushin Club and several defectors from the Seiyūhontō, the Seiyūkai held 161 seats—only 4
fewer than the ruling Kenseikai and nearly double the Seiyūhontō's 87
seats. Some Seiyūkai members favored a visibly progressive stance on
labor legislation, lest the reformist Kenseikai reap all the benefits of
expanded suffrage.[31] Yet Seiyūkai president Tanaka Giichi and other top
leaders resolved that no labor union law could possibly conform to "our

nation's circumstances" at the present time.[32] And it was highly unlikely that those circumstances would change, at least in the eyes of the ambitious Seiyūkai leader, Mori Kaku, a former executive of Mitsui and Company. A member of the Lower House committee on labor legislation, Mori attacked the very essence of the labor union bill—the provision protecting union members from yellow-dog contracts and arbitrary dismissal. Like other businessmen and Seiyūkai spokesmen, Mori adroitly combined Japan's exceptionalism with its similarities to capitalist America. Why not, he suggested, adopt U.S. Steel's successful policy of barring all trade unionists as a better model for Japan?[33]

The Seiyūkai's opposition to the union bill and labor disputes conciliation bill placed the deciding vote in the hands of the unpredictable Seiyūhontō. Party president Tokonami Takejirō personally favored enactment of the government's labor union bill. Although, as home minister in 1920, he had discouraged such legislation, the politically astute Tokonami now presented himself as the sponsor of Nambara Shigeru's "Home Ministry draft."[34] Other party elders remained irreconcilable. Of the three major political parties, the Seiyūhontō most consistently spoke for the interests of industry during the parliamentary deliberations. Charging that the conciliation bill would actually encourage industrial disputes, one committee member with a business background called instead for a legal ban on all strikes.[35] To the entrepreneur Kuribayashi Gosaku, the Social Bureau spoke, not for the government, but for the labor unions—especially Sōdōmei, which he insisted was a dangerous Marxist organization.[36] Worried cabinet officials and Kenseikai floor managers redoubled their efforts to win the Seiyūhontō's support for the government's labor union bill, but to no avail. The 1926 session ended with the union bill deadlocked in the Lower House committee.[37] When the Wakatsuki cabinet resubmitted the measure to the Lower House in March 1927, the Seiyūhontō was still "currying favor with the capitalists," according to the *Tōkyō asahi shimbun*.[38] Once again, the labor union bill died unceremoniously in committee.

The defeat of its labor union legislation notwithstanding, the Wakatsuki cabinet achieved several successes in the campaign to reform industrial relations and social policy. Thanks to the Kenseikai's negotiations with the Seiyūhontō during the 1926 Diet, the Lower House passed the path-breaking labor disputes conciliation bill over the opposition of the Seiyūkai. By a unanimous vote, the Lower House also repealed Article 17 (and supplementary Article 30) of the 1900 Police Regulations.[39] Contrary to the fears of many, both bills cleared the

House of Peers without revision. In addition, Kenseikai ministers and Home Ministry officials stepped up efforts to protect labor unions by administrative means. In April 1926, Home Minister Wakatsuki instructed prefectural governors to carry out the spirit of the recently defeated labor union bill: "the government's policy toward labor unions has not changed in the least and earnestly aims at their sound development. I urge you to understand this and give careful consideration to this policy when dealing with the labor movement."[40] Pursuing this policy, the government ordered all factories employing fifty workers or more to submit a list of shop regulations to the prefectural governors. In December, the Social Bureau partially reinstated the union bill's key protective clause by directing governors to void shop regulations equivalent to yellow-dog contracts.[41]

The Wakatsuki cabinet and the Home Ministry also cooperated on a series of labor-related welfare measures. In 1926, the cabinet activated the long-delayed 1922 Health Insurance Law and concurrently created a Health Insurance Division within the Social Bureau. Moreover, the Kenseikai government overcame opposition in the conservative Privy Council to enforcing the 1923 revision of the Factory Law.[42] The Kenseikai cabinets, it is true, often imposed budgetary and political constraints on the Social Bureau's ambitious proposals for unemployment programs, poor relief, and slum clearance. Nonetheless, the Kenseikai had established social policy as a central concern for party governments.

REINTERPRETING THE PEACE PRESERVATION LAW

No discussion of the Kenseikai's reformism would be complete without mention of the infamous Peace Preservation Law of 1925. Article 1 abounded in dangerous ambiguities for any social protest movement:

> Anyone who has organized an association with the objective of radically altering the national polity (*kokutai o henkaku shi*) or denying the system of private property, or anyone who has joined such an association with full knowledge of its object, shall be liable to imprisonment with or without hard labor for a term not exceeding ten years.
> Any attempt to commit the crimes in the preceding clause will [also] be punished.[43]

Indeed, from 1926 to 1945, the authorities invoked the Peace Preservation Law to arrest tens of thousands, ranging from Communist Party members to liberal intellectuals and followers of religious groups. Ironically, Katō's coalition cabinet sponsored the Peace Preservation Law at the same time as universal manhood suffrage. To most Japanese scholars, the simultaneous passage of repressive and reform legislation was no coincidence. In their view, the established parties and the bureaucracy extended the vote while arming the state with new powers to check any truly democratic challenge that might result.[44] American specialists, on the other hand, tend to play down the relationship between the Kenseikai's liberal measures and the Peace Preservation Law. They commonly note that the law was a long-standing piece of legislation prepared by the conservative Justice Ministry.[45]

However, neither set of historians seriously relates the Peace Preservation Law to the overall social policies of the party governments. The few scholars who have done so demonstrate that the key issue dividing the rival parties and bureaucratic cliques in 1925 was not *whether* to control "radical" labor and socialist organizations. Virtually all elites agreed on that. Rather, the controversy concerned *how* the state balanced repression versus reform, and *where* one drew the line between "radical" and "sound" groups.[46] In a debate that would profoundly influence labor policy over the next half decade, the Justice Ministry and its Seiyūkai allies squared off against the Home Ministry and the Kenseikai.

As one historian has noted, officials of the Justice Ministry and the Home Ministry adopted significantly different strategies toward the advance of democratic and socialist movements after World War I. Justice bureaucrats tended to rely on force to preserve the emperor-centered polity, whereas their colleagues in the Home Ministry strove to recognize and accommodate most popular organizations.[47] In 1922, for example, Justice Ministry leaders persuaded the Seiyūkai's Takahashi cabinet to sponsor the highly repressive bill to control radical social movements (*kageki shakai undō torishimari hōan*). Although some of the Home Ministry's "new men" participated in preparing the measure, they tried but failed to restrict the bill to unlawful *actions* by anarchist and Communist organizations. Justice Ministry officials defined "radicalism" in much broader and more moralistic terms. The final draft would punish anyone who simply "propagandizes, or attempts to propagandize, to subvert the laws of the state." Even more nebulous was the crime of propagandizing "to destroy the foundations of the social structure by means of a riot, violence, intimidation, or in other illegal ways."[48] The legislation's open-ended nature was repellent to Kenseikai and Kokumintō representatives, who feared such phrases could also be used against academics, advocates of universal suffrage, and the opposition parties themselves. The Seiyūkai cabinet was forced to shelve the bill.[49]

Furthermore, Justice Ministry leaders indiscriminately included all forms of workers' organization and popular discontent in their category of subversive activities. The Home Ministry was primarily responsible for the local police, yet the Justice Ministry's procurators could also direct police to make arrests. At the time of the rice riots in 1918, Home Minister Mizuno Rentarō emphasized a "social policy" solution in his instructions to governors: "Although some agitators have taken part in these disturbances, most [incidents] result entirely from problems of living conditions, and we should truly be sympathetic." He was promptly challenged by the administrative vice-minister of justice, Suzuki Kisaburō, who argued for the ample use of force over social policy: "I don't see anything worthy of sympathy."[50] Beginning in 1919, Justice officials similarly sabotaged the Home Ministry's attempts to restrict the application of Article 17's "instigation or incitement" clause to outside strike organizers. During the big strikes of 1921, Vice-Minister Suzuki ordered police to "arrest without fail . . . *anyone* instigating or inciting others by means of radical speech."[51] Finally, as members of the Investigative Commission on Administration in 1925, Justice Ministry representatives vigorously opposed the Social Bureau's proposed labor union bill and the repeal of Article 17. They not only sought the total elimination of labor's protections against union-busting employers, but also proposed a provision to empower state officials to dissolve any union that the authorities feared *might* "infringe on the public interest."[52]

By the mid-1920s, the Justice Ministry functioned as the general staff for the respectable Right. Unlike the Ministry of Commerce and Industry, there was nothing inherently antilabor about the Justice Ministry, which staffed the nation's procurators' offices and judgeships. Rather, the ministry's ideological cast resulted largely from its long-time domination by two of the era's most prominent conservatives, Hiranuma Kiichirō and Suzuki Kisaburō.[53] Together, the two officials virtually monopolized the top posts of procurator-general and vice-minister between 1911 and 1924, and they successively served as justice minister in 1923 and 1924. Beginning with Hiranuma's prosecution of anarchists in the Great Treason Trial of 1910, he and Suzuki endeavored to safeguard Japan's "national polity" (*kokutai*) by eradicating Western influences, from anarchism and Communism to trade unionism and social democracy.

In December 1923, an assassination attempt on the crown prince, coming on the heels of massive arrests of Communists and anarchists, further aroused the two officials' fears of social revolution. In response, Hiranuma and Suzuki organized the National Foundation Society (Kokuhonsha), a group composed mainly of Justice Ministry officials, military men, and Seiyūkai politicians. Their mission was to block the "winds of self-indulgence" and "radical doctrines."[54] Suzuki also served as advisor and then chairman emeritus of the Greater Japan National Essence Society (Dai Nihon Kokusuikai), whose patriotic toughs specialized in breaking strikes.[55] The growing political influence of Hiranuma and Suzuki was closely linked to their friendly ties to the Seiyūkai and the Hara cabinet. Suzuki went on to become president of the Seiyūkai.

The Justice Ministry clique united a broad array of conservative forces that rejected labor unions as a product of "dangerous thought" from the West. Upon appointment to the Privy Council in 1924, Hiranuma allied himself with the surviving Meiji oligarchs, Itō Miyoji and Kaneko Kentarō. The three adroitly combined nativism and capitalism the following year when the Privy Council delayed the enforcement of the 1923 revision of the Factory Law on the grounds that it favored workers over owners. The councilors also denounced the Social Bureau's draft labor union bill, claiming that the encouragement of unions invited "dangerous political revolution" and would "saddle the nation with misfortune for the next hundred years."[56]

One of their staunchest allies was the Seiyūkai politician, Ogawa Heikichi, who as justice minister cosponsored the Peace Preservation Law in 1925. By his own admission, Justice Minister Ogawa bore a great deal of responsibility for blocking the introduction of a labor union bill and other labor legislation during the period of the coalition cabinet.[57] Ogawa was a leading figure in the right-wing societies that had sprung up to resist labor and socialist movements after World War I. His newspaper, the Nihon shimbun, crudely portrayed all strikes as "auxiliary movements of Red ideology." Like Suzuki Kisaburō, he believed social unrest to be the product of a contagious "disease in thought," and he pointedly rejected the claims of social bureaucrats and Kenseikai politicians that poverty constituted the principal source of radicalism.[58] As Ogawa, Suzuki Kisaburō, and other outspoken conservatives rose to leadership within the Seiyūkai after 1925, they furthered the party's reliance on antisubversive measures as a solution to social problems.

The Peace Preservation Law, in short, arose from two sharply differing approaches. Kenseikai leaders and Home Ministry officials unequivocally supported a tough anti-Communist law in 1925, but they differentiated more carefully between most popular organizations and truly subversive associations. Home Minister Wakatsuki assured the Diet that the Peace Preservation Law would not restrict labor union activities.

> It is completely permissible for workers to engage in the labor movement in order to elevate their position. Furthermore, we in the government today, *especially those of us in the Home Ministry, the responsible agency,* do not, by any means, believe in restraining such activities. However, as I have stated, at issue is a control law which is designed so that anarchism and Communism will not succeed. As long as workers do not call for anarchism or Communism, this bill will not, in the least, inhibit their participation in the labor movement (applause).[59]

Wakatsuki had earlier explained that the bill's phrase "denying the system of private property" simply served as a legal definition of the Communist Party and would not proscribe discussion of the nationalization of certain industries.[60] Always conscious of foreign models, he and Home Ministry spokesmen likened the peace preservation bill to measures taken by Western democratic states to prevent infiltration by the Communist International. They expected such attempts to increase upon the imminent resumption of Japanese relations with the Soviet Union.[61]

While the Justice Ministry attempted to restore the sweeping language of the 1922 bill to control radical social movements, the Kenseikai and the Home Ministry worked to limit the scope of the peace preservation bill during early 1925. Joined by officials of the Kenseikai-linked Bureau of Legislation, Home Ministry representatives attempted to clarify the Justice Ministry's murky phrase, "to destroy the foundations of the social structure." The law, they insisted, should control only those groups that specifically and *by illegal means* sought to alter the parliamentary system, the judicial and administrative structures, the system of taxation, military service, and the system of private property. These officials redefined the legislation's central crime from "to subvert the laws of the state" to the clause, "radically altering the national polity."[62] Home Minister Wakatsuki equated the term "national polity" with the emperor's formal (but not de facto) sovereignty according to the Meiji Constitution. Because almost all labor unions and socialist organizations accepted the institution of constitutional monarchy, Home Ministry officials employed this phrase to isolate anarchist groups and the Communist Party, which explicitly advocated the overthrow of the emperor. Although "national polity" may seem dangerously ambiguous, Professor Okudaira Yasuhiro reminds us that most officials and politicians at the time found the term precise and uncontroversial. Not until the 1930s would the Japanese government expand the meaning of "national polity" to silence liberal and social democratic critics.[63]

Needless to say, the Home Ministry and the Kenseikai did not entirely succeed in narrowing the scope of the Peace Preservation Law. In his new capacity as justice minister, the Seiyūkai's Ogawa Heikichi pressed Wakatsuki to sponsor a more encompassing bill. From within the Privy Council, former Justice Minister Hiranuma warned Wakatsuki that the councilors would veto the cabinet's suffrage reform and possibly would not ratify the recent treaty establishing diplomatic relations with the Soviet Union unless the government enacted a Peace Preservation Law, presumably in the form of the harsh Justice Ministry draft.[64] The Kenseikai leader yielded, and the government's final version significantly broadened the definition of subversion. The coalition cabinet eliminated the Home Ministry's list of specific crimes, as well as a safeguard permitting organizations to seek changes in the system of private property by legal means. The Justice Ministry also successfully inserted Article 3, which made it a crime to "incite" others with the object of radically altering the national polity or denying the system of private property.

Led by Vice-Minister Yuasa Kurahei, officials in the Home Ministry and Bureau of Legislation denounced Article 3 for permitting the unwarranted suppression of those who were not active members of the Communist party, that is, those who simply "incited" without organizing or joining an association. In a dramatic display of disaffection, several higher civil servants from the two agencies urged the government to withdraw the entire bill.[65] Within the cabinet itself, Chief Secretary Egi Tasuku of the Kenseikai and Tsukamoto Seiji, director of the Bureau of Legislation, protested the inclusion of Article 3 in similar tones. It is noteworthy that Egi, Tsukamoto, and Yuasa had long advocated legally protected trade unionism as a more effective antidote to social unrest than blind repression.

According to the irascible Ogawa Heikichi, he and the rest of the

cabinet eventually overcame these objections and gave "the noisy opposition of the Lower House and the newspapers a swift kick."[66] Kenseikai leaders quelled a vocal rebellion by members of their progressive
wing in the process, although the Lower House did remove the ambiguous phrase of radically altering "the form of government" (seitai) from
the stipulated crimes. The house then approved the peace preservation
bill by the overwhelming vote of 246 to 18 on 7 March 1925.[67] Although the law easily passed, Japan's political and bureaucratic elites by
no means agreed on its interpretation. Following the formation of the
Seiyūkai's Tanaka cabinet in 1927, the Peace Preservation Law became
the focus of more bitter debate between the two parties and their bureaucratic allies.

MINSEITŌ AND SEIYŪKAI:
DIVERGENT RESPONSES TO UNIVERSAL
MANHOOD SUFFRAGE

The passage of the Universal Manhood Suffrage Law in 1925 offered
new hope to the proponents of social reform. The electorate quadrupled
from 3,288,000 (1924) to 12,409,000 at the time of the general election
of 1928. Few Japanese, of course, expected the emergence of a viable
labor or socialist party in the near future. Citing the nineteenth-century
British experience, most commentators instead believed that political
realignment would begin with the reorganization of the established parties into a conservative and a liberal party. There were few doubts about
which party merited the "conservative" label. In terms of both foreign
and social policy, the Seiyūkai had moved considerably to the right since
the days of the Hara cabinet. In a symbolic departure from the general
civilianization of Japanese politics since World War I, the Seiyūkai selected a former general, Tanaka Giichi, to serve as president in 1925. As
prime minister between 1927 and 1929, Tanaka dedicated himself to
stamping out Communism at home and in China. He decisively reversed
the noninterventionist China policy developed by Shidehara Kijūrō, the
foreign minister under the Kenseikai cabinets. On three occasions in
1927 and 1928, Tanaka dispatched several thousand Japanese troops to
stop Chiang Kai-shek's drive for the unification of China.[68]

While the Seiyūkai became more "reactionary" in the eyes of its
many critics, the Kenseikai and its successor, the Minseitō, took on the
trappings of a liberal party intent on attracting the new votes of workers, tenant farmers, and middle-class urbanites. Formed in June 1927

from a union of the Kenseikai and the Seiyūhontō, the Minseitō was the first major Japanese party to title itself the "democratic party." The party's opening platform pledged the "firm establishment of parliament-centered politics under the sovereign power of the Emperor, in which the general will of the people is reflected in the Imperial Diet." Socially, the Minseitō advocated state regulation to "root out the sources of social unrest by increasing production and ensuring equitable distribution."[69]

The new party won uncharacteristically high marks from progressive critics. The *Tōkyō asahi shimbun* expressed concern over the conservative influence of Tokonami's old Seiyūhontō clique, but nevertheless welcomed the absorption of the Seiyūhontō for bringing about the "much desired two-party system."[70] To many commentators, the selection of Hamaguchi Osachi as Minseitō president confirmed the dominance of the Kenseikai's liberal tendencies over those of the Seiyūhontō. Of the Kenseikai's former bureaucrats, Hamaguchi had been the most enthusiastic advocate of expanding the party's popular base. In his inaugural address, the new president called on the Minseitō to "rally the rising forces" and "respond to the demands of the times."[71] The formation of the Minseitō impressed even the socialist politician Asō Hisashi and the former Communist Party member Aono Suekichi. Both contrasted the Minseitō's popular "liberal" programs with the Seiyūkai's "conservative" positions.[72]

Indeed, the advent of universal manhood suffrage significantly deepened past cleavages over social policy as the Minseitō and Seiyūkai set out to attract different constituencies. Contemporary observers often ascribed the contrasts between the "liberal" Minseitō and the "conservative" Seiyūkai to the Minseitō's popularity in the cities, relative to the Seiyūkai's strength among landlords and small landowners.[73] Between 1920 and 1930, the Kenseikai/Minseitō steadily expanded its urban electoral base, particularly in the six largest cities (see table 6). In the 1928 general election, the first parliamentary contest held under manhood suffrage, the Minseitō won a majority of the seats in the six metropolitan centers. Nationally, the Minseitō triumphed in two-thirds (69) of Japan's 102 cities.[74] In prefectural and city-assembly races, as well, the Minseitō overwhelmed the Seiyūkai in Tokyo, Osaka, Kobe, and Hiroshima during 1928 and 1929.[75] The press variously attributed the Minseitō's strong showing in the cities to the Kenseikai's historic urban appeal, the party's social policies, the absorption of the Seiyūhontō, or to urban voters' disgust with the corruption and intervention-

TABLE VI   ELECTORAL PERFORMANCE IN THE SIX
LARGEST CITIES, GENERAL ELECTIONS, 1920–30
(seats won)

Election year	Total metropolitan seats[a]	Kenseikai		Seiyūkai		Seiyūhontō	
		Seats	%	Seats	%	Seats	%
1920	40	14 (110)[b]	35% (24%)[c]	10 (278)	25% (60%)		
1924	40	14 (152)	35 (33)	5 (102)	13 (22)	5 (111)	13% (24%)
		Minseitō				Proletarian parties	
1928	50	26 (216)	52 (46)	15 (217)	30 (47)	5 (8)	10 (2)
1930	50	31 (273)	62 (59)	13 (147)	26 (37)	1 (5)	2 (1)

SOURCES: Masumi Junnosuke, *Nihon seitō shi ron,* 5:296–97; Tōyama and Adachi, pp. 198–212.
[a]Tokyo, Osaka, Kyoto, Nagoya, Yokohama, and Kobe (excluding environs).
[b]Seats won, nationwide.
[c]Percentage of seats won, nationwide.

ist election tactics of the Tanaka government. Whatever the reasons, the electoral results of 1928 strengthened the respective urban and rural orientations of the Minseitō and the Seiyūkai.

Like Hara Takashi before him, Prime Minister Tanaka and the Seiyūkai appealed to rural voters with social policies that offered sizable subsidies to the countryside. The cabinet proposed to transfer revenues from the national land tax to local governments on the grounds that these funds would relieve hard-pressed rural communities and overtaxed farmers. In addition, Tanaka pledged to transform tenants into small landowners by financially assisting them to buy land. With three-fourths of its parliamentary delegation representing rural districts, the opposition Minseitō also recognized the problems of local government and tenancy. Yet its social policies differed from those of the Seiyūkai in two important respects. First, the Minseitō reaffirmed the importance of the cities and labor. During the general election of 1928, Minseitō candidates emphasized their campaign pledge to "institute social welfare measures, improve the living standards of workers, and rationalize labor-management relations."[76] The Minseitō further proposed to relieve local governments by having the central government directly pay the full salaries of elementary-school teachers. This measure would have benefited the cities, which theretofore had received a much lower national subsidy than rural towns and villages.[77] Second, drawing parallels to labor relations, Minseitō leaders championed the enactment of a tenancy law that would grant legal rights to tenant farmers vis-à-vis landlords.[78]

In addition to the urban-rural cleavage, manhood suffrage accelerated prior divergences between the two major parties in the respective influence of big business. The Seiyūkai's veteran industrialists occupied an unusually strong position in the Tanaka cabinet and among the party's top executives.[79] Seeking new sources to finance the soaring costs involved in appealing to the expanded electorate, the Seiyūkai redoubled its efforts to recruit wealthy candidates from the business community. In the election of 1928, according to one survey, the Seiyūkai accounted for all twenty of the new candidates from big business.[80] Kuhara Fusanosuke personified the growing political influence of heavy industry. The powerful industrialist had founded Kuhara Mining, the parent company of the better-known Nissan combine and the Hitachi Engineering Works. Kuhara literally bought his way into the Seiyūkai. Thanks to lavish contributions to his friend Tanaka Giichi, Kuhara was appointed communications minister in the Tanaka cabinet—a remarkable feat for a first-term Diet member.[81]

The Tanaka cabinet also refined a practice, begun under the Kenseikai cabinets, of nominating friendly businessmen to the House of Peers as imperial appointees. These included some of the Japan Industrial Club's most outspoken foes of labor unions.[82] Kuhara had himself broken a vigorous effort by the Yūaikai to organize workers in his Hitachi Mines in 1919.[83] Several of the Seiyūkai's other new industrialist candidates later led the fight against the Minseitō cabinet's labor union bill in 1931.[84]

Conversely, universal suffrage made the Minseitō more attentive to the needs of the working class than ever before. Although the Seiyūhontō entered the new party with a sizable contingent of industrial tycoons, the influence of big business over labor policy was offset by other elements in the leadership. The Minseitō, like the Kenseikai, possessed a vigorous progressive wing, which consistently pressed party elders to sponsor women's suffrage, labor legislation, a tenancy law, and other reform measures. Attracted by the Kenseikai/Minseitō's commitment to democratization, a number of liberal publicists joined the party and won Diet seats in the elections of 1924, 1928, and 1930. The press commonly called them the Minseitō's "young politicians" (shōsō-ha), for most were in their late thirties and early forties. Reinforcing the new crop were the Kenseikai's original "Radicals," several of whom had since assumed leadership positions in the Minseitō.

Parliamentary vice-ministers in the Hamaguchi cabinet included the two most prominent young politicians—the fiery orator, Professor Nagai Ryūtarō of Waseda University, and his former Waseda classmate, the journalist Nakano Seigō. As in 1920, the Radicals and young politicians influenced the Minseitō's priorities disproportionately to their numbers. This was largely a factor of their professions as metropolitan journalists, lawyers, and professors. Even those who represented outlying constituencies, such as Nagai from the city of Kanazawa, spent most of their time in Tokyo, where they had been educated or currently worked.[85] Accordingly, they were able to serve on the Minseitō's policy-making committees on a full-time basis—an opportunity not enjoyed by the party's truly provincial representatives and active businessmen.[86]

Nagai Ryūtarō and Nakano Seigō were chiefly responsible for the democratic and socially reformist thrust of the Minseitō's inaugural platform.[87] At times, they and fellow young politicians appeared indistinguishable from Professors Yoshino Sakuzō, Abe Isoo, and other intellectuals associated with the moderate Social Democratic Party. Nagai and Nakano were simply two of the Minseitō's several Waseda University graduates who had developed social democratic consciousness under the tutelage of Professor Abe. The Social Democratic Party and the affiliated labor federation Sōdōmei, in turn, worked closely with the young politicians to strengthen the Minseitō's commitment to progressive labor legislation.[88] Nevertheless, the young politicians identified strongly with the Minseitō's dedication to rationalizing, rather than eliminating, capitalism. Nakano presented his case for labor, tenancy, and social welfare legislation in terms of a new "philosophy of state regulation" that stood between the "twin evils of capitalism and socialism." Recognizing the workers' right to form unions against existing federations of employers, Nakano insisted that the state regulate both sides, particularly the "high-handedness of the capitalists."[89]

Prompted by the young politicians, the Minseitō developed new social legislation in a spirited drive to win the votes of the working class in the 1928 election. Minseitō spokesmen offered their party as the workers' best hope because the Minseitō was in a much better political position than the socialist parties to improve the lot of the proletarian classes.[90] The logic was irrefutable. The internecine struggles of 1925–26, it will be recalled, resulted in a slew of similar-sounding, yet stubbornly independent, proletarian parties. From left to right, there was the Labor-Farmer Party, the Japan Labor-Farmer Party, and the Social Democratic Party—as well as a Japan Farmers' Party (Nihon Nōmintō) and several local parties. In the general election of 1928, they divided up 5 percent of the popular vote to win a mere eight seats (or 1.7 percent of the Lower House).

Aided by the disarray of the socialist parties, the Minseitō made significant inroads among the working class. The vast majority of unorganized workers represented one source of votes. Moderate labor organizations and company unions were another. In 1928, for example, leaders of the naval labor unions in the Kure and Sasebo arsenals split into Social Democratic and Minseitō factions.[91] Moreover, in provincial cities, where the proletarian parties were weak, workers often belonged to pro-Minseitō "citizens' associations" and "young men's parties," together with white-collar employees and professionals.[92]

Members of the more politicized unions also succumbed to the Minseitō's appeal. Although the Social Democratic Party possessed the strongest labor union base with an affiliated union membership of some 190,000, the party in 1928 received only 120,000 votes, many of which came from metropolitan intelligentsia and salaried employees. On the eve of the 1930 general election, the Social Democrats and the Sōdōmei warned members: "Don't vote for the established parties." But as Sōdōmei leaders sadly admitted upon examining the results, the Minseitō had taken much of the floating vote among the proletarian classes by successfully presenting itself as the most viable progressive party.[93]

The Minseitō's growing interest in social issues reflected one final aspect of expanded suffrage. The parliamentary election of 1928 was unique in the history of interwar party rule. For the first and only time, the governing party failed to gain a majority in the Lower House, despite blatant interference by the Tanaka cabinet. The Seiyūkai emerged with a mere one-seat advantage over the popular Minseitō, as table 7 indicates. Although the Seiyūkai won the cooperation of a minor party, the Businessmen's Association (Jitsugyō Dōshikai), and four independents, Tanaka entered the Fifty-fifth Diet that April still short of a majority of 234. The parliamentary stalemate vastly elevated the political influence of the small progressive bloc composed of the proletarian parties, Ozaki Yukio's Meiseikai (Association for Enlightened Government), and the Kakushintō (the liberal rump of the Kakushin Club). The

TABLE VII   PARTY STRENGTHS IN THE
LOWER HOUSE, 1928
(seats)

Party	Election results (February 20)	55th Diet (April 20)
Seiyūkai	217	221
Minseitō	216	216
Proletarian parties	8	8
Businessmen's Association	4	3
Kakushintō	3	3
Meiseikai	—	7
Independents	18	7
Total	466	465

SOURCE: Shūgiin-Sangiin, *Gikai seido shichijūnen shi: Teikoku gikai shi,* 2:220.

Minseitō aggressively lured these elements to the opposition with promises to act upon some of their major demands. Cooperation between the
Minseitō and the socialist parties was not entirely new. The first
prefectural-level elections held under manhood suffrage occurred in September 1927. Tight contests between the two large parties produced a
number of prefectural assemblies in which the Minseitō and proletarian
parties allied to achieve a majority.[94]

Representatives of the left-wing Labor-Farmer Party summarily dismissed the Minseitō's promises of social legislation as a capitalist-
landlord trick, but the Lower House's four Social Democrats discerned
the advantages of working with the Minseitō. Shortly before the opening of the 1928 Diet, the Social Democrats urged fellow socialists to
cooperate with the Minseitō on a no-confidence motion against the
Tanaka cabinet. They also proposed a joint conference with the Minseitō and other opposition parties to discuss the revision or repeal of
several repressive laws and the enactment of legislation covering labor
unions, tenancy, and social insurance.[95]

Party chairman Abe Isoo had earlier organized the Japanese Fabian
Society to promote a legal, gradualist form of socialism on the English
model.[96] He and other Social Democrats recognized the practical problems of socialist parties in a nation where unions accounted for a mere
300,000 workers and 365,000 farmers. Abe shrugged off the Social

Democrats' failure to obtain more than four seats in 1928. In Britain, he noted, only two labor representatives won seats in the first election held after workers gained the vote in 1867.[97] Convinced that the proletarian parties must initially ally with the relatively liberal bourgeois party, Abe lavishly praised the reform policies of the newly formed Minseitō in 1927. He further pledged his party's support in organizing the next Diet.[98]

As in late-nineteenth-century Britain, an alliance of mutual benefit seems to have developed between the more liberal party and the mainstream of the labor movement. Trade unionist leaders such as Nishio Suehiro of Sōdōmei favored collaboration with the Minseitō to advance the interests of workers, just as similar objectives had earlier dictated close ties with the social bureaucrats. At the opening of the Diet in 1928, the Minseitō lost a critical vote for speaker of the Lower House by only two votes (230 to 228). Nishio and the three other Social Democrats had supported the Minseitō candidate, yet the four other socialist deputies deliberately abstained. The "realistic" labor leader took the opportunity to chide his comrades for their errant dogmatism: "If you can't get the best, take the second best."[99] Unlike the "Lib-labs" in the early stages of the British trade union movement, Sōdōmei leaders chose to remain formally independent of the Minseitō. Nor did the Minseitō's young politicians ever take the additional step of joining the proletarian parties, in contrast to the many British Liberals who switched to the Labour Party after World War I.[100] Yet it was undeniable that new support from labor and the cities was propelling the Minseitō in a noticeably reformist direction.

THE BUREAUCRATS ENTER POLITICS

Policy cleavages between the Minseitō and the Seiyūkai became even sharper as bureaucrats from the Home and Justice Ministries joined the rival parties. By 1929, several progressive labor specialists from the Home Ministry and Kyōchōkai had joined the Minseitō. Many others openly identified with the party from within the bureaucracy. Home Ministry officials flocked to the Minseitō for various reasons. Most had been administrative vice-ministers, bureau chiefs, and prefectural governors, whose high-ranking positions limited the avenues for further promotion within the Home Ministry. Some entered the Minseitō in the hope of becoming ministers of state or colonial administrators. The

Tanaka cabinet's massive suspension of Home Ministry officials in-
duced others to seek assurances of reappointment in future Minseitō
governments.

Whatever the motives, the politicization of Home Ministry bureaucrats sparked the formation of another potent lobby for social reform
within the Minseitō. The major parties prized the former civil servants for
their bureaucratic expertise and ongoing ties to the administrative policy-
making process. Such attributes had previously catapulted Katō Takaaki,
Wakatsuki Reijirō, Hamaguchi Osachi, and Egi Tasuku to the leadership
of the Kenseikai, and Takahashi Korekiyo and Tokonami Takejirō to the
presidencies of the Seiyūkai and Seiyūhontō. To Kamei Kan'ichirō, a
Social Democratic deputy and himself a former Foreign Ministry official,
bureaucratic alliances were pivotal in distinguishing the "progressive"
Minseitō from the "reactionary" Seiyūkai. The Seiyūkai allied itself with
"conservative bureaucratic forces," "provincial bourgeoisie," and "reactionary capitalist forces." Conversely, the Minseitō united "progressive
bureaucrats," "liberal political activists" (the young politicians), and
"modern commercial and industrial capital" on behalf of "bourgeois
democracy" and "fairly bold" social policies.[101]

The Minseitō's association with the social policy initiatives of the
Home Ministry and the Kyōchōkai evolved from the political realign-
ments of the mid-1920s. Kenseikai leaders had previously developed
their labor proposals independently of the bureaucracy. The party's
friendly relations with the Home Ministry had lapsed during its eight
years out of power (1916–24). The Home Ministry's pro-Kenseikai
contingent was confined to a small group of retired senior officials led
by Izawa Takio, who served as chief of the Metropolitan Police under
the Ōkuma cabinet (1914–16). Although he refused to affiliate formally
with the Kenseikai/Minseitō, Izawa emerged as the party's *éminence
grise* or, in Japanese, the *kuromaku* ("the man in black").[102] While the
Kenseikai remained in opposition, a Seiyūkai clique headed by Tokonami Takejirō and Mizuno Rentarō dominated the senior posts of the
Home Ministry after 1916.

The Kenseikai's accession to power in 1924 marked the beginning of
a new relationship with the Home Ministry's progressive bureaucrats.
At the senior level, Tsukamoto Seiji, the chief cabinet secretary and a
past Social Bureau director, entered the Kenseikai upon retirement. So
did the Home Ministry's current Police Bureau chief and the vice-
minister. Izawa also won the allegiance of Gotō Fumio and Maruyama
Tsurukichi, two of the ministry's most prominent "new men." Gotō

served as director-general in Taiwan under Inspector-General Izawa. Maruyama became a trusted deputy when Izawa next became mayor of Tokyo.[103]

The Seiyūhontō is usually dismissed as the era's most backward-looking party, yet the Kenseikai's merger with Tokonami's party was another shot in the arm for the Minseitō's social programs. Tokonami at the time commanded the loyalty of many social bureaucrats in the Home Ministry and the Kyōchōkai.[104] By entering the Minseitō, Tokonami transferred much of this progressive bureaucratic support to the new party. His most valuable contribution to labor reform was Soeda Keiichirō, the innovative executive director of the Kyōchōkai from 1920 to 1931. Soeda became sole executive director in 1926.

With some justification, the press regarded the Kyōchōkai as Tokonami's political fief.[105] Home Minister Tokonami had originally staffed the foundation with several trusted subordinates, including Soeda's fellow executive director, Tazawa Yoshiharu. Soeda himself had been Tokonami's chief of the Local Affairs Bureau. In 1923, the politically ambitious Soeda successfully contested a by-election for the Diet on the Seiyūkai ticket. The following year, Soeda and Mutō Shichirō, a Kyōchōkai section chief, followed Tokonami into the Seiyūhontō.

In 1927, Soeda and other retired Home Ministry officials once again accompanied Tokonami—this time into the Minseitō, where they remained, unlike their restless patron. Assisted by his staff in the Kyōchōkai, Soeda became the Minseitō's most knowledgeable proponent of a labor union law, a tenancy law, and unemployment relief.[106] He also worked to improve the status of unions and collective bargaining by personally mediating some of the largest disputes of the 1920s. During the long strike at the Noda Soy Sauce Company (1927–28), for example, Sōdōmei requested Soeda's good offices, whereas the Seiyūkai-affiliated owners initially dismissed the Kyōchōkai as an arm of the Minseitō.[107]

Soeda Keiichirō and other former Home Ministry officials formulated the Minseitō's social policies as full-fledged party members. Tazawa Yoshiharu, Maruyama Tsurukichi, and Gotō Fumio represented the Home Ministry's many social bureaucrats, who, though declining to enter the Minseitō, actively supported and influenced the party's programs from posts within the government and semigovernmental organizations. After leaving the Kyōchōkai in 1924, Tazawa joined Maruyama and Gotō in a drive to clean up party politics and disseminate "political education" (seiji kyōiku) in preparation for universal manhood suffrage.

Believing that young men in their teens and twenties would best respond
to these calls, the three served as directors of the Japan Young Men's Hall
(Nihon Seinenkan), a coordinating agency for the nation's young men's
associations. In 1925, the trio founded the Alliance for a New Japan (Shin
Nihon Dōmei), a group of young bureaucrats, journalists, and Diet members, who pledged to reform the parties by offering new programs.[108]

Tazawa, Maruyama, and Gotō assigned labor reform a central role
in their campaign for political education. Like many in the Home
Ministry's Local Affairs and Social Bureaus, they linked popular discontent in Japan to the absence of true "local autonomy" and "organizational autonomy." In their view, Japanese elites had historically denied
the people, including workers, the rights to choose their own leaders,
form their own associations, and, in general, control their own lives.
The advent of labor unions and manhood suffrage thus found the
masses and the working class unprepared to participate in politics and
the economy in a responsible manner. As an executive director of the
Kyōchōkai, Tazawa had earlier attempted to remedy this situation by
improving communications between workers and managers through
"workmen's seminars" (rōmusha kōshūkai). He also energetically promoted a labor union law and protective labor legislation. Most exceptional, Tazawa denounced both the Peace Preservation Law and the
1925 dissolution of the Farmer-Labor Party by his former employer, the
Home Ministry. In his view, these were illiberal and counterproductive
measures, which would simply force the outlawed Communists to join
the more moderate labor party.[109]

Led by men like Tazawa Yoshiharu, the Alliance for a New Japan
campaigned for "new liberalism" after 1925. Tazawa predicted the
development of a "rational" three-party system along British lines. He
valued a moderate labor party as the vehicle for elevating the political
discussion of social questions. But above all, he and other Alliance
members favored the formation of a centrist, British-style liberal party
that would unite small businessmen, farmers, professionals, and white-
collar workers behind programs of "democratic liberalism," "social
reformism," and "international cooperation."[110] In 1928, Tazawa and
Maruyama Tsurukichi attempted to organize independents within the
deadlocked Lower House into a small liberal party. When that failed,
they concluded that the Minseitō, despite its deficiencies, offered the
most realistic liberal alternative to the "shameful conduct" and "misgov-
ernment" of the Seiyūkai. Hamaguchi and Tokonami had nearly persuaded Maruyama to run as a Minseitō candidate in 1928, and Tazawa

had previously described the socially reformist Kenseikai as the potential liberal party.[111] Minseitō leaders, for their part, displayed keen
interest in the social bureaucrats. The succeeding Hamaguchi cabinet
chose Maruyama to head the Metropolitan Police and invited Tazawa
and Gotō Fumio to direct the Social Bureau. The latter two declined,
but Gotō accepted the Minseitō cabinet's appointment to the House of
Peers. The three officials enjoyed tremendous prestige among the Home
Ministry's social policy experts.[112] Their close ties to the Minseitō furthered the party's own drive to broaden its mass base through liberal
social legislation.

Although the Home Ministry's progressive bureaucrats preferred the
Minseitō, most wished to maintain a simple working relationship. The
Tanaka cabinet unwittingly drove many into a more active affiliation
with the Minseitō. The composition of the Tanaka cabinet reflected the
rising influence of the rival Justice Ministry clique. The ministry's reactionary Suzuki Kisaburō, who had since joined the Seiyūkai, held the
key post of home minister. Whereas home ministers ordinarily appointed the Home Ministry's own civil servants to subordinate offices,
Suzuki selected the Justice Ministry's Yamaoka Mannosuke, a no-less-
conservative protégé, to head the Police Bureau. Hara Yoshimichi, a
lawyer and active member of Hiranuma Kiichirō's National Foundation
Society, became justice minister with the strong backing of Hiranuma.
The new railways minister was none other than Ogawa Heikichi, the
former justice minister and leading sponsor of the Peace Preservation
Law.[113]

Home Minister Suzuki and Police Bureau Chief Yamaoka behaved
like foxes in the proverbial chicken coop, defiantly undercutting the
Home Ministry's more accommodative approach to labor problems.
The two Justice Ministry veterans utilized their newly acquired control
over the police to arrest strike organizers and political radicals. Their
responses to proposed legislation from the Social Bureau varied from
apathy to antipathy. Although some Seiyūkai leaders supported Social
Bureau director Nagaoka Ryūichirō, Suzuki viewed him as a long-time
enemy of the Justice Ministry.[114] Social Bureau officials in turn regarded
Suzuki Kisaburō with contempt. According to Kitaoka Juitsu, a section
chief at the time, Suzuki not only vetoed all proposals opposed by
employers' federations but also refused to support the Social Bureau's
less controversial recommendations.[115]

Railways Minister Ogawa Heikichi provided reinforcements in the
campaign against the social bureaucrats. His *Nihon shimbun* savagely

attacked the "pinkish thought" of the Social Bureau's Nagaoka and the Kyōchōkai's Soeda Keiichirō.[116] These public servants allegedly "ingratiated themselves with the rioters" in their open dealings with union leaders. Ogawa, by his own admission, cooperated closely with Police Chief Yamaoka and employers to check the rising tide of "pernicious strikes."[117] In a thinly veiled reference to Ogawa, Nagaoka Ryūichirō later complained that "a certain cabinet minister who loathed the Social Bureau" shamelessly attempted to block the Social Bureau's widely supported Poor Relief Law (Kyūgohō) in 1929.[118]

If any doubts remained of the Justice Ministry clique's disdain for liberalism and social democracy, they were dispelled by Home Minister Suzuki's statement to the press on the eve of the general election of 1928:

> According to our Constitution, the Cabinet is organized principally upon the august invocation of imperial sovereignty. It is inexcusable that our country be compared to others where Cabinets are directly formed by the majority party. From its inception, the Seiyūkai has been obedient to the principle of government centered on the emperor. . . . By contrast, the present platform of the Minseitō cites "a need to carry through politics centered on the parliament." This is a most disquieting concept, which I must say violates the great spirit of our nation's sacred Constitution. The governance of imperial Japan is completely subject to the control of the emperor; it is very clearly politics centered on the emperor.
>
> Concepts like parliament-centered politics are Anglo-American notions flowing from the current of democracy, and are inconsistent with our nation's *kokutai* (national polity).[119]

The Minseitō greeted Suzuki's declaration with incredulity. Seiyūkai members were equally stunned by their leadership's suicidal urges. No member of a party cabinet had ever before asserted that the parliamentary basis of party cabinets was incompatible with the national polity.[120]

The Seiyūkai's Justice Ministry group alienated many of the Home Ministry's less politicized officials, as well. During the prefectural and parliamentary elections of 1927–28, Home Minister Suzuki Kisaburō and Police Chief Yamaoka Mannosuke directed the most strident campaign of governmental interference in the history of party cabinets. Police zealously enforced Japan's strict electoral laws against candidates from the Minseitō and proletarian parties while ignoring similar transgressions by the Seiyūkai. Authorities confiscated Minseitō pamphlets and frequently prevented socialist candidates from speaking. To ensure compliance, Suzuki and Yamaoka replaced the governors and police chiefs of nearly every prefecture with officials loyal to the Seiyūkai. Although preceding Kenseikai cabinets had suspended pro-Seiyūkai and pro-Seiyūhontō governors, Suzuki's purge was unprecedented in its scale and ruthlessness. The Home Minister demoted several talented bureaucrats, besides furloughing or forcing the resignations of twenty-four governors. A typical victim was Yamagata Jirō, an able civil servant who had never identified with either party. By reactivating a number of less competent but fiercely pro-Seiyūkai officials, Suzuki further blocked the advancement of promising junior bureaucrats.[121]

The Minseitō skillfully exploited the Seiyūkai's lack of support within the Home Ministry. Prior to the prefectural elections of 1927, Izawa Takio organized retired Home Ministry officials into "election-surveillance squads" to check the Tanaka government's drive against opposition candidates at the local level. Over thirty former officials manned Izawa's squads during the following year's general election. Among the recently dismissed governors and bureau chiefs were the former "new men"—Yamagata Jirō, Ōtsuka Isei, and Tsugita Daisaburō, a past chief of the Social Bureau's Health Insurance Division. Ōtsuka and a future Social Bureau director, Matsumoto Manabu, joined the Minseitō outright. Suematsu Kaiichirō, another ex-governor, successfully ran for the Diet in 1928 and thereafter championed social programs from within the Minseitō.[122]

By 1928, the bureaucratic and partisan debates over how to deal with Japan's postwar social problems had converged. Personal, jurisdictional, and policy-related differences were polarizing the nation's political forces into two major camps. The Minseitō and Home Ministry formed the core of a progressive alliance that included friendly members in the House of Peers, the Social Democratic Party, and liberal intellectuals. The Seiyūkai and the Justice Ministry dominated a highly conservative coalition consisting of the Privy Council, like-minded peers, right-wing societies, and much of the army high command.[123] The two blocs would soon skirmish over the Tanaka cabinet's repressive approach to social dissatisfaction.

SOCIAL POLICY OR ANTISOCIALISM?: THE PARLIAMENTARY DEBATE, 1928–29

Upon assuming power in June 1927, Prime Minister Tanaka Giichi instructed prefectural governors to work for the "cultivation of a healthy spirit among the people," a spirit untainted by the "depraved and deca-

dent tendencies" of "a minority of society."[124] Commentators expected
the Seiyūkai and the Justice Ministry to take a hard line toward labor
unions and socialist associations, but few anticipated the Tanaka cabinet's crusade to eradicate alleged Communist organizations.

On 15 March 1928, the government invoked the Peace Preservation
Law and other statutes to arrest more than fifteen hundred suspected
Communist Party members and sympathizers throughout the nation.
Whereas thought crimes had previously lain within the jurisdiction of the
Home Ministry's Special Higher Police, Home Minister Suzuki Kisaburō
and Police Bureau Chief Yamaoka Mannosuke delegated the primary
responsibility for the raids to their former colleagues in the Justice Ministry. On 10 April, the government lifted a month-long news ban on details
of the arrests. That same day, Home Minister Suzuki ordered the dissolution of the Hyōgikai, the Labor-Farmer Party, the Japan Farmers' Union,
and the All-Japan Proletarian Youth League (Zen Nihon Musan Seinen
Dōmei). These groups, charged Suzuki, served as fronts for the pro-
scribed Japanese Communist Party in a conspiracy to alter the "national
polity," the "life blood of our people's spirit" for the past three thousand
years.[125] The Education Ministry simultaneously struck at the universi-
ties, forcing the resignations of Kawakami Hajime and other well-known
professors linked to the Communists.[126]

Minseitō leaders did not object to the use of force against the Communist Party. Even the Social Democratic Party and the Sōdōmei con-
doned the arrests, pointing to the Communist Party's illegal plot to
"inhibit the sound development" of the nation's labor unions and the
socialist movement.[127] Later evidence confirmed that several Communist leaders, in consultation with Comintern, had in fact infiltrated
Hyōgikai and the Japan Farmers' Union. Moreover, the clandestine
Communist Party had collaborated with the legal Labor-Farmer Party
to run eleven of its own candidates in the recent election of 20 February
1928.[128] The Minseitō nonetheless censured the government's methods
and motivations. Party spokesman Adachi Kenzō accused the Seiyūkai
cabinet of exaggerating the Communist threat for political reasons.
Indeed, the timing of the government's announcement, just ten days
before the start of the deadlocked Fifty-fifth Diet, suggested that Seiyūkai leaders had manufactured a Red scare to split the ranks of the
opposition parties.[129] Adachi called on Home Minister Suzuki to prove
a direct link between the legal Labor-Farmer Party and the Communist
Third International. Radical language in the party's platform was not in
itself a crime, he insisted.

Minseitō leaders and their Home Ministry allies emphatically blamed the Tanaka cabinet for shattering their more subtle efforts to isolate the Communists from labor unions and popular organizations. Kawasaki Takukichi and Matsumura Giichi had successively headed the Police Bureau under the Kenseikai-led cabinets. Both were content to monitor the activities of a few top leaders of the Communist Party.[130] Although Kenseikai cabinets had rigorously prosecuted Hyōgikai members for strike violations, they at least recognized Hyōgikai locals as legitimate trade unions. Former Home Minister Wakatsuki disbanded the Farmer-Labor Party in 1925, yet Kenseikai ministers took no action against the succeeding Labor-Farmer Party, which contained many Communists. By contrast, the Tanaka cabinet struck at the entire labor and tenant movement by dissolving the 21,000-member Hyōgikai and the 62,000-member Japan Farmers' Union. The government also destroyed the Labor-Farmer Party, which had drawn 190,000 votes in the February election, more than any other proletarian party. In all three cases, Home Minister Suzuki obliterated legal, mass-based organizations on the grounds that they contained a handful of Communist Party members, or simply people who sympathized with the Communist Party.[131]

Egi Tasuku most forcefully articulated the Minseitō's outrage at the Tanaka cabinet's preoccupation with suppression. The author of the Kenseikai's original labor legislation, Egi denounced the "hasty, frenzied suppositions and emotions" underlying the government's actions. The liberal ex-bureaucrat argued that only participatory democracy and respect for minority opinions would prevent the people from turning to radical ideologies. Looking at world developments, Egi bemoaned the tendency of "the Right" to crush "the Left," notably in Fascist Italy. This, he likened to "fighting poison with poison." The Right might win in Europe, but he warned that there was as much to fear from the antidote as from the poison. Fortunately, concluded Egi sarcastically, no one in Japan endorsed a Fascist solution.[132]

Blinded by their hatred of socialism, leaders of the cabinet's Justice Ministry clique followed excess with excess. Justice Minister Hara Yoshimichi next moved to revise the Peace Preservation Law, with the backing of Home Minister Suzuki Kisaburō and Railways Minister Ogawa Heikichi. According to Hara, the law's maximum sentence of ten years at hard labor was insufficient to deter the Communist Party.[133] Incredibly enough, the justice minister proposed the death penalty as the ultimate punishment for those who formed an association aimed at radically altering the national polity (the ten-year prison term for denying the system of private property was maintained). The cabinet's revision bill also broadened the scope of the original Peace Preservation Law by punishing those who did not actually belong to the Communist Party—that is, those who merely "furthered the objects" of an illegal association.[134] In addition, the Seiyūkai government requested the huge sum of two million yen to establish a nation-wide Special Higher Police network for the control of subversive movements. Special Higher Police sections had previously been confined to metropolitan and industrial prefectures.[135] Seiyūkai ministers could not have chosen a worse time to introduce the two antisocialist measures. The Tanaka cabinet not only lacked a parliamentary majority, but the Fifty-fifth Diet (April–May 1928) was a special two-week session—hardly the forum for controversial legislation.

True to its new progressive image, the Minseitō combated the government's repressive legislation in alliance with the proletarian parties and the liberal Kakushintō and Meiseikai. The Minseitō vigorously opposed Tanaka's budgetary request for funds to finance both the expansion of the Special Higher Police and the second military expedition against the Chinese Nationalists. The Seiyūkai finally passed the appropriation, but only after Minseitō and socialist representatives walked out of the budget committee.[136] Minseitō leaders were more successful in stopping the revision of the Peace Preservation Law in a Lower House committee.[137] Yet Ogawa Heikichi and Hara Yoshimichi were not about to admit defeat. At the end of the special session, the two ministers persuaded the cabinet to seek the Privy Council's approval of the revised Peace Preservation Law as an emergency imperial ordinance. The Meiji Constitution empowered the Privy Council to issue ordinances to deal with emergencies arising when the Diet was not in session. Such ordinances were subject to approval by the next Diet. As chairman of the Privy Council's screening committee, the conservative Hiranuma Kiichirō guaranteed smooth passage for the revised Peace Preservation Law. The measure was promulgated as an imperial ordinance during the summer of 1928.[138]

By dispensing with parliamentary approval, the Tanaka cabinet provoked a constitutional confrontation, in addition to the debate over antisubversive controls. Minseitō members were particularly incensed over the Seiyūkai's collaboration with the Privy Council, the undemocratic body that had forced the resignation of the Wakatsuki cabinet in 1927. While some sympathized with the contents of the revision of the Peace Preservation Law, they condemned the emergency ordinance on constitutional grounds.[139]

Furthermore, many Home Ministry officials refused to support their own government's revision, either as legislation or ordinance. They bluntly criticized Home Minister Suzuki and Police Bureau Chief Yamaoka for forcing the police to carry out the Justice Ministry's highly repressive policies against social movements. Officials of the Police Bureau were, at best, lukewarm to the expansion of the Special Higher Police. The prime movers were the outsiders Suzuki and Yamaoka, who wished to give Justice's procurators greater control over the new police force.[140] Suzuki and Yamaoka resigned in May after the Lower House censured both for electoral interference. However, the incoming home minister, Mochizuki Keisuke, proved no less committed to revising the Peace Preservation Law. A Seiyūkai advisor warned Mochizuki that the promulgation of the emergency ordinance would alienate the entire Home Ministry, especially the progressive young bureaucrats. The Home Minister eventually quelled the revolt in a manner that did little to endear the Seiyūkai cabinet to his bureaucratic subordinates.[141]

One of the most powerful critiques of the emergency ordinance came from a group of retired officials in the Privy Council. Although the council overwhelmingly approved the ordinance, five councilors voted in opposition. They pointed to the absurdity of executing those who simply organized an association with illegal objects, when the Criminal Code stipulated a maximum sentence of only ten years for the more serious crime of armed insurrection. The Privy Council's minority also dwelt on the government's failure to demonstrate the constitutional necessity for an emergency ordinance. Egi Kazuyuki, a former education minister and Egi Tasuka's father through adoption, advised the Tanaka cabinet to forego sterner penalties against radical ideologies in favor of preventive educational and social programs.[142] Such arguments legitimized the Minseitō's case against the revision ordinance, emanating as they did from venerable bureaucratic leaders of the Meiji era.[143]

The Fifty-sixth Diet (early 1929) provided the arena for the final clash between the two major parties over the revision of the Peace Preservation Law. The Minseitō waged a vigorous defense of civil liberties and constructive social policy, whereas Seiyūkai representatives attempted to defame the Minseitō for cooperating with the proletarian parties. To Ogawa Heikichi, the only opponents of the revision were the Communist Party and "its comrades, the liberals and socialists."[144] Although Minseitō speakers did not repudiate the original Peace Preservation Law of 1925, they condemned the emergency ordinance for its content, as well as its unconstitutionality. One liberal member captured the basic paranoia underlying the revision: "If a mere twenty or so students who have taken up Communism return to Japan [from the Soviet Union], is that a major incident?" The revision, in his words, was a "murder law" that sanctioned the death of the emperor's "Japanese subjects."[145]

Despite spirited opposition, the Minseitō and its socialist allies were unable to stop the Seiyūkai from ratifying the emergency ordinance in the Lower House by a vote of 249 to 170. The opportunistic Tokonami Takejirō made the difference. After leading some thirty Diet members out of the Minseitō the previous August, Tokonami formed the New Party Club (Shintō Kurabu). The club voted with the Seiyūkai on this and other crucial matters. The more conservative House of Peers approved the ordinance over the vocal dissent of Izawa Takio and other pro-Minseitō veterans of the Home Ministry.[146] On 16 April 1929, as if to prove the existence of an ever-present Communist menace, the government arrested survivors of the previous raids.

If nothing else, the Seiyūkai's reactionary policies created greater solidarity among the Minseitō, the Home Ministry, and the proletarian parties. On 9 March, only four days after the vote on the revision, the cabinet drove its rivals closer together when Tokonami's New Party Club and the Seiyūkai cosponsored an electoral redistricting measure. Eager to rejoin the Seiyūkai, Tokonami sought to restore the small-district system, which had singularly benefited the Seiyūkai during the Hara cabinet. This electoral scheme would replace the larger districts (three to five members), created by Katō Takaaki's coalition in 1925. Dismissed as a "Toko-mander" by the opposition parties, the bill deliberately assigned single-member districts to the Seiyūkai's rural strongholds; two- or three-member districts were placed in the opposition's urban bailiwicks, where the Seiyūkai could expect to win one additional seat in each.[147]

The ensuing parliamentary debate was noteworthy for the Minseitō's vigorous defense of the proletarian parties. Minseitō members naturally feared the consequences of the electoral revision for their own party. Yet they also blasted Tokonami and the Seiyūkai for conspiring to block the inevitable advance of the socialist parties. Such a revision, they argued, would dangerously alienate the proletarian classes from parliamentary politics by preventing the development of a moderate British-style labor party.[148] Led by the young politicians Nakano Seigō and Nagai Ryūtarō, Minseitō members joined with Social Democrats and liberal intellectuals to organize the National League to Protect Universal

Suffrage. The league sponsored a series of public rallies against the small-district bill during March. The Home Ministry's social bureaucrats felt so strongly about the new threat to "sound" social movements that Maruyama Tsurukichi spoke at the league's protest meetings, and Gotō Fumio and others lent their support.[149] Similarly angered by the naked partisanship behind the redistricting bill, the House of Peers allowed the legislation to die in committee after the measure passed the Lower House.[150]

The Tanaka cabinet's lackluster sponsorship of social legislation during the 1929 Diet stood in marked contrast to its enthusiasm for checking the Left. Home Minister Mochizuki Keisuke maintained his party's policy of opposing a labor union law. The Seiyūkai halfheartedly cosponsored a bill to establish vertical "industrial councils" on the order of Tokonami's 1920 works council bill and a similar Kyōchōkai draft of 1921. The legislation failed after employers' organizations objected to its compulsory features.[151] The House of Peers also shelved the cabinet's long-standing proposal to transform tenants into small landowners, citing the plan's unworkability and exorbitant cost.[152] The Poor Relief Law constituted the cabinet's only successful social policy, according to the *Tōkyō asahi shimbun*. Even this legislation, the daily added, resulted from a political deal with the welfare-minded industrialist, Mutō Sanji of the Businessmen's Association—not from any real commitment by the Tanaka government.[153] Moreover, Home Minister Mochizuki was unwilling to provide sufficient political backing for other Social Bureau initiatives, such as a proposed seamen's insurance bill. Three representatives from the Japan Industrial Club managed to stall the draft insurance bill within the Social Bureau's advisory board. The Kenseikai's Home Minister Wakatsuki Reijirō had easily overcome the objections of these same advisors to the bureau's far more controversial labor union bill in 1925. Mochizuki, on the contrary, abandoned the seamen's measure without a fight.[154] Likewise, the cabinet offered little protest when a committee of the House of Peers buried the Social Bureau's workmen's compensation bill (*rōdō saigai fujo hōan*).[155] Social welfare for workers was clearly not one of Tanaka's higher priorities.

The Tanaka cabinet dealt the Japanese labor movement a blow from which it never fully recovered. Led by the Justice Ministry clique, the Seiyūkai created a vast administrative network for the suppression of deviant thought and behavior. Seiyūkai leaders convinced many Japanese that labor unions were Communist fronts and therefore incompatible with the national polity. Governmental harassment explains in large part why total union membership dropped in 1928 for only the second time during the 1920s (see appendix 6). Ominous though they were, the storm clouds contained something of a silver lining. Prime Minister Tanaka Giichi unwittingly demonstrated the limits of repression as a solution to social problems. The Seiyūkai's excessive reliance on force had antagonized even conservative peers and privy councilors. To many Japanese, an equally reckless approach governed Tanaka's pork-barrel politics and the army's repeated incursions into China. During the spring of 1929, widespread censure of the Tanaka cabinet emboldened the Minseitō to draw up detailed labor and social policies in anticipation of taking power.[156]

The Minseitō's opportunity to act was not long in coming. On 2 July 1929, the Seiyūkai cabinet fell after Tanaka disregarded the emperor's order to disclose a report linking Japanese army officers to the previous year's assassination of the Manchurian warlord Zhang Zuolin. The nation's labor unions breathed a collective sigh of relief. The Social Democratic Party declared that the proletarian classes had "broken the tempest and are under clear skies now."[157] Hamaguchi Osachi organized the succeeding Minseitō cabinet. Determined to repair the damage wrought by the Seiyūkai and its reactionary allies, Hamaguchi embarked on the era's boldest drive for liberal reform.

CHAPTER V

The Limits of Liberal Reform, 1929–31

Viewing the state of society today, one is confronted by an
accelerating gap between rich and poor in both city and village, and by mutual antagonism between Labor and Capital.
Rising unemployment and tenant disputes have also inun-
dated all areas of society as the "social question" grows
daily in complexity and intensity. Our nation's urgent task,
as I see it, is to rectify and prevent [these problems]. We
must bring about a spirit of harmony (*kaiwa kyōchō*) in our
lives together, lay the foundations for peace and stability in
actual living conditions in society, and induce all of the people to bear responsibility for the development of the country's fortunes.

> —*Prime Minister Hamaguchi Osachi to his cabinet's*
> *Commission on Social Policy, 9 August 1929.*[1]

Amid a general critique of the interwar parties, the eminent political and
intellectual historian Maruyama Masao once wrote that the Minseitō's
Hamaguchi cabinet and the succeeding Wakatsuki cabinet possessed
"the strongest complexion of *bourgeois* liberalism in the recent history of
Japanese politics."[2] Others have similarly remarked on the coherent liberal worldview put forward by the Hamaguchi government (July 1929–
April 1931).[3] Shidehara Kijūrō, who previously served the Kenseikai
cabinets as foreign minister, returned to his post determined to further policies of close cooperation with the Anglo-American powers. In contrast
to the interventionist Tanaka Giichi, Shidehara and Hamaguchi adopted
a conciliatory position toward China's new Nationalist government.

"Cooperative diplomacy" combined with sound finance to form the

Hamaguchi cabinet's two central policies. The new government quickly returned the Japanese yen to the gold standard, long a symbol of the liberal world order. And in 1930, the cabinet placed the highest priority on securing ratification of the London Naval Treaty, by which Japan, Great Britain, and the United States agreed to contain a dangerous and expensive race for naval supremacy. Domestically, Hamaguchi proposed the most comprehensive program of social and political reform to date. In addition to a progressive labor union bill, the Minseitō government formulated tenancy legislation, tax reform, unemployment measures, and a path-breaking bill to enfranchise women in local elections.

Prime Minister Hamaguchi himself was like no other political leader in interwar Japan. In an age when Japanese politicians were routinely criticized for venality and lack of principle, progressive journalists praised Hamaguchi for combining the idealism and practical political skills necessary for reform. He was known as the "lion," in part for his white hair and bushy mustache, but more significantly because of his singular courage and tough-minded liberalism. The Social Democratic Party commentator Baba Tsunego called Hamaguchi one of Japan's few "constitutional" politicians, for the prime minister was not afraid to mobilize public opinion against the undemocratic opponents of parliamentary government and civilian control.[4] The most dramatic case involved his confrontation with the conservative Privy Council. When the Privy Council, backed by the Naval General Staff, balked at ratifying the London Naval Treaty, Hamaguchi became the first prime minister to threaten the removal of obstreperous councilors. Cautious party elders recommended negotiation, but Hamaguchi countered: "It doesn't matter if the Privy Council opposes us. I intend to request an Imperial sanction [against the council] and will take no steps toward reaching an understanding."[5] Such determination caught the nonparty elites off guard, although it was to cost Hamaguchi his life.

Hamaguchi's faith in the popular basis of party government also distinguished him from fellow retired bureaucrats in the Kenseikai/ Minseitō. For all their administrative acumen, Wakatsuki Reijirō, Egi Tasuku, and the late Katō Takaaki knew little of grass-roots politics. The three dominated the Dōshikai, the Kenseikai, and the Minseitō from nonelected seats in the House of Peers. Hamaguchi, on the other hand, rejected a peerage and chose from the start to run for election to the Lower House from his native Kōchi prefecture. His democratic sensibilities won him tremendous respect from party regulars and energized the Minseitō's quest for a mass base.

DYNAMIC BEGINNINGS

Hamaguchi came to office in July 1929 on a wave of popular ac-
claim. Leading newspapers complimented his new cabinet ministers on
their administrative expertise and progressiveness. The Minseitō president had taken the unprecedented step of forming a shadow cabinet
during the past two years in opposition. He was thus able to put together a minority government within eight hours, or, in the words of the
Tōkyō asahi shimbun, "more quickly than the British Labour cabinet"
of the same year.[6] Prime Minister Hamaguchi thereupon unveiled an
unusually detailed ten-point program, which accentuated the "implementation of social policies." Toward this end, the cabinet immediately
created an authoritative Commission on Social Policy (Shakai Seisaku
Shingikai) for the purpose of preparing a labor union bill and a farm-
tenancy bill.[7]

Never had a Japanese government been so favorably disposed to the
passage of a labor union law. Besides Hamaguchi, the cabinet contained
several veteran proponents of labor union legislation: Adachi Kenzō
(Home Affairs), Egi Tasuku (Railways), Koizumi Matajirō (Communications), and Matsuda Genji (Colonies).[8] As home minister, Adachi advanced the government's social policies with unparalleled vigor. He
shared Hamaguchi's commitment to reform, albeit with a more home-
spun flair. Adachi Kenzō (1864–1948) was not an urbane former bureaucrat, but a thirty-five-year veteran of the gritty world of party politics.
The product of a traditional education that emphasized Confucian values
and loyalty to the emperor, the young Adachi had played a leading role in
the patriotic societies that sought to extend Japanese influence in Korea
during the mid-1890s. While in Korea, he helped recruit the Japanese
adventurers who brutally murdered Queen Min in 1895 when she
showed signs of siding with the Russians against the Japanese.[9]

His chauvinism notwithstanding, Adachi was a consummate politician, and he championed labor legislation and other democratic reforms
with an eye toward attracting the masses to his party. Called the "god of
elections," he had long functioned as his party's most successful campaign strategist. The home minister became known for such statements
as: "I'd like to see a second Minseitō formed in the [Social] Democratic
Party."[10] He took up the cause of women's suffrage with the same
electoral considerations in mind. Adachi moreover led a sizable Minseitō faction of older Radicals and "young politicians," which similarly
associated social reform with political gain.[11]

Labor union legislation appealed to Hamaguchi's ministers on economic, as well as political, grounds. Social policy became intimately linked to the Minseitō's key program of returning the yen to the gold standard at its value on the eve of World War I. Like many of his Western counterparts, Hamaguchi viewed the readoption of the gold standard as more than an economic policy. It was a matter of international prestige. The prime minister noted with considerable shame that "in the West, . . . all of the world's civilized nations with the exception of one or two like Spain" had already removed the embargo on shipping gold.[12] In his eyes, Japan's embargo, combined with deficit spending by Seiyūkai governments, resulted in postwar inflation and eroded the nation's trading position.

To remedy these ills, Hamaguchi and his finance minister, Inoue Junnosuke, took measures that deflated prices and raised the value of the yen a full 11 percent, prior to returning to gold in January 1930.[13] In addition to drastic retrenchment in administrative expenses, the cabinet sponsored a thoroughgoing program of industrial rationalization patterned after German efforts during the 1920s. A Provisional Industrial Rationalization Bureau was established within the Ministry of Commerce and Industry in June 1930. The goal was to rechannel investment, prevent overproduction, and cut production costs. With the passage of the Important Industries Control Law in 1931, the government gained the power to encourage, and in some cases to compel, cartelization in such designated industries as cotton-spinning, iron and steel, and chemicals. For individual firms, rationalization commonly meant the adoption of new equipment and technologies, coupled with drastic cuts in labor costs through lower wages, extended hours, and massive dismissals.[14]

Hamaguchi acknowledged that his deflationary measures would bring "temporary hardships" for workers and other low-income groups.[15] In an age of pre-Keynesian economic thought, Minseitō leaders and Home Ministry officials accepted such dislocations as a necessary evil in the process of economic recovery. Nonetheless, they recognized the imperative of assisting the victims with positive social policies. In his charge to the Commission on Social Policy, the director of the Social Bureau stated: "In light of the imminent removal of the embargo on gold, we cannot afford to delay the enactment of a labor union law and a tenant law."[16] Wedded to the notion of cheap government, Hamaguchi was reluctant to spend large sums on the relief of unemployment and poverty. A good liberal, he preferred to make the rules of the game fairer. Labor-union and tenant laws offered workers and tenant farmers the rights with which to defend their interests in negotiation with employers and landlords. Minseitō spokesmen were fond of rhetorically coupling industrial rationalization with the "rationalization of Labor-Capital relations." Many hard-nosed businessmen agreed, led by Finance Minister Inoue Junnosuke, the recent president of the Bank of Japan and a prominent figure in the financial community. Inoue and Hamaguchi expected the passage of a union law to foster greater communication between labor and management during the difficult process of industrial rationalization.[17]

Meeting in the autumn of 1929, the cabinet's select Commission on Social Policy demonstrated just how respectable the recognition of labor unions had become within Minseitō circles. In 1925, Kenseikai cabinet ministers had done little to save the Social Bureau's progressive draft union bill from the generally hostile Investigative Commission on Administration. By contrast, Prime Minister Hamaguchi strongly encouraged his Commission on Social Policy to formulate a more prolabor union bill, and he named several outspoken advocates to serve on the panel. Home Minister Adachi personally chaired the body's special committee on labor union legislation. Two other Minseitō committeemen, Koizumi Matajirō and Takagi Seinen, were veteran Radicals who drew substantial labor support from constituencies in Yokosuka and Tokyo, respectively. But it was the party's retired social bureaucrats who played the most prominent role within the special committee. Soeda Keiichirō, the Kyōchōkai's executive director, set the course of the deliberations. His own liberal draft union bill formed the basis of the commission's recommended legislation.[18] Two other former officials, Tsukamoto Seiji and Suematsu Kaiichirō, also proved spirited defenders of the rights of unions at several critical junctures. The special committee's only spokesman for the interests of employers was Tawara Magoichi, who served as minister of commerce and industry.[19]

The reformist thrust of the Commission on Social Policy further reflected the heightened influence of Social Bureau officials within the bureaucracy. In 1925, they held a lowly position within the Investigative Commission on Administration; in 1929, they dominated the bureaucratic secretarial panel, which counseled the special committee in framing its union bill. The Social Bureau's new director, Yoshida Shigeru, enjoyed the reputation of a dynamic official who could deftly work with all sides on behalf of labor reform. Yoshida (not to be confused with the postwar prime minister of the same name) came to his post with considerable experience in handling urban social problems. He had successively served as a deputy mayor of Tokyo and in the

Reconstruction Bureau, which the government set up after the Kantō earthquake of 1923.[20] To "realistic" labor leaders such as Nishio Suehiro, Yoshida was progressive even among Social Bureau personnel: "Bureau Chief Yoshida, in particular, was unsurpassed in political ability, and he assertively stood up to the Diet members" in defense of the labor union bill of 1931.[21] As we shall see, Yoshida continued to shape labor policy throughout the 1930s and early 1940s.

Guided by Yoshida Shigeru and the Minseitō's former officials, the special committee gave new meaning to the concept of bureaucratic autonomy vis-à-vis employers. The remaining panelists reinforced the image of expertise and political neutrality. Professor Kuwata Kumazō's name was virtually synonymous with the Social Policy Association, which he had cofounded in the 1890s. Another professor, Fujisawa Rikitarō of the House of Peers, was almost as well known for his defense of the rights of the proletarian parties.[22] Conspicuously absent were committeemen from the business community. Cabinet ministers had originally hoped to include representatives of labor and management, but employers objected to sitting down with trade unionists and socialists lest that imply de facto recognition.[23] Although members of the special committee voiced concern over occasional excesses committed by the labor movement, most directed their criticisms at the "high-handedness of the capitalists."[24] When the minister of commerce and industry claimed that a progressive union bill would destroy labor-management harmony, Tsukamoto Seiji vehemently echoed the sentiments of his former colleagues in the Home Ministry: "We must protect workers and their organizations to some degree if there is to be *true* labor-management harmony."[25]

The special committee strove to fashion union legislation that would curb rampant union-busting, yet could be passed by the business-oriented Diet. The recommended bill was considerably more prolabor than the Kenseikai cabinet's labor union bill of 1926. Panel members unanimously restored two protective features deleted by the Kenseikai cabinet—the legal recognition of all unions, including federations, and a clause permitting unions to eschew incorporation if they so chose. Committeemen further endorsed a previously controversial article that would exempt unions from liability for strike-incurred damages. On the other hand, the special committee toned down some features of the Social Bureau's more progressive draft union bill of 1925. Whereas the Social Bureau draft would have recognized collective agreements as legally binding, Director Yoshida Shigeru and Soeda Keiichirō realistically argued that such a provision would block the enactment of the Hamaguchi cabinet's entire union bill. Besides, as they observed, collective bargaining had yet to play a major role in Japanese industrial relations.

Indeed, most members favored significant controls over wayward unions. The home minister would be given the power to dissolve any union that violated the law or its own rules, or that engaged in actions "contrary to the public interest." The most divisive issue concerned the enforcement of the crucial prohibition against making employment contingent on nonmembership in a union. Soeda and Tsukamoto Seiji warned that the right to organize unions would be meaningless unless the law levied a fine against managers who prevented workers from entering or remaining in unions. Confronted by determined opposition from the minister of commerce and industry, however, Soeda agreed to the weaker wording that an employer "must not" discriminate against union members.[26]

The Commission on Social Policy approved the special committee's generally liberal report without modification. The Social Bureau thereupon drafted the recommendations into a labor union bill that provided more safeguards for unions than any measure previously introduced to the Diet by the government or an opposition party (see appendix 5).[27] Although the bill was popularly called the "Social Bureau draft" and likened to the Social Bureau draft of 1925, it represented more than a bureaucratic proposal. Prime Minister Hamaguchi made it clear that the cabinet had informally approved the commission's recommendations before instructing the Social Bureau to draft the legislation.[28]

The government's labor union bill formed part of a comprehensive social program drawn up by the committees of the Commission on Social Policy. Despite a general promise to reduce spending, Hamaguchi supported the commission's urgent request for the expansion of government-subsidized employment offices and public-works projects for the jobless.[29] Faced with soaring unemployment, the Hamaguchi cabinet increased spending on public works in 1930 tenfold over the Tanaka government's expenditures for fiscal 1928.[30] On the basis of the commission's report, the government also prepared the long-postponed seamen's insurance bill. Lastly, the cabinet accepted the commission's proposal for a tenancy bill. Pressed by the worsening recession in agriculture, landlords were repossessing tenanted lands at an accelerated rate. These evictions contributed to a sharp increase in landlord-tenant disputes during 1929. Like the labor union bill, the draft tenancy bill promised to restructure social and economic relationships. At the initiative of progressive bureaucrats in the Ministry of Agriculture and Forestry, the government proposed to guarantee the rights of tenants to remain on leased land and to negotiate rent reductions in years of poor harvests.[31]

Hamaguchi's agenda for social reform won unprecedented praise from progressive intellectuals and leaders of the moderate labor unions. While acknowledging the limitations of the proposed union bill, the liberal *Ōsaka mainichi shimbun* congratulated the Minseitō on going beyond the Kenseikai cabinets' previous legislation. The act of legal recognition, the daily stated, could only accelerate unionization.[32] The Social Democratic Party's large labor federations, which affiliated with the pragmatic Council to Promote Labor Legislation, expressed similar opinions. Leaders of Sōdōmei and the council's four other federations immediately met with the Social Bureau's Yoshida Shigeru in an attempt to strengthen the proposed union bill. They requested the inclusion of collective-bargaining guarantees, the imposition of tough penalties against anti-union employment practices, and restrictions on the home minister's power to dissolve unions.[33] Nonetheless, Sōdōmei officials indicated support for the government's union bill because such a law would "undoubtedly exert a revolutionary influence from the standpoint of trade unionism."[34]

Rising unemployment, exacerbated by industrial rationalization, convinced Social Democratic unions that the Minseitō's labor policies offered workers the only realistic means of protecting their position.[35] The Hamaguchi cabinet, for its part, was the first party government in which the prime minister and other ministers of state occasionally met with union leaders to discuss labor and social issues.[36] Hamaguchi and Home Minister Adachi established another precedent in 1930 when they appointed Abe Isoo of the Social Democratic Party to serve on the Home Ministry's Council to Prevent Unemployment (Shitsugyō Bōshi Iinkai).[37]

Support from the liberal press and the small labor movement did not ensure passage of the labor union bill, but it clearly contributed to the Minseitō's popular image as an innovative, reformist party. In January 1930, Hamaguchi dissolved the Lower House, in which the Seiyūkai still held a majority. The Minseitō won an overwhelming victory in the February election, obtaining 273 seats to the Seiyūkai's 174. Neither the Minseitō nor the Kenseikai had ever before enjoyed a parliamentary majority. Contemporary observers attributed much of the Minseitō's evident popularity among the urban classes and tenant farmers to the party's promises of social legislation and tax reform.[38] The Seiyūkai was no longer a formidable obstacle to labor reform. But Hamaguchi had yet to confront the most powerful interest in the debate.

THE EMPLOYERS' OFFENSIVE

It may be difficult in retrospect to understand why Minseitō leaders believed that employers would accept the legal recognition of labor unions. One must recall, however, that the party's interest in a labor union law arose as much (or more) from a capitalistic desire to stabilize and rationalize industrial relations as it did from electoral considerations. As in 1919, businessmen by no means agreed on the question of recognizing unions, and the Hamaguchi government paid particular attention to those employers' associations that favored or at least did not oppose the enactment of labor-union legislation.

In his comments to the Commission on Social Policy in October 1929, Soeda Keiichirō acknowledged that Mitsui executives and other powerful industrialists in Tokyo opposed the passage of any union bill. Yet he and Yoshida Shigeru of the Social Bureau emphasized the "very progressive" positions taken by the Osaka business community and the Sumitomo *zaibatsu*. According to Soeda, Osaka's leading industrialists expressed agreement with most of the items in his proposed draft. Yoshida concurred: "Capitalists generally regard the enactment of a union law as inevitable in this day and age."[39] After the commission issued its report in December, Soeda set off for the Osaka and northern Kyushu areas, where he convinced many businessmen of the benefits of the government's labor union bill.[40] Lest they miss the point, Soeda issued the following warning:

> We have entered the era of universal suffrage elections. From now on, the proletarian parties will steadily gain in strength. If we do nothing, we may not be able to enact any kind of labor union law three or five years hence. But it is presently possible to effect a moderate union law while the proletarian parties have yet to make major gains. It is in your best interests, I believe, to assent to a bill of this degree.[41]

Indeed, the signs of business support were encouraging during the autumn of 1929. Although the Tokyo-based Japan Industrial Club totally rejected the government's proposal, several other employers' associations took more favorable positions. As they had throughout the 1920s, organizations representing smaller enterprises tended to advocate some form of legal recognition, whereby unions would receive certain rights in exchange for stipulated duties and official supervision. The Osaka Industrial Association, the Osaka Chamber of Commerce and Industry, and the Electric Power Industry Association essentially endorsed the Commission on Social Policy's recommended labor union bill with only minor revisions. Most notably, the influential Osaka Industrial Association moved far beyond its earlier support of the simple legal recognition of labor unions. Association leaders now favored the recognition of labor federations, as well as that of individual craft and industrial unions. They also approved of a union's right to choose whether it would legally incorporate, arguing that if incorporation were made compulsory, the red tape involved would drive some unions to evade recognition and thus make supervision more difficult. Equally remarkable was the Osaka Industrial Association's support for union legislation that would invalidate both the discriminatory dismissal of union members and any employment contract that forbade union membership.[42]

Cheered by the backing of influential employers, Prime Minister Hamaguchi resolutely defended his union bill against the more intractable foes of labor legislation. The first confrontation occurred in late December, when executives of the Japan Industrial Club visited the prime minister to protest the proposed union bill. Most existing unions were dedicated to class struggle, they maintained; recognition would therefore "greatly intensify class struggle in Japanese industry in the future." Hamaguchi promised consideration of the industrialists' views, but he firmly challenged their assumptions: "I don't believe the enactment of a Labor Union Law will intensify class struggle; rather, it will give meaning to Labor-Capital harmony in industry."[43]

Hamaguchi's confidence also derived from the good will of the banking world. His key ally was Ikeda Seihin, president of the Mitsui Bank and probably the most prominent banker in Japan. Ikeda and most big bankers reportedly kept their distance from the Japan Industrial Club's opposition movement as late as July 1930.[44] In a 1949 interview, Ikeda claimed that he mobilized fellow bankers in favor of a labor union law because he believed workers needed unions to resist dismissals and improve working conditions.[45] Ikeda perhaps exaggerated his progressive credentials, but his stated commitment to long-term stability in industrial relations accorded well with that of such financially minded Minseitō leaders as Hamaguchi and Finance Minister Inoue Junnosuke.

It soon became clear, however, that the cabinet had badly misgauged the extent of the industrial community's opposition. Commanded by Chairman Dan Takuma of Mitsui, the Japan Industrial Club embarked on an unprecedented nationwide campaign to unify employers against the legal recognition of unions. During the first months of 1930, the Electric Power Industry Association and several other organizations shifted to positions of unqualified opposition to the government's draft labor union bill.[46] Yet it was the relatively progressive Osaka Industrial Association that executed the most dramatic turnaround. Adopting the language of the Japan Industrial Club, the Osaka industrialists condemned the cabinet's proposed legislation for blindly recognizing all unions, including those whose principles were "incompatible with our nation's social system and economic organization." A new demand surfaced. The Osaka Industrial Association might support a weaker union bill if it were coupled to a "bill to control labor disputes" (rōdō sōgi torishimari hōan).[47] As clarified by the Osaka Chamber of Commerce and Industry, the bill should prohibit public-enterprise strikes, sympathy strikes, disputes with objects other than employment conditions, and strikes by minors. It should also restrict participation by "third parties" and severely punish "actions obstructing industry."[48] Whereas Osaka employers had previously looked to the state as a referee, they now called on the government to protect them from organized labor.

Several developments lay behind the new unity among employers. First, industrialists faced an unparalleled surge in labor disputes between 1929 and 1931 (see appendix 1). Although economic downturns usually inhibit strike activity, the worsening recession was unquestionably the precipitant in this case. Hamaguchi desired labor union legislation to lessen the social costs of his austerity and rationalization programs, but businessmen could not conceive of a worse time to bolster the unions.

The Japanese began feeling the full effects of the worldwide Great Depression after the government returned the yen to the gold standard at its expensive prewar value in January 1930. An overvalued yen and the sharp decline in the American market severely strained Japan's export-oriented manufacturing sector.[49] Already engaged in rationalization efforts, industrialists undertook deeper wage cuts and more sweeping dismissals. Excluding the hard-hit silk industry and mining sectors, total industrial employment dropped 10 percent in 1930 (from 1929) and another 9 percent in 1931 from the previous year.[50] Moreover, money wages declined nearly 20 percent in general manufacturing during the same years, with unskilled workers in textiles and other industries enduring deeper cuts. The defensive character of the resulting strike wave is also apparent. In 1930, 76 percent of all strikes and lockouts centered on workers' defensive attempts to resist layoffs and lower wages or to gain severance pay; by contrast, in the strike-ridden year of 1921, workers in 73 percent of the incidents struck primarily for positive demands—higher wages, shorter hours, or the right to organize unions (see appendix 1).

What particularly alarmed employers was the unexpected growth of labor unions during the acute recession. Despite a substantial shrinkage in the work force, total union membership increased 23,300 and 14,700 in 1930 and 1931, respectively. The rate of unionization reached its pre-1945 high of 7.9 percent in 1931. Amid economic adversity, unions found converts among such previously unorganized elements as automobile workers, salaried employees, and even employees in the motion-picture industry. Slightly less than 1 percent of factory women belonged to unions in 1930, but they, too, began to play a major role as rationalization took its toll in the textile industry. Two of the largest disputes in 1930 occurred at the Tōyō Muslin Company, where female workers struck to defend their jobs and seniority allowances against company cutbacks. The second strike, which lasted nearly two months, involved 2,050 women and 449 men. Sōdōmei and the centrist Federation of Japanese Labor Unions actively assisted the workers, succeeding in organizing a few hundred of the women. Tempers mounted as the second strike wore on. On 24 October, hundreds of angry workers clashed with right-wing thugs recruited by the company. The crowds went on to stop streetcar service and throw rocks at the police, who arrested 209 strikers.[51] The shocked business community viewed the incident as evidence of escalating "street fighting" and Communist infiltration of the mainstream of organized labor.[52]

Although unions were more active than ever before, employers greatly exaggerated the political radicalization of the labor movement. In actuality, Communist influence was confined to the few thousand members of the harassed and loosely organized remnants of the Hyōgi-kai. Sōdōmei and other "right-wing" unions, on the other hand, recognized organized labor's vulnerability in the face of high unemployment, and their leaders intensified the commitment to "realistic" strategies that advanced the economic position of members. They concluded more collective agreements, further centralized control over strike-making, and, for the first time, amassed some sizable strike funds. According to the Social Bureau, the leadership's report to Sōdōmei's annual convention in 1930 "happily counted 285 incidents—an increase—which saw peaceful solutions stopping short of strikes."[53] The rapidly expanding centrist unions relied on strikes to a much greater extent. Yet their strikes, too, focused on economic objectives and were a far cry from the politicized actions of the labor movement during the early 1920s. As viewed by the Social Bureau, labor's centrist and right wings converged around realistic policies by 1931. Both groups avoided struggle for its own sake while increasingly cooperating with the government and capitalists to better the lives of workers.[54]

Second, whether radicalized or not, the new wave of disputes and unionization struck hardest at smaller companies, which had previously rejected the harsh anti-union line advanced by the large employers of the Japan Industrial Club. Pushed out of the big companies, unions had long concentrated on the weaker small and medium-sized firms. But 1930 saw something of a quantum leap in the number of extremely small-scale disputes. The average number of participants per dispute fell from 237 in 1921 to 84 in 1930, dropping further during the next two years (see appendix 1). An astounding 69 percent of strikes in 1930 involved fewer than fifty workers; only 3 percent involved more than five hundred participants. To provide an international perspective, one Social Bureau researcher demonstrated that Japan experienced over twice as many strikes and lockouts as Great Britain in 1930, yet with less than one-third the number of participants.[55]

Frustrated in their attempts to cut labor costs during the recession, smaller employers grew resentful of a government that seemed more concerned about protecting labor unions than them. Complained one owner who had recently suffered a strike: "There are the police, but you can't trust them. Then there are the governmental officials, but they can't be relied on, either."[56] The tycoons of the Japan Industrial Club adroitly played upon the fears of their less powerful comrades to forge a common front. All could agree on one point: the legal protection of unions would "result in the withering of entrepreneurial spirit and bring about the decline of small and medium-sized business."[57]

Third, industry's shift to total opposition emerged from successful efforts to drive horizontal trade unions out of large private enterprises during the 1920s. Zaibatsu affiliates in heavy industry had been experimenting with various types of company unions ever since Home Minister Tokonami Takejirō presented his plan to set up works councils in

1919. Many took the form of factory councils, in which representatives of labor and management discussed matters of mutual concern. Others were looser workers' organizations geared to mutual assistance, educational activities, accident prevention, or simply socializing. To woo workers from trade unions, an increasing number of employers allowed some discussion of wages, hours, and working conditions within factory councils in the latter half of the 1920s. Sōdōmei and other moderate labor unions managed to transform a few councils into vehicles for collective bargaining. Yet even the Kyōchōkai, which envisioned the coexistence of factory councils and horizontal labor unions, was forced to admit that most councils existed to ward off genuine trade unions.[58]

Judging by the rhetoric of the Japan Industrial Club in 1930 and 1931, factory councils also existed to ward off trade-union legislation. The club's chairman, Dan Takuma, pointed with pride to the "cooperative unions" (kyōai kumiai) in his Mitsui Mines and Miike Mines; affiliated workers allegedly welcomed "paternalism" and eschewed socialism. According to Industrial Club spokesmen, the government's union bill ignored all company unions while legitimizing "militant" labor unions—a category defined to include the reformist Sōdōmei. To emphasize the anomalous nature of the trade unions, one club director contrasted the 180,000 workers in "militant" unions with the 500,000 employees in factory councils and other company unions:

> These organizations [company unions] should be considered unions. I have already asked why the Social Bureau is incapable of recognizing them as such. . . . At any rate, there are factory councils encompassing 450,000 members, or [if one includes other non-trade-union organizations] cooperative associations which aim at education, mutual assistance, and improved welfare for their 500,000 members. We should guide these organizations and establish a type of labor union appropriate to Japan.[59]

Although the Industrial Club's figures lacked precision, the Social Bureau counted 641,197 members in non-trade-union organizations as of June 1934.[60]

Lastly, much had changed since 1919, when many employers looked upon English-style labor unions and labor union legislation as part of "the trends of the world." Japanese industrialists discovered America. With Dan Takuma at their head, twenty-four of the nation's top businessmen spent six months observing postwar economic conditions in the West in 1921 and 1922. They were most impressed by talks with corporate executives and Republican Party leaders in the United States. Herbert Hoover, then secretary of commerce, warned against recognizing industrial unions because workers thus organized would surely emerge victorious. Elbert Gary of U.S. Steel lectured his Japanese guests on the evils of collective bargaining and the virtues of his firm's factory councils. Anticipating and no doubt inspiring the Japan Industrial Club's case against union legislation, Gary emphasized the high degree of public support behind the steel companies' battle to keep the unions out. He further contrasted the small proportion of trade unionists with the great majority of American workers who valued the liberty to conclude individual contracts free from union bosses.[61] Irony of ironies, much of what we now consider the uniquely "Japanese employment system"—that is, company-linked benefits, loyalty to the firm, and enterprise-based unions—was influenced in part by American employers' experiments with the anti-union "American Plan" and "welfare capitalism" during the 1920s.[62]

Among Japanese employers, the American model advanced in prominence as the British model receded during the latter half of the 1920s. Taking a cue from his counterparts in the United States, Dan Takuma blamed assertive trade unions for economic stagnation in Great Britain and "other nations which have imported the English system." Japanese businessmen were especially heartened by the failure of the British General Strike in 1926. They observed that even the Labour Party cabinet (1929–31) had come to recognize the need to revive industry and cooperate with industrialists. Just as Japanese bureaucrats and entrepreneurs had toured the West in search of solutions, Dan and others gleefully noted that in 1930, British unions and managerial groups dispatched fact-finding teams to the United States, continental Europe, and Japan itself. They were particularly fond of quoting the story of the trade unionists who, sent by the *Daily Mail,* reported that American prosperity was based on nonunionized labor working for high wages.[63]

In the judgment of Japanese employers, it was Japan's militant labor leaders, not they, who failed to understand the new "trends of the world." A 1930 survey by the Tokyo Chamber of Commerce and Industry juxtaposed the upsurge in strikes in Japan since 1926 with their sharp decline in the United States and Great Britain after the latter's General Strike. Departing from their earlier glorification of Japan's incomparable "beautiful customs" of social harmony, chamber leaders concluded: "Whereas labor unions have turned toward Labor-Capital harmony in the United States and Britain, only in our country have the unions maintained attitudes based on class struggle. Recognition of the [government's] radical labor union bill at this time would be abhorrent."[64]

THE "SOCIAL BUREAU DRAFT"

In the face of growing opposition from the nation's employers during the spring of 1930, the Hamaguchi cabinet dug in to save its labor union bill. Speaking for the cabinet in May, Home Minister Adachi Kenzō promised to introduce the union bill at the next regular session of the Diet in early 1931, without revision and regardless of opposition from management or labor. Adachi scornfully compared the industrialists' resistance to earlier arguments that universal manhood suffrage would destroy the nation. Just as Japan had easily survived the enactment of the Suffrage Law, so, too, would Japanese industry prosper by legally recognizing labor unions, he predicted. In interviews with reporters, representatives of the government minced no words in attacking the absolute opposition of employers to labor union legislation. Such hostility was based on "unadulterated conservative thought" and "absurd arguments which totally misunderstand modern politics." Spokesmen acknowledged that capitalists would in the short run be constrained from cutting wages and personnel at will, but "to oppose the union bill on that ground is to think only of one's profits while ignoring the rest of society." In the long run, they insisted, a union law benefited capitalists because it also contained supervisory features that guide the labor movement along "the correct path."[65]

Into the fray rushed officials of the Home Ministry with by far the harshest criticisms of the employers' position. Tensions between businessmen and social bureaucrats reached a new high during a fifty-five-day strike against the Kanegafuchi Spinning Company (Kanebō) from April to early June. Some seven thousand workers, a majority of them women, walked off the job at four Kanebō plants after the company reduced wages and instituted other rationalization measures. Begun by the welfare-minded entrepreneur Mutō Sanji, Kanebō's mills had been considered a model of paternalistic industrial relations without unions.

Home Ministry officials accordingly seized upon the strike to claim that the vaunted managerial policy of paternalism in Japan rested on "the whims of capitalists" and offered no solution to growing labor problems. Kanebō's directors, they complained, had "cruelly" cut wages rather than reduce stockholders' dividends and Mutō's three-million-yen pension fund. Only a labor union law would protect workers from the "high-handedness of the capitalists."[66] Moreover, Home Minister Adachi restrained the police from intervening in the dispute, thus fulfilling a promise made to Sōdōmei's Nishio Suehiro, who led the strike at the Osaka mill.[67] Following the Kanebō strike, Social Bureau director Yoshida Shigeru conveyed a blunt message to one group of businessmen from the Osaka area: "True Labor-Capital harmony results only when both sides are placed on an equal level. That is, the legal recognition of workers' organizations will produce such equality. If you oppose the aims of this bill, you deny labor unions and are fundamentally in disagreement with the authorities."[68]

Nevertheless, the government's pledge to introduce the union bill to the next Diet simply solidified the opposition campaign of the industrialists. On 22 May, the Japan Industrial Club hosted representatives from the nation's commercial and industrial associations to map out a common strategy against the labor union bill. Throughout June, the Industrial Club assisted the formation of regional federations of industrial organizations in the Keihin (Tokyo-Yokohama), Kinki (Osaka-Kyoto-Kobe), Nagoya, northern Kyushu, and Hokkaido areas. No issue had ever before united the full gamut of Japanese business interests—industrial and financial, large and small, Tokyo-based industrial associations, and local chambers of commerce. The Kinki Area Federation of Industrial Organizations, for example, absorbed twenty existing associations representing fifteen thousand factories. Coordinated by Dan Takuma and Gō Seinosuke, president of both the Japan Chamber of Commerce and Industry and its Tokyo affiliate, the regional federations sent numerous delegations to lobby cabinet ministers, members of the House of Peers, and leaders of the two major parties.[69]

These efforts forced Hamaguchi's first retreat from the proposed labor union bill. On 24 June 1930, Dan and Gō paid the prime minister a visit. The *Tōkyō asahi shimbun* suspected a deal, and its front page featured a photograph taken at Hamaguchi's official residence of Dan, his hat held seemingly to hide his lips, engaged in conversation with Gō. Two days later, Hamaguchi met with representatives from the Kinki Area Federation of Industrial Organizations, and he repeated his pledge to submit the draft bill to the next Diet. This time, however, the prime minister intimated that the draft might be somewhat altered. He went one step further on 28 June, declaring that the proposed union bill constituted no more than the "Social Bureau's draft" and should not be equated with the government's final bill or even with a formal draft by the Home Ministry. While acknowledging the basis of the Social Bureau draft to be the report by the Commission on Social Policy, Hamaguchi posed the distinct possibility of producing a "better bill" in consultation with the interested parties.[70]

The influence of employers within the Minseitō clearly contributed to the cabinet's crumbling defense of the so-called Social Bureau draft. Although industrial magnates played a lesser role in the Minseitō than in the Seiyūkai, businessmen of all types accounted for fully 59 percent of the Minseitō's delegation to the Lower House in 1930 (see appendix 4). Most occupied leading positions within their local chambers of commerce, and few Minseitō politicians relished the thought of losing campaign contributions from business groups in their districts. As local employers' associations flocked to the banner of the Japan Industrial Club, Minseitō members worried that the proposed union bill would incur the wrath of the entire business community. Party executive Usawa Uhachi, an entrepreneur from Chiba, spoke for many provincial businessmen in the Minseitō when he openly challenged the need for any union law amidst a recession.[71]

Narrow partisan considerations did not alone explain Hamaguchi's efforts to placate employers. Contemporary commentators often wrote of tensions between the Minseitō cabinet's commitment to "finance capitalism" and retrenchment, on the one hand, and progressive social policies, on the other.[72] Hamaguchi's program to rationalize and revitalize the economy necessitated close cooperation with powerful Tokyo industrialists. The Commission on Social Policy was only one of the cabinet's blue-ribbon panels convened during its first year. The prime minister based his economic policies on recommendations from four other commissions. As shown below, the commissions included several leading employers from the Japan Industrial Club and other Tokyo-Yokohama associations:

> *Commission on International Accounts (Kokusai Taishaku Shingikai):* Gō Seinosuke (Japan Industrial Club; president, Japan and Tokyo Chambers of Commerce and Industry); Watanabe Tetsuzō (Tokyo Chamber)
>
> *Commission on Tariffs (Kanzei Shingikai):* Ōhashi Shintarō, Yasukawa Yūnosuke (both Industrial Club), Miyakegawa Hyakutarō (Yokohama Chamber)

Ministry of Commerce and Industry's Council on Commerce and Industry (Shōkō Iinkai): Gō Seinosuke, Dan Takuma, Kimura Kusuyata, Nakajima Kumakichi (all Industrial Club), Isaka Takashi (Industrial Club; president, Yokohama Chamber), Fujita Ken'ichi (past president, Tokyo Chamber)

Advisory Board to the Ministry of Commerce and Industry's Provisional Industrial Rationalization Bureau (Rinji Sangyō Gōrikyoku): Nakajima Kumakichi, Isaka Takashi, Makita Tamaki (all Industrial Club).[73]

Although Home Ministry officials attacked these industrialists for their opposition to the union bill, the staff of the Ministry of Commerce and Industry met daily with the same men to formulate a national program of industrial rationalization. Symbolic of the relationship, the Commission on Commerce and Industry held its last meeting at the Japan Industrial Club.[74] Persons close to the business community increasingly advised Minseitō leaders that the union bill stood in the way of continued industrial support for the cabinet's economic policies. By early July, many party members privately questioned the costs of defending the Social Bureau draft.[75]

By pressuring Hamaguchi into reexamining the Social Bureau draft, the forces of management drove a wedge between the cabinet and the most progressive advocates of labor reform within the Home Ministry and the Minseitō. Outraged at the prime minister's change of policy, Home Ministry officials protested that the Social Bureau's "private draft" was in fact the government's bill and that the Social Bureau had dutifully followed the recommendations of the Commission on Social Policy and the cabinet itself. These civil servants cautioned the government against surrendering to big business. The proposed union legislation, they claimed, already balanced the rights of organized labor against the need for governmental controls.[76] The Hamaguchi cabinet and the Home Ministry thus pursued divergent policies during the remainder of 1930. Whereas the cabinet neither promoted nor revised the Social Bureau draft, the Home Ministry zealously defended its bill against all critics.[77] When the nation's business associations mounted a new offensive in October, Social Bureau officials threatened to supplement the union bill with a measure to guarantee collective agreements.[78]

Hamaguchi's tilt toward employers similarly angered the Minseitō's supporters of the Social Bureau draft. Home Minister Adachi and Communications Minister Koizumi Matajirō warned of the political conse-

quences of abandoning the proposed union bill after the cabinet had so
enthusiastically promoted the measure. Adachi chose to ignore Hamaguchi's statement of June, firmly backing his subordinates in the Home
Ministry. Throughout the rest of 1930, Adachi reaffirmed the government's intention to introduce the Social Bureau draft to the next Diet
without revision.[79] Within the Minseitō, the Kyōchōkai's Soeda Keiichirō rallied the party's former Home Ministry bureaucrats behind the
Social Bureau draft. As chairman of the Minseitō's special committee on
social policy, Soeda repeatedly denounced attempts by employers and
his fellow party members to weaken the government's union legislation.
The Minseitō's progressive young politicians, many of whom were allied with Adachi, went further to support the Social Bureau's call for a
supplementary collective agreements bill.[80]

The fight to save the Social Bureau draft was notable for the paucity
of mass support. In contrast to the Home Ministry and the Minseitō's
social reform wing, the labor movement itself proved unwilling and
unable to back the cabinet's liberal legislation against the forces of
capital. Unions affiliated with the moderate Social Democratic Party
and the "centrist" Japan Masses' Party did collaborate to organize several demonstrations against the Japan Industrial Club and other business associations between May and July. Yet compared with the employers' campaign, labor's protests were small in size and confined to the
major cities. The proletarian parties had obviously lost the political
clout enjoyed during the Seiyūkai-Minseitō deadlock of 1928–29. The
Minseitō's electoral victory in 1930 lessened the party's dependence on
the socialist movement. The Minseitō's young politicians had eagerly
joined socialists in the anti-Tanaka rallies of 1929, but they played no
role in the labor movement's demonstrations of 1930.

The political impotence of organized labor stemmed partly from
internal disunity and partly from the continued preoccupation with
ideological purity. Whereas industrialists presented a united front to the
cabinet, the labor union movement remained fragmented into right-
wing, centrist, and left-wing blocs grouped around the three major
proletarian parties. Revived in December 1929, the left-wing New
Labor-Farmer Party camp totally rejected the Social Bureau draft. The
Japan Masses' Party appeared privately satisfied with the Social Bureau's bill, yet felt compelled in public to agitate for an "independent"
labor union law. The right-wing Social Democratic Party pursued the
most pragmatic course, requesting the prime minister's good offices to
persuade businessmen to accept the Social Bureau draft.[81] But clearly,

the Social Democrats relied more on Hamaguchi than he on them. According to Yamanaka Tokutarō, a prolabor scholar of the time, the Japan Industrial Club's well-orchestrated drive convinced the public that labor unions were destroying Japanese industry. The labor movement, on the other hand, failed to demonstrate the importance of the right to organize unions.[82]

Nonetheless, the employers' offensive had not crushed all hopes of progressive labor union legislation in the last months of 1930. The Minseitō's overwhelming majority ensured passage of the bill in some form by the Lower House and discouraged a veto by the House of Peers. No one, however, anticipated the tragedy that was to befall the prime minister. Hamaguchi, it must be understood, was extremely unpopular in right-wing circles. His government had signed the London Naval Treaty in April 1930 over the strenuous objections of the Naval General Staff, which insisted on a higher ratio of heavy cruisers and other ships vis-à-vis the United States and Great Britain. Allying with the Seiyūkai and conservative privy councilors, the Naval General Staff and various patriotic societies launched a nationwide campaign to persuade the public that the cabinet had dangerously compromised Japan's national security. Hamaguchi fought back. Championing the right of civilian cabinets to determine military strength, he skillfully rallied the navy minister and the elder statesman Prince Saionji behind the accord. The outmaneuvered Privy Council reluctantly ratified the treaty in September. Yet Hamaguchi paid dearly for his victory. Assassination was an ever-present danger for Japanese leaders who challenged the military's "right of supreme command." On 14 November, an angry young man from a right-wing society shot the prime minister at the Tokyo train station. Mortally wounded, Hamaguchi somehow remained in office throughout the crucial Fifty-ninth Diet. His fate and that of liberal reform had become very much intertwined.

PARLIAMENTARY DEBACLE

Prior to the attempt on his life, Hamaguchi looked forward to the Fifty-ninth Diet (24 December 1930–27 March 1931) as an opportunity to fulfill the Minseitō's promises of further democratization. In addition to labor-union and tenancy legislation, he offered a set of tax reforms that would more equitably distribute burdens and reduce levies, on the basis of the savings achieved by the London Naval Treaty. His cabinet also prepared two measures to broaden the franchise. The first, a revision of the Election Law, would lower the voting age for males to twenty. The much-publicized women's civil rights bill (*fujin kōmin hōan*) proposed to enfranchise adult women in elections at the city, town, and village level. These controversial bills would have faced formidable opposition under the best of circumstances from employers, landlords, the Seiyūkai, and conservatives in the House of Peers and the Privy Council.

The terrorist attack on Hamaguchi tremendously compounded the government's difficulties on the eve of the parliamentary session. Hamaguchi had been the bridge between the Minseitō's leadership group of former bureaucrats, led by Egi Tasuku, and Adachi Kenzō's band of Radicals and young politicians. Within hours of the shooting, a succession dispute broke out to divide the supporters of Egi and Adachi. Minseitō elders forestalled an open rift on 15 November by selecting Foreign Minister Shidehara Kijūrō to serve as acting prime minister until the hospitalized Hamaguchi could resume his duties. A career diplomat who had never formally joined the Minseitō, Shidehara woefully lacked Hamaguchi's parliamentary skills and dedication to domestic reform. The foreign minister, moreover, personified the pro-Anglo-American diplomacy and conciliatory China policy so detested by many in the armed forces, the Privy Council, the House of Peers, and the Seiyūkai. Upon assuming his new duties, Shidehara reaffirmed the government's commitment to introducing Hamaguchi's reform legislation, but the journalist Baba Tsunego aptly judged the cabinet "more dead than alive."[83]

To make matters worse, the cabinet's liberal bills faced an unusually hostile reception in the Diet. The Fifty-ninth Diet was one of the most acrimonious sessions in the history of modern Japan. Within the Lower House, the jingoist Seiyūkai seized upon Hamaguchi's acceptance of the London Naval Treaty in an effort to topple the Minseitō cabinet. The minority party's reliance on unparliamentary methods seemed to know no bounds. In the "slip of the tongue" incident, rioting Seiyūkai representatives disrupted parliamentary business for over a week during February 1931. They accused Shidehara of dishonoring the imperial institution after he simply observed that the emperor had personally approved the London treaty. Shidehara himself was physically assaulted in the halls of the Diet by toughs hired by the Seiyūkai.[84]

As the Great Depression worsened, Hamaguchi's orthodox economic policies became another target. Unemployment, as measured by the Social Bureau, rose from 294,000 to 413,000 between the beginning of

1930 and the end of 1931, although most independent observers agreed that the real figure was much higher.[85] Seiyūkai spokesmen also pointed to the devastating recession in agriculture, where the price of rice, and especially that of silk cocoons, plummeted. They pinned the principal blame on the cabinet's return to the gold standard just as the American silk market was collapsing. The Minseitō government, to be sure, did not rigidly adhere to its retrenchment program, and it did float over 34 million yen in emergency unemployment bonds for public works and railway maintenance. Yet against the backdrop of highly visible unemployment, the Seiyūkai had little difficulty portraying these remedies as too little, too late.[86] Similarly angered by the London Naval Treaty and Hamaguchi's ineffectual economic policies, conservative leaders in the House of Peers threatened to defeat the proposed labor union bill and the government's other liberal measures.[87] Cabinet ministers further feared that the Privy Council would spitefully block the slated revision of the Election Law.[88]

The question of introducing labor union legislation under these unfavorable circumstances divided an already factionalized Minseitō. Some Minseitō leaders advised postponement. Others, like Railways Minister Egi Tasuku and Finance Minister Inoue Junnosuke, recommended strategic revisions in the draft prepared by the Social Bureau.[89] Led by Soeda Keiichirō, the party's social reformers condemned both positions and urged Shidehara to introduce a progressive union bill close to the Social Bureau draft. The young politicians and former Home Ministry officials also called on the fiscally orthodox cabinet to fund the long-postponed Poor Relief Law of 1929.[90] Although Soeda and other socially minded ex-officials were members of Egi's "bureaucratic faction" (kanryō-ha), most proponents of the Social Bureau draft belonged to Adachi Kenzō's "party politician faction" (tōnin-ha). Adachi's clique included a sizable group of first- to third-term Diet members associated with the reformist mavericks, Nakano Seigō and Nagai Ryūtarō. Following the attack on Hamaguchi, twenty-nine of these backbenchers bitterly protested the appointment of Baron Shidehara, a bureaucrat and nonparty man, over their patron Adachi. They suspected Egi and the bureaucratic faction of plotting to humiliate Home Minister Adachi by shelving the Home Ministry's labor union bill and the two suffrage reforms.[91] The ambitious Adachi found himself in a quandary. A strong commitment to the Social Bureau draft would solidify his support within the Home Ministry and among the younger stratum of the Minseitō. Yet such a stand would provoke the wrath of the business community and probably cost him the party presidency.[92] Adachi's political fortunes depended in part on his ability to unite the forces of capital and labor behind the proposed labor union bill.

Adachi's solution was audacious in its vision of industrial relations. On 22 December, two days before the opening of the Diet, the Home Minister sponsored Japan's first national-level talks between representatives of the unions and employers. Assisted by the Home Ministry's staff, several distinguished retired officials served as third-party mediators. Ministry officials modeled the conference after the 1928 Mond-Turner talks, at which British industrialists and trade union leaders discussed ways of restoring industrial peace and efficiency.[93] But could such a scheme work in Japan? From organized labor, Adachi carefully selected those whom he called the "most moderate, reliable, and representative" spokesmen: Nishio Suehiro, Matsuoka Komakichi, Yonekubo Mitsusuke, Abe Isoo (all Social Democrats), and Miwa Jusō and Kamijō Aiichi (centrist union leaders).[94] Employers were nonetheless suspicious. The Japan Industrial Club adamantly refused to have any dealings with the trade unionists. Tokyo-based industrial organizations boycotted the talks, claiming that the invited labor leaders represented unions that espoused "an ideology at variance with the nation and industry and one which we cannot recognize as representative of the true spirit of most workers."[95] Five employers—three from Osaka and one each from Nagoya and Yokohama—did attend the labor-management conference, only to walk out after stating their position of absolute disapproval. Having failed to mollify his business critics, Adachi prepared to jettison the Social Bureau draft. On 17 January, the Home Minister conferred exclusively with industrial representatives in the hope of framing a more passable bill. Their intractable opposition, however, left little room for maneuver.[96]

Stymied, the cabinet at long last agreed to revise the draft labor union bill. Adachi Kenzō and Egi Tasuku were assigned the task of rewriting. Adachi subsequently charged his factional rival with willfully sabotaging the government's union legislation.[97] In actuality, Egi functioned as an honest broker in a badly divided cabinet. The author of the Kenseikai's original labor legislation, he wished to make only those revisions necessary to guarantee passage. Other cabinet members, notably Colonial Minister Matsuda Genji, sought to shelve the union bill itself or, failing that, to remove such key protective clauses as Article 12, which prohibited employers from dismissing union members and requiring yellow-dog contracts.[98] Although Matsuda's group severely weakened the Social Bureau draft, Egi and Adachi did succeed in saving Article 12 and winning cabinet approval for the introduction of the revised labor union bill to the current parliamentary session.[99]

In its final form, the Hamaguchi cabinet's labor union bill of 1931 marked more than a retreat from the 1929 Social Bureau draft. It was even more restrictive than the Wakatsuki cabinet's union bill of 1926 (see appendix 5). Besides prohibiting political contributions by unions, the cabinet struck the article exempting unions from liability for dispute-incurred damages. The 1931 union bill also limited union membership to workers and former workers, although anyone could be a union official. Reflecting the employers' opposition to the legal recognition of militant federations, Article 1 restricted recognition to unions and federations based on a single craft or industry. It further excluded highly politicized unions that did not also pledge in their stated objects to work for the "mutual assistance and education" of members. As in 1926, however, Egi and Adachi softened these restrictions with a proviso by which all existing unions and federations would be recognized.[100]

Home Minister Adachi introduced the labor union bill to the Lower House on 24 February. The press reported a great deal of interest in the fate of the legislation. The galleries were packed, and Prince Chichibu, the emperor's younger brother, sat in the spectators' box with class-mates from the War College.[101] The diluted bill predictably disappointed labor and progressive intellectuals. The liberal press caustically wrote of this "pure and simple law to control labor unions."[102] The labor unions and socialist parties staged a series of angry demonstrations, in which scuffles resulted and police detained several, including Diet member Asanuma Inejirō. The centrist National Masses' Party (Zenkoku Taishūtō), successor to the Japan Masses' Party, directed most of the protests. The moderate Social Democratic unions pursued a more ambiguous course. Publicly, their Council to Promote Labor Legislation circulated tens of thousands of posters with the caption: "The Ringleaders of the Willful Murder of the Labor Union Bill: Down with Gō and Dan! Watch Out for the Zaibatsu's Clerk, Hamaguchi!"[103] Privately, Sōdōmei's chairman, Matsuoka Komakichi, agreed with Nishio Suehiro that the enactment of the union bill, despite its defects, would benefit the labor movement. The practical Nishio thereupon met with Home Minister Adachi. The two collaborated on a script whereby Nishio attacked the government's bill in the Diet, so that Adachi could maintain that the legislation pandered to neither labor nor capital.[104]

The cabinet inflamed progressive opinion further by introducing a revision to the 1926 Labor Disputes Conciliation Law alongside the labor union bill. The original law had stipulated compulsory conciliation proceedings only in public-enterprise disputes. The proposed revision empowered the authorities to mediate any private-sector dispute that, in their judgment, threatened the public interest. Although the legislation flowed from the Home Ministry's long-standing efforts to arbitrate the crippling strikes of the recession years, critics accused the cabinet of capitulating to industrialists' demands for a total prohibition of strikes.[105]

If Minseitō leaders thought the two labor bills would placate the business community, they were sorely mistaken. The Keihin and Kinki Area Federations of Industrial Organizations rejected the weakened labor union bill, just as they had the Social Bureau draft.[106] As Baba Tsunego observed, employers feared that any legal recognition of the right to organize would open the door to rapid unionization.[107] Moreover, the directors of the Japan Industrial Club reacted coolly to the proposed revision of the Labor Disputes Conciliation Law. They demanded an outright ban on strikes, not conciliation by possibly prolabor officials from the Home Ministry.[108] In terms of organization, the country's employers succeeded where the labor movement failed. During the Diet session, they completed preparations for a permanent, centralized lobbying association, and in April they founded the National Federation of Industrial Organizations (Zenkoku Sangyō Dantai Rengō-kai or Zensanren). The primary model was the vigorously anti-union National Association of Manufacturers in the United States.[109]

The Minseitō majority notwithstanding, the two labor bills encountered substantial resistance within the Lower House. The Minseitō's young politicians charged the government with surrendering to the capitalists, and their labor experts initially refused to serve on the committee on labor legislation. They also threatened to challenge the revision of the Disputes Conciliation Law on the Diet floor.[110] With only a month remaining in the session, Seiyūkai members stalled the measures in committee another two weeks. As in 1926, Seiyūkai representatives opportunistically attacked the union bill with contradictory arguments. The industrialist Matsumura Kōzō opposed any recognition of unions at a time when many labor organizations subscribed to radical ideas, whereas Tago Ichimin condemned the Minseitō cabinet for emasculating the progressive features of the original Social Bureau draft.[111] In the end, the Minseitō's leaders restored discipline within their own party and mobilized the majority. After years of bureaucratic proposals and parliamen-

tary debates, the Lower House finally passed the labor union bill, along
with the equally controversial tenancy bill and the women's civil rights
bill. The revision of the Conciliation Law was also approved.

The Minseitō's reform legislation then moved to the House of Peers.
According to the Meiji Constitution of 1889, the House of Peers possessed the power to quash any measure approved by the popularly elected
Lower House. The titled peers, who constituted nearly one-half of the
upper house, generally hailed from an older, less liberal Japan. Yet, despite their loathing of labor unions, most titled peers were reluctant to
defy the Minseitō's large majority in the Lower House. They remembered
all too well the events of 1924, when Count Kiyoura's unpopular "cabinet of peers" united the major parties and public against the upper chamber.[112] By contrast, Seiyūkai sympathizers in the House of Peers mounted
an openly partisan campaign against the Minseitō's entire legislative
program. Like the Minseitō, the Seiyūkai drew its principal strength from
nonhereditary peers—retired bureaucrats (imperial appointees) and local
notables elected from among those Japanese paying the highest direct
national taxes.[113] Seiyūkai activists included such vehement opponents of
labor union legislation as the former Justice Ministry officials, Suzuki
Kisaburō and Yamaoka Mannosuke.[114]

Although "House of Peers" conjures up the image of doddering old
conservatives, modern businessmen made up the most fundamental
source of opposition to labor legislation. In mid-February, some fifty of
the chamber's industrialists and landlords formed the Shōwa Discussion
Group (Shōwa Kondankai) to defeat both the labor union bill and the
tenancy bill. The roster of participating industrialists reveals the im-
mense influence enjoyed by leaders of the Japan Industrial Club and
other powerful employers within the 400-member House of Peers:

Barons: Gō Seinosuke, Nakajima Kumakichi (both Industrial Club),
Nagamatsu Atsusuke, Kondō Shigeya, Akamatsu Norikazu

Imperial appointees: Naitō Hisahiro, Fujiwara Ginjirō, Nezu Kai-
chirō, Ōhashi Shintarō, Isomura Toyotarō, Hattori Kintarō, Ōkawa
Heisaburō, Makoshi Kyōhei (all Industrial Club), Inahata Katsutarō
(Osaka Chamber of Commerce and Industry), Yukawa Kankichi (Sumitomo enterprises), Imai Gosuke (Matsumoto Chamber)

Representatives of highest taxpayers: Mori Heibei (Osaka Chamber), Isogai Hiroshi (Nagoya Chamber), Mori Hirosaburō, Morita
Fukuichi, Tsuchida Mansuke, Kobayashi Kaheiji.[115]

The prominent role of big business in the House of Peers reflected the transformation of Japan's political leadership amid rapid industrialization. The fifty members of the Shōwa Discussion Group accounted for only a portion of the peers who felt economically threatened by labor unions. Baron Gō Seinosuke and Baron Nakajima Kumakichi represented the growing class of second-generation noblemen who had channeled their families' wealth and prestige into industry. Combined with other industrialists who had entered the House of Peers as untitled imperial appointees or highest taxpayers, they posed a formidable obstacle to the enactment of progressive labor legislation.

The coalition of businessmen, conservative peers, and Seiyūkai supporters proved more than sufficient to stop the labor union bill and the revision of the Labor Disputes Conciliation Law in committee. To ensure defeat, upper house leaders packed the committee with a Who's Who of leading industrialists—notably the Industrial Club's Gō Seinosuke, Nakajima Kumakichi, Naitō Hisahiro, Fujiwara Ginjirō, and Isomura Toyotarō. Seiyūkai partisans completed the antigovernment majority.[116] Landlords and businessmen shelved the tenancy bill in another committee. The women's civil rights bill was overwhelmingly voted down by the House of Peers, and the Privy Council had earlier bottled up the bill to lower the male voting age to twenty.[117]

THE DEATH OF LIBERAL SOCIAL POLICY

The House of Peers bore direct responsibility for the defeat of the labor union bill, but progressive journalists placed equal blame on the inept parliamentary tactics employed by the cabinet under Shidehara's direction. Baba Tsunego maintained that the government should have threatened the upper chamber with peerage reform, a threat that the Katō Takaaki cabinet had successfully used to pass the universal manhood suffrage bill in 1925.[118] The two issues, however, were quite different. Katō could count on widespread public support in the fight with the House of Peers over manhood suffrage. There is little reason to believe that the Minseitō in 1931 could have similarly united popular opinion behind the union bill against the well-organized business community, given the minuscule size of the labor movement.

The Minseitō's inability to enact labor union legislation stemmed from far more profound sources than factional strife or a lack of will on the part of Shidehara. The Fifty-ninth Diet marked the end of the decade of liberal reform. A Japanese government would not again introduce a labor union bill until the American Occupation in 1945. Hamaguchi had been defeated despite having forged the interwar era's strongest consensus on behalf of social and political reform, cooperative diplomacy, and the return to the gold standard. Since his ascendancy to the Minseitō presidency in 1927, he had attracted support from a broad constellation of forces, including the party's young politicians, moderate socialists, liberal intellectuals, prominent businessmen, Home Ministry officials, and other higher civil servants. These allies may not have favored every aspect of Hamaguchi's liberal program, yet they preferred the Minseitō's spirit of accommodation and reform to the Tanaka cabinet's reliance on military expansion and suppression of dissent.

Once in office, however, Prime Minister Hamaguchi discovered the costs of attempting even mild reform in a divided society and a rather tenuous parliamentary democracy. International disarmament and a conciliatory China policy antagonized powerful elements in the military, the Privy Council, and the House of Peers. His labor policy likewise ran into a brick wall of employers' opposition and conservative reaction in the House of Peers. Although historians often criticize the interwar parties for failing to advance meaningful changes, Hamaguchi's liberal proposals were vetoed for their boldness, not their insufficiency.

The onset of the Great Depression further discredited Hamaguchi's classically liberal blend of tight fiscal policy and social reform centered on the simple legal recognition of labor unions. The public, and parts of his own party, increasingly blamed the prime minister's return to the gold standard for intensifying the economic crisis. Alarmed at the growing incidence of rural poverty and failing small businesses, politicians and bureaucrats turned their attention away from labor problems to channeling direct relief to farmers and shopkeepers, who formed well over half of the population. Among the workers themselves, the most immediate need became relief and state-sponsored employment programs, not a labor union law that placed responsibility for one's welfare solely on the union.

With the close of the disastrous Fifty-ninth Diet in March 1931, most observers were skeptical of the Minseitō's ability to undertake significant social and political reforms in the near future. But few expected the total collapse of the party's progressive agenda. Wakatsuki Reijirō formally replaced the ailing Hamaguchi as prime minister in April. The Minseitō's trials on the home front soon paled before a graver challenge to the party's brand of liberalism. In September 1931, the Imperial Army occupied southern Manchuria in defiance of the cabinet. The

Manchurian Incident precipitated the fall of the Wakatsuki cabinet in December and ushered in a decade and a half of military expansion and war. The institution of party cabinets lingered on another five months in the form of a Seiyūkai government headed by Inukai Tsuyoshi. Following Inukai's assassination by young naval officers in May 1932, party cabinets gave way to a series of nonparty cabinets consisting of military men, career bureaucrats, and a dwindling number of party politicians.

The tumultuous events of 1931 and 1932 shattered the Minseitō-led coalition that supported labor legislation. Moderate labor leaders backed away from the bourgeois party that made lavish promises yet delivered little. Home Ministry officials began experimenting with more interventionist approaches to labor problems that did not involve cumbersome legislative approval. And the Minseitō lost most of its reformist leadership in a remarkably short span of time. Hamaguchi succumbed to his wounds in August 1931. Inoue Junnosuke, the former finance minister, was gunned down by right-wing terrorists the next January, and Egi Tasuku died in September 1932. Perhaps most devastating was the loss of Adachi Kenzō. The home minister left the Minseitō in December 1931, after party elders thwarted his plans to form an emergency coalition cabinet with the Seiyūkai.[119] The twenty-one Lower House members who followed Adachi had, in large part, been associated with the socially reformist "young politician" faction.

Against the backdrop of the Manchurian crisis, the Depression, and threats to the survival of the parties, Yoshioka Shigeyoshi, a proponent of trade unionism, sadly proclaimed the death of liberal labor policy in 1932: "labor union legislation, which had attracted the attention of all of society as a major historical issue, has become an exquisite luxury. Having no bearing on the grave times, it has been totally eliminated from the political agenda."[120] What had shortly before occupied a central position in Hamaguchi's plans to liberalize Japanese society vanished with scarcely a trace under the increasing authoritarianism of the 1930s.

CHAPTER VI

The Statist Solution, 1931–45

HENRY R. SACKETT [United States prosecutor]:	I would like to ask you to explain in your own words the difference between the rightists and leftists in Japan? I might say in my country we consider the rightists as conservatives and the leftists as liberals but you keep referring to the military group and others associated with it as being rightists. I can't bring myself around to think of them as conservatives. . . .
MARQUIS KIDO KŌICHI [Lord Keeper of the Privy Seal]:	In Japan, the rightists are those generally equivalent to the Fascists and the leftists are the socialists and communists. . . .
SACKETT:	Where do the conservatives fit into that group? . . .
KIDO:	The Zaibatsu is economically conservative and the two political parties, the Minseitō and the Seiyūkai, are both conservative parties.
SACKETT:	They are conservative as distinguished from the rightists? They would be called leftists, so the leftists are really the conservatives?
KIDO:	No. They are right in the middle. . . . And there are liberals in the conservatives. . . .

*—Preliminary interrogation, International
Military Tribunal for the Far East,
25 February 1946*[1]

Mr. Sackett may be forgiven his confusion regarding Japanese politics during the country's "Fifteen-Years War" (1931–45). It was a time when the press bandied ideological labels about, when self-styled "renovationists" (*kakushin-ha*) of various stripes struggled to rescue the state from "liberal" politicians and capitalists. To American Occupation authorities in 1945, the Japanese transgressions against liberal democracy were apparent enough. The parliamentary parties had steadily lost influence in successive "whole-nation cabinets" and were eventually pressured to dissolve themselves in 1940. The imperial government also engineered the dissolution of the nation's labor unions that same year and set up in their place the state-run Greater Japan Industrial Patriotic Association (Dai Nihon Sangyō Hōkokukai). But just *who* bore responsibility for Japan's authoritarian New Order was another matter. There was no Nazi or Fascist party, no takeover of the state by outside elements. Although nativist military officers and civilian rightists sought to overthrow parliamentary government and crush all Western ideologies, their influence waned following the failure of an attempted coup d'état by young army officers on 26 February 1936. The United States Occupation later singled out the Imperial Army's systematic intrusion into domestic politics. Yet it is clearer today that the military never attained the manpower or expertise necessary to rule at home.

Most evidence now points to the central role of the civilian bureaucracy in framing the authoritarian programs that would dominate Japan's home front from the early 1930s to 1945. The higher civil service crossed into the 1930s and 1940s fundamentally unchanged in terms of personnel and recruitment patterns. The phenomenon of bureaucratic continuity calls to mind Robert Paxton's observation about the contemporary Vichy regime: "At its height, . . . Vichy was more the creation of experts and professionals than of any other social group, and to judge Vichy is to judge the French elite."[2]

Beginning around 1934, numerous articles appeared in Japan describing the rise of powerful "new bureaucrats" or "renovationist bureaucrats" (*kakushin kanryō*), who proposed sweeping controls over economy and society. Indeed, several labor leaders looked to the "new military men" and "new bureaucrats" to "drive back the present bourgeois parties" and introduce the type of "totalitarian controlled economy" found in Fascist Italy, Nazi Germany, and the Soviet Union.[3] In actuality, the "new bureaucrats" were not new at all. Many had been known as progressive "new men" within the Home Ministry as far back as 1920 or had subsequently served in the Social Bureau. With the fall of party cabinets in 1932, some of those who came to be called "new bureaucrats" advanced to ministerial rank in the whole-nation cabinets, in part because of their recognized ability to deal with social problems. The great irony was that several of the social bureaucrats who championed the recognition of labor unions during the 1920s later pursued policies that led to the demise of organized labor in 1940.

One cannot hope to understand the nature of Japanese authoritarianism in the 1930s without considering the thought and behavior of the social bureaucrats during the previous decade. The New Order represented more than a victory for capitalists or the conservative unification of the Japanese people against foreign influences. In their search for a more totalitarian approach to industrial relations, the social bureaucrats exhibited many of the boldly "progressive" characteristics seen since 1919. Officials not only maintained their earlier faith in the predominance and autonomy of state interests (for example, social order, public health, and welfare), but substantially expanded their powers to regulate managerial actions regarding labor. Second, the bureaucrats recognized that the state could not simply revert to the conservative Meiji-era program of repressing workers' organizations. In the interests of promoting smooth labor-management relations, the wartime regime would have to grant workers a new type of organized voice. And third, a foreign model once again influenced the debate over domestic policy to an impressive degree. This time, however, the government's cosmopolitan specialists discovered the latest "trends of the world" in Nazi Germany.

We must not, on the other hand, lose sight of the changes that transformed labor policy after 1931. The 1930s were, above all, a time of war and preparation for war. The Japanese occupation of Manchuria in 1931–32 was followed by the outbreak of full-scale hostilities with China in 1937 and with the Western powers in 1941. Mindful of the country's international isolation, the "new bureaucrats" and union leaders alike retreated into a nationalistic "Japanism" that explicitly repudiated Anglo-American liberalism. Moreover, although the social bureaucrats formulated labor policy both before and after 1931 from the perspective of the state's interests, their definition of those interests changed significantly.

During the 1920s, the Home Ministry primarily aimed at social stabilization—that is, reducing the appeal of Communism and other radical ideologies by improving public welfare, encouraging labor unions, and extending the franchise. By the early 1930s, such social disorder was no longer a problem. The government had eradicated the Communist Party and affiliated associations, and the remaining labor and farmer organizations were undeniably moderate. Wartime mobilization of industrial labor became the leading priority. The new labor policy was decidedly statist in the sense that officials asserted controls over a relationship that previously had been conducted between workers and managers on a more or less autonomous basis. For the Japanese worker, the authoritarian labor measures resulted in what one labor scholar has termed a "dark valley" between the better times of the 1920s and the post-1945 era.[4] Yet, given the striking continuities in bureaucratic personnel, the war years were less of an aberration in terms of policy. The social bureaucrats devised the statist program in response to the perceived failures of liberal labor policies after 1931. But the search for solutions to the "labor question" in twentieth-century Japan was far from over.

LABOR'S TURN TO THE STATE

The bureaucrats did not revise labor policy entirely from above. Although the government's dissolution of the unions in 1940 followed the Nazi script in some respects, the underlying circumstances could not have been more different. One of Hitler's first acts in 1933 was to destroy Germany's free unions because the large, class-conscious labor movement represented a direct challenge to the consolidation of the Nazi party-state. No such threat existed in Japan, where organized labor enthusiastically embraced nationalism and state socialism during the 1930s. Stephen Large has taken Sōdōmei leaders to task for abandoning the "political struggle on behalf of socialism" in favor of the "narrow cause of unionism."[5] Yet he neither shows how the weak forces of labor could have stopped the drift toward authoritarianism and war, nor does he gauge the advantages of the movement's nationalist strategy. Ironically, union officials gained their greatest influence over governmental policy from 1932 to 1936 amid stagnation in actual unionization. To understand the movement's carefully conceived, if short-sighted, turn to the state, one must recognize the leadership's fears of isolation following the defeat of the 1931 labor union bill and the Manchurian Incident.

At the shopfloor level, the labor unions paid dearly for their failure to penetrate the large private enterprises. The Japanese economy rapidly recovered from the Great Depression after 1931, fueled in part by the government's crash armament program. A disproportionate amount of the expansion in the heavy industrial work force occurred in large companies with over one thousand employees.[6] Because the labor movement remained confined to small and medium-sized firms, the proportion of union members began declining after 1931, despite modest increases in the number of organized workers. Unions represented only 6.2 percent of industrial workers in 1937, down from 7.9 percent in 1931.

On the political front, too, labor leaders found themselves cut off from erstwhile allies in the Minseitō. Socialist deputies ritualistically introduced labor union legislation to a hostile Diet throughout the first half of the 1930s. Even if a nonparty cabinet wished to sponsor labor reform, it faced formidable opposition from the Seiyūkai, which held an enormous majority in the Lower House from 1932 to 1936. Above all, industrialists formed a far more potent and united pressure group than in the previous decade. Japanese employers had organized the National Federation of Industrial Organizations in 1931 specifically to resist future labor union legislation. The National Federation prevented the government from introducing any major labor bills until 1936 and thereafter weakened most such legislation.[7] Except for a few social policy experts and younger politicians, Minseitō members also adopted the language, if not the positions, of the National Federation. On the eve of the 1936 general election, the Minseitō's campaign platform blasted the notion of "Labor-Capital harmony, which is based on labor unions," for having "exacerbated class struggle, destroyed industry, and deepened the instability in living conditions." Concluded the once liberal party: "The existence of labor unions has taken on the appearance of a cancerous growth in industry."[8]

At the same time, politicians and bureaucrats shifted their attention to other social problems amid the widely perceived "state of emergency" (hijōji) associated with the Manchurian Incident and the Depression. In 1934, Sōdōmei chairman Matsuoka Komakichi lamented that the "problems of the farm villages have been on everyone's lips of late, but the problems of factory workers are equally acute."[9] No government had ever extended a Diet session over labor legislation, yet the cabinet of Okada Keisuke called a special session in August 1932 to approve several relief measures for hard-pressed farmers. Under the new leadership of former Social Bureau director Yoshida Shigeru, the Kyōchōkai devoted the November 1932 issue of its journal to "A Reexamination of Social Policy." In his preface, Yoshida decreed that relations between labor and capital no longer were the sole object of social policy.[10] Over the next two years, the Kyōchōkai and Social Bureau turned to the pressing issues of rural poverty and failing small businesses.[11] Declared a spokesman for the Social Bureau in 1935:

> These are not the times to be discussing the enactment of a Labor Union Law, revision of the [Labor] Disputes Conciliation Law, or any other legal system for organized labor which would grant powerful rights to workers who [already] generally enjoy a much higher standard of living than the destitute farmers.[12]

Finally, socialist union leaders confronted a new challenge from the emerging ultrarightist labor movement. The patriotic labor organizations may be roughly divided into two categories—the "national socialists" and the "Japanists." The national socialists vocally supported the use of military means to protect Japan's economic interests in Manchuria and China, while looking to European fascism for models of a totalitarian state. Most had been socialists before breaking with the proletarian parties after the Manchurian Incident, and they maintained their antipathy toward capitalists. The national-socialist unions, however, failed to overcome sectarian divisions and the stigma of their European inspiration. By 1934, most had either faded away or adopted the less radical rhetoric of "Japanism."[13]

The Japanist labor movement represented a far more potent threat to trade unionism, for it denied the existence of conflicting interests between Labor and Capital. In the judgment of some scholars, the Japanist unions came the closest to constituting a truly fascist movement in the sense of a vehemently antisocialist, mass-based front.[14] The phenomenon, moreover, had an indigenous character, predating the Manchurian Incident and the vogue of fascist models. The founding father was Kamino Shin'ichi, a skilled workman and foreman at the large Ishikawajima Shipyard. As a result of a company-sponsored trip to Europe via Asia in 1920, Kamino became convinced that all Japanese must cooperate against Western colonialism and racial discrimination. To break the hold of Ishikawajima's strike-prone leftist union, he subsequently joined forces with management to instill loyalty and patriotism in the workers. In 1926, Kamino formed the pioneer patriotic union, the Ishikawajima Jikyōkai Labor Union. He gradually drew similar unions at other shipyards into the Japan League of Shipbuilding Workers (Nihon Zōsen Rōdō Remmei), whose obvious interests in naval expansion had much to do with surging nationalism among the workers.[15] The league in turn united the Japanist movement into the Japan Industrial Labor Club (Nihon Sangyō Rōdō Kurabu). In April 1936, the club joined with like-minded organizations to form the National Association of Patriotic Labor Unions (Aikoku Rōdō Kumiai Zenkoku Konwakai), which altogether counted 47,000 members.

The Japan Industrial Labor Club rejected nearly every tenet of the Sōdōmei-led trade union movement. Putting national productivity before self-interest, the Japanist activists repudiated the standard unionist goal of the "unconditional maintenance and improvement of working conditions." Preferring the "fusion" (yūgō) of labor and capital to the goal of mere "harmony," they attacked the Sōdōmei's dedication to "industrial cooperation" and collective agreements. Both objectives allegedly stemmed from Sōdōmei's "class-oriented perspective." Japanist labor organizations made no demands for structural changes in the capitalist order; they simply sought to "purify the hearts" of employers. The horizontal links between Japanist unions caused concern among some industrialists, who feared the rise of another class-conscious movement. With a few exceptions, however, Japanist organizations avoided strikes and remained based on company unions, which collaborated with managers against outside trade unions.[16]

In an effort to escape further isolation, the trade union movement took two major steps. After years of feuding, an alliance was concluded between the rival labor blocs affiliated with the Social Democratic Party and the centrist National Labor–Farmer Masses' Party. Formalized in September 1932, the Congress of Japanese Labor Unions (Nihon Rōdō Kumiai Kaigi) encompassed eleven organizations and 220,000 members (or 64 percent of the nation's unionists). As leader of the larger Social Democratic bloc, Sōdōmei infused the congress with its longstanding mission of economically oriented "sound trade unionism." The two major proletarian parties merged that same year into the Social Masses' Party (Shakai Taishūtō).

Second, Sōdōmei and the Congress of Japanese Labor Unions adopted a strategy of tactical nationalism. Put simply, labor leaders appropriated the language of the patriotic Right, asserting that the needs of national unity demanded that the state place unions on an equal level with capitalists. Although Sōdōmei and the Social Masses' Party publicly opposed "fascism," they found the doctrine of national socialism useful in practice. Sōdōmei's journal sounded the call for a "totalistic planned economy" and the "development of whole-nation industry," just one month after the Manchurian Incident.[17] Federation spokesmen blessed the nation's mission in Manchuria much as many Western socialists had earlier supported "social imperialism."[18] They criticized the army's specific plans to create an "independent" Manchukuo, but endorsed Japan's economic control of Manchuria because "the large advanced nations—the United States, Great Britain, and France—have monopolized the world's important territories and resources, blocking the free development of the people of other nations." In the "struggle for racial survival," they stressed, Japanese labor favored greater national self-sufficiency at a time when Western workers demanded tariffs against Japanese goods and the expulsion of Japanese immigrants.[19]

The real enemy, however, was not the West, but what the Congress of Japanese Labor Unions termed the "nonproductive, nonsocial, and nonnational character of capitalism." To help check these tendencies, the congress pledged to "participate in the state administration of industry."[20] On 17 November 1933, the organization presented cabinet ministers with a remarkable "Memorial on the Control of Industry and Labor." The labor movement essentially offered to surrender a large degree of autonomy to state officials in exchange for legal recognition and the regulation of employers. The petition naturally requested enactment of a labor union law and a collective agreements law. Yet it also proposed a revision of the 1926 Labor Disputes Conciliation Law that would allow officials to order conciliation, and, if necessary, arbitrate any dispute in the private, as well as public, sectors. In addition to the eventual nationalization or national management of important industries, the plan called for cartelizing small and medium-sized manufacturers into trade associations, in which labor unions would participate. Because workers and employers could not do so on their own, the government was to create "industrial cooperation councils" at the national, prefectural, and industrial levels. Responsible for negotiating collective agreements and other matters, the councils would be chaired respectively by a minister of state, prefectural governors, and lower officials, and they would consist of representatives of labor, management, and consumers.[21] The memorial inspired the leading demands of the congress over the next several years.

The "Memorial on the Control of Labor and Industry" introduced the concept of corporatism into the Japanese debate concerning the restructuring of industrial relations. As elucidated by the political scientist Philippe Schmitter, corporatism is a system of interest representation in which the constituent units are organized into a limited number of singular, compulsory, noncompetitive, hierarchically ordered and functionally differentiated categories, recognized or licensed (if not created) by the state and granted a deliberate representational monopoly within their respective categories in exchange for observing certain controls on their selection of leaders and articulation of demands and supports.[22]

Indeed, the authors of the memorial freely acknowledged the influence of Fascist Italy's system of national syndicates and corporations. In the case of Italian industry, the state officially recognized and granted exclusive rights to conclude labor contracts to two national syndicates, one representing employers and the other the Fascist Party's unions.[23] Nonetheless, the Japanese labor leaders preferred what Schmitter labels "societal corporatism" (versus "state corporatism") in their insistence on the continued existence of independent trade unions. Having formed the National Federation of Industrial Organizations in 1931, Japanese employers already possessed a hierarchy of industrial associations to unify and convey their positions on labor policy.[24] The founding of the Congress of Japanese Labor Unions offered the prospect of state-supervised negotiations between labor and employers' associations at various levels. Or so union leaders hoped.

The labor movement's corporatist vision did not stop at theory. Led by Sōdōmei, the congress launched an "industrial cooperation campaign" that resulted in a record number of collective agreements. In 1931, Sōdōmei had a mere 23 accords covering 3,669 workers; the totals jumped to 62 (9,418 workers) in 1934 and peaked in 1937 at 120 (10,780). The increase was related to the unions' successes in dealing directly with the trade associations of small and medium-sized producers on an industry-wide basis. Employers in smaller industries were sometimes willing to grant concessions to unions if their competitors did the same. In 1934, for example, a Sōdōmei union negotiated a pact with the Bulb Association (Barubukai), covering 210 separate shops and 1,012 workers in the electric-bulb industry of the Tokyo-Yokohama area.[25]

To facilitate communication with managers, Sōdōmei and the congress concurrently sponsored a series of regional "industrial cooperation conferences" during 1933 and 1934. Labor leaders routinely included sympathetic officials from the Social Bureau, the police, and the Kyōchōkai.[26] At a typical conference held in Hiroshima prefecture, Sōdōmei's chairman, Matsuoka Komakichi, explained how collective bargaining averted strikes and saved companies money. He was followed by the prefectural governor and former Social Bureau official, Yuzawa Michio, who praised Matsuoka as a patriot "steeped in the Japanese spirit."[27] Some have pronounced the campaign for collective bargaining a "dismal failure" because the agreements covered less than 10 percent of Japanese unionists, excluding seamen and their officers.[28] Nevertheless, the labor unions gained unprecedented legitimacy in the eyes of officials and many smaller employers.

The movement's drive to implement socialism through the state made for strange bedfellows. The most famous case involved the Army Ministry's release of a pamphlet entitled "The Basic Principles of National Defense and Proposals to Strengthen It" in October 1934. Prepared by officers associated with the army's "Control Faction," the document denounced laissez-faire liberalism as an obstacle to national mobilization. The officers instead proposed a controlled economy and "national defense in the broad sense." The pamphlet provoked a torrent of criticism from the press, the two major parties, and other opponents of military interference in domestic politics. In contrast, it received the enthusiastic support of Asō Hisashi, secretary-general of the Social Masses' Party. At the annual convention of the Congress of Japanese Labor Unions in 1934, Asō lauded the "young officers" for realizing that a good defense required improvements in the health and welfare of farmers and workers. Sloughing off his party's commitment to "antifascism," the secretary-general also cheered on the "new bureaucrats" in their struggle against the "bourgeois parties."[29]

Although many in the Social Masses' Party condemned Asō's ties to right-wing army officers, socialist and labor leaders held the "new bureaucrats" in much greater esteem. The definition of a new bureaucrat varied considerably according to the observer and the year.[30] In 1935, the term referred primarily to the Home Ministry group surrounding the former social bureaucrats, Gotō Fumio and Yoshida Shigeru. Gotō served as the dynamic home minister in the nonparty Okada Keisuke cabinet (1934–36), and Yoshida headed the new Cabinet Research Bureau (Naikaku Chōsakyoku). The Okada cabinet created the supraministerial bureau in 1935 to formulate policies for the nation's quasi-wartime society. Echoing Asō, an official of Sōdōmei was effusive in his praise of the "new military men" and "new bureaucrats" of the Cabinet Research Bureau. He acknowledged that the new bureaucrats sought to revise, rather than dismantle, capitalism, but he believed that their social policies would "little by little liberate the working class from the yoke of capitalism."[31]

Organized labor's turn to the state did not go unrewarded. Home Ministry officials viewed the Social Masses' Party and its affiliated labor movement as political allies against the opponents of greater governmental intervention. In the general election of 20 February 1936, the Social Masses' Party won an unprecedented eighteen seats in the Lower House. The momentum continued, and the party garnered thirty-seven seats in April 1937. These substantial gains were due, in part, to the unification of the proletarian parties and to the party's ability to appeal beyond trade unionists to farmers and salaried employees. However, the Home Ministry also appears to have played a major role, at least in 1936. Police officials not only refrained from the usual harassment of proletarian candidates, but actually provided assistance.[32] One generally reliable newspaper dubbed the Social Masses' Party the "pet of the Home Ministry's new bureaucrats." To check the strength of the established parties, officials of the Home Ministry and the Ministry of Agriculture and Forestry reportedly attempted to forge a mass party based on the Social Masses' Party and the growing movement of agricultural and producers' cooperatives (sangyō kumiai). Several socialist candidates received speakers and money from the government-sponsored cooperative organizations.[33]

The national-socialist strategy paid additional dividends in the form of new social legislation. On 26 February 1936, ultranationalist young officers affiliated with the army's Imperial Way Faction attempted to overthrow the Okada cabinet for placing restraints on the military's soaring budget. Rebel troops murdered several national leaders, including the finance minister and the preceding prime minister. Although loyal troops suppressed the uprising, the outcome was of small consolation to the enemies of authoritarian rule. The succeeding Hirota Kōki cabinet (March 1936–February 1937) introduced "fascism from above," in the words of one scholar.[34] Allied with the army's Control Faction, the new government significantly reduced the established parties' influence in the cabinet and effectively prohibited the socialist movement's celebration of May Day 1936. Incredibly enough, Sōdōmei's top officials, Matsuoka Komakichi and Nishio Suehiro, vigorously defended Hirota before their comrades in October. The Hirota cabinet was far from "reactionary," protested Chairman Matsuoka; on the contrary, its commitment to "national defense in the broad sense" had finally elevated the issues of national health and sanitation and other "renovationist" policies. (When a skeptical labor leader asked about the ban on May Day, Nishio replied that Hirota had surely not known about it beforehand!)[35]

Matsuoka had a point. The Hirota cabinet breathed new life into a number of labor bills earlier proposed by the Social Bureau but effectively bottled up by the National Federation of Industrial Organizations and other business groups. In May 1936, the government introduced the first of these, the retirement fund bill (*taishoku tsumitatekin oyobi taishoku teate hōan*). The debate was the clearest evidence to date of the realignment of forces supporting social policy. Prompted by the National Federation, the Seiyūkai and most of the Minseitō attacked the measure as yet another military-bureaucratic encroachment on managerial autonomy. By contrast, the Social Masses' Party and the Congress of Japanese Labor Unions actively supported the Home Ministry's bill, both inside and outside the Diet. Union leaders had resolved not to repeat the past mistake of opposing or appearing to oppose any governmental legislation that was less than perfect. Following the passage of a compromise version, grateful Home Ministry officials appointed Matsuoka and two other Sōdōmei members to serve on the committee charged with drafting the crucial ordinances to implement the Retirement Fund Law.[36]

The irony did not escape contemporary observers. The Social Masses' Party had become the "quasi-governmental party."[37] By collaborating with the government, Sōdōmei soon realized other longstanding legislative demands—the revision of the Seamen's Law (1937), a protective Shops Law (1938) for commercial employers, and the National Health Insurance Law (1938). Whereas the established parties and big business put up determined resistance to the wartime regime's attempts to usurp parliamentary prerogatives and regulate private enterprise, the Social Masses' Party enthusiastically backed the Electric Power Control Law and the sweeping National General Mobilization Law in 1938.[38] The labor movement's proponents of "realism" appeared vindicated in their reliance on the bureaucracy to improve the lot of the worker. But if they believed that organized labor had finally become a pillar of the state apparatus, they were greatly deluded.

SEARCH FOR A NEW LABOR POLICY, 1931–36

The labor movement's turn to the state largely explains why governmental policy toward organized labor did not change dramatically between 1932 and 1936, despite increasing authoritarianism. As they had throughout the 1920s, Home Ministry officials welcomed each new step toward "sound trade unionism" and "industrial cooperation." By 1934, representatives of the Social Bureau regularly attended the annual conventions of Sōdōmei and the Congress of Japanese Labor Unions, and the home minister and the bureau director sent warm words of greeting.[39] The authorities were particularly gratified by the public commitment of most federations to "minimize strikes" following the Manchurian Incident.[40]

The social bureaucrats' continued encouragement of labor unions retained key elements of what they themselves termed the "liberal" policies of the 1920s. Visions of a controlled economy aside, officials acknowledged that the state could not simply impose industrial peace from above. Ideally, Home Ministry officials wished to see all workers represented by some type of labor organization that could advance members' welfare and rationally resolve differences with employers. In actuality, there were few alternatives to the trade unions. Factory councils and company unions did not exist in the vast majority of small and medium-sized firms, the scene of most labor disputes.[41] The limits of the Japanist labor movement were equally apparent by 1936. Hampered by managerial suspicions of horizontal linkages, the patriotic unions failed to form a strong central organization.[42] According to a spokesman for the Social Bureau, the declining patriotic unions numbered a mere 44,000 members in June 1936. By contrast, the social democratic Congress of Japanese Labor Unions counted 220,000 members, and its political influence was strengthened by the recent electoral success of the Social Masses' Party.[43]

Indeed, the Social Bureau and the Kyōchōkai closely paralleled the Congress of Japanese Labor Unions in their corporatist vision of labor-management relations during the first half of the 1930s. Recognizing the benefits of a united labor movement, Kyōchōkai officials had served as go-betweens in the formation of the Social Masses' Party in 1932. They provided the same service in January 1936, when Sōdōmei and the largest centrist federation merged into the All-Japan General Federation of Labor (Zen Nihon Rōdō Sōdōmei), or Zen Sōdōmei.[44] Soon after the failure of the labor union bill in the spring of 1931, the Social Bureau embarked on an "industrial cooperation campaign." Anticipating organized labor's "Memorial on the Control of Industry and Labor," bureau leaders looked forward to sponsoring a series of central and local "labor-management conferences," at which industrialists and union representatives could discuss methods of setting standards for wages and hours, lowering production costs, and settling disputes.[45] In contrast to their more passive stance during the 1920s, Home Ministry and Kyōchō-kai personnel actively encouraged employers to conclude collective agreements with the unions.[46] Hoping to improve conditions in small and medium-sized companies, officials especially welcomed the labor movement's commitment to bargaining with trade associations.[47]

Nonetheless, for all the official sympathy for "sound trade union-ism," it was becoming clear that unions no longer constituted the cen-tral focus of labor policy. Labor unions, after all, accounted for less than 8 percent of industrial workers. Furthermore, the defeat of the 1931 labor union bill had prompted a serious reexamination of past policy. Home Ministry officials conceded the hopelessness of passing a progressive labor union law in the foreseeable future.[48] The previous decade's English model of minimizing labor-management conflict was, for all practical purposes, dead. Without actually repudiating trade unionism, the Social Bureau and police began experimenting with more interventionist methods of maintaining industrial harmony and improv-ing workers' welfare.

The search for a new labor policy was also bound up with the "renovationist" ideology of the "new bureaucrats." The Japanese occu-pation of Manchuria unleashed a wave of extreme nationalism, which only intensified in the face of international criticism and Japan's with-drawal from the League of Nations in 1933. Previous accounts of Japa-nese ultranationalism have focused on right-wing ideologues and the military while generally neglecting the civilian bureaucracy. The Home Ministry in fact emerged at the head of a massive bureaucratic drive to apply indigenous solutions or the "Japanese spirit" to domestic prob-lems, including labor questions.

In January 1934, the Tōkyō nichinichi shimbun described the great interest in the "Japanese spirit" among the Home Ministry's junior and senior bureaucrats, some of whom collaborated with young military officers.[49] Although Social Bureau officials were known for their knowl-edge of the West, the Social Bureau's young administrative officers reportedly formed groups to study the "Japanese spirit" more quickly than in any bureau other than the Police Bureau. One such activist was Kurihara Minoru. Returning from his tour of the West in 1932, the twenty-nine-year-old labor specialist took on the task of promoting a "Japanese-style labor movement." He became an active contributor to the journal Shakai undō ōrai (Comings and goings of the social movement), whose editors similarly worked to unite the various Japanist and national-socialist unions. The journal brought together a broad array of "renovationist" bureaucrats in the Social Bureau, the Police Bureau, and especially the Kyōchōkai.[50]

At the most senior level, Yoshida Shigeru emerged as the high priest of administrative Japanism. He wielded considerable influence over the social bureaucrats through his successive leadership of the Social Bureau (1929–31), the Kyōchōkai (1931–34), and the Cabinet Research Bureau (1935–36). Unlike the Home Ministry's more specialized labor experts, Yoshida had worked closely with the military and civilian Right since his days as an administrator of the state-sponsored Shinto shrines. While he favored governmental protection of workers, he also sought to reduce social unrest by using the shrines to "unify the people's spirit around the Emperor." Moreover, he returned from his tour of the United States and Europe in 1923 less impressed with foreign models than were his peers. The Westerners' insistence on rights and self-interests bothered him the most.[51] In January 1932, Yoshida and another Home Ministry veteran, Gotō Fumio, helped to found the National Mainstay Society (Kokuikai), a discussion group of leading army officers and "new bureaucrats." The well-known nationalist and Confucian scholar, Yasuoka Masaatsu, provided the spiritual inspiration. In addition to lecturing on the incomparable nature of Japan's imperial institution and Shinto traditions, Yasuoka called for purging the nation of the alleged Western imports of selfishness and materialism.[52]

The cult of Japanism affected the course of labor policy in two significant ways. First, although their nationalism was undoubtedly genuine, Home Ministry officials happily rode its crest to win unprecedented autonomy for the state and themselves vis-à-vis private interests— parties, capitalists, and labor unions. After a decade of accepting a subordinate role under party cabinets, the ambitious civil servants now asserted that, as classless "officials of the Emperor," they alone possessed the traditional neutrality and talent necessary to alleviate pressing social and economic problems. The Home Ministry's disdain for capitalists (though not capitalism itself) was evident in such slogans as "Eradicate the evils of the parties and the zaibatsu" and "Let the officials take a strong role in building the New Japan."[53]

The statist thrust of Japanism thus made it more than an escape into conservative nativism. Yoshida Shigeru might trumpet the glories of indigenous solutions, yet as director of the Cabinet Research Bureau in 1935, he immediately ordered detailed studies of authoritarian policies in Germany, Italy, and the Soviet Union. As Yoshida admitted, the "Japanese spirit" was not a precise "doctrine or set of demands defined in opposition to other theoretical 'isms.'" Rather, one studied the "Great Way of our gods" to understand all other knowledge.[54] Japanism was further equated with the rejection of Anglo-American liberalism. To justify their abandonment of "liberal" labor union legislation, Social Bureau officials unflinchingly pointed to the world-wide ascendancy of "ideologies of statism and control that have superseded past ideas of socialism and liberalism."[55]

Second, the rising tide of nationalism discredited the very concept of trade unionism, predicated as it was on the recognition of conflicting interests between classes. The Home Ministry and the Kyōchōkai actively patronized the Japanist labor organizations.[56] Yoshida and others viewed Kamino Shin'ichi's Jikyō Labor Union as a prototype for a national movement of patriotic unions in every workplace. Kamino himself had long been the darling of the National Mainstay Society and the *Shakai undō ōrai* crowd. In the judgment of Gotō Fumio, Kamino "has ensured the existence of the nation's industry by awakening both workers and capitalists to the fact that they are Japanese and must together cast off their selfish motivations."[57] The policy of supporting Japanist labor was not so much intended to supplant the trade unions as to pressure them into similarly placing "service to the nation and industry" (*sangyō hōkoku*) above class interests. In May 1935, the Home Ministry formally abandoned the concept of "harmony between Labor and Capital" in favor of the Japanist objective of the "unity of Labor and Capital" (*rōshi ittaishugi*). Home Minister Gotō Fumio instructed police to "foster a moral spirit by which both Labor and Capital work for all of the nation and industry, oblivious to private advantage."[58]

Imbued with a mission to control capitalists as well as workers, the Home Ministry intruded on the shopfloor to a degree undreamed of before 1931. The extralegal regulation of smaller firms was a notable example. A permanent feature of Japan's industrial structure, family-based manufacturing and handicraft shops mushroomed amid the post-1932 export boom. By 1934, the Social Bureau regarded the poor working conditions in the shops as the foremost labor problem, blaming excessive competition for the exceptionally low wages and appallingly long hours. Yet the state's only corrective, the Factory Law, excluded 20 percent of all workers in private industry, most of whom labored in the smallest undertakings. Then there was the international dimension. To the embarrassment of the Japanese government, Western delegates to the 1934 International Labor Conference complained bitterly of Japan's reliance on sweated labor and "social dumping" to flood their markets with inexpensive goods.

As a remedy, the Social Bureau ordered prefectural officials to "guide and encourage" trade associations in the worst industries to restrict hours and correct other abuses.[59] The government achieved far greater success than the labor unions in this regard. Factory inspectors and the police persuaded several trade associations to adopt regulations covering member firms throughout entire prefectures or regions. Dressmakers in kimono shops, for example, sometimes worked from 7:00 A.M. to 1:30 or 2:00 the next morning. Thanks to official intervention in Osaka prefecture, the Kimono Merchants' and Manufacturers' Association agreed in September 1934 to a number of restrictions, including limiting daily hours to nine, eleven, or thirteen, depending on the season. The pact regulated conditions for five thousand employees, or over half of the prefecture's kimono workers.

In the absence of a widespread labor movement, state officials took it upon themselves to represent workers' interests in direct bargaining with employers' organizations. The Social Bureau soon sought a more systematic solution. In February 1935, the bureau revealed plans to sponsor a bill to strengthen agreements on working conditions (rōdō jōken ni kansuru kyōtei ni kansuru hōritsuan). If two-thirds of a trade association's members petitioned the authorities, prefectural officials could legally extend the provisions of the association's agreement on improving working conditions to all firms engaged in the same industry within the locale.[60] To the manufacturers' associations, the bill opened the door to unrestrained compulsion by the state. The powerful National Federation of Industrial Organizations pointed to existing agreements as evidence that accords often arose from "pressure on the part of the authorities rather than the voluntary initiative of the employers concerned."[61] Sōdōmei's labor leaders supported the Social Bureau's draft, but resolute opposition from the business community prevented the legislation from being introduced.[62]

Although the bill to strengthen agreements on working conditions failed, the Home Ministry's determination to protect workers resulted in the previously mentioned flurry of social legislation from 1935 to 1938. The first measure passed was the controversial Retirement Fund Law of 1936. In its final form, the act required all companies with fifty or more employees to establish a retirement fund, to be financed by joint contributions by workers and employers. Upon leaving the firm, workers received a lump sum, the amount depending on whether they had reached retirement age, were dismissed, or had quit. The Social Bureau had been exploring methods of insulating workers from the recurrent dangers of unemployment since the Depression days of 1931. The Retirement Fund Law also emerged from the Home Ministry's concern for employees in small and medium-sized firms. Whereas most enterprises with more than three hundred employees had already implemented some form of retirement or severance pay, few smaller firms had such provisions. The Social Bureau's initial public draft in 1935 would have extended the practice to all companies employing ten or more persons.[63] In keeping with the nationalist spirit of the times, the bureaucrats astutely promoted the retirement fund bill as a "Japanese" alternative to Western-style unemployment insurance.[64]

Nonetheless, the National Federation of Industrial Organizations attacked the retirement fund bill with a fury not seen since the battle over labor union legislation. Social Bureau officials were vociferously denounced as "Reds."[65] The objections of the industrialists and fellow travelers in the Diet are by now familiar. The legislation would (1) take "our country's beautiful customs" of employer benevolence and reduce them to the worker's right to retirement and severance pay; (2) hurt small and medium-sized manufacturers; and (3) encourage strikes to force employers to contribute more to the fund, inasmuch as the measure required companies to contribute at least 2 percent of a worker's wages.[66] The National Federation retreated from total opposition only after the renovationist Hirota cabinet pledged to enact measures to "stabilize the people's livelihood" at all costs. In the final compromise, the business lobby managed, among other things, to restrict the provisions of the law to enterprises with fifty or more employees. But the bureaucrats gained as well. The law resulted in the creation of new retirement funds in a majority of large companies and in almost all the small and medium-sized firms covered.[67]

The Social Bureau successfully sponsored two other major bills, which significantly broadened the scope of social legislation beyond blue-collar workers in factories and mines. Enacted in 1938, the Shops Law (Shōtenhō) marked the government's first attempt to regulate working hours and set safety standards in commercial establishments. The statute affected 1,395,000 employees working in stores and hairdressing shops in cities and their environs. The prime targets were neighborhood stores and shops, which stayed open well into the night, seven days a week, in order to compete with department stores and each other. With a few exceptions, the Shops Law compelled all affected establishments to close at 10:00 nightly and to shut down entirely once a month. In stores with fifty or more employees, women and children under sixteen were restricted to an eleven-hour work day with at least two days of vacation per month. Small shopkeepers tended to oppose the constraints on flexible operating hours, but most metropolitan chambers of commerce supported the rather mild legislation because it promised to curb the worst abuses of competition.[68]

The Diet also passed the National Health Insurance Law in 1938. The measure represented Japan's most comprehensive piece of social legislation before 1945, for it offered benefits to the general population. First drafted by the Social Bureau in 1934, the legislation specifically aimed at arresting the alarming deterioration of health in the economically depressed countryside. The original Health Insurance Law of 1922 had set up a compulsory insurance system only for wage earners in larger factories and mines (extended in 1934 to those in industrial enterprises employing five or more). The new National Health Insurance Law facilitated the creation of health insurance associations by cooperatives and trade associations, besides cities, towns, and villages. The government supplemented members' contributions with subsidies. Participation and the establishment of insurance associations was originally voluntary, although the wartime regime soon made both compulsory.[69] Taking stock of the Home Ministry's legislative offensive of 1936, one yearbook of labor affairs described the advent of "totalitarian" or "statist social policy" as the government assumed more and more responsibility for activities previously sponsored by employers, private social services, and labor and farmer groups.[70]

Finally, the lure of statist solutions influenced the Home Ministry's actions regarding labor disputes more than in any other area. The trend toward official arbitration was not entirely new. Police officers had long played a prominent role in mediating disputes. Prefectural conciliation officers assumed primary responsibility in 1926. Between 1930 and 1934, major strikes in public transportation prompted Home Ministry leaders to order conciliation proceedings six times under the previously unused Labor Disputes Conciliation Law of 1926. Committees chaired by Yoshida Shigeru of the Kyōchōkai settled two such strikes by Tokyo streetcar workers in 1932 and 1934.[71] Although the number of strikes noticeably declined after 1931, authorities feared a resurgence as massive rearmament fueled inflation and workers' demands for higher wages.

During 1934 and 1935, the Social Bureau again attempted to strengthen the ineffectual Labor Disputes Conciliation Law. The existing statute prevented the government from legally settling the era's many strikes in strategic firms that produced for the military yet were not actually managed by the state. The proposed revision would have granted officials sweeping discretionary powers to compel conciliation and, in effect, arbitrate in disputes involving privately owned companies.[72] Whereas Sōdōmei leaders wholeheartedly supported the Social Bureau's revision, the National Federation of Industrial Organizations pressured the government into killing the bill before it reached the Diet.[73] As in 1931, employers were dead set against empowering officials to impose settlements.

When a revised Conciliation Law did not seem be forthcoming, the assertive Home Ministry stepped up efforts to arbitrate disputes at the administrative level. In a departure from the previous policy of mediating strikes after they broke out, the Social Bureau in 1935 ordered police and conciliation officers to "prevent disputes from occurring" (funsō o mizen ni bōshi suru). Officials were instructed to intervene at the earliest possible moment, even to organize "labor-management discussion councils" (rōshi kondankai) to bring the two sides together beforehand.[74] Table 8 indicates the profound impact on the resolution of disputes. The proportion of all disputes settled by outside, primarily

TABLE VIII   MEDIATION OF LABOR DISPUTES, 1929–36

		Disputes mediated		Mediator/Disputes mediated		
	Total disputes	No.	Percent	Conciliation officers	Police officers	Others
1929	1,419	386	27%	33%	24%	43%
1930	2,283	658	29	37	24	39
1931	2,456	684	28	37	26	37
1932	2,217	626	28	29	33	39
1933	1,897	600	32	25	35	40
1934	1,915	600	31	25	40	35
1935	1,872	746	40	22	56	22
1936	1,975	817	41	20	62	18

SOURCE: Nishinarita, "Manshū," pp. 288–89.

governmental, mediation jumped in 1935 to 40 percent. Also noteworthy, the Home Ministry became so committed to preventing strikes
that most of the mediated disputes were again settled by ordinary
police officers, rather than professional conciliation officers. Official
conciliation was often heavy-handed, to say the least. By 1935, mediators intervened without any formal request from either interested party
in 75 percent of all conciliated settlements.[75] Japanese scholars have
appropriately called such practices "saber mediation."[76]

The Japanese state had staked out a position of relatively great autonomy by the beginning of 1936. Its propensity to control both labor and
management rose in proportion to the perceived need for unimpeded
military-industry mobilization. The policy of preventing strikes emerged
in part from fears of future hostilities with the Anglo-American powers
following Japan's decision to abrogate the Washington Naval Treaty
(notice given in December 1934) and its withdrawal from the London
Naval Conference in January 1936.[77] Yet how did these state actions
respectively affect employers and workers? A great deal of antipathy
clearly existed between Home Ministry bureaucrats and capitalists. In
their instructions to prefectural police, directors of the Social Bureau
typically praised the labor unions for promoting "industrial patriotism
and industrial cooperation." On the other hand, they ordered police to
exert pressure on the many employers who "have taken advantage of
the present social situation to harden their attitudes" against organized
labor.[78] Managers particularly resented "saber mediation" by the Special Higher Police, whose officers took pride in their ability to distinguish between cooperative trade unionists and dangerous Communists.
One veteran of the elite force recalled how angry he would become
when "some stubborn company president" refused to talk to union
leaders.[79]

Nevertheless, the new statism hardly elevated the position of workers
to the extent predicted by "realistic" union leaders. One need only look
at the outcome of conciliation in the 1934 Tokyo streetcar strike, often
cited as a prime example of bureaucratic even-handedness. Yoshida
Shigeru rammed a "compromise" settlement through the conciliation
committee that would reduce wages 20 percent. When the social democratic union rejected the proposal and resumed the strike, Yoshida simply negotiated with a Japanist union that stayed on the job. The police,
for their part, arrested several strike leaders and protected scabs until
the hapless union agreed to accept Yoshida's terms.[80] In the face of the
Home Ministry's aggressive drive to regulate working conditions and

prevent disputes, the labor unions were rapidly losing not only the right to strike, but also their central function of representing the interests of workers.

UNIONS BYPASSED: THE INDUSTRIAL PATRIOTIC MOVEMENT, 1936–40

For all their experimentation with more interventionist labor policies between 1931 and 1935, officials at least recognized the contributions of the existing unions to orderly industrial relations. The year 1936 marked the beginning of an assault on the raison d'être of trade unionism by various groups within the government and semigovernmental agencies. All sides agreed on the desirability of an alternative model of labor organization to the trade unions, though they differed on specifics. The reexamination of industrial relations emerged from the long-term drift toward statist policies, but key developments during 1936 and 1937 provided the immediate impetus. The most apparent of these involved new pressures from the army to place the entire economy, including labor policy, on a total wartime footing. Although junior officers failed in the attempted coup of 26 February 1936, the army high command persuaded the succeeding Hirota cabinet to expand the military in preparation for a probable war with the Soviet Union.[81] Moreover, the threat of another insurrection by the young officers furnished the new government with a convenient excuse to cancel the socialist movement's May Day celebrations.[82]

The emerging debate pitted the uncompromising opponents of trade unions—the army and the large industrialists—against civilian bureaucrats and outside labor experts who favored the establishment of labor-management councils in every plant, with some powers to discuss working conditions. If the latter's plans tended toward the theoretical, the army's approach was brutally direct. On 10 September 1936, the army ordered all workers in its arsenals to withdraw from unions. The directive gutted the venerable Japan General Federation of Workers in Governmental Enterprises, which together with Sōdōmei had led the moderate Social Democratic camp since the mid-1920s. The federation instantly lost eight thousand workers or half of its membership.

A spokesman for the army likened horizontal unions to the rebellious officers who fomented the recent putsch: "The army has made special efforts to maintain discipline since the February 26 Incident and has strictly prohibited the formation of so-called horizontal organizations within any command. . . . It has simply extended military discipline to [civilian] workers in the arsenals."[83] The high command specifically feared the formation of a European-style "antifascist" Popular Front among labor unions and the proletarian parties. Three Osaka arsenal unions had agreed to form such a front at the local level in August.[84] The army's ban was not without precedent. Naval and National Railway officials had steadily weakened the negotiating powers of horizontal unions in their enterprises after 1931. But army authorities became the first to challenge directly the government's long-time policy of recognizing labor unions.[85]

The army's actions placed it firmly on the side of powerful employers. Factory councils in the big army arsenals had functioned as forums for genuine bargaining between labor and management during the early 1930s. Workers elected representatives, and each council contained several members of unions affiliated with the General Federation of Workers in Governmental Enterprises. In the wake of the Manchurian Incident, the army gradually stripped the factory councils of their negotiating role while diminishing the union presence. Following the prohibition of arsenal unions in 1936, officers established "familial workmen's councils," whose functions were limited to welfare activities. They further segmented labor organization at the arsenal level by basing the new bodies on the smaller unit of the workshop. Workers lost the power to vote for representatives, whom the foreman now appointed.[86] The army thenceforth opposed the creation of any factory council that would give arsenal workers a voice in discussing working conditions. In addition, officers sought to weaken labor organization in the many private firms that produced for the military. Such attitudes played a major role in crippling the later efforts of the Kyōchōkai and civilian bureaucrats to establish elected labor-management councils in all enterprises.[87]

The army's ban on unions unleashed a new offensive against organized labor in the private sector as well, during the autumn of 1936. Complained one prefectural conciliation officer to his superiors in the Home Ministry: "The army's denial of unions has unquestionably influenced the attitudes of factory owners in recent labor disputes. It really pains me . . . that employers have become so brazen in refusing recognition to unions."[88] Company managers, moreover, paralleled the army in the drive to eliminate the collective voice of workers within the enterprise. Factory (works) councils quickly spread to the big non-*zaibatsu* firms after 1931. The greatest growth occurred between 1933 and 1936.

During the latter half of the 1920s, employers had generally permitted labor-management councils to debate and often negotiate wages, hours, and other conditions of employment. But as the threat of strikes and militant unions diminished after 1931, many councils lost the power to make decisions. Most new councils were simply organs for the "informal discussion" (*kondan*) of nonsubstantive issues (see table 9).[89]

The factory council at the Kobe plant of Mitsubishi Electric Machinery was typical. By 1937, employers had limited the agenda to matters of productivity, accident prevention, and improved hygiene and welfare. Meeting in 1938, council members nostalgically looked back to the 1920s when worker representatives made demands that were often met. Now, they lamented, few items were discussed, and the council lacked the authority to make decisions. Fellow representatives deemed the council a "waste."[90]

The Home Ministry publicly distanced itself from the campaign to crush labor unions and undermine factory councils. Irate ministry officials accused the army of radicalizing the mainstream of the labor movement and the Social Masses' Party, which they feared would join the left-wing Popular Front. Home Ministry leaders immediately warned the Ministries of Navy, Finance, and Communications not to follow the army's lead, and they vowed to prevent all acts of union-busting by private employers.[91] In a statement to the Privy Council shortly after the demise of the arsenal unions, the Social Bureau reaffirmed that "under the present circumstances in which the protection of workers and their welfare is still inadequate, [labor unions] must exist to some degree as a means of self-defense for workers. We find no grounds to refuse to recognize their moderation in thought and behavior."[92]

TABLE IX   GROWTH OF FACTORY COUNCILS, 1925–36

	Number of councils	Format of deliberations	
		Decision-making	*Informal discussion*
1925	168	—	—
1928	171	—	—
1933	196	126	70
1936	274	63	211

SOURCES: Nishinarita, "Manshū," p. 267; NRUS, 10:435–37. The figures include both works councils and quasi-works-councils (*jun rōdō iinkai*).

Yet the Social Bureau's reluctance to dissolve the unions in September 1936 was a far cry from its previous encouragement of trade unionism. The bureau's reply to the Privy Council also rhetorically asked "whether trade unionism can conclusively solve the labor problems of our nation?" Japan's frenzied military build-up had apparently made the social bureaucrats impatient. So would the acceleration of dispute activity that autumn. During the first six months of 1937 alone, 109,749 workers took part in strikes, slowdowns, and lockouts—a total that surpassed the previous peak of 81,329 for *all* of 1931 (see appendix 1).[93]

The government had itself to blame for the unrest. Upon coming to power in February 1936, the Hirota cabinet embarked on a program of massive armament with little regard for its inflationary consequences. Tokyo retail prices rose 4.6 percent in 1936 and 9.4 percent during 1937.[94] A majority of disputes accordingly centered on workers' demands for wage increases. What particularly alarmed the government was the occurrence of most disputes in the military-related heavy industries and transportation. Officials did not accuse the labor movement of instigating most job actions. On the contrary, some 60 percent of strikes, slowdowns, and lockouts in 1936–37 took place in nonunion plants (whereas unions were involved in nearly three-quarters of such disputes in 1931). The problem, so far as the social bureaucrats were concerned, was that neither the trade unions nor any other type of labor organization existed on a sufficient scale to mediate between employers and workers.[95]

And if such organizations did not exist, they would have to be created. Even as they criticized the army's actions in September 1936, Home Ministry officials were rumored to be considering a "final solution" to the problem of labor unions. Social Bureau leaders readied a "distinctively Japanese labor union law" for introduction to the next Diet. The projected law would no longer deal with labor problems as "purely economic," but would instead regulate industrial relations on the basis of "familialism, a beautiful custom of our country." The guiding principle was to be "the primacy of the economic and ethical state in which the state employs compulsion to restrict capitalists and protect workers."[96] Rather than legally recognize the "labor unions of the past," the measure mandated the establishment of one labor-management council per enterprise, effectively banning separate organizations for workers and employers. The councils would in turn form regional labor-management bodies, capped by a tripartite central organization under the domination of officials. Participating managers and owners would be discouraged from working only for profit, and workers were expected to "cast off the consciousness that they are selling their labor and realize the reality of service to the nation through labor (*kinrō hōkoku*)." Although this "labor union bill" never made it to the Diet, the press described widespread support for it among young officials throughout the bureaucracy.[97]

Official claims to the contrary, the Social Bureau's councils scheme was not "distinctively Japanese" at all, but an obvious imitation of Nazi Germany's 1934 Law for the Organization of National Labor (Gesetz zur Ordnung der nationalen Arbeit).[98] Historians have tended to take the nativist rhetoric of Japanese authoritarianism at face value. They thus overlook the profound impact of Nazi models on contemporary Japanese policies, particularly those relating to the demise of labor unions.[99] In addition to impressing Home Ministry officials, Hitler's labor program attracted the attention of a number of nonbureaucratic labor specialists associated with the Kyōchōkai, the Cabinet Research Bureau, and the Shōwa Research Association, an influential brain trust of the future prime minister, Konoe Fumimaro.[100] Just as British and Weimar German precedents systematized the social bureaucrats' quest for a new labor policy after World War I, the Nazi model provided an empirically tested and ruthlessly simple answer to the problem of wartime industrial tensions.

Although some Japanese looked to the innovations of Italian Fascism, most labor experts deemed German National Socialism a better fit. As the Kyōchōkai's researchers explained, the Fascist state reorganized industry into one *corporazione,* yet maintained separate syndicates for employers and workers, as well as the institution of collective bargaining. How, asked the incredulous Japanese, would the Italians reconcile the rights of capital with those of the state and the totality?[101]

The Nazis, on the other hand, denied the existence of conflicts of interest between labor and management. Hitler smashed the socialist unions, abolished collective contracts, and prohibited strikes and lockouts. Industrial relations were placed under the supervision of the party-state's German Labor Front. Restructured by the Law for the Organization of National Labor in January 1934, the Labor Front combined all industrial and commercial employees and employers into enterprise units. Called "shop communities" (*Betriebsgemeinschaft*), the units summoned up the popular German ideal of a classless Volksgemeinschaft. The law required workers, termed the "followers," to obey the employer (the "leader"). The leader was in turn obligated to look after the workers' welfare. To harmonize differences, the statute established purely advisory Councils of Trust, composed of the employer and representatives of the employees, in all plants employing more than twenty. Although the workers themselves lost their collective voice, the Labor Front and the Reich Trustees of Labor occasionally intervened on behalf of workers, or what they perceived to be the workers' interests. Less concerned with the material conditions of labor, the Labor Front harangued managers to respect the dignity of workers.[102]

The transmission of Nazi ideas on labor can be most directly traced to Minami Iwao. Like many Japanese proponents of state controls, Minami was not a civil servant by training. He came to the attention of the Social Bureau's Yoshida Shigeru in the early 1930s while serving as the chief labor manager at Japan Electric. Eager to study the latest in labor policy, Minami left his job and set off for Germany in the summer of 1934. He was accompanied by the Kyōchōkai's highest-ranking labor expert and future executive director, Machida Tatsujirō. Admiration is too weak a word to describe Minami's impressions of the German Labor Front. He became fascinated with the Labor Front's "Strength through Joy" program, which sought to raise workers' morale by sponsoring inexpensive entertainment and group travel. His mission, recalled Minami, was to "form an organization and system uniting the nation's fifteen million workers, from enterprises large and small, into one body in which they would be happy in their work and happy outside the workplace."[103]

His chance came soon. Yoshida Shigeru, director of the Cabinet Research Bureau, summoned Minami back to Japan the following summer to join the new bureau. When the Hirota cabinet sought out ideas for a "renovationist" program following the 26 February 1936 rebellion, Yoshida personally directed Minami to finalize his draft for a Nazi-style labor front. Entitled "Policy for the Adjustment of Labor-Capital Relations," Minami's ambitious plan formed the basis of the Social Bureau's "Japanese labor union bill" and the later Industrial Patriotic movement.[104]

Minami's proposal was a thinly veiled version of the Nazi labor program. In place of the German Labor Front would be a hierarchically ordered Japanese Labor Service Cooperative Body (Nihon Kinrō Kyōdō-dan). The fate of existing labor unions was unambiguous. The state would dissolve all unions and employers' associations. Minami had no difficulty in translating the German concepts of "shop community" and Volksgemeinschaft. Invoking the Japanese ideal of the organic village, or *kyōdōtai,* he functionally grouped all "industrial producers"—whether employers, staff, or workers—into plant-level units. Shareholders or "capitalists" were excluded. As in the case of the Reich Trustees of Labor, ultimate power would rest with the newly created Labor Inspectorate Bureaus at the prefectural level. Inspectors could authorize minimum wages, arbitrate disputes, and discipline both employers and workers for unfair practices. Minami even proposed the establishment of a Japanese Patriotic Labor Service Party (Nihon Aikoku Kinrōtō), to be based on the enormous membership of the labor body and a parallel agricultural front.[105]

The Minami plan and subsequent bureaucratic proposals sought above all to prevent labor disputes by means of "plant discussion councils" (*keiei kondankai*). Identical in spirit to the Nazi Councils of Trust, the discussion councils were designed to "cultivate moral notions of trust and mutual dependence between Labor and Capital." They would be legally mandated in all firms employing thirty or more. The discussion councils represented the first line of conflict resolution. If councilors failed to reach a settlement, the issue would be forwarded to a conciliation committee in the Japanese Labor Service Cooperative Body and finally to arbitration by special courts or the labor inspector. The plant councils could also discuss working conditions, employment rules, productivity, and welfare.

But Minami no more intended to give workers' representatives an equal say than did his Nazi counterparts. He in fact endorsed existing factory councils in the large companies as a model. Moreover, the proposed councils could not make binding decisions, nor was the employer, who served as advisor, under any obligation to obey the majority opinion. Past collective agreements would be invalidated. Minami further weakened the position of workers by permitting managerial staff to represent the "working people" (*kinrōsha*) on the councils.

Nonetheless, the Minami proposal was not simply a smoke screen to preserve the hold of private management over labor. Employers sensed a radical challenge to their authority. Like the Nazis, Minami and his bureaucratic allies proposed to subordinate individual firms to the needs of the nation. Officials found existing company unions inadequate because the organizations embodied "the egoism of the firm and often succumb to the absolute control of the entrepreneur."[106] Minami roundly condemned capitalism itself. Such "evils of capitalism" as "the omnipotence of profit" and "enslavement of labor" ran "contrary to the Japanese spirit," he maintained. To these renovationists, the solution to labor problems lay in nothing less than a Nazi-like revolution in the status of workers. Management must thenceforth respect "brawn work" as much as white-collar "brain work."[107]

What industrialists feared most was the prospect of compulsory discussion councils supervised by the state. Inspired by Minami, several prefectural police departments drew up plans to require discussion councils as a means of preventing work stoppages after the outbreak of war with China in July 1937. In the best-known case, Arakawa Mataichi, the factory-section chief of Aichi prefecture, proposed the now familiar system of hierarchical councils, ranging from factory discussion councils to a supreme committee of arbitration officials. Area businessmen reacted with outrage, forcing Arakawa's transfer in early 1938.[108]

The various bureaucratic initiatives for restructuring industrial relations culminated in the Industrial Patriotic movement in 1938. The war with China had intensified official concern with industrial peace and the conservation of manpower. The government expanded the Social Bureau into a full-fledged Welfare Ministry on 1 January 1938. The new ministry's Labor Bureau assumed primary jurisdiction over labor administration, although the Home Ministry retained important functions through control of local government and the police.

The Welfare and Home Ministries clearly had little to fear from the labor unions. In December 1937, the Home Ministry crushed what survived of labor-based opposition to Japanese expansionism when it dissolved the small left-wing National Council of Japanese Labor Unions (Nihon Rōdō Kumiai Zenkoku Hyōgikai). The remaining unions enthusiastically endorsed the nation's mission in China just as they had in 1931. At its annual convention in October 1937, the Zen Sōdōmei patriotically pledged to launch no strikes for the duration of hostilities. Such sentiments broke the back of the unparalleled wave of labor disputes during the first half of 1937. Only 14,000 workers took part in strikes, slowdowns, and lockouts in the six months following the outbreak of war in July (compared with 110,000 for the first half). Yet the social bureaucrats and the police feared a recurrence of labor dissatisfaction as Japanese troops bogged down and inflation continued unabated.[109] The time had come to reorganize labor and management.

The government launched the Industrial Patriotic movement after receiving a report from the Kyōchōkai's Emergency Countermeasures Commission (Jikyoku Taisaku Iinkai) in April 1938. The "Prospectus for Policies to Adjust Labor-Capital Relations" represented a compromise between the social bureaucrats and large-scale industrialists. Although the commission was dominated by officials or retired officials from the Home and Welfare Ministries, the influential National Federation of Industrial Organizations also placed a number of representatives on the subcommittee of experts. Matsuoka Komakichi of the Zen Sōdōmei constituted the sole voice of the social democratic unions. The commission's final report fell short of the Minami and Arakawa plans in terms of state control over management and labor. Its provisions, however, did require all enterprises to establish an organ to bring about "mutual understanding between managers and employees."

On 24 August, the Welfare and Home Ministries specifically instructed prefectural officials to promote the universal formation of plant-level "industrial patriotic units" (sangyō hōkokukai), which would consist of the employer and all employees. To give meaning to "the spirit of industrial patriotism," the joint directive insisted that each unit create a labor-management discussion council with powers to engage in "frank discussion" of various matters, including "treatment" (taigū)—that is, wages, hours, and working conditions. Councils would generally include some members elected by the employees. A semigovernmental Industrial Patriotic Federation (Sangyō Hōkoku Remmei) had already been established three weeks earlier for the purpose of coordinating activities among the enterprise units.[110]

Like their German counterparts, industrialists viewed the emerging Japanese labor front with considerable apprehension. The movement's sponsors were essentially the same social bureaucrats who once championed labor union legislation. To the Chūbu (Nagoya area) Federation of Industrial Organizations, "the Kyōchōkai [commission]'s proposal is even more socialistic than the systems of Nazi Germany and England."[111] Managers repeatedly expressed fears that the compulsory organization of councils and mandated discussion of "treatment" issues would lead to labor unions in their plants.[112]

Nonetheless, the leaders of the National Federation of Industrial Organizations adopted a policy of general support for the Industrial Patriotic movement. Rather than directly resist the bureaucrats as they had done over previous labor legislation, they strove to temper the government's campaign from within the Kyōchōkai commission and the Industrial Patriotic Federation. The industrialists' moderation stemmed, in part, from the passage of the sweeping National General Mobilization Law in March 1938. They recognized that officials could simply impose the discussion councils by fiat if business refused to cooperate.[113] The National Federation of Industrial Organizations accordingly participated in the drive, but made every effort to restrict the industrial patriotic units to such nonmaterial activities as sports, education, and accident prevention. Employers demanded that the new organizations conform to the existing "chain of command" within each enterprise and, in practice, simply renamed their mutual-aid societies and company unions.[114]

Recent scholarship has dwelt on the divergent approaches of the social bureaucrats and businessmen toward the Industrial Patriotic movement. In actuality, the two sides were not far apart by 1938. Although the Labor Bureau (Welfare Ministry) initially fought the employers' attempts to remove all substantial questions of "treatment" from the agenda of discussion councils, the social bureaucrats demonstrated no burning desire to give workers an effective voice in freely elected factory councils. In a key directive of November 1938, bureau officials clarified that the joint directive of 24 August did not require that workers' representatives to the discussion councils be elected by the employees themselves. If it "fit the circumstances of the individual enterprise," a factory head could directly appoint all councilors.[115] Moreover, despite talk of promoting "frank discussions" between managers and workers, at no point did Labor Bureau officials recommend granting the councils real powers to pass binding resolutions. Like Minami Iwao and the Nazis, the bureaucrats tossed employees the sop of "informal discussion" (kondan) while denying them any checks over management.

The social bureaucrats soon dropped the mere mention of elections and discussions of "treatment" issues following the government's complete takeover of the Industrial Patriotic movement in April 1939. A joint directive from the Welfare and Home Ministries made industrial patriotic units directly responsible to newly created prefectural federations headed by governors. Officials increasingly viewed the enterprise associations as the lowest level of wartime labor administration—not as autonomous bodies for settling disputes. Military conscription and war-related production resulted in an acute shortage of skilled labor, accompanied by longer hours, absenteeism, intense interfirm mobility, and rising wages. The government hoped to use the industrial patriotic units to rally grass-roots support for its new ordinances to regulate wages, hours, employment, and dismissals.[116] Lest the point be missed, the Labor Bureau repeatedly distinguished the discussion councils from the dynamic factory councils of the past:

It is a social democratic idea to think of the discussion councils as forums for making demands about working conditions or simply for reaching mutual understanding when feelings of unfairness and dissatisfaction arise. . . . The question of treatment that appeared in initial explanations of the movement was based on a misunderstanding of the nature of the discussion councils. If the discussion councils are not so-called decision-making bodies, neither are they simply advisory bodies. They are discussion bodies that will realize the spirit of industrial patriotism and the unity of the enterprise.[117]

By removing the check of effective councils, the bureaucrats confirmed the authority of private management within the enterprise even as they asserted control over the Industrial Patriotic movement.[118] To some scholars, the potent resistance of business was decisive in weakening the even-handed approach of the Welfare Ministry.[119] Yet such conclusions ignore the continuities in bureaucratic thought dating back to Nazi-influenced plans by Minami Iwao and the Social Bureau in 1936. The persistence of managerial supremacy under the Industrial Patriotic movement was the logical outcome of administrative proposals that not only denied workers any restraint over employers, but also repudiated the legitimacy of conflicting interests.

THE FAILURE OF STATE CORPORATISM, 1940–45

If the Industrial Patriotic movement did not substantially alter the position of management and capital, the same could hardly be said for that of organized labor. The social bureaucrats, it must be noted, did not explicitly sponsor the Industrial Patriotic drive to crush the trade unions. In their joint directive of 24 August 1938, the Home and Welfare Ministries warned local officials not to resort to the "forcible dissolution of labor unions" when instituting industrial patriotic units.[120] It was clear from the start, however, that the government refused to grant the existing labor movement a positive role in wartime mobilization. Given the patriotism and cooperative nature of the social democratic unions, one must question why the bureaucrats so totally circumvented the labor unions, even in the plants and industries where the organizations maintained a major presence. In so doing, officials abandoned their pre-1936 strategy of pragmatically relying on a variety of workers' associations, including trade unions. Unlike the British and Americans during World War II, they also ruled out the "societally" corporatist possibility of placing union leaders and employers on governmental boards charged with settling strikes, determining wages, and allocating manpower.[121] As subsequent statements revealed, the authorities refrained from forcibly dissolving the unions only because they did not wish to provoke resistance. "Spontaneous" or voluntary dissolution became the articulated objective. Local police and individual companies organized over nineteen thousand industrial patriotic associations with three million members by the end of 1939. The unions had every reason to fear their redundancy.

Whether premeditated or not, the government's Industrial Patriotic campaign irrevocably split the ranks of the union movement and the Social Masses' Party. Although labor historians often criticize the narrow economic unionism of the old Sōdōmei and the Social Democratic Party, the "realistic" leaders of those groups never wavered in the principled defense of independent trade unions. Led by Chairman Matsuoka Komakichi and Nishio Suehiro, the Sōdōmei mainstream of the Zen Sōdōmei recognized the dangers of the Industrial Patriotic movement from its inception. Matsuoka reluctantly supported the formation of industrial patriotic units on the condition that the unions continue to exist alongside the new associations. However, he and his Sōdōmei clique proved powerless to stop the mass defections of members and entire affiliates to the bureaucratic movement.

The Congress of Japanese Labor Unions, through which Sōdōmei leaders had dominated the social democratic labor movement since 1932, was the first to fragment. During the last three months of 1938, the congress lost four of its largest federations. The Japan Seamen's Union and the Maritime Officers' Association both withdrew in October upon forming a patriotic seamen's federation. The Japan Steelworkers' Union bolted two weeks later and became one of the first unions to dissolve into industrial patriotic associations the following April. Union leader Itō Ushirō had recently returned from Germany, strangely ecstatic about the position of labor under Nazi rule.[122]

Matsuoka's defense of autonomous trade unionism was further undercut by the old "centrist" faction headed by Asō Hisashi in the Social Masses' Party and Miwa Jusō within the Zen Sōdōmei. The centrist unions, it will be recalled, had criticized Sōdōmei's "realistic" tactics from an ideological left-wing perspective during the late 1920s, but Asō and Miwa opportunistically leapfrogged Sōdōmei to support renovationist military officers and "socialism from above" from the time of the army pamphlet incident in 1934. Miwa Jusō similarly threw his labor faction's unqualified support behind the bureaucrats' Industrial Patriotic movement in 1938. The founders of the Industrial Patriotic Federation rewarded Miwa with a seat on the board of directors, whereas they relegated the wary Matsuoka Komakichi to a weaker advisory panel. Eager to impress these new-found friends, Miwa's clique demanded the dissolution of Zen Sōdōmei itself in July 1939 because the federation allegedly constituted a "sectional, class-based, and conflictual organization."[123] Matsuoka Komakichi and the Sōdōmei faction immediately expelled the centrist unions. The Zen Sōdōmei lost 40 percent of its membership in one fell swoop. The rump federation renamed itself the Sōdōmei and stubbornly refused to disband. In contrast, Miwa's breakaway unions prepared for imminent dissolution, forming the transitional Industrial Patriotic Club in November.

The suicidal impulses of the Asō-Miwa clique can be understood partly in terms of its quest for influence under a new national-socialist order. Together with renovationist bureaucrats, younger party politicians, and several progressive intellectuals, Asō and other socialists worked closely with the charismatic prime minister, Prince Konoe Fumimaro, to form a single mass party.[124] Konoe's cabinets (June 1937–January 1939; July 1940–October 1941) presided over the birth and growth of the Industrial Patriotic system. The group surrounding Konoe dreamed of creating a totalitarian "New Order" along Nazi and Italian Fascist lines. Echoing European state-corporatist thinkers, advocates of the New Order sought to mobilize national energies by reorganizing all private associations into pyramidal organizations demarcated by "function" (for example, industry), not class or interest.

The New Order became a reality in the weeks preceding and following the formation of the second Konoe cabinet in early July 1940, when the government and sympathetic politicians pressured generally reluctant party elders into dissolving the nation's established parties. Asō and Miwa disbanded the Social Masses' Party and the Industrial Patriotic Club with much greater enthusiasm on 6 July 1940. Japanist unions similarly dissolved into industrial patriotic associations if they had not already done so.[125] Officials then established the Imperial Rule Assistance Association. In addition to serving as a political association, the IRAA reorganized the entire work force into functional *hōkokukai* (patriotic associations) covering industry, mining, agriculture, commerce, naval workers, and seamen. Initially headed by the welfare minister, the Greater Japan Industrial Patriotic Association assumed control of the some fifty-four thousand industrial patriotic units and their 4.5 million members in November 1940.

Opportunism and patriotism cannot totally explain the collapse of the labor movement, however. The fact remains that the government employed a great deal of coercion—some subtle, some not. As he had throughout the 1930s, Welfare Minister Yoshida Shigeru enunciated the evolving policy on 16 February 1940: although the government refrained from forcibly dissolving the unions, the authorities were expanding and "guiding" the Industrial Patriotic movement so that the "necessity for labor unions to oppose capitalists and to maintain and improve livelihood is *naturally* disappearing."[126] Such "guidance" often involved the use of civilian and military police to harass unions into dissolution. The case of the Tokyo Transportation Workers' Union (Tōkyō Kōtsū Rōdō Kumiai) is instructive. The historically militant union organized one of the first industrial patriotic units in August 1938 to fend off pressures for outright dissolution from a growing faction supported by municipal authorities. One year later, when union leaders attempted to defend the union's right to exist alongside the unit, they were promptly visited by officials of the Metropolitan Police. The beleaguered labor activists announced their intention to disband in the near future, although it required direct threats from the police before the union finally dissolved itself on 7 July 1940.[127]

A similar fate awaited the Sōdōmei, heir to the pioneering Yūaikai and long the symbol of sound, independent unionism. On 7 May 1940, the Home Ministry prohibited the formation of the Labor Service Nationalist Party (Kinrō Kokumintō). Sōdōmei and the veterans of the Social Democratic Party had sponsored the new party after Asō Hisashi's mainstream expelled them from the Social Masses' Party.[128] The Home Ministry's rationale demonstrated the totalitarian mentality of the formerly sympathetic bureaucrats. The new party's greatest sin was to be a "class party, based ideologically on socialism and organizationally on the so-called proletarian class."[129]

Without spelling out the consequences, Welfare Minister Yoshida Shigeru strongly advised Matsuoka Komakichi a few days later to dissolve Sōdōmei "voluntarily."[130] Faced with governmental threats and the rapid loss of affiliates, Matsuoka and Nishio Suehiro reluctantly disbanded the Sōdōmei on 8 July 1940. Federation leaders struck a defiant tone even in defeat. Acknowledging the weakness of the labor unions, they reminded officials of their contributions to industrial peace and mobilization: "Yet governmental authorities refused to recognize our program. They regard its existence as an enormous obstacle to the Industrial Patriotic movement and have pursued a policy of destroying the labor unions."[131] The remaining unions quickly followed Sōdōmei's lead or were forced to dissolve. True to the Nazi model, the bureaucrats saw to it that the Industrial Patriotic Association inherited the unions' funds. By 1943, only three unions survived, with a combined membership of 155.[132]

The eradication of Japanese labor unions presents a series of puzzling continuities that link the larger phenomenon of Taishō democracy to the authoritarianism that followed. Yoshida Shigeru had actively promoted the Social Bureau's progressive union legislation in the early 1930s, and labor leaders regarded him as a sympathetic ally. Yasui Eiji once crafted the Social Bureau's proposals to guarantee the rights to strike, to form unions, and to bargain collectively. His eloquently liberal vision of labor-management relations placed him in a class by himself. Yet this same Yasui became an enthusiastic proponent of state corporatism, or the compulsory reorganization of all interest groups into the functional patriotic associations. As Konoe's trusted home minister during the latter half of 1940, he personally directed the absorption of the unions into the Industrial Patriotic Association.[133]

The historian may offer various explanations for these transformations, but there is much to be gained by listening to the rationalizations of the social bureaucrats themselves. Most resembled Yoshida. They claimed, then and since, to have consistently encouraged the formation of truly "autonomous" popular organizations, whether trade unions or patriotic workers' associations. Officials never tired of noting the inadequacy of "heavy-handed controls" from above without "spontaneous" organized activity from below.[134] In the words of the Nazi-inspired Minami Iwao, "You can lead a man to water, but you can't make him drink."[135] Social bureaucrats such as Yasui Eiji further insisted that the government bore no responsibility for crippling the labor movement, because the unions, including Sōdōmei, "spontaneously dissolved" themselves into industrial patriotic associations.[136] The former Social Bureau official, Kitaoka Juitsu, was one of the few who hoped that the government would grant union leaders a positive role under the New Order. Nevertheless, he, too, drew the following conclusion:

> In this year [1940], our nation's labor unions were effectively eliminated without the slightest application of compulsion by the government. The Industrial Patriotic Association, as a large-scale institution embracing all workers and employers, originated without any use of force. This was much like the Tokugawa [shogun] returning authority to the Emperor in the Meiji Restoration. Although such great changes in foreign nations have

resulted from legal or de facto compulsion, nothing like that occurred in our country. The Tokugawa shogunate returned authority to the Emperor without bloodshed.[137]

Kitaoka was somewhat mistaken about the Meiji Restoration, in which fierce fighting took some ten thousand lives, and he was surely wrong about the autonomous nature of the Industrial Patriotic movement.[138]

Such tortured rationalizations point up the centrality of corporatist thought in the odyssey of the social bureaucrats. These officials sought new ways of minimizing the conflicts of modern industrial society during both the 1920s and the 1930s, and as members of a relatively independent higher civil service, they firmly believed in the capacity of the state to do so. In this respect, the social bureaucrats resembled the proponents of "state corporatism" in Fascist Italy, Vichy France, and Salazar's Portugal. Like many European corporatists, the Home Ministry officials initially favored a more liberal or societal form of corporatism from 1919 to 1935—that is, the government best promoted harmonious social relations by encouraging the development of independent, nationwide workers' organizations and employers' associations. However, as Schmitter has described, European state corporatists became caught up in a "built-in contradiction" between their vision and the actual policies pursued. As a result,

> there is scarcely a single state-corporatist theorist who does not proclaim his opposition to statism, his commitment to decisional decentralization and his desire for eventual associational autonomy. Nevertheless, our theorist is aware that given the fragmented, ideologically charged and class-divided nature of the political system he is operating within, singular, non-conflictive, hierarchically ordered and functionally compartmentalized associations are not likely to be spontaneously forthcoming. He therefore advocates the temporary use of state authority to establish these compulsory structures—and to remove voluntaristic, competing ones—all, of course, in the name of national and/or public interest.[139]

The Japanese government similarly launched the Industrial Patriotic scheme as a rational mechanism for settling disputes in lieu of a widespread union movement. But here, too, the logic of compulsion overpowered the sponsors' visions of organizational autonomy. Japanese bureaucrats quickly transformed the plant associations into passive support groups, all the while insisting on the associations' mission to promote "frank discussion" between workers and managers.

Despite attacks on the flaws of capitalism by its bureaucratic champions, the Industrial Patriotic movement displayed another common feature of state corporatist systems: the asymmetric treatment of the concerned interests. Italy's Fascist regime, for example, restricted the already eviscerated workers' syndicates to the local and regional level, while permitting the industrialists' national confederation to continue alongside the corporatist structure.[140] By the same token, the Industrial Patriotic Association did not so much incorporate, as obliterate, the collective labor interest.

The fate of the National Federation of Industrial Organizations presents a striking contrast. To begin with, federation chairman Fujiwara Ginjirō held the strategic post of minister of commerce and industry in the same Yonai cabinet that cleansed Japan of labor unions during the first half of 1940. According to the federation's chief secretary, Welfare Minister Yoshida Shigeru gently whispered to Fujiwara at a cabinet meeting in July: "Now that we've gotten Sōdōmei to dissolve, I'd like you to disband the National Federation of Industrial Organizations as well." Fujiwara reportedly responded with stony silence, and the matter was immediately dropped. The National Federation did in fact dissolve itself some two years later in May 1942, but only after officials assured the association of a continued organizational identity within the Labor Service Council (Kinrō Kyōgikai) of the Greater Japan Industrial Patriotic Association.[141] The powerful Japan Industrial Club and the Japan Economic League (Nihon Keizai Remmeikai) survived the Pacific War completely intact.

In the realm of industrial policy, the government's creation of compulsory control associations (tōseikai) similarly reinforced the dominance of large companies within most industrial groups.[142] The limits of state autonomy vis-à-vis the capitalists were clear. The wartime regime required the cooperation of producers. Industrialists controlled production and effectively organized themselves; the labor movement had accomplished neither. Dream as they might, the social bureaucrats fell far short of the Nazi model of eradicating the organized interests of both business and labor.

This is not to say that the social bureaucrats abandoned the cause of labor protection. On the contrary, the China and Pacific wars heightened the government's concern for the health and welfare of workers, particularly those in military-related industries. Moreover, the Konoe cabinet created the Welfare Ministry in January 1938 primarily at the initiative of the army, whose medical officers had grown alarmed at the deteriorating health of recruits.[143] Bolstered by an expanded labor inspectorate, Welfare Ministry bureaucrats acquired powers over company managers that would have dazzled the overworked factory inspectors of the old Social Bureau. Their most effective weapon was the Ordinance on Labor Management in Essential Industries (Jūyō Jigyōjo Rōmu Kanrirei), promulgated in February 1942. The ordinance empowered labor inspectors to order designated companies to make changes regarding hiring, firing, hours, wages, and most other labor matters. The measure significantly affected managerial practices and probably contributed to the emergence of some features of postwar Japan's famed employment system, according to Andrew Gordon. Officials systematically directed firms to pay family allowances, extend seniority wages to all workers, and expand welfare programs.[144]

On balance, however, the tremendous expansion of state power gave workers little to cheer about. The wartime social bureaucrats strove above all to allocate manpower and increase productivity. The government nationalized all private and municipal employment agencies in 1938. Studiously emulating the Nazis, the Welfare Ministry dealt with the worsening labor shortage by steadily denying workers the freedom to change jobs.[145] The bureaucrats even adopted the Nazi innovation of the "workbook" or labor passport, which most workers were compelled to show to new employers. To prevent workers from leaving jobs in strategic industries, one ordinance in 1942 required permission from the head of a governmental employment agency in all cases of hiring, dismissal, or voluntary separation. Furthermore, despite some efforts to improve wages, officials generally imposed wage ceilings to reduce production costs and to prevent companies from poaching workers from competitors. Whereas the real wages of German workers fell only 2 percent between 1939 and 1944, those of the Japanese labor force dropped 33 percent. Deprived of their own organizations, the demoralized workers protested in the only ways possible—absenteeism, job switching, slowed production, and the manufacture of defective goods. Worried police noted numerous cases of disputes or "near disputes" in the final years of the war.[146]

In this otherwise dismal story, there was perhaps one positive development for the future. It gradually dawned on the social bureaucrats that the wartime industrial patriotic organizations were proving no more, and possibly less, effective than the labor unions they replaced.[147] The corporatist reorganization of labor had failed to improve production, resolve labor-management differences, and secure the vital cooperation of workers for the war effort. The Industrial Patriotic Association appeared every bit the equivalent of the German Labor Front, boasting 5,800,000 members and 86,000 units by the end of 1943.[148] Recent case studies demonstrate, however, that few factory associations dealt with the material and treatment issues that most concerned workers.[149] A majority had not established discussion councils as late as the middle of 1941, and in those that had, most managers simply exhorted members to work hard and be patriotic. A survey of conditions in 1942 by the Home Ministry's Police Bureau described workers as indifferent, even contemptuous, toward the discussion councils.[150] Although workers increasingly took advantage of the labor shortage to press demands on employers after 1942, they generally formed ad hoc organizations rather than use the moribund industrial patriotic units.[151]

The perceived failure of the Industrial Patriotic structure prompted many of the original sponsors to propose a more autonomous voice for the workers at the height of the Pacific War. In 1941, prominent labor specialists within Konoe's brain trust, the Shōwa Research Association, emphatically warned that workers would not voluntarily cooperate unless the factory units permitted genuine discussion of material issues.[152] Curiously enough, several social policy experts criticized the government for not better emulating the German Labor Front. The Labor Front, claimed Professor Hattori Eitarō, enjoyed "social autonomy" in the sense that it pursued the collective interests of workers against those of other groups and institutions. In Japan, however, the bureaucrats simply imposed controls from above, working through the companies' existing personnel departments, not the new industrial patriotic units.[153]

As productivity plummeted during the last year of the Pacific War, others contemplated a more democratic alternative. At one subcommittee meeting of the Labor Service Council in July 1944, the chairman, a manager, asked: "Why haven't [the working masses] become excited about the Industrial Patriotic movement the way they used to be about the labor union movement?" The reply was all the more revealing, coming as it did from Minami Iwao, the original architect of the Japanese labor front and now Kantō Regional Director of the Industrial Patriotic Association: "The Industrial Patriotic movement's [lack of] appeal is a real problem. I believe the time has come to consider Mr. Nishio Suehiro's call for reviving labor unions."[154]

The reintroduction of unions may also have appealed to the social bureaucrats during the final months of the war as they sought to rally the workers. American bombing compounded the difficulties of maintaining the already demoralized work force. According to one former official of the Welfare Ministry, the Labor Service Bureau began preparing a genuine labor union law in May or June 1945, weeks before the August surrender to the United States.[155] Although unsubstantiated, the story is not as far-fetched as it sounds. If there was one trait of the social bureaucrats that had remained constant since 1918, it was their flexibility in responding to the perceived failures of past policies.

In May 1942, the chief of the Labor Bureau, Mochinaga Yoshio, had confidently proclaimed:

> We hail July 1940 when the labor unions dissolved and we no longer recognized their existence in fact. Labor unions ceased to exist in Japan from that time. When I think about it today, I cannot contain my happiness for the nation. Just look at the United States now. The labor unions have erected tremendous barriers to the expansion of production. They say that Roosevelt himself sought the support of the labor unions at the time of the recent presidential election. And that's how the United States has gotten into its present difficulties.[156]

By late August 1945, as Welfare Ministry officials hurriedly burned their wartime records in preparation for the coming of the victorious Americans, they apparently thought otherwise.

Epilogue: Legacies for Postwar Japan

The postwar Occupation forces adopted the foolish policy of
liberating the Communist Party and placing it at the head of
the labor movement. Had they not done so, I [along with
my colleagues in the Social Bureau] believe that the postwar
labor movement [like that of the prewar period] could have
followed a sound pattern of development led by the
Sōdōmei.

> —Kitaoka Juitsu (former Social Bureau official and
> advisor to the postwar Labor Ministry), 1961[1]

It used to be the custom to conclude historical studies of twentieth-
century Japan in 1940 or 1941. The tragic endpoints of war and authoritarian rule presented the historian with a difficult choice. One could
point to the "road not taken"—for example, to the failure of the political parties and socialist movement to resist militarism. Or one could
more positively conclude that the interwar parties or labor unions made
respectable inroads, considering their novelty. The historian's singular
focus on the prewar era was natural in the years immediately following
Japan's defeat in 1945. However, more than forty years have passed,
and it seems rather pointless to continue to treat prewar and postwar
Japan as if they were two different societies. For all the changes introduced by the Occupation (1945–52), the Americans maintained the
prewar civilian elites in large part, relying on the bureaucracy in particular to implement reforms. The United States did not so much create new
political forces as somewhat shift the balance between existing groups.
The tensions of the presurrender past quickly resurfaced to affect relations among the bureaucracy, the parties, the business community, and
organized labor.

Historians and political scientists are only now beginning to demonstrate the impressive continuities in policies and politics between pre-

1945 and postwar Japan.[2] Rather than judge Japanese labor policy and state-society relations in exclusively prewar terms, I offer an overview of postwar developments as my conclusion. Many of the protagonists in this story underwent a series of seemingly abrupt shifts during the prewar and war years. How the same people dealt with labor questions after 1945 under a very different set of circumstances helps to clarify their positions within the longer-term debate. The following examination of transwar continuities also places contemporary Japan within its historical context.[3] We cannot hope to understand postwar changes without appreciating the persistent influence of prewar and wartime labor policy and political behavior.

The salient features of the evolving relationship between the state and labor questions before 1945 may be summarized as follows:

(1) *Central role of the social bureaucrats.* The Home Ministry's social bureaucrats had come a long way since the 1890s, when officials of the small Bureau of Health and Sanitation struggled to persuade industrialists and economic bureaucrats that the state had an obligation to protect workers from exploitative employers and the uncertainties of life. Bureaucratic social policy acquired its dynamic and relatively autonomous character after World War I, in part because the government placed labor administration in the prestigious Home Ministry rather than the industrially oriented Ministry of Agriculture and Commerce.

World War II ended with the social bureaucrats of the Home and Welfare Ministries at the peak of their power. The actual content of their policies presents a more mixed picture. On the one hand, the Home Ministry attached great importance to enacting the Social Bureau's progressive labor union bills between 1925 and 1931. Influenced by the liberal British model, officials believed that workers would become responsible members of society and industry when they gained the rights to organize unions and elect their own representatives. But there was no mistaking the social bureaucrats for genuine liberals. The prime movers in the Social Bureau and later the Welfare Ministry had, for the most part, served or would serve as elite officers in the Home Ministry's police and Special Higher Police, the latter of which specialized in the control of radical socialist and labor organizations. They accordingly regarded liberal labor policy and democratization as instrumental means to preserve public order and advance state objectives. These were not men content to wait for a "sound" labor movement to develop on its own. By 1940, officials switched to the policy of eliminating all unions after convincing themselves that state-sponsored industrial patriotic units would better advance wartime mobilization.

(2) *Rise and fall of the bourgeois liberal alternative.* Interwar labor reform and political democratization, in general, depended on the policies of the established bourgeois parties. In addition to encouraging the administrative protection of union rights, Kenseikai and Minseitō governments successfully sponsored universal manhood suffrage, the repeal of Article 17 of the Police Regulations, the Labor Disputes Conciliation Law, and other labor measures. The big question was whether the Minseitō would evolve into a viable, socially reformist liberal party, standing between the nascent proletarian parties and the conservative Seiyūkai. As contemporary observers acknowledged, the liberal alternative was fraught with potential contradictions.

The Hamaguchi cabinet's spirited promotion of the labor union bill and other social legislation rested on two related suppositions: first, that its capitalist allies favored the legal rationalization of labor-management relations and, second, that a reformist Minseitō could forge a mass base of workers and tenants, besides drawing the moderate Social Democratic Party into a lasting "Lib-lab" relationship. The first pillar of Minseitō liberalism came crashing down in 1931, when small and medium-sized employers shifted to total opposition to the labor union bill amid the unprecedented strike wave of the Depression. The party had become caught between its business and labor constituencies. Given the former's preponderance, the Minseitō naturally chose business, bringing the interwar era of reform to a close, several months before the Manchurian Incident and the collapse of party rule.

(3) *Emergence of the "realistic" labor leaders.* The division of the interwar labor movement into clashing left and right wings was closely related to the debate over labor's attitudes toward the state. The Communist-linked Hyōgikai and other leftist unions organized workers in a struggle against the political and economic system, and they condemned the government's labor legislation as a smoke screen for controlling the unions. Their rivals in Sōdōmei and the large rightwing federations insisted instead on collective bargaining and the primacy of workers' economic interests. Led by Nishio Suehiro and Matsuoka Komakichi, these pragmatic trade unionists placed enormous trust in the state's ability to improve workers' lives and to elevate labor vis-à-vis management.

Aided by the government's unrelenting crusade against Communists, the moderate unions gained control of the labor movement by the early 1930s. But they soon discovered that the admired autonomy of their erstwhile bureaucratic allies was a double-edged sword that could be used against labor realists as well as capitalists and radical organizers. Although the wartime dissolution of unions discredited the value of "sound trade unionism" in the eyes of many left-wing labor activists after 1945, Nishio's mix of cautious economic unionism and anti-Communism would continue to exert a powerful hold over the postwar labor movement.

(4) *Tensions between business and the state*. Prewar employers occasionally sought state intervention in the realm of labor relations. The first generation of manufacturers demanded legislation to restrain labor mobility in the early 1880s. Alarmed at the sharp rise in labor unrest after World War I, leading employers' associations again called on the government, this time to rationalize industrial relations by means of a labor union law. In general, however, industrialists were confident of their abilities to resolve labor problems, and they increasingly united to oppose the efforts of the social bureaucrats to recognize labor unions and regulate working conditions. It must also be remembered that employers did not constitute the driving force behind the Industrial Patriotic movement and wartime controls, both of which they viewed as threatening bureaucratic intrusions.

Nonetheless, management clearly benefited from the actual operation of the wartime labor system. Wages were frozen, mobility was curtailed, and workers lost the rights to strike and organize. Although businessmen resented the autonomous labor initiatives of the Home and Welfare Ministries, the wartime experience reassured them that the bureaucrats did not seek a socialistic transformation of the economic structure.

In short, any discussion of the Japanese government's policies toward the labor movement after World War II must consider the complex legacy of these earlier programs and relationships.

PERSISTENCE OF THE SOCIAL BUREAUCRATS

The legacies were most apparent in the continuity in bureaucratic personnel. The triumphant Americans arrived in September 1945, determined to dismantle Japan's authoritarian wartime apparatus. Intent on encouraging the unionization of labor, Occupation authorities, or SCAP

(Supreme Commander for the Allied Powers), ordered the Japanese government to nullify existing repressive laws and to enact positive labor legislation. The next January, SCAP mandated the exclusion from labor administration of "all persons who were directly connected in the past in a responsible capacity with the obstruction or suppression of trade union organization or activity."[4]

The so-called labor purge coincided with the general purge of the civil bureaucracy, by which the Americans singled out officials and former officials of the Home Ministry and affiliated police agencies. The Occupation had earlier disbanded the Special Higher Police. The purges removed some 60 percent of the Home Ministry's highest officials during 1946.[5] The coup de grâce came at the end of 1947, when the Japanese government abolished the mighty Home Ministry and scattered its functions to the Welfare Ministry, the Labor Ministry, the Construction Ministry, the Local Autonomy Agency, and the newly decentralized police system. The cabinet had created the Labor Ministry in September.

Yet the Occupation never attempted to remove the vast majority of higher civil servants who had dealt with labor matters during the war. Many entered the new Labor Ministry, where the wartime generation held the posts of vice-minister and key bureau chiefs as late as 1969. While insisting on the authoritarian mentality of the police and Home Ministry, SCAP treated the staff of the wartime Welfare Ministry with surprising restraint, considering its central role in dissolving the unions and administering the Industrial Patriotic system. The persistence of the social bureaucrats owed much to the technocratic nature of presurrender labor policy. SCAP leaders, having committed themselves to labor reform, of necessity turned to those most knowledgeable in industrial relations, unemployment programs, and factory inspection. American labor experts (located in the Labor Division of the Economic and Scientific Section) were further impressed by their Japanese colleagues' sophisticated understanding of labor policies in the United States, Britain, and other democracies.[6]

Second, the Americans quickly recognized the futility of trying to purge former police officers from the ranks of the apparently enlightened labor bureaucrats. Nearly all of the Welfare Ministry's talented civil servants in 1946 had previously served as elite police officials. These included five of the first seven vice-ministers of the future Labor Ministry, as well as the principal drafters of the progressive Trade Union Law (1945) and Labor Standards Law (1947). SCAP officials finally threw up their hands after discovering that more than six hundred former officers of the regular police and Special Higher Police were working in prefectural labor sections.[7]

As the wartime labor bureaucrats became entrenched in the postwar Labor Ministry, a more senior group of former Home Ministry officials surfaced to guide the labor policies of the ruling political parties. Most entered politics after being depurged in 1951. Their eagerness to become party members signified a new relationship between social bureaucrats and politicians. Although some Home Ministry officials had joined the Minseitō and Seiyūkai during the 1920s, the great majority had kept their distance. The frequent alternation of power made open partisanship much too risky for the ambitious higher civil servant. The end of party cabinets in 1932 confirmed that elite bureaucrats, not parties, were the true spokesmen for the state. Wrapping themselves in the mantle of state autonomy, Home Ministry officials denounced the two parties and their capitalist allies for ignoring the needs of workers and small farmers. Several went beyond to assist the Social Masses' Party and agricultural cooperatives as counterforces to the established parties.

Political alignments and the very nature of the Japanese state changed markedly under the Occupation. The Home Ministry ceased to exist, and the American-imposed postwar constitution guaranteed party control of the cabinet. In contrast to the prewar pattern of party competition, the two major bourgeois parties—the Liberals and the Democrats (initially called the Progressives)—gradually coalesced into the business-oriented Liberal Democratic Party (LDP), which has ruled Japan ever since its formation in 1955. Although a small group of former Ministry of Agriculture and Forestry officials joined the postwar Japan Socialist Party, nearly all veterans of the Home, Welfare, and Labor Ministries have affiliated with the ruling LDP or its bourgeois predecessors.

Even more than the civil servants of the Labor Ministry, the politicized Home Ministry clique functioned as the bridge between interwar social policy and the bourgeois government's controversial measures toward the labor movement during the 1950s. Recent attention has focused on the influence of retired economic bureaucrats within the LDP, but journalists at the time were more likely to sensationalize the political "revival of the Home Ministry."[8] Over thirty depurged Home Ministry veterans won Lower House seats in 1952, and the total Home Ministry contingent within both houses of the Diet came to 54 in 1960.

With the end of the Occupation in 1952, the Labor Ministry and, indeed, the cause of labor reform lost the prestige enjoyed under American rule. Thereafter the cabinet and the governing party decided major questions of labor policy.

Because a large number of Home Ministry veterans had once held posts in the Social Bureau or Welfare Ministry, party leaders turned to them to staff cabinet and party-level positions related to labor and social welfare.[9] The social bureaucrats had survived and so had their prewar notion of "social policy," which combined reform and control. Postwar labor policy would be dominated by civil servants and retired officials who had been trained to determine the parameters of sound trade union activity.

THE OCCUPATION REFORMS

The dual aspects of prewar social policy were very much in evidence during the Occupation years. A tendency prevails on both sides of the Pacific to assume that the Americans unilaterally established the main features—good and bad—of postwar Japanese labor policy. Such explanations routinely divide Occupation policy into an initial liberal phase and a later "reverse course." In the first phase, SCAP ordered the Japanese government to enact the Trade Union Law and other progressive legislation while it actively promoted labor's freedom to organize, strike, and bargain collectively. But beginning in 1947, the argument continues, the Americans systematically diluted labor's new rights in the face of Cold War tensions and growing Communist influence within the Japanese labor movement.

Although the Americans undeniably set the broad policy outlines, officials of the Labor Ministry (and the Welfare Ministry before September 1947) played a vital role in advancing the initial progressive policies and, later, in rolling many of them back. Ironically, the labor bureaucrats achieved their greatest autonomy under the aegis of the American state. Like their colleagues in other ministries, these officials became more powerful during the Occupation than ever before or ever again.[10] Thanks to the United States military, the bureaucrats no longer contended with the forces that had resisted labor legislation in the past. The Imperial Army had been disbanded; employers were temporarily forbidden to organize national associations; and a cowed Diet uncharacteristically passed every labor measure approved by SCAP. Under such circumstances, Welfare and Labor officials enthusiastically cooperated with their American counterparts, reviving the 1920s agenda of labor and social legislation in the process.

Japanese initiative and bureaucratic continuity were central to the formulation of the Labor Standards Law of 1947. Social Bureau officials had worked throughout the interwar period to broaden the scope of protective legislation beyond the 1911 Factory Law. Their efforts resulted in several revisions of the original law, plus the Workmen's Compensation Law (1931), the Retirement Fund Law (1936), and the Shops Law (1938). To improve productivity and worker morale during World War II, the Welfare Ministry further attempted to inhibit dismissals while forcing management to pay minimum "living wages."[11] This administrative drive did not succeed, but after the war, the staff of the ministry's Labor Policy Bureau threw itself into the task of drafting a comprehensive Labor Standards Law that did establish minimum wages and other major protections. To the surprise of SCAP's labor experts, the resulting law significantly exceeded the United States's Fair Labor Standards Act in coverage. Building upon their wartime policy to increase job security, Welfare Ministry bureaucrats, for example, required employers to give dismissed workers thirty days' notice, whereas American officials had favored no more than fifteen days.[12]

The prewar experience similarly guided the Welfare Ministry's promotion of the crucial Trade Union Law (enacted in December 1945). Amid the social dislocations of defeat, officials sought a legal framework for union-management relations for essentially the same instrumental reasons that had earlier produced the Home Ministry's reformism after World War I. In both cases, bureaucrats proposed the legal recognition of labor union activities to prevent industrial breakdown and the emergence of a radical labor movement. Drawing on the programs of the 1920s, the Higashikuni cabinet set up a commission to draft detailed trade union legislation in early October, several days before General Douglas MacArthur directed the government to encourage unionization. The Labor Legislation Commission (Rōmu Hōsei Shingikai) included employers, Diet members, and civil servants from other ministries. Yet the real work of formulating the Trade Union Law fell to a small group of anti-Communist labor leaders, legal scholars, and Welfare Ministry officials, which had been associated with the Social Bureau's prewar labor union legislation.[13] By appointing Nishio Suehiro and Matsuoka Komakichi to the strategic drafting subcommittee, the social bureaucrats once again indicated their preference for the "realism" of the old Sōdōmei.

Impressed by the depth of Japanese sentiment for a trade union law, SCAP stood aside while the Labor Legislation Commission drafted the union bill. The final Trade Union Law bore a striking resemblance to the Social Bureau's progressive drafts of 1925 and 1929. Among its liberal features, the law guaranteed the rights of unions in both the private and public sectors (except for the police and firefighters), and it strictly prohibited employers from discriminating against union members. Even the seemingly new guarantees of collective-bargaining rights had their origins in the Social Bureau's 1925 draft and the Home Ministry's encouragement of collective agreements during the early 1930s. On the restrictive side, the 1945 Trade Union Law resurrected earlier proposed provisions that would empower the government to monitor union activities and finances. The postwar Trade Union Law introduced only one truly novel feature. It created tripartite labor relations commissions—consisting of labor, management, and "public interest" representatives—to conciliate disputes and adjudicate cases of unfair labor practices.[14] As in the 1920s, powerful officials within the government were determined to establish a liberal, yet supervised, framework within which unions would develop.

THE "REVERSE COURSE" AND JAPANESE HISTORY

If the policies of the interwar years help explain the labor bureaucrats' commitment to the Trade Union Law system in 1945, they also illuminate the pivotal role of the Japanese state in the subsequent "reverse course." From the perspective of the Japanese bureaucrats and ruling bourgeois parties, no reversal occurred. Although, in the wake of defeat, the civilian elites generally favored the legal recognition of labor unions, they never ceased to oppose the development of a highly politicized or Communist-dominated labor movement. The Japanese government required neither American advice nor the new Cold War to arrive at this position. Its anti-Communist labor policy was firmly rooted in the Social Bureau's interwar concept of "sound trade unionism." While patronizing the moderate Sōdōmei, the Home Ministry had ruthlessly repressed the militant, Communist-backed Hyōgikai. The vision of a sound labor movement led by the revived Sōdōmei continued to inspire

surviving social bureaucrats and bourgeois politicians after 1945.
Viewed in historical terms, the "reverse course" represented a second
attempt by the Japanese state to reshape the labor movement along anti-
Communist lines.

Japanese authorities might very well have forged a moderate union
movement in the early postwar months had SCAP not intervened. The
presurrender imperial state emerged remarkably intact and fully capable
of suppressing left-wing labor elements. In the weeks following defeat in
August 1945, the government looked with favor upon the efforts of the
anti-Communist labor leaders, Nishio Suehiro and Matsuoka Komakichi, to reactivate the Sōdōmei. Back in operation by January 1946, the
Sōdōmei (renamed the Nihon Rōdō Kumiai Sōdōmei) again emphasized
cautious trade unionism and cooperation with managers. Politically, it
affiliated with the moderate Japan Socialist Party, which Nishio and
others had concurrently organized.

SCAP, too, preferred the social democratic leadership of Sōdōmei,
but the Americans demanded that the Japanese police refrain from ha-
rassing left-wing labor organizers. The Occupation moreover released
several hundred Communist Party members from jail and lesser detention in October 1945. SCAP officials desired a strong union movement
as a political counterweight to the entrenched presurrender elites, and
they were initially willing to tolerate some Communist Party influence
within organized labor.[15]

As it turned out, American authorities were just as shocked as their
Japanese counterparts by the labor militancy that followed the lifting of
the imperial government's controls. From an insignificant base of five
thousand in October 1945, union membership soared to nearly five
million by December 1946, against the postwar backdrop of hyperinfla-
tion, massive layoffs, and acute food shortages. During the first six
months of 1946, thousands of workers engaged in "production control," whereby employees took over the management of enterprises in
dispute actions. By May, high-level United States officials were charging
collusion between the Soviet Union and the left wing of Japanese labor.

The newly liberated Japanese Communist Party did not in fact instigate most incidents of production control, nor did it propose the immediate overthrow of capitalism by workers' soviets. Nonetheless, the party
posed a clearly perceived threat to Japan's political and economic establishment. In August 1946, Communists and left-wing socialists organized
the Sambetsu Kaigi (Japanese Congress of Industrial Organizations),
whose membership greatly outnumbered that of the rival Sōdōmei

(1,630,000 to 850,000). Beginning in October, Sambetsu leaders spearheaded a series of crippling strikes aimed at resisting the government's program of personnel and wage retrenchment. Politically, they sought to topple the Liberal Party cabinet of Yoshida Shigeru (not to be confused with the Home Ministry official of the same name). Prime Minister Yoshida's blanket condemnation of organized labor helped drive even the moderate Sōdōmei into a tenuous alliance with the left-wing Sambetsu. Thus united, Japanese labor planned a nationwide general strike, scheduled for 1 February 1947, to demand the immediate formation of a popularly based government that would include Communists.[16]

In the face of larger, increasingly political strikes, American and Japanese authorities began to sound more and more alike in their defense of "democracy" and "sound" unions against Communism. The social bureaucrats breathed a collective sigh of relief when MacArthur banned the projected general strike in late January 1947. In the ensuing months, the Labor Ministry and SCAP mounted a joint counteroffensive against Communist elements in a manner recalling the interwar Home Ministry's divide-and-control tactics. Together with the Sōdōmei, United States and Japanese officials assisted the formation of internal "democratization leagues" (Mindō) by Sambetsu organizers who had come to resent Communist Party interference. Both sets of authorities actively lectured workers on the need for free, responsible, and autonomous unions. Labor Division Chief James Killen equated "freedom" and "autonomy" with freedom from the domination of political parties.[17] Leaders of the Labor Ministry heartily agreed. In an article entitled "What is a Sound Union Movement?" the ministry's Labor Policy Bureau explained:

> With reference to the key objectives laid out in the Trade Union Law, a union has an obligation, first and foremost, to economic reconstruction. . . . Second, a sound union is an autonomous (jishuteki) one. The union movement must be as free as possible. Accordingly, it must not suffer from domination and interference from any other quarter. . . . Third, a [sound] union is a thoroughly democratic one. A labor union must truly be a union for all of its members, and, for example, must absolutely avoid dictatorship by its leaders or domination by a few.[18]

Determined to isolate militant groups from the rest of the labor movement, SCAP and the Japanese government proceeded to weaken many of the protections guaranteed by the 1945 Trade Union Law. In 1948, the conservative Yoshida cabinet took on the left-wing public-employees' unions by sponsoring legislation that prevented workers in public enterprises from striking. An accompanying law denied to civil servants the rights to strike and to bargain collectively.[19] Yoshida's government completed the overhaul of labor legislation in 1949, with the revisions of the original Trade Union Law and the 1946 Labor Relations Adjustment Law. Modeled after the Taft-Hartley Act of 1947, key amendments gave the government and labor relations commissions greater control over the certification and internal procedures of unions. Both SCAP and the Labor Ministry regarded the revised legislation as an important instrument for denying trade union rights to Communist-backed organizations.[20]

The stage was set for the Red Purge, in which SCAP, the Japanese state, and employers joined forces in the postwar era's most ambitious attempt to reshape the labor movement. The locus of labor policy-making had meanwhile shifted from SCAP to the Yoshida cabinet, the ruling Liberal Party, and big business. Although SCAP had initially prevented businessmen from organizing a nationwide association on the order of the prewar National Federation of Industrial Organizations, the Americans removed the shackles in 1948. The newly created Nikkeiren (Japan Federation of Employers' Associations) immediately coordinated an enterprise-level campaign to renegotiate early postwar collective contracts, limit the scope of union activities, and reassert managerial authority.

By the latter half of 1950, the Yoshida cabinet felt strong enough to carry out its own Red Purge. In a crackdown reminiscent of Prime Minister Tanaka Giichi's blow against the far Left in 1928, the government not only encouraged the dismissal of thousands of alleged Communists in the public and private sectors, but went further to dissolve the Sambetsu-dominated Zen Rōren (National Council for the Coordination of Labor Unions). Continuities abounded as Ōhashi Takeo, an influential social bureaucrat in the wartime Home and Welfare Ministries, directed the anti-Communist crusade in his new capacity as Yoshida's attorney general. Labor Ministry officials cautioned employers against settling scores with non-Communist union members, yet they pledged not to interfere with efforts to dismiss "Communistic, subversive elements."[21] The state's policies, active and passive, proved crucial to the destruction of the left-wing Sambetsu at the factory level. Bolstered by the Red Purge, managers vigorously supported the formation of more cooperative, anti-Communist "second unions" within enterprises.[22]

As in the late 1920s, the Japanese government appeared to have successfully reinforced moderate tendencies within the labor movement.

Leaders of the anti-Communist democratization leagues hastily withdrew their organizations from the beleaguered Sambetsu in 1949 and
1950. Sambetsu's membership plummeted from 1,372,000 in 1948 to
47,000 in 1951. In July 1950, the Labor Ministry and SCAP openly
supported the consolidation of Sōdōmei and the democratization
leagues into the present Sōhyō (General Council of Japanese Trade
Unions). The Red Purge did not, however, eliminate the sources of
tensions that divided the government and much of organized labor.
Sōhyō itself soon came under the domination of left-wing socialists who
vehemently protested the 1951 United States-Japan Security Treaty and
often resorted to large-scale political strikes. In retaliation, Attorney
General Ōhashi Takeo warned in 1951 that the Yoshida cabinet was
considering both a "public peace-preservation law" and a law to prohibit general strikes. The legislation never materialized, but in June
1952 the cabinet succeeded in passing the Subversive Activities Prevention Law, which many believed was ambiguous enough to be applied to
trade union activity.[23] Disturbed by the rising wave of strikes in the coal
and electric-power industries, the government also pushed through the
so-called Strike Regulation Law of 1953 that effectively outlawed work
stoppages in those industries.

Following the end of the Occupation in 1952, the former social bureaucrats of the ruling bourgeois parties played an increasingly powerful role
in the government's numerous confrontations with the labor movement.
Whereas the Labor Ministry was confined to the narrow sphere of labor
administration, the retired Home Ministry officials dealt with labor questions in the sweeping prewar fashion, as problems of public order, political education, and basic governance. During the first half of the 1950s, no
issue concerned the bureaucratic politicians more than the recentraliza-
tion of the nation's police forces, which Occupation reforms had placed
under local control. Decentralization, they protested, stripped the state of
its most potent weapon against the Communist Party and left-wing labor
unions. Nadao Hirokichi, the chief proponent of the government's cen-
tralizing Police Law of 1954, had been, appropriately enough, a senior
official in the wartime Welfare and Home Ministries.[24] In the latter half
of the decade, the Liberal Democratic Party's social bureaucrats turned to
another familiar issue—the "thought problem" in education—locking
horns with the militant Japan Teachers Union. Once again, Nadao led the
charge in his capacity as education minister under Prime Minister Kishi
Nobusuke. In the calm that followed the uproar over the revision of the
Security Treaty in 1960, some Home Ministry veterans, including Ōhashi

Takeo (labor minister, 1962–64), favored a compromise with Sōhyō on the issue of broadening the rights of public employees. However, just as many, led by Nadao, joined former Education Ministry figures to form the LDP's "education–public peace" (*bunkyō-chian*) group, which rejected any accommodation with Sōhyō and especially with the despised Japan Teachers Union.[25]

The persistence of these higher civil servants offers the historian a rare opportunity to examine how the twentieth-century Japanese state has balanced its interests against those of Capital and Labor. The LDP's social bureaucrats had clearly changed since their prewar and wartime days. No longer were they the impressively autonomous "officials of the Emperor" who advanced state initiatives, often in direct defiance of employers; now they appeared little more than spokesmen for Nikkeiren's industrialists. And yet, in one important respect, they had not changed. Even as politicians, they continued to behave as officials of the Home Ministry in their vigorous defense of the established order against the leftist threat. Prior to 1945, the social bureaucrats could afford to experiment with new modes of labor organization—whether "sound" trade unions or industrial patriotic units—precisely because they had little to fear from below, particularly after the Home Ministry eradicated remaining Communist groups in 1928. But the tremendous growth and politicization of the early postwar labor movement dispelled any doubts that state officials might have had about what side they were on. As the social-bureaucrats-turned-politicians openly allied themselves with businessmen, defense of the state and social order came to be equated with defense of the capitalist economic system that supported that order.

TOWARD CORPORATISM WITH LABOR?

The protracted struggles between Sōhyō and the bourgeois party governments of the 1950s are past history, but the theme of mutual hostility continues to pervade discussions of the contemporary Japanese state and labor. In a suggestive comparative essay, T. J. Pempel and Tsunekawa Keiichi argue that postwar Japan constitutes an anomalous case of "corporatism without labor." That is, the Japanese state pursues its paramount goal of economic growth in close cooperation with officially recognized, hierarchically ordered associations that represent big business, small business, agriculture, and virtually every other major interest *except* labor. According to Pempel and Tsunekawa, the exceptional status of labor stems most directly from the unions' failure to establish a single national federation that could function as a peak association in economic policy-making or bargaining with comparable business associations. As of June 1985, the largest national labor center, Sōhyō, represented only 35.2 percent of organized workers, whereas the second largest, Dōmei (Japan Confederation of Labor), accounted for a mere 17.4 percent. The overwhelming majority of Japanese unions remain based on the enterprise unit, and most bargain with employers at the plant level, regardless of affiliation with national federations.

The voice of labor appears to be fragmented politically, as well. Sōhyō supports the Japan Socialist Party and, to a lesser extent, the Communist Party, whereas Dōmei backs the breakaway Democratic Socialist Party. The Socialists headed the short-lived Katayama cabinet (April 1947–March 1948) and thereafter participated in a second coalition government, the Ashida cabinet (March–October 1948). Yet no labor-based party has obtained a single cabinet post since then. Nor, contend Pempel and Tsunekawa, do labor representatives sit on many of the government's advisory councils or exercise much influence in the LDP-dominated parliamentary committees. Throughout most of the postwar era, they conclude, the "anti-labor coalition" of the LDP, big business, and bureaucrats consciously excluded labor from policy-making, and the labor movement itself generally rejected inclusion as tantamount to co-optation.[26]

Although the case for corporatism without labor is compelling in several respects, I propose a different, more historical reading of twentieth-century trends.[27] The state and organized labor have rarely been as far apart in the postwar era as one might think. The interwar experience is instructive on two counts. First, despite the antigovernment stance taken by Sambetsu and then Sōhyō, the postwar labor movement has increasingly come under the influence of the direct successors of the prewar Sōdōmei and other organizations with similar commitments to "realistic" trade unionism. Labor's right wing has consistently sought an institutionalized role in policy-making and bargaining, just as Sōdōmei strove to define and participate in a corporatist scheme of conflict resolution during the mid-1930s. Second, the postwar coalition surrounding the ruling parties contains many who, like interwar social bureaucrats and Minseitō politicians, do wish to incorporate labor at the national level. They are, to be sure, hostile to left-wing political unionism and have occasionally involved the state in weakening militant unions, particularly those composed of public employees.

Nonetheless, the policies of the dominant coalition have seldom aimed at the fragmentation of organized labor as a collective interest. Rather, bureaucrats, bourgeois politicians, and businessmen have regularly expressed the hope that right-wing union leaders would once again unify the labor movement. Their reasoning echoes that of the prewar generation. Some point out the partisan advantages of absorbing or allying with a moderate social democratic party; others emphasize the necessity of bringing labor into the existing order from the standpoint of social harmony; still others favor a truly tripartite system of corporatism to deal with pressing problems of productivity.

The Sōdōmei-style reunification of the labor movement has been most apparent in the development of Sōhyō's chief rival, Dōmei. Inaugurated in 1964, Dōmei inherited the spirit of "trade unionism" advanced by Nishio Suehiro, Matsuoka Komakichi, and the prewar Sōdōmei. Matsuoka was still chairman of Sōdōmei in 1952, when his anti-Communist lieutenants led the rump of their federation out of the left-leaning Sōhyō. In 1954, Sōdōmei cofounded Dōmei's immediate predecessor, Zenrō Kaigi (All-Japan Labor Union Congress). The loose confederation included several other unions that had since left Sōhyō out of dissatisfaction with the latter's propensity for politicized and singularly unsuccessful strikes. Although no longer active in Sōdōmei, the indefatigable Nishio Suehiro furthered the process of consolidation.

In 1960, forty Lower House members accompanied Nishio out of the Japan Socialist Party to form the less doctrinaire Democratic Socialist Party, which in turn encouraged the merger of Sōdōmei and Zenrō Kaigi into Dōmei. A distinguishing feature of the Sōdōmei/Dōmei organizations has been their unflagging commitment to cooperating with big business and the state on behalf of increased productivity. In 1955, for example, the nation's leading business associations and the government set up the Japan Productivity Center and invited the unions to support the campaign to modernize Japanese production. The militant Sōhyō denounced the campaign as a stratagem to cut wages, dismiss workers, and "Industrially Patrioticize" the unions. Sōdōmei and Zenrō Kaigi, on the other hand, endorsed increased productivity as the best means of raising real wages, and they eagerly joined in the productivity movement at the national and enterprise levels. The productivity campaign is often considered the springboard for postwar Japan's astounding economic growth.[28]

Although Dōmei is smaller than Sōhyō, it and like-minded organizations now constitute the mainstream of the Japanese labor movement in the private sector. Dōmei surpassed Sōhyō in members from privately owned industries as early as 1967. Sōhyō currently faces the prospect of further isolation as official policies of administrative retrenchment and privatization, particularly of the National Railways, weaken its dominant public-sector unions. The economic boom of the 1960s and early 1970s also saw the emergence of a second center of pragmatic trade unionism, the International Metalworkers Federation–Japan Council. The IMF–JC's potential as a unifier lies in its transcendence of the existing national centers. It managed to attract leading private-sector labor organizations from all four major national centers, including Sōhyō. These affiliates were moreover placed in the strategic core of Japan's export-driven economy—iron and steel, automobiles, electrical machinery, and shipbuilding. In alliance with Dōmei, the IMF–JC has vigorously criticized the confrontational tactics of Sōhyō's leadership and has instead associated the fortunes of the working class with maintaining Japan's competitive position.[29]

The growth of the Dōmei/IMF–JC bloc clearly strengthened the corporatist tendencies inherent in the labor movement's annual Spring Offensive (Shuntō). Begun by Sōhyō in 1955 to coordinate the wage demands of its unions, the Spring Offensive soon expanded to include the affiliates of the three other national centers. A national coordinating committee or representatives of major industrial federations typically negotiate with comparable employers' associations, and influential unions are chosen to lead the bargaining. These settlements then become the basis of contracts between participating enterprise unions and managers. The IMF–JC unions emerged as the national pattern-setters in the late 1960s. Japan's continued competitiveness after the 1973 oil crisis owed much to the central leadership of the IMF–JC's Federation of Iron and Steel Workers' Unions (Tekkō Rōren), which remains nominally in Sōhyō despite its moderation. Since 1975, the federation has annually persuaded the nation's unions to scale down wage demands in exchange for employment-maintenance measures, pension reform, and governmental commitments to tax cuts.

In addition to the Spring Offensive, the Dōmei/IMF–JC unions have successfully established several bodies for industry-wide joint consultation with employers in an effort to cope with the problems of industrial restructuring, such as those plaguing the depressed shipbuilding industry. Employers generally like the rationality of the Spring Offensive and joint consultation. So apparently do governmental officials, who have played a greater, if behind-the-scenes, role in promoting anti-inflationary wage settlements since 1974.[30]

As the new "realists" consolidate their hold over the private-sector unions, they have revived the prewar Sōdōmei's quest for inclusion in policy-making. Chaired by Nishio Suehiro until 1967, the Democratic Socialist Party furnishes these unions with an institutionalized political voice. Although critics describe the DSP as conservative and unprincipled in its collaboration with the ruling LDP, the DSP has often been an effective lobby for welfare measures for workers and the general public. In a recent study of the Japanese legislative process, Mike Mochizuki demonstrated how the DSP was responsible for the enactment of the innovative Employment Insurance Law (1974), by which the state subsidizes employers to maintain employment. DSP leaders and the unions not only persuaded the Labor Ministry and cabinet to reintroduce the bill after its first failure, but also succeeded in patching together a compromise between the LDP and the opposition parties within the Diet committee. Mochizuki notes that representatives of the unions and socialist parties further affect policy by regularly serving on preparliamentary advisory councils attached to the Labor Ministry and other agencies.[31]

Finally, one must not ignore the growing tendency of private-sector unions to advance policies in direct negotiation with bureaucrats and the governing LDP. In 1976, the IMF–JC unions founded the Trade Union Council for Policy Promotion (Seisaku Suishin Rōso Kaigi), which began meeting regularly with LDP representatives and officials of the various ministries.[32] Forty-one unions from all four national centers founded its successor, the All-Japan Council of Private-Sector Labor Organizations (Zemmin Rōkyō), in December 1982. Member unions counted 5,400,000 workers in January 1986. The Zemmin Rōkyō recently approved plans to transform the council by November 1987 into a truly national federation encompassing all of organized labor in the public as well as private sectors. The drive has drawn support from two of Sōhyō's leading public-employees' unions—Jichirō (prefectural and municipal workers) and Zentei (postal workers)—and several observers predict the long-awaited unification of the Japanese labor movement. Equally important, Zemmin Rōkyō has been unequivocal in its pursuit of a policy-making role at the national level. The labor council has held a series of meetings and conferences with the Labor Ministry, with the Ministry of International Trade and Industry on industrial policy and industrial relations, and with the Economic Planning Agency on price issues. Governmental officials are said to rate the Zemmin Rōkyō more highly than any other labor organization. Some scholars now speak of the emergence of "neo-corporatism" *with* labor.

The LDP, for its part, has viewed the reformist consolidation of the labor movement with keen interest. The vision of a "Lib-lab" centrist party did not die with the Minseitō in 1931. The bourgeois forces remained divided between the Liberal Party and the Democratic (Progressive) Party during the first ten years of the postwar era, and both parties frequently eyed the right-wing socialists and their allies in Sōdōmei as coalition partners. Within days of the surrender in August 1945, the former Seiyūkai politician, Hatoyama Ichirō (prime minister, 1954–56), approached Sōdōmei's Nishio Suehiro about such an alliance. Nishio and other leaders of the Socialist Party (JSP) declined both this and a subsequent invitation to participate in the Liberal Party's Yoshida cabinet in January 1947.[33] The rival Democratic Party, the one more closely identified with the old Minseitō, was more successful in its overtures. Like their predecessor, the Democrats campaigned on a platform of "modified capitalism" and social policy, and in 1947 and 1948 they cooperated with the right wing of the JSP and a smaller bourgeois party to organize the coalition Katayama and Ashida cabinets. The quest for a socialist-labor ally ebbed after the bourgeois parties united in 1955 to form the Liberal Democratic Party, which maintained comfortable parliamentary majorities over the next fifteen years.

However, the LDP's hold eroded during the 1970s, and the party fell short of Lower House majorities in three general elections since 1976. Following the third such setback, in December 1983, speculation grew that the ruling party would bring the Dōmei-backed DSP into the cabinet as a coalition partner. The LDP and DSP in fact agreed to establish a committee to coordinate policy demands in February 1984.[34] Determined to cultivate better ties with the private-sector unions, the LDP had already resolved to "deepen exchange with labor unions as friendly groups" in its 1980 action policy.[35] In the most recent general election, in July 1986, the Liberal Democrats won an unprecedented 304 seats in the Lower House (total, 512), while the JSP and DSP lost 25 and 11 seats, respectively. The possibility of a labor representative in the cabinet again appears remote. On the other hand, the virtual collapse of the Sōhyō-supported Socialist Party may well drive the unions into a closer relationship with the governing party and bureaucracy, besides accelerating the unification of organized labor by Zemmin Rōkyō.

Whether these developments will lead to the full incorporation of labor is, of course, an open question. Yet this much is clear. Labor questions have rarely been confined to shopfloor relations between workers and employers. Throughout the twentieth century, the Japanese state has played a major role, be it in the form of labor union legislation, the Industrial Patriotic movement, or suppressive red purges. Moreover, the relationship among the state, Labor, and Capital has been complex, involving alliances between fractions of the three. Rival parties and bureaucratic cliques competed to define the interests of the state; employers' associations divided over recognizing and incorporating unions; and organized labor invariably formed left and right wings. All sides have occasionally adopted extreme measures with disastrous results. The left-wing Hyōgikai and postwar Sambetsu chose to confront the combined anti-Communist forces of the state, employers, and the rest of the labor movement. The wartime social bureaucrats likewise discarded a cooperative labor union movement in preference for unworkable totalitarian organizations and controls.

But all sides have also learned from previous experiences. In the years since the Occupation, the government and business have not attempted to roll back the basic union rights of private-sector workers. Nor does the present mainstream of organized labor view the state as an uncompromising foe. The precise relationship between the state and labor issues will continue to change as it has since the days of the first draft factory legislation in the 1880s. The postwar record of economic success notwithstanding, the Japanese, too, are beginning to face the problems of declining heavy industries as more recently industrialized countries compete for world markets. A new sense of crisis pervades the vital export sector as a result of the staggering appreciation of the yen against the dollar since September 1985. How the government, business, and labor unions interact to resolve these questions will no doubt determine the next phase in this ongoing story.

APPENDIX I   INDUSTRIAL STRIKES, 1897–1941

Year	Strikes	Participants	Year	Strikes	Participants
1897[a]	32	3,510	1907	60	11,483
1898	43	6,293	1908	13	823
1899	15	4,834	1909	11	310
1900	11	2,316	1910	10	2,934
1901	18	1,948	1911	22	2,100
1902	8	1,849	1912	49	5,736
1903	9	1,359	1913	47	5,242
1904	6	897	1914	50	7,904
1905	19	5,013	1915	64	7,852
1906	13	2,037	1916	108	8,413

Year	Strikes and lockouts		Demands[b]		Wages[c] (1934–36 = 100)		Partici-pants per strike
	Inci-dents	Partic-ipants	Posi-tive	Defen-sive	Actual	Real	
			Percent	Percent			
1917[d]	398	57,309	84	4	41.8	54.4	144
1918[d]	417	66,457	87	4	53.7	51.9	159
1919	497	63,137	89	3	79.1	57.4	127
1920	282	36,371	69	23	104.5	72.6	129
1921	246	58,225	73	16	106.7	80.8	237
1922	250	41,503	48	38	112.7	86.7	166
1923	270	36,259	66	17	109.0	84.6	134
1924	295	48,940	53	17	112.7	86.7	166
1925	270	32,472	47	18	115.7	87.9	120
1926	469	63,644	56	17	117.9	93.9	136
1927	366	44,478	42	37	115.7	93.5	122
1928	357	38,099	40	33	117.9	99.1	107
1929	522	65,299	24	48	117.2	100.9	125
1930	853	72,045	13	76	106.0	101.5	84
1931	940	59,261	23	66	98.5	106.6	63
1932	823	47,719	26	63	95.5	102.2	58
1933	551	37,394	50	39	97.8	101.5	68

Year	Strikes and lockouts		Slowdowns		Total participants in all disputes
	Incidents	*Participants*	*Incidents*	*Participants*	
1930	853	72,045	53	9,284	81,329
1934	578	42,561	48	6,975	49,536
1935	545	32,421	45	5,313	37,734
1936	511	27,204	36	3,696	30,900
1937	553	55,972	75	67,758	123,730
1938	227	13,257	35	5,084	18,341
1939	294	20,762	64	52,073	72,835
1940	240	24,184	31	8,765	32,949
1941	—	—	—	—	10,867

SOURCES: Rōdōshō, RGS, 1:1310–11; for 1917–33 figures, Miwa Ryōichi, p. 259.
[a]Covers only July through December.
[b]Positive demands include higher wages, shorter hours, and the right to organize; defensive demands include resistance to wage reductions and personnel cuts.
[c]Index below estimates the average wage for male and female workers in manufacturing.
[d]Strike figures do not include lockouts.

APPENDIX II   CABINETS AND MINISTERS RELATED TO LABOR POLICY, 1908–32

Cabinet	Year formed	Party[a]	Home Affairs	Agriculture-Commerce	Justice
Katsura Tarō (II)	1908	—	Hirata Tōsuke	Ōura Kanetake	
Saionji Kimmochi (II)	1911	S[b]	Hara Takashi	Makino Nobuaki	
Katsura Tarō (III)	1912	—	Ōura Kanetake	Nakashōji Ren	
Yamamoto Gonnohyōe (I)	1913	S[b]	Hara Takashi	Yamamoto Tatsuo	
Ōkuma Shigenobu (II)	1914	D[b]	Ōura Kanetake Ichiki Kitokurō	Taketomi Tokitoshi Minoura Katsundo	

Cabinet	Year formed	Party[a]	Home Affairs	Agriculture-Commerce	Justice
Terauchi Masataka	1916	—	Gotō Shimpei Mizuno Rentarō	Nakashōji Ren	
Hara Takashi	1918	S	Tokonami Takejirō	Yamamoto Tatsuo	Hara Takashi Ōki Enkichi
Takahashi Korekiyo	1921	S	Tokonami Takejirō	Yamamoto Tatsuo	Ōki Enkichi
Katō Tomosaburō	1922	—	Mizuno Rentarō	Arai Kentarō	Okano Keijirō
Yamamoto Gonnohyōe (II)	1923	—	Gotō Shimpei	Den Kenjirō	Hiranuma Kiichirō
Kiyoura Keigo	1924	—	Mizuno Rentarō	Maeda Toshisada	Suzuki Kisaburō
Katō Takaaki (I)	1924	K, S, KC	Wakatsuki Reijirō	Takahashi Korekiyo Noda Utarō[c]	Yokota Sennosuke Ogawa Heikichi
Katō Takaaki (II)	1925	K	Wakatsuki Reijirō	Kataoka Naoharu	Egi Tasuku
Wakatsuki Reijirō (I)	1926	K	Wakatsuki Reijirō Hamaguchi Osachi	Kataoka Naoharu Fujisawa Ikunosuke	Egi Tasuku
Tanaka Giichi	1927	S	Suzuki Kisaburō Mochizuki Keisuke	Nakahashi Tokugorō	Hara Yoshimichi
Hamaguchi Osachi	1929	M	Adachi Kenzō	Tawara Magoichi	Watanabe Chifuyu
Wakatsuki Reijirō (II)	1931	M	Adachi Kenzō	Sakurauchi Yukio	Watanabe Chifuyu
Inukai Tsuyoshi	1931–32	S	Nakahashi Tokugorō Suzuki Kisaburō	Maeda Yonezō	Suzuki Kisaburō Kawamura Takeji

[a]S = Seiyūkai; D = Dōshikai; K = Kenseikai; KC = Kakushin Club; M = Minseitō.
[b]Sympathy toward a party, as indicated by the inclusion of that party's leaders in the cabinet.
[c]Those named in this column from here on headed the Ministry of Commerce and Industry, which replaced the Ministry of Agriculture and Commerce in April 1925.

APPENDIX III STRIKE-RELATED ARRESTS UNDER ARTICLE 17 OF THE POLICE REGULATIONS AND OTHER CHARGES, 1914–26

Year	Strikes[a] (parti-cipants)	Total arrests	Art. 17, "instiga-tion, in-citement"	Art. 17, other clauses[b]	Sedition and other charges
1914	7,904	32	18	—	14
1915	7,852	65	9	55	1
1916	8,413	59	30	10	19
1917	57,309	174	104	34	36
1918	66,457	1,965	159	197	1,609
1919	63,137	536	58	61	417
1920	36,371	378	131	54	193
1921	58,225	634	16	68	550
1922	41,503	213	6	37	170
1923	36,259	237	11	10	216
1924	54,526	383	26	54	303
1925	40,742	331	—	17	314
1926	67,234	993	—	—	993

SOURCE: Kamii, "Chian keisatsuhō," p. 172.
[a]Figures for 1924–26 include slowdowns.
[b]Includes the application of the "instigation or incitement" clause and Article 17, in general, in tandem with other laws.

APPENDIX IV   OCCUPATIONAL BACKGROUND
OF THE NONPROLETARIAN PARTIES, LOWER HOUSE
REPRESENTATIVES, 1920–30
(percentages)[a]

Election year and party	Business[b]		Professions[c]		Higher civil service		Unclear	
1920								
Kenseikai	68%	(73)[d]	32%	(35)[d]	12%	(13)[d]	6%	(6)[d]
Seiyūkai	67	(188)	28	(78)	13	(36)	4	(11)
Kokumintō	45	(13)	55	(16)	10	(3)	7	(2)
House total	65	(303)	31	(142)	13	(58)	5	(25)
1924								
Kenseikai	65	(102)	38	(59)	10	(15)	7	(11)
Seiyūkai	58	(59)	32	(32)	8	(8)	11	(11)
Seiyūhontō	63	(70)	31	(35)	15	(17)	6	(7)
Kakushin Club	59	(17)	52	(15)	21	(6)	0	(0)
House total	62	(286)	35	(162)	12	(54)	8	(38)
1928								
Minseitō	59	(126)	40	(85)	19	(41)	5	(10)
Seiyūkai	62	(138)	34	(76)	16	(36)	7	(15)
House total	59	(272)	37	(173)	18	(83)	6	(29)
1930								
Minseitō	59	(159)	39	(105)	16	(43)	5	(14)
Seiyūkai	60	(103)	34	(59)	19	(32)	11	(19)
House total	58	(267)	38	(174)	17	(77)	8	(37)

SOURCE: Masumi, *Nihon seitō shi ron*, 5:255–59.

[a]Because members often represented more than one occupational category (e.g., a lawyer-businessman), each party's percentages total more than 100 percent.

[b]Business encompasses company and bank presidents, board members, and managers. It includes most agricultural representatives, who commonly headed agricultural firms and served on the boards of local banks and companies.

[c]Includes lawyers, journalists, publishers, educators, doctors, priests, and monks.

[d]Figures in parentheses indicate the number of representatives.

	Agriculture & Commerce Ministry draft (1920)	Home Ministry draft (1920)	Kenseikai bill (1921)	Kokumintō bill (1922)	Social Bureau draft (1925)	Wakatsuki cabinet bill (1926)	Hamaguchi cabinet draft bill (1929)	Hamaguchi cabinet bill (1931)
Act of incorporation	Compulsory	Voluntary	Compulsory	Compulsory	Voluntary	Compulsory	Voluntary	Voluntary
Unions recognized	Craft, industrial unions (within prefectural borders)	All unions, federations	Craft, industrial unions (federations?)	All unions, federations	All unions, federations	Craft, industrial unions	All unions, federations	Craft, industrial unions
Those excluded from membership	None	None	None	None	None	Military personnel, civilian employees of the military, plant managers	Military personnel, civilian employees of the military, plant managers	Military personnel, civilian employees of the military

Enforcement of clause against union-busting	None; no protection of right to organize	Levies fine	None	Levies fine	Levies fine	None	None	None
Union exempted from liability for strike damages	No	Yes	No	Yes	Yes	Yes	Yes	No
Guarantees collective agreements	No	No	No	No	Yes	No	No	No
Governmental controls on unions	Annul union decisions; dissolve union	Annul, revise decisions	Annul decisions; dissolution	Annul, revise decisions	Annul, revise decisions	Annul, revise decisions; dissolution	Annul, revise decisions; dissolution (union can appeal)	Annul, revise decisions; dissolution (union can appeal); forbid political contributions

APPENDIX VI   LABOR UNIONS AND UNION
MEMBERSHIP, 1918–41

Year	Number of unions	Union membership	% of industrial work force
1918	107	—	—
1919	187	—	—
1920	273	—	—
1921	300	103,442	—
1922	389	137,381	—
1923	432	125,551	—
1924	469	228,278	5.3%
1925	457	254,262	5.6
1926	488	284,739	6.1
1927	505	309,493	6.5
1928	501	308,900	6.3
1929	630	330,985	6.8
1930	712	354,312	7.5
1931	818	368,975	7.9
1932	932	377,625	7.8
1933	942	384,613	7.5
1934	965	387,964	6.7
1935	993	408,662	6.9
1936	973	420,589	6.9
1937	837	395,290	6.2
1938	731	375,191	5.5
1939	517	365,804	5.3
1940	49	9,455	0.1
1941	11	895	—

SOURCE: Rōdōshō, RGS, 1:1306–7.

Abbreviations Used in the Notes

KKZ   *Keisatsu kyōkai zasshi*
NRUS   *Nihon rōdō undō shiryō* (Rōdō undō shiryō iinkai)
RGS   *Rōdō gyōsei shi* (Rōdōshō)
RUN   *Rōdō undō nempō* (Naimushō shakaikyoku rōdōbu)
SGS   *Sōdōmei gojūnen shi*
SSJ   *Shakai seisaku jihō*
TAS   *Tōkyō asahi shimbun*
TGSGS   *Teikoku gikai shūgiin giji sokkiroku*
TGSIG   *Teikoku gikai shūgiin iinkai giroku*

Notes

NOTES TO THE INTRODUCTION

1. Notably, Ezra F. Vogel, *Japan as Number One: Lessons for America* (Cambridge: Harvard University Press, 1979); William G. Ouchi, *Theory Z: How American Business Can Meet the Japanese Challenge* (Reading, Mass.: Addison-Wesley Publishing, 1981); Richard Tanner Pascale and Anthony G. Athos, *The Art of Japanese Management: Applications for American Executives* (New York: Simon and Schuster, 1981).

2. In English, the classic statement of this position appears in James Abegglen, *The Japanese Factory: Aspects of its Social Organization* (Glencoe: The Free Press, 1958); for an excellent, historically based critique of such culturalist explanations, see Andrew Gordon, *The Evolution of Labor Relations in Japan: Heavy Industry, 1853–1955* (Cambridge: Council on East Asian Studies, Harvard University, 1985).

3. M. Y. Yoshino, *Japan's Managerial System: Tradition and Innovation* (Cambridge: M.I.T. Press, 1968).

4. See the official history of the leading interwar labor federation, Sōdōmei gojūnen shi kankō iinkai, ed., *Sōdōmei gojūnen shi*, 3 vols. (Tokyo: Kōyōsha, 1964–68) (hereafter cited as SGS).

5. F. M. L. Thompson, "Social Control in Victorian Britain," *Economic History Review* 34 (May 1981): 189–208.

6. Robert Scalapino, *Democracy and the Party Movement in Prewar Japan: The Failure of the First Attempt* (Berkeley: University of California Press, 1953); Peter Duus, *Party Rivalry and Political Change in Taishō Japan* (Cambridge: Harvard University Press, 1968); Gordon Mark Berger, *Parties out of Power in Japan, 1931–1941* (Princeton: Princeton University Press, 1977).

7. E.g., Tetsuo Najita, "Some Reflections on Idealism in the Political Thought of Yoshino Sakuzō," in *Japan in Crisis: Essays on Taishō Democracy,*

ed. Bernard S. Silberman and H. D. Harootunian (Princeton: Princeton University Press, 1974), pp. 29–66.

8. Harry Wray, "How Democratic Was Taishō Democracy?" in *Japan Examined: Perspectives on Modern Japanese History*, ed. Harry Wray and Hilary Conroy (Honolulu: University of Hawaii Press, 1983), p. 172.

9. With the welcome exceptions of Chalmers Johnson, *MITI and the Japanese Miracle* (Stanford: Stanford University Press, 1982); Kenneth Pyle, "Advantages of Followership: German Economics and Japanese Bureaucrats, 1890–1925," *Journal of Japanese Studies* 1 (Autumn 1974): 127–64; and Robert M. Spaulding, Jr., "Japan's 'New Bureaucrats,' 1932–45," in *Crisis Politics in Prewar Japan*, ed. George M. Wilson (Tokyo: Sophia University, 1970), pp. 51–70.

10. Theda Skocpol, "Bringing the State Back In: Strategies of Analysis in Current Research," in *Bringing the State Back In*, ed. Peter B. Evans, Dietrich Rueschemeyer, and Theda Skocpol (Cambridge: Cambridge University Press, 1985), p. 9.

11. W. J. Mommsen, ed., *The Emergence of the Welfare State in Britain and Germany, 1850–1950* (London: Croom Helm, 1981); Hugh Heclo, *Modern Social Politics in Britain and Sweden* (New Haven: Yale University Press, 1974).

12. Berger, chap. 1.

13. Duus, *Party Rivalry*, p. 248; Masumi Junnosuke, *Nihon seitō shi ron*, 7 vols. (Tokyo: Tōkyō daigaku shuppankai, 1965–80), 5 (1979): 230, 236.

14. Kimbara Samon, "Seitō seiji no hatten," in *Iwanami kōza: Nihon rekishi*, vol. 18 (Tokyo: Iwanami shoten, 1975), pp. 255–96; for one such claim by a former official, see Gotō Fumio, *Gotō Fumio shi danwa dai 1-kai sokkiroku*, Naiseishi kenkyū shiryō, no. 4 (Tokyo: Naiseishi kenkyūkai, 1963), pp. 25–26.

15. J. Reulecke, "English Social Policy around the Middle of the Nineteenth Century as Seen by German Social Reformers," and E. Peter Hennock, "The Origins of British National Insurance and the German Precedent 1880–1914," both in Mommsen, pp. 32–49, 84–106; Charles S. Maier, "Between Taylorism and Technocracy: European Ideologies and the Vision of Industrial Productivity in the 1920s," *Journal of Contemporary History* 5, no. 2 (1970), pp. 27–61.

16. For a suggestive new approach, see D. Eleanor Westney, "The Emulation of Western Organizations in Meiji Japan: The Case of the Paris Prefecture of Police and the Keishi-chō," *Journal of Japanese Studies* 8 (Summer 1982): 307–42.

17. Peter Duus and Daniel I. Okimoto, "Fascism and the History of Pre-War Japan: The Failure of a Concept," *Journal of Asian Studies* 39 (Nov. 1979): 65–76.

18. H. V. Emy, *Liberals, Radicals and Social Politics, 1892–1914* (Cambridge: Cambridge University Press, 1973); J. Roy Hay, *The Origins of the Liberal Welfare Reforms, 1906–1914* (London: Macmillan, 1975).

NOTES TO CHAPTER ONE

1. Takahashi Yūsai, *Takahashi Yūsai shi dai 2-kai danwa sokkiroku*, Naiseishi kenkyū shiryō, no. 17 (Tokyo: Naiseishi kenkyūkai, 1964), pp. 10–11.

2. Kawai Eijirō, *Meiji shisōshi no ichidammen—Kanai Noburu o chūshin to shite* (1941; reprint ed., Tokyo: Shakai shisōsha, 1969), p. 225.

3. Ōkuma Shigenobu, "Ōkuma haku no rōdō mondai dan," *Rōdō sekai* 6 (3 Apr. 1902): 7–8.

4. R. P. Dore, "The Modernizer as a Special Case: Japanese Factory Legislation, 1882–1911," *Comparative Studies in Society and History* 11 (Oct. 1969): 448.

5. Mikio Sumiya, "The Emergence of Modern Japan," in *Workers and Employers in Japan*, ed. Kazuo Okochi, Bernard Karsh, and Solomon B. Levine (Tokyo: Tokyo University Press, 1973), p. 33.

6. William W. Lockwood, *The Economic Development of Japan* (Princeton: Princeton University Press, 1968), p. 33.

7. Yasue Aoki Kidd, *Women Workers in the Japanese Cotton Mills: 1880–1920,* Cornell University East Asia Papers, no. 20 (Ithaca: Cornell China-Japan Program, 1978), p. 2.

8. Ibid., pp. 6–7; Gary R. Saxonhouse, "Country Girls and Communication among Competitors in the Japanese Cotton-Spinning Industry," in *Japanese Industrialization and Its Social Consequences,* ed. Hugh Patrick (Berkeley: University of California Press, 1976), pp. 100–101.

9. Nōshōmushō shōkōkyoku, *Shokkō jijō* (1903; reprint ed., Tokyo: Kōseikan, 1971), p. 45.

10. Thomas Dublin, *Women at Work: Transformation of Work and Community in Lowell, Massachusetts, 1826–1860* (New York: Columbia University Press, 1979), p. 23.

11. Saxonhouse, p. 101.

12. Ibid., p. 99. Comparable percentages are as follows: France, 31.5 percent (1901), India, 17.5 percent (1921), and Italy, 46.2 percent (1911).

13. Hiroshi Hazama, "Historical Changes in the Life Style of Industrial Workers," in Patrick, *Japanese Industrialization,* pp. 23–24.

14. *Jiji shimpō,* 21 Oct. 1897, and *Rōdō sekai,* 15 Dec. 1897, cited by Gordon, *Evolution,* pp. 28–29.

15. Rōdōshō, *Rōdō gyōsei shi,* 2 vols. (Tokyo: Rōdō hōrei kyōkai, 1961–69), 1:164–65 (hereafter cited as RGS).

16. Quoted in Kazuo Okochi, *Labor in Modern Japan* (Tokyo: The Science Council of Japan, 1958), p. 14.

17. Nōshōmushō, *Shokkō jijō,* pp. 78–79.

18. Saxonhouse, p. 103; *Shokkō jijō,* pp. 70–72.

19. Hazama, "Historical Changes," pp. 32–33.

20. Murakami Nobuhiko, *Meiji josei shi,* vol. 3 (Tokyo: Rironsha, 1971), pp. 188–89; Okochi, *Labor,* p. 15.

21. Mikiso Hane, *Peasants, Rebels, and Outcastes* (New York: Pantheon, 1982), pp. 180–81.

22. Kidd, p. 2; Hazama, "Historical Changes," pp. 30–31; Okochi, pp. 7–9.

23. Sumiya Mikio, *Nihon chinrōdō shi ron* (Tokyo: Tōkyō daigaku shuppankai, 1955), pp. 290–91, 295–96.

24. Dublin, p. 88.

25. Rōdō undō shiryō iinkai, ed., *Nihon rōdō undō shiryō,* 11 vols. (Tokyo: Chūō kōron jigyō shuppan, 1959–68), 10:424 (hereafter cited as NRUS).

26. Kidd, p. 3.

27. RGS, 1:99–100.

28. Ironworkers' Union and Katayama, quoted in Sumiya Mikio, *Nihon no rekishi*, vol. 22: *Dai Nihon teikoku no shiren* (Tokyo: Chūō kōron: 1966), pp. 111–13.

29. Ibid.; Thomas C. Smith, "The Right to Benevolence: Dignity and Japanese Workers, 1890–1920," *Comparative Studies in Society and History* 26 (Oct. 1984): 587–613; Gordon, *Evolution*, pp. 47–48.

30. Gordon, *Evolution*, pp. 22–24, 47–49.

31. Oka Minoru, *Kōjōhō ron*, rev. ed. (Tokyo: Yūhikaku, 1917), pp. 136–37.

32. E.g., Nakamura Masanori, *Nihon rekishi*, vol. 29: *Rōdōsha to nōmin* (Tokyo: Shōgakkan, 1976), p. 176; Kagoyama Takashi, "Kōjōhō no seiritsu to jisshi ni okeru kanryōgun," in *Nihon kindaika no kenkyū*, ed. Takahashi Kōhachirō, vol. 2 (Tokyo: Tōkyō daigaku shuppankai, 1973), pp. 67–68; International Labour Office, *Industrial Labour in Japan* (Geneva: International Labour Office, 1933), p. 137; Dore, "Modernizer," pp. 433–50.

33. Kenneth B. Pyle, "Advantages of Followership: German Economics and Japanese Bureaucrats, 1890–1925," *Journal of Japanese Studies* 1 (Autumn 1974): 127–64; Robert A. Scalapino, *The Early Japanese Labor Movement: Labor and Politics in a Developing Society* (Berkeley: Institute of East Asian Studies/Center for Japanese Studies, University of California, 1984), p. 6.

34. See Byron K. Marshall, *Capitalism and Nationalism in Prewar Japan* (Stanford: Stanford University Press, 1967), pp. 10, 13–29; Arthur J. Tiedemann, "Big Business and Politics in Prewar Japan," in *Dilemmas of Growth in Prewar Japan*, ed. James W. Morley (Princeton: Princeton University Press, 1972), pp. 268–73.

35. F. G. Notehelfer, "Japan's First Pollution Incident," *Journal of Japanese Studies* 1 (Spring 1975): 351–83.

36. Johnson, pp. 84–88.

37. Hazama Hiroshi, *Nihon no shiyōsha dantai to rōshi kankei* (Tokyo: Nihon rōdō kyōkai, 1981), pp. 45–46.

38. Koji Taira, *Economic Development and the Labor Market in Japan* (New York: Columbia University Press, 1970), p. 111.

39. Ikeda Makoto, *Nihon shakai seisaku shisō shi ron* (Tokyo: Tōyō keizai shimpōsha, 1978), pp. 92–93.

40. For surveys of business opinion in 1898–99, see Taikakai (Gotō Fumio), ed., *Naimushō shi*, 4 vols. (Tokyo: Chihō zaimu kyōkai, 1971–72), 1:247–48; Obama Ritoku, ed., *Meiji bunka shiryō soshō*, vol. 1 (Tokyo: Fūkan shobō, 1961), p. 12.

41. Quoted in Hazama, *Nihon no shiyōsha*, p. 47.

42. Andō Tarō, "Shokkō no torishimari oyobi hogo," *Taiyō* 2 (5 December 1896): 58; Ikeda, pp. 21–24, 94.

43. Marshall, *Capitalism*, pp. 55–76; Dore, "Modernizer," pp. 440–42. The minutes of the First and Third Higher Councils appear in Obama.

44. Shimura Gentarō (former Industrial Bureau chief), *Tōyō keizai shimpō*, 25 Oct. 1897, cited by Ikeda, p. 88.

45. Andō Tarō, p. 57.

46. Ministry of Agriculture and Commerce statement to First Higher Council on Agriculture, Commerce, and Industry, 1896, in Obama, p. 21.

47. Ikeda Makoto, pp. 86–87.

48. Ariga Nagafumi, "Shokkō jōrei seitei no jiki ni tsuite," *Kokka gakkai zasshi*, no. 129 (Nov. 1897), p. 933.

49. Obama, pp. 89–90.

50. Ibid., pp. 113–14.

51. The revised draft lowered the age of protected young workers from fourteen to ten and extended the maximum daily hours from ten to twelve. The subcommittee did, however, strengthen protections in some areas. Women received the same hours restrictions as youths, and the Industrial Bureau's heavy-handed provisions on work permits were removed. The revised draft appears in Obama, 1:146–48; see also Koji Taira, "Factory Legislation and Management Modernization during Japan's Industrialization 1896–1916," *Business History Review* 44 (Spring 1970): 95.

52. Kanai Noburu in Kawai, *Meiji*, pp. 165, 167.

53. Abe Isoo, *Shakai mondai kaishakuhō* (1901); reprinted in *Meiji bunka shiryō*, vol. 5, ed. Kaji Ryūichi (Tokyo: Fūkan shobō, 1960), pp. 51–52.

54. Yoshida Kyūichi, *Nihon shakai jigyō no rekishi* (Tokyo: Keisō shobō, 1966), pp. 147–48.

55. Masayoshi Chūbachi and Koji Taira, "Poverty in Modern Japan: Perceptions and Realities," in Patrick, *Japanese Industrialization*, pp. 396, 400–404; see biography of Yokoyama by Tachibana Yūichi, *Hyōden: Yokoyama Gennosuke* (Tokyo: Sōjusha, 1979).

56. Kazuo Okochi, *Labor*, p. 28; Hyman Kublin, *Asian Revolutionary: The Life of Sen Katayama* (Princeton: Princeton University Press, 1964).

57. Position of Taguchi Ukichi, quoted in Kawai, p. 171.

58. James J. Sheehan, *The Career of Lujo Brentano* (Chicago: University of Chicago Press, 1966), chaps. 3–4; Pyle, "Advantages."

59. Kawai, pp. 166–76, 221–22.

60. Andō Tarō, p. 57.

61. Obama, 1:38, 55; for Soeda's thought, see Ikeda Makoto, pp. 29–30, 43–45.

62. Taikakai, pp. 69–71, 107–8, 139.

63. Tsurumi Yūsuke, *Gotō Shimpei*, 4 vols. (Tokyo: Gotō Shimpei haku denki hensankai, 1937–38), 1:434–36; Kagoyama, pp. 68–69.

64. Tachibana, pp. 168–70.

65. Ikeda Makoto, p. 214.

66. Yokoyama Gennosuke, *Nihon no kasō shakai* (1899); reprinted in *Yokoyama Gennosuke zenshū*, vol. 1 (Tokyo: Meiji bunken, 1972), pp. 139–40.

67. Ikeda Makoto, pp. 217, 214.

68. Ishiwara Osamu, *Jokō to kekka* (1914; reprint ed., Tokyo: Kōseikan, 1970), pp. 87–88; Kagoyama, pp. 76–77.

69. Text of the law appears in RGS, 1:51–54. Special clauses established a fifteen-year transitional period, during which the law permitted (1) light work

by boys aged ten and eleven, (2) night work by women and minors, and (3) exceptional two-hour extensions per working day for women and minors.

70. Sumiya Mikio, "Kōjōhō taisei to rōshi kankei," in *Nihon rōshi kankei shi ron* (Tokyo: Tōkyō daigaku shuppankai, 1977), pp. 12–17; Andrew Gordon, "Business and the Corporate State: The Business Lobby and Bureaucrats on Labor," in *Essays in Japanese Business History*, ed. William D. Wray (Cambridge: Council on East Asian Studies, Harvard University, forthcoming).

71. Gotō to Prime Minister Itō Hirobumi, 15 Aug. 1896, in Tsurumi, 1:769.

72. Oka, pp. 142–43.

73. Sumiya, "Kōjōhō," pp. 27, 29–31, 38.

74. Oka, pp. 1152, 143.

75. RGS, 1:97–102.

76. Kamii Yoshihiko, "Dai ichiji taisen chokugo no rōdō seisaku: Chian keisatsuhō 17-jō no kaishaku tekiyō mondai o chūshin to shite," *Rōdō undō shi kenkyū*, no. 62 (1979), pp. 154–57.

77. Nimura Kazuo, "Rōdōsha kaikyū no jōtai to rōdō undō," in *Iwanami kōza: Nihon rekishi*, vol. 18 (Tokyo: Iwanami shoten, 1975), pp. 95–98.

78. See F. G. Notehelfer, *Kōtoku Shūsui, Portrait of a Japanese Radical* (Cambridge: Cambridge University Press, 1971).

79. Richard H. Mitchell, *Thought Control in Prewar Japan* (Ithaca: Cornell University Press, 1976), pp. 25–27.

80. Quoted in Shinobu Seizaburō, *Taishō demokurashii shi*, 3 vols. (Tokyo: Nihon hyōronsha, 1954–58), 1:122.

81. Miyachi Masato, "Nichirō zengo no shakai to minshū," in *Kōza Nihon shi*, ed. Rekishigaku kenkyūkai and Nihon shi kenkyūkai, vol. 6 (Tokyo: Tōkyō daigaku shuppankai, 1970), pp. 156–58.

82. Yoshida Kyūichi, pp. 192–93, 198–99.

83. Excepting the national railways, which in 1907 organized its 90,000 employees into the Employees' Mutual Aid Association (Gengyōin Kyōsai Kumiai) and the Staff Employees' Relief Association (Shokuin Kyūsai Kumiai). Tsurumi, 3:195–96.

84. Kenneth B. Pyle, "The Technology of Japanese Nationalism: The Local Improvement Movement 1900–1918," *Journal of Asian Studies* 33 (Nov. 1973): 51–65.

85. Kiyoshi Ogata, *The Co-operative Movement in Japan* (London: P. S. King and Son, 1923), pp. 316, 89–91; Bismarck's flirtation with producers' cooperatives is described by Theodore S. Hamerow, *The Social Foundations of German Unification 1858–1871: Struggles and Accomplishments* (Princeton: Princeton University Press, 1972), pp. 204–20.

86. Miyachi, "Nichirō zengo," pp. 160–61; Kawai, *Meiji*, pp. 223, 228.

87. Shakai seisaku gakkai, ed., *Rōdō sōgi*, record of 7th Congress (1914; reprint ed., Tokyo: Ochanomizu shobō, 1977), pp. 9–33.

88. Matsuo Takayoshi, *Taishō demokurashii no kenkyū* (Tokyo: Aoki shoten, 1966), pp. 151–52, 162.

89. Stephen S. Large, *The Yūaikai, 1912–1919: The Rise of Labor in Japan* (Tokyo: Sophia University, 1972), pp. 43, 74–75.

90. Oka, pp. 136–37.

91. See Tetsuo Najita, *Hara Kei and the Politics of Compromise, 1905–1915* (Cambridge: Harvard University Press, 1967).

92. Yoshida Kyūichi, pp. 151–53, 177, 198–99.

93. Mitani Taichirō, "Seiyūkai no seiritsu," in *Iwanami kōza: Nihon rekishi,* vol. 16 (Tokyo: Iwanami shoten, 1976), pp. 169–70.

94. Kuwata Kumazō, "Kōjōhō no seitei oyobi jisshi no yūrai," *Rōdō oyobi sangyō,* no. 58 (June 1916), p. 39.

95. Tanabe Kumaichi, in *Dai Nihon teikoku gikai shi,* vol. 8 (Tokyo: Dai Nihon teikoku gikai shi kankōkai, 1928), 4 Feb. 1911, p. 307.

96. Sumiya, "Kōjōhō," pp. 10–20, 33–34.

97. Yoshida Kyūichi, p. 153.

98. Narusawa Akira, "Hara naikaku to dai ichiji sekai taisengo kokunai jōkyō," pt. 2. *Hōgaku shirin* 66, no. 3 (February 1969), pp. 59–60.

99. Obama, pp. 179–81.

100. Ōoka Ikuzō, "Kōjōhō jisshi hantai ron," *Rōdō oyobi sangyō,* no. 61 (Sept. 1916), p. 33.

101. Sumiya, "Kōjōhō," pp. 24, 32, n. 1; also RGS, 1:46.

102. *Tōkyō asahi shimbun,* 17 May 1914, p. 2 (hereafter cited as TAS); Sumiya, "Kōjōhō," pp. 34–36.

103. Tomita Kōjirō, "Sangyō teikoku no kempō to shite no kōjōhō," *Rōdō oyobi sangyō,* no. 61 (Sept. 1916), p. 35.

104. Reform activities of the Kokumintō and Shimada are discussed by Miyachi Masato, *Nichirō sensōgo seiji shi no kenkyū* (Tokyo: Tōkyō daigaku shuppankai, 1973), p. 283; Akamatsu Katsumaro, *Nihon shakai undō shi* (Tokyo: Tsūshin kyōkai shinkōkai, 1949), pp. 53–55, 74; Itō Takashi, *Taishō-ki "kakushin"-ha no seiritsu* (Tokyo: Hanawa shobō, 1978), pp. 113, 155; Tachibana, p. 38.

105. Kawai, *Meiji,* p. 27.

106. Wakatsuki Reijirō, *Kofūan kaikoroku* (Tokyo: Yomiuri shimbunsha, 1950), pp. 162–63.

107. Duus, *Party Rivalry,* pp. 52–68.

108. TAS, 15 Apr. 1916, p. 4.

109. Yasuda Hiroshi, "Seitō seiji taiseika no rōdō seisaku—Hara naikaku-ki ni okeru rōdō kumiai kōnin mondai," *Rekishigaku kenkyū,* no. 420 (May 1975), p. 26.

110. Oka, p. 142.

NOTES TO CHAPTER TWO

1. *Yomiuri shimbun,* 17 Feb. 1919, in *Nihon rōdō nenkan,* 1920, ed. Ōhara shakai mondai kenkyūjo (Tokyo: Ōhara shakai mondai kenkyūjo shuppanbu, 1920), p. 836 (hereafter cited as *Nihon rōdō nenkan*).

2. Katō Takaaki, "Katō sōsai no enzetsu," *Kensei* 2, no. 6 (26 July 1919), 2–3.

3. Kawarada Kakichi (chief, Public Security Section of Police Bureau),

cited by Suzuki Bunji, *Rōdō undō nijūnen* (Tokyo: Ichigensha, 1931), pp. 186–87.

4. Mitani Taichirō, *Taishō demokurashii ron* (Tokyo: Chūō kōronsha, 1974), p. 29.

5. Statistics by Ministry of Agriculture and Commerce. The figures would show an even greater increase if one included workers in mines, governmental enterprises, transportation, and communications. Nimura, "Rōdōsha," pp. 104–5.

6. See Inoue Kiyoshi and Watanabe Tōru, eds., *Kome sōdō no kenkyū, 5* vols. (Kyoto: Yūhikaku, 1959–62).

7. Kamii, "Chian keisatsuhō," p. 170.

8. SGS, 1:278; Hyōdō Tsutomu, *Nihon ni okeru rōshi kankei no tenkai* (Tokyo: Tōkyō daigaku shuppankai, 1971), pp. 338–44, 356, 362; Nimura, pp. 106–7.

9. SGS, 1:222, 229–31; Large, *Yūaikai*, pp. 136–37.

10. Kimura Teikichi, "Seikatsu to futsū senkyo," *Rōdō oyobi sangyō* 8 (April 1919): 22–23.

11. *Den Kenjirō nikki*, Aug. 17, 1918, cited by Kimbara, "Seitō seiji," p. 258.

12. Nimura, "Rōdōsha," p. 108.

13. *Nihon rōdō nenkan*, 1920, pp. 657, 664.

14. Nimura, "Rōdōsha," pp. 108–9.

15. Iwao F. Ayusawa, *A History of Labor in Modern Japan* (Honolulu: East-West Center Press, 1966), pp. 121–26.

16. Morita Yoshio, *Nihon keieisha dantai hatten shi* (Tokyo: Nikkan rōdō tsūshinsha, 1958), pp. 59–60.

17. Gordon, *Evolution*, pp. 101, 109–12.

18. Report of 27 May 1919, *Nihon kōgyō kurabu nijūgonen shi*, ed. Nihon kōgyō kurabu nijūgonen shi hensan iinkai, 2 vols. (Tokyo: Nihon kōgyō kurabu, 1943), 1:133–36.

19. Position paper of 7 Oct. 1919, ibid., 1:151.

20. Hyōdō, *Nihon*, p. 367.

21. *Nihon rōdō nenkan*, 1920, p. 905.

22. *Nihon rōdō nenkan*, 1920, pp. 934–35.

23. Position paper of 14 Aug. 1920, *Ōsaka kōgyōkai gojūnen shi*, ed. Ōsaka kōgyōkai gojūnen shi hensan iinkai (Osaka: Ōsaka kōgyōkai, 1964), p. 186.

24. Morita, pp. 60, 63; International Labour Office, p. 84.

25. Petition of 9 Dec. 1919, *Nihon rōdō nenkan*, 1920, p. 226.

26. Ibid., pp. 226, 934–35; Miwa Ryōichi, "Rōdō kumiaihō seitei mondai no rekishiteki ichi," in *Ryōtaisenkan no Nihon shihonshugi*, ed. Andō Yoshio (Tokyo: Tōkyō daigaku shuppankai, 1979), pp. 257–58.

27. *Nihon rōdō nenkan*, 1920, pp. 928, 935.

28. Ibid., p. 225.

29. *Nihon kōgyō kurabu*, 1:147; Morita, pp. 70–71.

30. *Nihon rōdō nenkan*, 1920, pp. 835–36.

31. Danshaku Dan Takuma denki hensan iinkai, ed., *Danshaku Dan Ta-*

kuma den, 2 vols. (Tokyo: Danshaku Dan Takuma denki hensan iinkai, 1938), 1:49–78, 132.

32. They included Yamamoto Teijirō, Noda Utarō (president, Miike Spinning), Nakahashi Tokugorō (president, Osaka Shipping and Ujikawa Electric), Okazaki Kunisuke (president, Keihin Electric Railways), and Mochizuki Keisuke (mining and shipping). Compiled from Tōyama Shigeki and Adachi Yoshiko, *Kindai Nihon seiji shi hikkei* (Tokyo: Iwanami shoten, 1961), p. 145.

33. Masumi, 4 (1968): 264–66. The Seiyūkai's most prominent business candidates in the 1920 elections were Sakurauchi Yukio (owner of several electricity companies), Mori Kaku (bureau chief, Mitsui and Company), Uchida Shin'ya (Uchida Shipping), Yamamoto Jōtarō (Nippon Hydroelectric, Nisshin Spinning), and Makoshi Kyōhei (beer companies).

34. Masumi, 4:266; details in Najita.

35. Matsuo Takayoshi, "Dai ichiji taisengo no fusen undō," in *Taishō-ki no seiji to shakai,* ed. Inoue Kiyoshi (Tokyo: Iwanami shoten, 1969), p. 163.

36. Duus, *Party Rivalry,* pp. 135–42.

37. Hara Takashi, *Hara Takashi nikki,* ed. Hara Keiichirō, 5 vols. (Tokyo: Fukumura shuppan kabushiki kaisha, 1965), 22 Oct. 1917, 4:328.

38. Mitani, *Taishō,* pp. 28–29.

39. See Maeda Renzan, *Tokonami Takejirō den* (Tokyo: Tokonami Takejirō denki kankōkai, 1939); Taikakai, 4:98–107.

40. Masumi, 4:226; Kuribayashi Teiichi, *Chihō kankai no hensen* (Tokyo: Sekaisha, 1930), pp. 229–31.

41. *Ōsaka asahi shimbun,* 30 Dec. 1918, in Watanabe Tōru, "Nihon ni okeru rōdō kumiai hōan no tōjō o megutte," pt. 1, *Nihon rōdō kyōkai zasshi,* no. 87 (June 1966), p. 4.

42. *Yomiuri shimbun,* 17 Feb. 1919, in *Nihon rōdō nenkan,* 1920, p. 836.

43. TAS, 13 Feb. 1919, p. 4.

44. Italics mine. *Ōsaka asahi shimbun* and *Ōsaka mainichi shimbun,* both of 4 Feb. 1919, quoted in Watanabe Tōru, pt. 1, p. 7.

45. Kamii, "Chian keisatsuhō," p. 177.

46. Kimbara Samon, *Taishō-ki no seitō to kokumin—Hara Takashi naikakuka no seiji katei* (Tokyo: Hanawa shobō, 1975), p. 165.

47. Letter to Marquis Saionji Kimmochi, "Wagakuni rōdō mondai kaiketsu hōshin," n.d. [ca. Feb. 1919], Kobashi Ichita kankei monjo, Tokyo University, Tokyo.

48. Suzuki, p. 189; also Large, *Yūaikai,* p. 174.

49. Yasuda, pp. 17, 18–20; Yano Tatsuo, "Taishō-ki rōdō rippō no ichidammen—rōdō sōgi chōteihō no seiritsu katei," *Hōseishi kenkyū,* no. 27 (1977), p. 109.

50. Cf. Suzuki, pp. 191–95; Large, *Yūaikai,* pp. 175–77. Labor historians often cite Suzuki's recollections of 1931 to claim that the Yūaikai leader broke off relations with Shibusawa in August 1919 because Shibusawa had undercut the unions' influence by having organized the Kyōchōkai. In reality, one month after the alleged incident, the two men held a press conference to announce their joint opposition to the government's refusal to send a trade

unionist as the workers' delegate to the International Labor Conference. TAS, 23 Sept. 1919, p. 2.

51. *Ryūmon zasshi*, no. 375 (Aug. 1919) and no. 376 (Sept. 1919), in *Shibusawa Eiichi denki shiryō*, ed. Shibusawa seien kinen zaidan ryūmonsha, vol. 31 (Tokyo: Shibusawa Eiichi denki shiryō kankōkai, 1960), pp. 630, 637.

52. *Nihon rōdō nenkan*, 1920, pp. 925–27.

53. TAS, 15 Oct. 1919, p. 7.

54. Watanabe Tōru, "Nihon ni okeru rōdō kumiai hōan no tōjō o megutte," pt. 2, *Nihon rōdō kyōkai zasshi*, no. 88 (July 1966), pp. 2–3.

55. *Nihon rōdō nenkan*, 1920, pp. 222–25, 876–77.

56. RGS, 1:143–44; Nishinarita Yutaka, "1920 nendai Nihon shihonshugi no rōshi kankei—Jūkōgyō rōshi kankei o chūshin ni," *Rekishigaku kenkyū*, no. 512 (Jan. 1983), pp. 2–3.

57. Kawarada Kakichi, "Iwayuru rōdō kumiai no kōnin to chian keisatsu-hō dai 17-jō ni tsuite," *Keisatsu kyōkai zasshi*, no. 227 (Apr. 1919), pp. 37–39.

58. Kawamura Takeji, "Rōdō mondai ni tsuite," *Keisatsu kyōkai zasshi*, no. 247 (Jan. 1921), pp. 35, 39.

59. A. Morgan Young, *Japan Under Taisho Tenno, 1912–1926* (London: Allen and Unwin, 1928), p. 285.

60. Quoted in SGS, 1:295.

61. Koyama Shojū, in *Dai Nihon teikoku gikai shi*, vol. 11, Lower House, 13 Mar. 1919, p. 1205.

62. *Ōsaka mainichi shimbun*, 20 Mar. 1919, in Watanabe Tōru, pt. 1, p. 7.

63. Kawamura Takeji, pp. 37–38; see also Sumiya, "Kōjōhō," p. 5, n. 6.

64. Especially Matsuo Takayoshi, *Taishō demokurashii no kenkyū* (Tokyo: Aoki shoten, 1966).

65. Duus, *Party Rivalry*, p. 135.

66. Hugh Heclo, *Modern Social Politics in Britain and Sweden* (New Haven: Yale University Press, 1974), p. 293.

67. Katō Masanosuke, in Kenseikai shi hensanjo (Yokoyama Katsutarō), ed., *Kenseikai shi* (Tokyo: Kenseikai shi hensanjo, 1926), p. 126.

68. Ibid., pp. 126–27.

69. Egi Tasuku, "Shippei hoken seido," *Kensei* 3 (Jan. 1920): 8–9.

70. TAS, 3 Feb. 1920, p. 2; Egi Tasuku kun denki hensankai, ed., *Egi Tasuku den* (Tokyo: Egi Tasuku kun denki hensankai, 1939), pp. 173, 195.

71. Shimizu Gen (formerly of Ministry of Agriculture and Commerce), in *Zen Keinosuke tsuisōroku*, ed. Yoshino Kōichi (Tokyo: Nihon dantai seimei hoken kabushiki kaisha, 1959), p. 11.

72. Uemura Kōsaku, "Rōdō hoken jisshi ni tsuite," *Kensei* 2 (February 1919): 10.

73. Ōsaka kōgyōkai, pp. 152–54, 192.

74. *Ōsaka asahi shimbun*, 2 Feb. 1919, p. 2.

75. Lower House, budget committee, 3 Feb. 1919, in *Ōsaka asahi shimbun*, 4 Feb. 1919, p. 2.

76. Watanabe Tōru, pt. 1, p. 5.

77. TAS, 16 Feb. 1920, p. 2.

78. Masumi, 5:261–62.

79. John Elliot Turner, "The Origin and Development of the Kenseikai (Constitutional Political Association) of Japan, 1913–1927," (M.A. thesis, University of Minnesota, 1949), p. 130.

80. Inoue Kiyoshi, ed., *Taishō-ki no kyūshinteki jiyūshugi* (Tokyo: Tōyō keizai shimpōsha, 1972), pp. 469–526.

81. TAS, 28 Aug. 1921, p. 2.

82. E.g., *Yomiuri shimbun*, 29 Jan. 1920, p. 3; on the British Radicals, see Emy, pp. 50–53, 100–103.

83. Matsuo, "Dai ichiji taisengo," pp. 165–66, 200.

84. Peter Duus, "Nagai Ryūtarō: The Tactical Dilemmas of Reform," in *Personality in Japanese History*, ed. Albert M. Craig and Donald H. Shively (Berkeley: University of California Press, 1970), pp. 403, 407.

85. Figure cited by Nimura, "Rōdōsha," p. 108.

86. Miyachi, *Nichirō sensōgo*, pp. 350, 373–74; Itō Takashi, *Taishō-ki* pp. 228, 232, 246; *Nihon rōdō nenkan*, 1920, pp. 385, 398; Matsuo, "Dai ichiji taisengo," pp. 179–80.

87. *Nihon rōdō nenkan*, 1920, pp. 462–63; Itō, *Taishō-ki*, pp. 243–45.

88. Ueno Terumasa, "Dai ichiji sekai taisengo no Nihon rōdō undō no tenkai—kaigun kōshō ni okeru rōdō seisaku," *Nihon shi kenkyū*, no. 163 (Mar. 1976), pp. 171–72, 181–83.

89. *Rōdō undō*, no. 6 (1 June 1920), p. 8. For a similar story in the district surrounding the Yokosuka Naval Arsenal, see Matsuo, "Dai ichiji taisengo," p. 202.

90. Duus, *Party Rivalry*, p. 240.

91. TAS, 22 Dec. 1919, p. 3; Watanabe Tōru, pt. 1, p. 10.

92. Stephen S. Large, *Organized Workers and Socialist Politics in Interwar Japan* (Cambridge: Cambridge University Press, 1981), p. 27.

93. Koizumi Matajirō, *Fusen undō hisshi* (Tokyo: Hirano shobō, 1928), pp. 111–12.

94. Henry D. Smith, II, "The Nonliberal Roots of Taishō Democracy," in Wray and Conroy, p. 192.

95. Emy, pp. 2–7, 147–48, 281.

96. *Nihon rōdō nenkan*, 1920, pp. 220–221.

97. Quoted in Itō Masanori, *Katō Takaaki*, 2 vols. (Tokyo: Katō haku denki hensan iinkai, 1929), 1:776.

98. Ibid., 1:776–80.

99. Shimada Saburō, "Jiyūshugi no shōri to senran no kyōkun," *Kensei* 2 (Jan. 1919): 11–25.

100. *Dai Nihon teikoku gikai shi*, vol. 11, Lower House, 1 Feb. 1919, pp. 995–96.

101. *Japan Weekly Chronicle*, 4 Sept. 1919, p. 372.

102. Taketomi Tokitoshi, "Sengo no sūsei to taiōsaku," *Kensei* 2 (Jan. 1919): 27–29.

103. See translated summaries of Japanese-language editorials in *Japan*

Times, 4 Oct. 1919, p. 4; *Tōkyō nichinichi shimbun*'s condemnation of the U.S. Government appears in ibid., 3 Dec. 1919, p. 2.

104. Edward Geary Griffin, "The Adoption of Universal Manhood Suffrage in Japan" (Ph.D. diss., Columbia University, 1965), pp. 45–46, 57–58.

105. Hamaguchi Osachi, "Kokumin seikatsu no kiki," *Kensei* 2 (Aug. 1919): 27; Suzuki Fujiya, in *Dai Nihon teikoku gikai shi,* vol. 11, Lower House, 11 Mar. 1919, p. 1179.

106. Katō Takaaki, "Katō sōsai," p. 2.

107. Speech to Nagoya Keizaikai, in *Japan Weekly Chronicle,* 29 May 1919, p. 815.

108. Koyama Shojū, in *Dai Nihon teikoku gikai shi,* vol. 11, Lower House, 13 Mar. 1919, p. 1205.

109. *Ōsaka asahi shimbun,* 2 Feb. 1919, p. 3; similarly, TAS, 16 Dec. 1919, p. 3.

110. *Nihon rōdō nenkan,* 1920, pp. 220–21.

111. Egi Tasuku, "Rōdō mondai," *Kensei* 2 (October 1919): 26–27.

112. Draft appears in RGS, 1:137–40.

113. Cf. Shinobu, *Taishō demokurashii,* 2:576–81; Miwa Ryōichi, p. 245; Yasuda, p. 27.

114. RGS, 1:140–42.

115. Report on the Forty-fifth Diet, *Kensei* 5, no. 3 (Spring 1922), p. 34.

116. Especially Mitsuchi Chūzō, "Rōdō kumiai no kenkyū ni tsuite," *Seiyū,* no. 236 (Dec. 1919), pp. 1–6.

117. Watanabe Tōru, pt. 2, p. 5; Kawamura Takeji, pp. 36–37.

118. Hara, 20 Feb., 3 Mar. 1920, 5:217, 22.

119. Matsuo, "Dai ichiji taisengo," p. 199; Yasuda, pp. 23–24.

120. Ayusawa, *History of Labor,* pp. 179–82.

121. House of Peers, 12 Mar. 1921, quoted in *Egi Tasuku den,* pp. 182–83.

122. International Labour Office, pp. 142, 146.

123. Miwa Ryōichi, pp. 262, 269.

124. *Nihon kin-gendai shi jiten,* 1978 ed., s.v. "Kawasaki-Mitsubishi zō-senjo daisōgi," by Watanabe Tōru.

125. Kamii, "Chian keisatsuhō," pp. 167–68, 175–77.

126. *Kensei* 4 (July 1921): 58.

127. TAS, 28 Aug. 1921, p. 2.

128. E.g., Higuchi Hideo, "Demokurashii to nōson no jikaku," *Kensei kōron* 1 (Aug. 1921): 2–4.

129. Egi Tasuku, in House of Peers, 12 Mar. 1921, in *Egi Tasuku den,* p. 185; Katō Takaaki, TAS, 28 Aug. 1921, p. 2.

130. TAS, 29 July 1921, p. 2.

131. Kōno Hironaka, "Futsū senkyo dankō no kyūmi," *Kensei* 5 (Mar. 1922): 2.

NOTES TO CHAPTER THREE

1. Yasui Eiji, *Rōdō undō no kenkyū* (Tokyo: Nihon daigaku, 1923), pp. 212–13, 247.

2. See Takemura Tamirō, "Jinushisei no dōyō to nōrin kanryō–Kosakuhō sōan mondai to Ishiguro Tadaatsu no shisō," in *Kindai Nihon shisō shi taikei,* vol. 5: *Kindai Nihon keizai shisō shi,* ed. Chō Yukio and Sumiya Kazuhiko (Tokyo: Yūhikaku, 1969), pp. 323–56.

3. Kawamura Teishirō, *Kankai no hyōri* (Tokyo: Yūsankaku shuppan, 1974), p. 135.

4. Nagaoka Ryūichirō, *Kanryō nijūnenkan* (Tokyo: Chūō kōronsha, 1939), p. 222.

5. Watanabe Osamu, "1920 nendai ni okeru tennōsei kokka no chian hōsei saihensei o megutte," *Shakai kagaku kenkyū* 27, nos. 5–6 (Mar. 1976), pp. 191–92.

6. Nicos Poulantzas, "The Problem of the Capitalist State," in *Ideology in Social Science,* ed. Robin Blackburn (New York: Vintage Books, 1972), p. 246.

7. Charles A. Beard, *The Administration and Politics of Tokyo: A Survey and Opinions* (New York: Macmillan, 1923).

8. Pyle, "Advantages," pp. 162–64.

9. For an excellent theoretical discussion, see Nora Hamilton, *The Limits of State Autonomy: Post-Revolutionary Mexico* (Princeton: Princeton University Press, 1982), pp. 3–25.

10. Bernard S. Silberman, "Bureaucratic Decision-making in Japan: 1868–1925," *Journal of Asian Studies* 29 (Feb. 1970): 353.

11. Ibid., pp. 352–53.

12. Masumi, 4:166–67.

13. Mori Ariyoshi, *Seinen to ayumu: Gotō Fumio* (Tokyo: Nihon seinenkan, 1979), pp. 52–53.

14. As recalled by a former official, Maeda Tamon, quoted in Tsurumi Yūsuke, *Gotō Shimpei,* 3:687.

15. See Sally Ann Hastings, "The Government, the Citizen, and the Creation of a New Sense of Community: Social Welfare, Local Organizations, and Dissent in Tokyo, 1905–1937," (Ph.D. diss., University of Chicago, 1980), pp. 26–48.

16. Masumi, 4:166, 174, 178.

17. Hata Ikuhiko, *Kanryō no kenkyū* (Tokyo: Kōdansha, 1983), p. 15.

18. Silberman, p. 353.

19. Fujinuma Shōhei, *Watakushi no isshō* (Tokyo: Fujinuma Shōhei kankōkai, 1957), pp. 25–26.

20. Masumi, 4:189.

21. Yasui Eiji, *Yasui Eiji shi danwa dai 1-kai sokkiroku,* Naiseishi kenkyū shiryō, no. 14 (Tokyo: Naiseishi kenkyūkai, 1964), pp. 6–7.

22. Akira Kubota, *Higher Civil Servants in Postwar Japan* (Princeton: Princeton University Press, 1969), pp. 156–57.

23. Yoshino Kōichi, p. 73; TAS, 26 Dec. (evening) 1924, p. 1.

24. Kurihara Minoru, *Kurihara Minoru shi danwa dai 1-kai sokkiroku,* Naiseishi kenkyū shiryō, no. 184 (Tokyo: Naiseishi kenkyūkai, 1977), p. 13.

25. Several social bureaucrats belonged to the "class of 1900," including Horikiri Zenjirō, Maeda Tamon, Tsugita Daisaburō, and Maruyama Tsurukichi. Refer to annual list of successful examination candidates in Senzenki

kanryōsei kenkyūkai (Hata Ikuhiko), ed., *Senzenki Nihon kanryōsei no seido, soshiki, jinji* (Tokyo: Tōkyō daigaku shuppankai, 1981), esp. pp. 466–69.

26. For details of Gotō's life, see Mori; Susan Beth Weiner, "Bureaucracy and Politics in the 1930s: The Career of Gotō Fumio" (Ph.D diss., Harvard University, 1984).

27. Gotō, *Sokkiroku,* pp. 6–7.

28. Ibid., p. 10.

29. Masumi, 4:213–15.

30. Gotō Fumio, "Sengo Ōbei ni okeru jinshin no dōyō to kikō," *Keisatsu kyōkai zasshi,* no. 239 (Apr. 1920), pp. 10–11.

31. Gotō, *Sokkiroku,* p. 36.

32. Horikiri Zenjirō, *Horikiri Zenjirō shi danwa dai 2-kai sokkiroku,* Naiseishi kenkyū shiryō, no. 8 (Tokyo: Naiseishi kenkyūkai, 1963), pp. 11, 15–17, 38–41.

33. Takahashi Yūsai, p. 42.

34. Ōno Rokuichirō, *Ōno Rokuichirō shi danwa dai 1-kai sokkiroku,* Naiseishi kenkyū shiryō, no. 61 (Tokyo: Naiseishi kenkyūkai, 1968), pp. 42, 47, 51, 90–91.

35. Yasui, *Sokkiroku,* pp. 20–21, 35.

36. Yasui Eiji, "Wagakuni rōdō undō no sūsei," pt. 2, *Shimin* 17 (Sept. 1922): 21; G. D. H. Cole, *The World of Labour,* 4th ed. (London: G. Bell and Sons, 1919), p. 165.

37. Other notable examples were Tsugita Daisaburō, vice-minister (1931), and Kawarada Kakichi, home minister (1936) and education minister (1939–40).

38. Gotō, "Sengo," p. 7.

39. Weiner, pp. 43–52; on Nagaoka, see Kurihara, p. 13.

40. Gotō, *Sokkiroku,* pp. 24, 27–28.

41. Taguchi Unzō, in Watanabe Haruo, *Omoide no kakumeikatachi* (Tokyo: Yoshiga shoten, 1968), pp. 63–64.

42. Baba Tsunego, *Seikai jimbutsu ron* (Tokyo: Chūō kōronsha, 1935), p. 228.

43. Yasui, *Sokkiroku,* p. 6.

44. Ōno, *Sokkiroku,* pp. 92–93.

45. Kitaoka Juitsu, *Wagaomoide no ki* (Kamakura: Kamakura insatsu kabushiki kaisha, 1976), pp. 86–88.

46. Kurihara, p. 14.

47. Kawanishi Jitsuzō, in Maruyama Masao and Fukuda Kan'ichi, eds., *Kaisō no Nambara Shigeru* (Tokyo: Iwanami shoten, 1975), p. 17.

48. Yasuda, pp. 20–21; Kawai Eijirō, "Kan o jisuru ni saishite," TAS, 17 Nov.–2 Dec. 1919, p. 3.

49. See Jeremiah Schneiderman, *Sergei Zubatov and Revolutionary Marxism: The Struggle for the Working Class in Tsarist Russia* (Ithaca: Cornell University Press, 1976).

50. Westney, pp. 331–32.

51. E.g., Ōtsuka Isei, "Okuyukashii Eikoku no kokuminsei," *Keisatsu*

kyōkai zasshi (hereafter cited as KKZ), no. 253 (July 1921), pp. 37–39; for a general discussion, see Watanabe Osamu, pp. 187–88; Elise Kurashige Tipton, "The Civil Police in the Suppression of the Prewar Japanese Left," (Ph.D. diss., Indiana University, 1977), pp. 181–90.

52. Maeda Tamon, "Ōbei shisatsu shokan," KKZ, no. 236 (Jan. 1920), pp. 22–23.

53. Amanoya Keiji, "Ōshū ni okeru genka no rōdō undō," pt. 2, KKZ, no. 258 (Dec. 1921), pp. 38–39.

54. Matsui Shigeru, "Kokumin to keisatsu," KKZ, no. 236 (Jan. 1920), pp. 13, 17.

55. Ibid., p. 16.

56. Nambara Shigeru, "Naimushō rōdō kumiai hōan no koto nado," in *Rōdō gyōsei shi yoroku,* supp. to vol. 1 of RGS (1961), pp. 27–30.

57. Nambara Shigeru, "Rōdō kumiaihō o ronzu," pt. 1, KKZ, no. 244 (Oct. 1920), pp. 3–6; pt. 2, no. 245 (Nov. 1920), pp. 2, 8.

58. Ibid., pt. 2, p. 9.

59. Nambara's (Home Ministry) draft appears in RGS, 1:135–37.

60. Nambara, "Rōdō kumiaihō," pt. 2, pp. 4, 7; on British trade union laws, see Charles Wooten Pipkin, *Social Politics and Modern Democracies,* 2 vols. (New York: Macmillan, 1931), 1:288–91.

61. TAS, 5 Dec. 1919, p. 3.

62. Watanabe Tōru, pt. 1, p. 8.

63. Ōsaka kōgyōkai, p. 183.

64. TAS, 26 Jan. 1920.

65. *Kokumin shimbun,* 22 Jan. 1920, cited by Watanabe Tōru, pt. 2, p. 4.

66. Quoted in RGS, 1:129; for draft, see 1:133–35.

67. TAS, 26 Jan. 1920, p. 2.

68. Yasuda, pp. 22–23; Scalapino, *Early Japanese Labor,* pp. 109–110.

69. Kamii Yoshihiko, "Dai ichiji taisengo no rōdō seisaku—1926 nen rōshi kankeihō o megutte," *Shakai seisaku gakkai nempō,* no. 23 (1979), p. 125.

70. Kawamura Takeji, Sanjikan gijiroku, 26 Mar. 1920, Records of the Rinji sangyō chōsakai, National Archives, Tokyo.

71. Kawamura Takeji, "Rōdō," pp. 29–30. Refer to p. 268, n. 58.

72. Interview with Kitaoka Juitsu, Zushi, 10 Apr. 1979; Nambara, "Naimushō," RGS, supp., pp. 29–30.

73. Watanabe Tōru, pt. 2, pp. 5–7.

74. Yoshino Kōichi, pp. 2, 23–24.

75. International Labour Office, p. 152.

76. Masumi, 4:172–73.

77. TAS, 25, 26 Aug. 1922, p. 2.

78. Iwao F. Ayusawa, *Industrial Conditions and Labour Legislation in Japan,* Studies and Reports, series B (Economic Conditions), no. 16 (Geneva: International Labour Office, 1926), pp. 18–20.

79. Kamii, "1926 nen," p. 128; Kitaoka Juitsu, "Shakaikyoku no setchi to rōdō gyōsei," in *Naimushō gaishi,* ed. Taikakai (Tokyo: Chihō zaimu kyōkai, 1977), pp. 147–48; TAS, 22 Sept. 1922, p. 2.

80. Kitaoka Juitsu, "Kyū-Shakaikyoku no omoide," in *Rōdō gyōsei shi yoroku*, supp. to vol. 1 of RGS (1961), p. 3.

81. Yasui, *Rōdō*.

82. George O. Totten, "Collective Bargaining and Works Councils as Innovations in Industrial Relations in Japan during the 1920s" in *Aspects of Social Change in Modern Japan*, ed. R. P. Dore (Princeton: Princeton University Press, 1970), pp. 209–10.

83. Yasui, *Sokkiroku*, p. 14.

84. Yasui, *Rōdō*, pp. 135, 156, 205–6; also, Kamii, "1926 nen," pp. 138–39.

85. Yasui, *Rōdō*, pp. 139–54.

86. Ibid., pp. 8–9, 207.

87. Ibid., pp. 204–6.

88. Kamii, "1926 nen," p. 129.

89. Nambara, "Naimushō," RGS, supp., p. 29.

90. Yasui, *Rōdō*, pp. 212, 241.

91. Bruno Ramirez, *When Workers Fight: The Politics of Industrial Relations in the Progressive Era, 1898–1916* (Westport, Conn.: Greenwood Press, 1978), pp. 160–72.

92. For a subtle statement of this position, refer to Kamii, "1926 nen," pp. 131–35.

93. In English, see Scalapino, *Early Japanese Labor*, pp. 97–142; Large, *Organized Workers*, chap. 2.

94. Hyōdō, *Nihon*, pp. 363–65.

95. Matsuo, "Fusen undō," pp. 188–89, 202.

96. Miwa Ryōichi, p. 269.

97. George M. Beckmann and Genji Okubo, *The Japanese Communist Party, 1922–1945* (Stanford: Stanford University Press, 1968), pp. 49–50, 54–57.

98. SGS, 1:569–70, 575–77, 642.

99. *Teikoku gikai shūgiin iinkai giroku* (hereafter cited as TGSIG), 51st sess., "Rōdō sōgi chōtei hōan," 25 Feb. 1926, pp. 19–21.

100. Yasui, *Rōdō*, pp. 112–15, 118–22; Naimushō shakaikyoku daiichibu, *Rōdō undō gaikyō, 1922*, p. 25.

101. Yasui, p. 119.

102. Ibid., p. 123.

103. Ayusawa, *History of Labor*, pp. 127–35.

104. TAS, 18 July 1923, p. 2; 16 Feb. 1924, p. 3.

105. Miwa Ryōichi, pp. 244, 254, n. 28.

106. Kitaoka, *Wagaomoide*, pp. 72–73.

107. Beckmann and Okubo, p. 68; Scalapino, *Early Japanese Labor*, p. 135.

108. Nimura Kazuo, "Kameido jiken shōron," *Rekishigaku kenkyū*, no. 281 (Oct. 1973), pp. 40–41; Kano Masanao, *Nihon no rekishi*, vol. 27: *Taishō demokurashii* (Tokyo: Shōgakkan, 1976), pp. 307–12.

109. Cf. Kamii, "1926 nen," pp. 131–34.

110. Gotō Fumio, *Sokkiroku*, p. 34.

111. Yasui, *Sokkiroku*, pp. 30–32.

112. Kitaoka, "Kyū-Shakaikyoku," p. 9; Watanabe Osamu, pp. 192, 196–203.

113. Nishio Suehiro, *Taishū to tomo ni—watakushi no hansei no kiroku* (Tokyo: Sekaisha, 1952), p. 177; SGS, 1:655.

114. Large, *Yūaikai*, pp. 172–73.

115. Yano Tatsuo, "Taishō-ki rōdō rippō no ichidammen—rōdō sōgi chōteihō no seiritsu katei," *Hōseishi kenkyū*, no. 27 (1977), pp. 108–9; *Rōdō* 9 (Sept. 1920): 213.

116. "Rōdō kaikyū no hanseiji-netsu," *Rōdō* 10 (Apr. 1921): 2–3.

117. Andrew D. Gordon, "Workers, Managers, and Bureaucrats in Japan: Labor Relations in Heavy Industry, 1853–1945" (Ph.D. diss., Harvard University, 1981), p. 271; Smith.

118. Naimushō, *Rōdō undō gaikyō, 1922,* p. 3; Nimura, "Rōdōsha," p. 130.

119. Scalapino, *Early Japanese Labor,* pp. 124, 139–40.

120. Stephen S. Large, "Nishio Suehiro and the Japanese Social Democratic Movement, 1920–1940," *Journal of Asian Studies* 36 (Nov. 1976): 37–56.

121. See Guenther Roth, *The Social Democrats in Imperial Germany: A Study in Working-Class Isolation and National Integration* (Totowa, N.J.: Bedminster Press, 1963).

122. Smith, p. 605.

123. Nishio, *Taishū,* pp. 187–91, 247–48.

124. Scalapino, *Early Japanese Labor,* p. 170, n. 45.

125. Kitaoka, "Kyū-Shakaikyoku," pp. 3–6; for a somewhat different version, see George Oakley Totten, III, *The Social Democratic Movement in Prewar Japan* (New Haven: Yale University Press, 1966), p. 47.

126. *Japan Chronicle,* 16 Jan. 1924, p. 5.

127. Toriumi Yasushi, "Hara naikaku hōkaigo ni okeru 'kyokoku itchi naikaku' rosen no tenkai to zasetsu," *Tōkyō daigaku kyōyōgakubu jimbun kagaku kiō,* no. 54 (1974), pp. 85–87, 98.

128. Beckmann and Okubo, p. 87; Nimura, "Rōdōsha," p. 133.

129. Naimushō, *Rōdō undō gaikyō, 1923,* pp. 54–55; *Rōdō undō gaikyō, 1924,* pp. 39–41.

130. *Japan Chronicle,* 10 Feb. 1924, p. 5; Nimura, "Rōdōsha," pp. 129–31.

131. TAS, 16 Feb. 1924, p. 3; Ayusawa, *History of Labor,* pp. 131–32.

132. TAS, 16 Feb. 1924, p. 3.

133. Cited by Hayashi Hiroshi, "Naimushō shakaikyoku kanryō no rōdō seisaku kōsō," *Hitotsubashi kenkyū* 7 (Apr. 1982): 89.

134. Large, *Yūaikai,* pp. 73–77; Young, pp. 150, 171, 234, 239.

135. For recent correctives to the conventional wisdom, see Fujino Yutaka, "Kyōchō seisaku no suishin—Kyōchōkai ni yoru rōdōsha no tōgō," in *Kindai Nihon no tōgō to teikō,* ed. Kano Masanao and Yui Masaomi, vol. 3 (Tokyo: Nihon hyōronsha, 1982), pp. 265–97; William Dean Kinzley, "The Quest for Industrial Harmony in Modern Japan: The Kyochokai, 1919–1946," (Ph.D. diss., University of Washington, 1984).

136. Yoshiharu Tazawa, "Moral Significance of 'Harmonious Cooperation,' " *Shakai seisaku jihō,* no. 21 (May 1922), English section, p. 1.

137. Kyōchōkai, ed., *Saikin no shakai undō* (Tokyo: Kyōchōkai, 1929), p. 994.

138. Nagai Tōru, "Rōdō undō to futsū senkyo," *Shakai seisaku jihō,* no. 40 (Jan. 1924), p. 27.

139. Draft and internal deliberations appear in Kyōchōkai, "Rōdō kumiai hōan kankei shorui," 1921–24, Ōhara Institute for Social Research, Tokyo; see also Fujino, pp. 285–87.

140. Fujino, pp. 288–90.

141. *Yomiuri shimbun,* 7 Mar. 1926, p. 3.

142. Kitaoka, "Kyū-Shakaikyoku," p. 9.

143. Directive of Dec. 1926, cited by Miwa Ryōichi, pp. 247, 255, n. 43.

144. Interview with Kitaoka, 19 Dec. 1978.

145. Hasegawa Kimiichi, "Chūshō kōgyō to rōdō mondai," *Shakai seisaku jihō,* no. 129 (June 1931), pp. 200–201.

146. Hyōdō, *Nihon,* pt. 3, chap. 2; Nimura, "Rōdōsha," p. 116; cf. Nishinarita, "1920 nendai."

147. Smith, p. 613; Gordon, *Evolution,* pp. 109–21.

148. Gordon, pp. 210–11; Kyōchōkai, *Saikin,* pp. 794–805.

149. Naimushō shakaikyoku rōdōbu, *Rōdō undō nempō, 1926,* pp. 73, 431–32 (hereafter cited as RUN); International Labour Office, pp. 125–26.

150. *Ōsaka asahi shimbun,* 17 Jan. (evening) 1925, p. 2.

151. Saitō Ken'ichi, "Jiji kaisetsu: sōgi chōteihō no kaisei," *Rōdō,* no. 279 (Oct. 1934), pp. 12–13.

152. Kitaoka, "Kyū-Shakaikyoku," pp. 3–4; regarding the ordinances to effect the 1931 Workmen's Compensation Law, see *Rōdō,* no. 241 (July 1931), p. 5.

153. Horikiri Zenjirō, *Horikiri Zenjirō shi danwa dai 3-kai sokkiroku,* Naiseishi kenkyū shiryō, no. 10 (Tokyo: Naiseishi kenkyūkai, 1964), p. 5.

154. Interview with Kitaoka, 19 Dec. 1978. The Association for International Labor was established in early 1925 to support the ILO and the enactment of Japanese labor legislation. It later became the Association for Social Legislation, a leading lobby for a progressive labor union law. Ayusawa, *Industrial Conditions,* pp. 110–11.

155. Akamatsu Katsumaro, *Nihon shakai undō shi* (Tokyo: Tsūshin kyōiku shinkōkai, 1949), p. 312; Nishio, *Taishū,* p. 273.

156. Ueno, pp. 177–78, 183; Naimushō, *Rōdō undō gaikyō, 1924,* pp. 22–23.

157. Scalapino, *Early Japanese Labor,* pp. 216–17; Beckmann and Okubo, pp. 87–92.

158. SGS, 2:26.

159. RUN, 1925, pp. 14–22; membership figures for the Sōdōmei and Hyōgikai are taken from RUN, 1925–28.

160. Shakai keizai rōdō kenkyūjo, ed., *Kindai Nihon rōdōsha undō shi* (Niigata: Hakurinsha, 1947), pp. 62–63.

161. RUN, 1928, pp. 410–14.
162. SGS, 2:26, 265–67, 290–91; also Totten, "Collective Bargaining."
163. E.g., Kyōchōkai, pp. 283–85; cf. Totten, "Collective Bargaining," pp. 210–25.
164. Large, *Organized Workers,* esp. pp. 107–11.
165. Nimura, "Rōdōsha," p. 133.
166. Totten, "Collective Bargaining," pp. 238–39.
167. RUN, 1928, pp. 41, 54.
168. Beckmann and Okubo, pp. 96–101; Totten, *Social Democratic Movement,* pp. 59–60.
169. TAS, 2 Dec. 1925, p. 2.
170. Iwamura Toshio, "Musan seitō no seiritsu," in *Iwanami kōza: Nihon rekishi,* vol. 18 (Tokyo: Iwanami shoten, 1975), p. 319.

NOTES TO CHAPTER FOUR

1. TGSIG, 51st sess., "Rōdō sōgi chōtei hōan," 2 Mar. 1926, pp. 18–19.
2. For an introduction to party politics during the 1920s, refer to Duus, *Party Rivalry,* chaps. 7–9.
3. Imai Seiichi, *Nihon no rekishi,* vol. 23: *Taishō demokurashii* (Tokyo: Chūō kōronsha, 1974), pp. 443–44.
4. Masumi, 5:230.
5. Kimbara, pp. 288, 290.
6. *Kensei* 7 (March 1924): 45; Koizumi Matajirō, "Minshū seiji e no kaidan e," ibid., pp. 13–14.
7. Speech of 5 Apr. 1924, in *Kenseikai shi,* pp. 598–99.
8. Details appear in Kuribayashi Teiichi, *Chihō kankai no hensen* (Tokyo: Sekaisha, 1930), pp. 277–88.
9. Kitaoka Juitsu, "Nagaoka Ryūichirō o omoide," *Taika,* no. 79 (Spring 1978), p. 15.
10. E.g., Duus, *Party Rivalry,* pp. 225–29.
11. Interview with Kitaoka, 19 December 1978.
12. Taikakai, pp. 440, 443, 451.
13. Miwa Ryōichi, p. 245.
14. TAS, 20 Oct. 1924, 9 Jan. 1925, p. 2.
15. Yano, "Taishō-ki," p. 117.
16. TAS, 26 Dec. 1924, p. 2; 10 Jan. 1925, p. 7.
17. TAS, 6 Aug. (evening) 1925, p. 1; 26 Feb. (evening) 1926, p. 1.
18. TAS, 12 Aug. 1925, p. 4.
19. Yano Tatsuo, "Rōdō hōan o meguru gyōsei chōsakai gijiroku," pt. 1, *Handai hōgaku,* no. 105 (Jan. 1978), pp. 143–46.
20. Draft appears in RGS, 1:421–23.
21. Yano, "Rōdō hōan," pt. 1, pp. 150–55.
22. Draft appears in RGS, 1:424–27.
23. Suehiro Izutarō, "Rōdō kumiai torishimari hōan o hyōsu," TAS, 10–14, 17, 19 Feb. 1926, p. 2.

24. [Kitahara Yasue], "Rōdō kumiaihō kara nukitotta hone," *Jiji shimpō,* 28 Feb.–7 Mar. 1926.

25. TAS, 26 Feb. (evening) 1926, p. 1.

26. SGS, 1:884.

27. See Nagaoka Ryūichirō, in *Teikoku gikai kizokuin iinkai giji sokkiroku,* 51st sess., "Rōdō sōgi chōtei hōan," 24 Mar. 1926, p. 2; for business positions on the conciliation bill, see Yano, "Taishō-ki," p. 135.

28. *Danshaku Dan,* 2:48–49.

29. *Nihon kōgyō kurabu nijūgonen shi,* 1:489–501.

30. Miwa Ryōichi, pp. 262–64.

31. TAS, 25 Feb. 1926, p. 2; 4 Mar. 1926, p. 3.

32. *Yomiuri shimbun,* 4 Mar. 1926, p. 2; TAS, 9 Mar. 1926, p. 3.

33. TGSIG, 51st sess., "Rōdō sōgi chōtei hōan," 2 Mar. 1926, p. 18.

34. *Chūgai shōgyō shimpō,* 15 Mar. 1926, p. 2.

35. Taki Kumejirō, in TGSIG, op. cit., 3 Mar. 1926, pp. 3–5.

36. Lower House committee, 25 Feb. 1926, in TAS, 26 Feb. 1926, p. 2.

37. Yano, "Taishō-ki," pp. 130–31.

38. TAS, 14 Mar. 1927, p. 3.

39. Ibid., 18, 23 Mar. 1926, p. 2.

40. Taikakai, 4:451.

41. Cited by Miwa Ryōichi, pp. 247, 255, n. 43.

42. *Nihon rōdō nenkan,* 1927, pp. 414–15.

43. Based on translation by Mitchell, p. 63.

44. Shinobu Seizaburō, *Taishō seiji shi,* 4 vols. (Tokyo: Keisō shobō, 1951–52), 4:1179–81.

45. Duus, *Party Rivalry,* p. 203; Mitchell, pp. 57–62.

46. See Watanabe Osamu; Okudaira Yasuhiro, *Chian ijihō shōshi* (Tokyo: Chikuma shobō, 1977).

47. Matsuo Takayoshi, "Dai ichiji taisengo no chian ijihō kōsō—Kageki shakai undō torishimari hōan," in *Ronsō gendai shi,* ed. Fujiwara Akira and Matsuo Takayoshi (Tokyo: Chikuma shobō, 1976), p. 159.

48. A more complete translation appears in Mitchell, p. 46.

49. Watanabe Osamu, pp. 198, 202–3; Report on the Forty-fifth Diet, *Kensei* 5, no. 3 (1922), pp. 39–40.

50. 22 Aug. 1918, cited by Watanabe Osamu, pp. 181–82.

51. Italics mine. Quoted in Kamii, "Chian keisatsuhō," pp. 167–68; also pp. 175–77.

52. Yano, "Rōdō hōan," pt. 1, pp. 153–54, 159, 164.

53. Mitchell, pp. 34–37.

54. Richard Anthony Yasko, "Hiranuma Kiichirō and Conservative Politics in Prewar Japan" (Ph.D. diss., University of Chicago, 1973), pp. 94–95; also Itō Takashi, *Shōwa shoki seiji shi kenkyū* (Tokyo: Tōkyō daigaku shuppankai, 1969), pp. 353–57.

55. *Nihon kin-gendai shi jiten,* 1978 ed., s.v. "Dai Nihon kokusuikai," by Watanabe Tōru.

56. For union bill, see TAS, 20 Aug. 1925, p. 3; 19 Oct. 1925, p. 2; for Factory Law revision, see 28 Nov. 1925, p. 2.

57. [Ogawa Heikichi], "Seikai bōyūryokusha no iken," *Nihon shimbun,* 1 Dec. 1930, p. 1; the Kenseikai's Suzuki Fujiya corroborated this version, TGSIG, 51st sess., "Rōdō sōgi chōtei hōan," 25 Feb. 1926, p. 7.

58. Memorandum of 25 June 1926, cited by Itō, *Shōwa shoki,* p. 398; also pp. 404, 223, 396.

59. Italics mine. Lower House, 19 Feb. 1925, cited in *Dai 50-kai Teikoku gikai chian iji hōan giji sokkiroku narabi iinkai gijiroku,* ed. Shakai mondai shiryō kenkyūkai (Kyoto: Tōyō bunkasha, 1972), pp. 13–14.

60. TAS, 19 Feb. 1925, p. 2.

61. *Dai 50-kai Teikoku gikai chian iji hōan,* p. 2; TAS, 9 Jan. 1925, p. 2.

62. Watanabe Osamu, pp. 213–15.

63. Okudaira, pp. 50–59.

64. Ogawa Heikichi, "Chian ijihō kinkyū chokurei happu made no keika," in *Nihon shimbun jūnen kinen—Nihon seishin hatsuyō shi,* ed. Komatsu Mitsuo (Tokyo: Nihon shimbunsha, 1934), p. 273.

65. Watanabe Osamu, pp. 216–17.

66. Ogawa, "Chian ijihō," pp. 270–75.

67. Kisaka Jun'ichirō, "Chian ijihō hantai undō—1925 nen ichi-sangatsu ni okeru," in *Taishō demokurashii,* ed. Yui Masaomi (Tokyo: Yūseidō, 1977), pp. 318–35.

68. Matsuo Takayoshi, "Seiyūkai to Minseitō," in *Iwanami kōza: Nihon rekishi,* vol. 19 (Tokyo: Iwanami shoten, 1976), pp. 88–95.

69. Shiba Teikichi, ed., *Rikken Minseitō shi,* 2 vols. (Tokyo: Rikken Minseitō shi hensankyoku, 1935), 2:724.

70. TAS, 26 Apr. 1927, p. 3.

71. Hamaguchi Osachi, "Rikken Minseitō sōsai shūnin no ji," *Minsei* 1 (July 1927): 3.

72. Asō Hisashi, "Minseitō, Kakushintō shutsugen ni taisuru hihan," *Kaizō* 9 (July 1927): 89–92; Aono Suekichi, "Saikin seikyoku no kansatsu," ibid., pp. 84–88.

73. Myōga Fusakichi, *Nihon seitō no gensei* (Tokyo: Nihon hyōronsha, 1929), p. 287; Kyōchōkai, pp. 683–84.

74. Matsuo, "Seiyūkai," p. 99.

75. TAS, 12 June (evening) 1928, p. 1; *Minsei* 3 (Apr., June, July 1929).

76. *Minsei* 2 (Feb. 1928): 79, 84.

77. Matsuo, "Seiyūkai," p. 96.

78. Kyōchōkai, pp. 886–88; Iinuma Jirō, "Seitō seiji to Shōwa nōgyō kyōkō," *Shisō,* no. 624 (June 1976), pp. 156–57.

79. At the cabinet level: Nakahashi Tokugorō (Commerce and Industry), Yamamoto Teijirō (Agriculture and Forestry), and Mochizuki Keisuke (Communications; later Home Affairs). Party executives included Yamamoto Jōtarō (secretary-general, 1927), Mori Kaku (secretary-general, 1929–31), Wakao Shōhachi, and Uchida Shin'ya.

80. TAS, 16 Feb. (evening) 1928, p. 1.

81. Kuhara Fusanosuke ō denki hensankai, ed., *Kuhara Fusanosuke* (Tokyo: Nihon kōgyō kabushiki kaisha, 1970), pp. 366–70, 400–402; for a general analysis of campaign contributions, see Masumi, 5:266–69.

82. I.e., Fujiwara Ginjirō, Wakao Shōhachi, Hattori Kintarō, and Isomura Toyotarō. Takahashi Kamekichi, *Nihon shihonshugi hattatsu shi* (Tokyo: Nihon hyōronsha, 1929), pp. 329–30; Morita, pp. 63–64, 70–71.

83. *Kuhara,* pp. 279–81; interview with Kageyama Shōzō (private secretary to Kuhara), Tokyo, 19 Mar. 1979.

84. Especially Katsuta Ginjirō (Katsuta Steamship), Matsumura Kōzō (Furukawa and Company), and Miyashima Seijirō (Nisshin Spinning).

85. "Nagai Ryūtarō" hensankai (Matsumura Kenzō), ed., *Nagai Ryūtarō* (Tokyo: "Nagai Ryūtarō" hensankai, 1959), p. 127.

86. These generalizations are based on my survey of Minseitō members in the Lower House, 1928–30, by age, education, occupation, political background, constituency, and party office; compiled from Shūgiin-Sangiin, *Gikai seido shichijūnen shi,* 12 vols. (Tokyo: Ōkurashō insatsukyoku, 1960–63), *Shūgiin giin meikan;* also from the monthly section on party news ("Rikken Minseitō tōhō") in *Minsei.*

87. Nakano Yasuo, *Seijika Nakano Seigō,* 2 vols. (Tokyo: Shinkōkaku shoten, 1971), 1:453–54; *Nagai Ryūtarō,* p. 254.

88. E.g., Hisa Shōhei, Uchigasaki Sakusaburō (Waseda graduates), Sugiura Takeo, Katō Taiichi, and Iwakiri Shigeo. Kamei Kan'ichirō, *Kizoku, shihonka, rōdōsha* (Tokyo: Chūseidō, 1931), p. 48; TAS, 25 Feb. 1927, p. 7.

89. Nakano Seigō, "Wagatō no kōchō suru kokka seichōshugi," *Minsei* 2 (Feb. 1928): 27–28; also Nakano Seigō, "Futsū senkyo no ronjin," *Kensei kōron* 5 (Apr. 1925): 13–14.

90. Katō Taiichi, "Rikken Minseitō no honryō," *Minsei* 1 (Sept. 1927): 33–35.

91. Ueno, pp. 183, 187, n. 33.

92. Matsuo, "Seiyūkai," p. 99.

93. *Rōdō,* no. 224 (Feb. 1930), p. 6; "Sōsenkyo no kyōkun," ibid., no. 225 (Mar. 1930), pp. 2–3; for a similar assessment by the Minseitō, see Yoshikawa Kan'ichi, "Fusen dai niji sōsenkyo to musan seitō," pt. 2, *Shakai undō ōrai* 2 (Apr. 1930): 40.

94. Shūgiin-Sangiin, *Gikai seido shichijūnenshi: Teikoku gikai shi,* 2:220–22; Masumi, 5:326–32; Iwamura, p. 329.

95. TAS, 26 Feb. 1928, p. 2; *Japan Chronicle,* 6 Apr. 1928, p. 5.

96. *Nihon kin-gendai shi jiten,* 1978 ed., s.v. "Nihon Fuebian kyōkai," by Matsuo Takayoshi.

97. *Trans-Pacific,* 25 Feb. 1928, p. 13.

98. Abe Isoo, "Rikken Minseitō no seikō o hyōsu," *Chūō kōron* 42 (July 1927): 88–91.

99. Nishio, *Taishū,* pp. 246–48.

100. See Emy, p. 289.

101. Kamei, pp. 62, 69.

102. See Izawa Takio denki hensan iinkai, ed., *Izawa Takio* (Tokyo: Haneda shoten, 1951).

103. Kuribayashi, pp. 246, 511.

104. Maruyama Tsurukichi, *Shichijūnen tokorodokoro* (Tokyo: Shichijū-

nen tokorodokoro kankōkai, 1955), pp. 30–32; Yasui, *Sokkiroku*, pp. 34, 37–38; Tazawa Yoshiharu kinenkai, ed., *Tazawa Yoshiharu* (Tokyo: Tazawa Yoshiharu kinenkai, 1954), pp. 104–5.

105. *Yomiuri shimbun*, 26 Mar. 1924, p. 5; *Hochi shimbun*, 26 Aug. 1924, p. 9.

106. Itō, *Shōwa shoki*, pp. 62–64.

107. George O. Totten, "Japanese Industrial Relations at the Cross-roads: The Great Noda Strike of 1927–1928," in *Japan in Crisis: Essays on Taishō Democracy*, ed. Bernard S. Silberman and H. D. Harootunian (Princeton: Princeton University Press, 1974), pp. 418, 426.

108. Itō, *Shōwa shoki*, pp. 48–60.

109. Yoshii Ken'ichi, "Tazawa Yoshiharu ron," *Jimbun kagaku kenkyū* (Niigata daigaku), no. 53 (Mar. 1978), pp. 9–10, 14; Tazawa Yoshiharu, *Seiji kyōiku kōwa* (Tokyo: Shinseisha, 1926), pp. 130–31; "Kyōchōkai" kaiwakai (Machida Tatsujirō), ed., *Kyōchōkai shi—Kyōchōkai sanjūnen no ayumi* (Tokyo: "Kyōchōkai" kaiwakai, 1965), p. 36.

110. Tazawa, *Seiji kyōiku*, pp. 114–37.

111. Maruyama Tsurukichi, pp. 126–34; Tazawa Yoshiharu, "Fusengo ni okeru seikai no bun'ya o ronjite, chihō gikai no oyobu," *Shimin* 22 (Jan. 1927): 4–6.

112. Interview with Kitaoka Juitsu, 19 Dec. 1978.

113. Matsuo, "Seiyūkai," p. 93.

114. Compare Kuribayashi, pp. 459–60; Kitaoka, "Nagaoka," pp. 14–16.

115. Interview with Kitaoka; Taikakai, 4:117–18.

116. Komatsu, pp. 60, 69, 77.

117. Ogawa, "Chian ijihō," p. 276.

118. Nagaoka, pp. 349–50.

119. Translated by Berger, p. 47.

120. Itō, *Shōwa shoki*, pp. 224–25.

121. Matsuo, "Seiyūkai," pp. 86–89; Kuribayashi, pp. 278, 282–85, 376–87.

122. Itō, *Shōwa shoki*, pp. 71–73.

123. For a similar schematization, see ibid., p. 460.

124. Tanaka Giichi, "Seiyūkai naikaku no shisei," *Seiyū*, no. 317 (July 1927), p. 3.

125. Cited by Okudaira, p. 91.

126. Details in Byron K. Marshall, "Growth and Conflict in Japanese Higher Education, 1905–1930," in *Conflict in Modern Japanese History*, ed. Tetsuo Najita and J. Victor Koschmann (Princeton: Princeton University Press, 1982), p. 292.

127. TAS, 11 Apr. 1928, p. 2; SGS, 2(1966): 78–79.

128. Masumi, 5:457.

129. Okudaira, p. 88.

130. Ebashi Takashi, "Shōwa shoki no tokkō keisatsu," *Kikan gendai shi*, no. 7 (June 1976), pp. 73–75, 78.

131. Okudaira, pp. 61, 89.

132. Egi Tasuku, "Shisō mondai hihan," TAS, 17–18 Apr. 1928, p. 3.

133. *Teikoku gikai shūgiin giji sokkiroku* (hereafter cited as TGSGS), 55th sess., 28 Apr. 1929, p. 63.

134. Text of revision appears in Okudaira, pp. 252–53.

135. Ebashi, pp. 78–79.

136. Furuya Tetsuo, "Dai 55-kai Teikoku gikai shūgiin kaisetsu," in *Teikoku gikai shi*, ed. Shakai mondai shiryō kenkyūkai, 1st ser., 40 vols. (Kyoto: Tōyō bunkasha, 1975–78), 1:268.

137. Ogawa, "Chian ijihō," p. 278.

138. Yoshimi Yoshiaki, "Tanaka (Gi) naikakuka no chian ijihō kaisei mondai," *Rekishigaku kenkyū*, no. 441 (Feb. 1977), pp. 2–4.

139. *Minsei* 2 (Aug. 1928): 92; Matsuo, "Seiyūkai," p. 104.

140. Ebashi, p. 79.

141. Mochizuki Keisuke den kankōkai, ed., *Mochizuki Keisuke den* (Tokyo: Haneda shoten, 1945), p. 339.

142. Yoshimi, pp. 3–5.

143. Saitō Takao, "Kinkyū shokureian shingi ni saishi: Sūfu arawaretaru giron ni tsuite," *Minsei* 2 (Aug. 1928): 37–41.

144. Ogawa, "Chian ijihō," p. 279; also Nagawa Kan'ichi, in TGSGS, 56th sess., 5 Mar. 1929, p. 555.

145. Saitō Takao, in TGSGS, 2 Mar. 1929, pp. 538–40.

146. TAS, 20 Mar. 1929, p. 3.

147. TAS, 8–9 Mar., p. 2; 13 Mar. (evening) 1929, p. 1.

148. TAS, 19 Mar. 1929, p. 2; "Gyakushi tōkō ni shōsenkyoku ron—musan kaikyū no kikensei zōka," *Minsei* 2 (Oct. 1928): 3.

149. TAS, 12, 14, 19 Mar. (all evening), p. 1; 20 Mar. 1929, p. 2.

150. TAS, 22 Mar. 1929, p. 2.

151. Miwa Ryōichi, p. 248.

152. *Japan Chronicle*, 27 Mar. 1929, p. 4.

153. TAS, 21 Feb. (evening) 1929, p. 1.

154. TAS, 26 Sept., 25 Oct. 1928, p. 4.

155. RGS, 1:296.

156. *Minsei* 3 (June 1929): 88.

157. Statement of 3 July 1929, cited by Kōno Mitsu, Akamatsu Katsumaro, and Rōnōtō shokikan, *Nihon musan seitō shi* (Tokyo: Hakuyōsha, 1931), p. 418.

NOTES TO CHAPTER FIVE

1. Quoted in Itō, *Shōwa shoki*, p. 61.

2. Masao Maruyama, *Thought and Behavior in Modern Japanese Politics*, ed. Ivan Morris (London: Oxford University Press, 1969), p. 81.

3. Sugihara Masami, *Atarashii Shōwa shi* (Tokyo: Shinkigensha, 1958), p. 39.

4. Baba Tsunego, *Seikai jimbutsu fūkei* (Tokyo: Chūō kōronsha, 1931), p. 204; also Baba's *Gendai jimbutsu hyōron* (Tokyo: Chūō kōronsha, 1930), pp. 7–13.

5. Cited by Itō, *Shōwa shoki*, p. 113.

6. TAS, 3 July 1929, p. 2.

7. Itō, pp. 15–16, 34, 61.

8. For Matsuda's espousal of a union law in 1919 while in the Seiyūkai, see Watanabe Tōru, pt. 2, pp. 2–3.

9. Hilary Conroy, *The Japanese Seizure of Korea: 1868–1910* (Philadelphia: University of Pennsylvania Press, 1960), p. 317.

10. Kamei, p. 54.

11. Itō, *Shōwa shoki*, pp. 25–29.

12. Hamaguchi Osachi, "Gōriteki keiki kaifuku no kichō," *Minsei* 3 (Sept. 1929): 2.

13. Details in Hugh T. Patrick, "The Economic Muddle of the 1920s," in *Dilemmas of Growth in Prewar Japan*, ed. James W. Morley (Princeton: Princeton University Press, 1971), pp. 211–66.

14. Nakamura Takafusa, *Shōwa kyōkō: Aru ōkura daijin no higeki* (Tokyo: Nihon keizai shimbunsha, 1978), pp. 100–8; Johnson, pp. 109–10.

15. Hamaguchi, "Gōriteki," p. 5.

16. Yoshida Shigeru to the commission's special committee on labor union legislation, 6 Nov. 1929, Shakai seisaku shingikai, "Shakai seisaku shingikai ni okeru rōdō kumiaihō shingi keika," Ōhara Institute for Social Research, Tokyo.

17. Conversation with Professor Nakamura Takafusa, Tokyo University, Tokyo, 2 Oct. 1978; on the government's desire to include representatives from the unions and proletarian parties on the advisory board to the Provisional Industrial Rationalization Bureau, see TAS, 3 June 1930, p. 2.

18. RGS, 1:447, n. 3.

19. See minutes of the special committee on labor union legislation, "Shakai seisaku shingikai."

20. Yoshida Shigeru denki kankō henshū iinkai, ed., *Yoshida Shigeru* (Tokyo: Yoshida Shigeru denki kankō henshū iinkai, 1969), pp. 46–47.

21. Nishio, *Taishū*, p. 273; for the view of a younger Social Bureau official, see Kurihara, p. 17.

22. See his opposition to the Tanaka cabinet's small-district electoral reform, House of Peers, 24 Mar. 1929, in TAS, 25 Mar. (evening) 1929, p. 1.

23. TAS, 12 Nov. 1929, p. 2; XYZ, "Shakai minshūtō no seitai," *Shakai undō ōrai* 2 (Feb. 1930): 60.

24. Fujisawa Rikitarō, special committee, 31 Oct. 1929, "Shakai seisaku shingikai."

25. Italics mine. Ibid., 13 Nov. 1929.

26. Ibid., 13, 22, 29 Nov. 1929.

27. Draft appears in RGS, 1:448–51.

28. Hamaguchi to leaders of the Japan Industrial Club, TAS, 22 Dec. 1929, p. 2.

29. Policy speech to the Lower House, 21 Jan. 1930, quoted in Shūgiin-Sangiin, *Gikai seido shichijūnen shi: Teikoku gikai shi*, 2:271.

30. RGS, 1:575–81, 585.

31. See Ogura Takekazu, *Tochi rippō no shiteki kōsatsu* (Tokyo: Nōrinshō nōgyō sōgō kenkyūjo, 1951), pp. 562–72.

32. *Ōsaka mainichi shimbun,* 7 Dec. 1929.

33. TAS, 13 Dec. 1929, p. 2.

34. "1930 nen o mukau," *Rōdō,* no. 223 (Jan. 1930), p. 3.

35. "Rōdō kumiaihō yōkyū no igi," *Rōdō,* no. 226 (Apr. 1930), pp. 2–3.

36. *Shakai undō ōrai* 1 (Nov. 1929): 42.

37. *Shakai seisaku jihō,* no. 117 (June 1930), p. 202.

38. Sassa Hiroo, "Seikyoku o shihai suru mono—kinkyū katō seiji no jissō," *Kaizō* 13 (May 1931): 81; see electoral analysis by Arthur E. Tiedemann, "The Hamaguchi Cabinet: First Phase, July 1929–February 1930: A Study in Japanese Parliamentary Government" (Ph.D. diss., Columbia University, 1959), pp. 174, 208.

39. Special committee, 31 Oct. 1929, "Shakai seisaku shingikai."

40. *Danshaku Dan,* 2:55; Morita, p. 169; also Soeda Keiichirō, "Rōdō kumiaihō no seitai ni tsuite taihō no jukuryo o yōbōsu," *Kōsei* (Feb. 1930), in Naimushō shakaikyoku rōdōbu, *Rōdō kumiai hōan ni kansuru shiryō* (Tokyo: Naimushō shakaikyoku rōdōbu, 1930), pp. 241–47.

41. Quoted in *Danshaku Dan,* 2:55.

42. Position paper of 25 Oct. 1929, in Naimushō, *Rōdō kumiai hōan,* pp. 64–67; see also opinions of the Osaka Chamber of Commerce and Industry (18 Oct. 1929) and the Electric Power Industry Association (28 Dec. 1929), pp. 63–64, 81–87.

43. TAS, 22 Dec. 1929, p. 2.

44. *Hochi shimbun,* 26 July 1930.

45. Ikeda Seihin, *Kojin konjin* (Tokyo: Sekai no Nihonsha, 1949), pp. 102–3.

46. *Danshaku Dan,* 2:66–67; Yamanaka Tokutarō, *Nihon rōdō kumiaihō kenkyū* (Tokyo: Moriyama shoten, 1931), pp. 86–87.

47. Position paper of 25 Feb. 1930, Naimushō, *Rōdō kumiai hōan,* pp. 105–7.

48. Petition of Nov. 1930, cited by Miwa Ryōichi, p. 268; Miwa's analysis on p. 265.

49. Patrick, "Economic Muddle," pp. 252–56.

50. Miwa Ryōichi, p. 267.

51. On unionization and the Tōyō Muslin strike, see RUN, 1930, pp. 2, 375–91; 1931, p. 4.

52. Miwa Ryōichi, p. 286.

53. RUN, 1930, p. 89.

54. Ibid., 1930, pp. 3–4 (preface), 88–90; 1931, pp. 4–6.

55. Britain: 415 strikes and 287,300 participants; Japan: 906 strikes and 81,329 participants. According to Hasegawa, the average Japanese strike in 1930 involved only 90 participants, as contrasted with 692 in Britain (510 for Germany and 255 for the United States during 1929). Hasegawa Kimiichi, pp. 202–3.

56. Nihon kōgyō kurabu, ed., *Saikin ni okeru rōdō sōgi no sōrei* (1930), cited by Nishinarita Yutaka, "Manshū jihen-ki no rōshi kankei," *Hitotsubashi daigaku kenkyū nempō: Keizaigaku kenkyū* 26 (Jan. 1985): 295.

57. Statement of "Fundamental Principles" by representatives of the na-

tion's business associations at the Japan Industrial Club, 22 May 1930, cited by Matsuo, "Seiyūkai," p. 119.

58. Kyōchōkai, pp. 528–30; also Nishinarita, "Manshū," pp. 267–70.

59. Fujiwara Ginjirō, in Naimushō shakaikyoku rōdōbu, *Rōdō rippō kondankai (dai 1, 2-kai) sokkiroku,* 2 vols. (Tokyo: Naimushō shakaikyoku rōdōbu, 1930–31), 2:30–31; also 2:19–20.

60. SSJ, no. 176 (May 1935), English supp., p. 3.

61. Morita, pp. 73–79.

62. David Brody, "The Rise and Decline of Welfare Capitalism," in *Change and Continuity in Twentieth-Century America: The 1920's,* ed. John Braeman, Robert H. Bremner, and David Brody (Columbus: Ohio State University Press, 1968), pp. 147–78.

63. Naimushō, *Rōdō rippō,* 2:5–6; *Danshaku Dan,* 2:52–53.

64. TAS, 11 June 1930, p. 4.

65. TAS, 26 May 1930, p. 2.

66. Ibid., 11 Apr. 1930, p. 3.

67. Nakamura Masanori, p. 304.

68. *Hochi shimbun,* 26 June 1930.

69. Yamanaka, pp. 86–87; Matsuo, "Seiyūkai," pp. 118–19.

70. TAS, 25, 29 June, p. 2; 27 June (evening) 1930, p. 1.

71. Minseitō's special committee on social policy, TAS, 10 June 1930, p. 2.

72. E.g., Sassa Hiroo, "Jiyūshugi ka, fuashizumu ka," *Kaizō* 13 (Jan. 1931): supp., 133–34.

73. TAS, 19 July 1929, p. 3; 26 Sept. (evening) 1929, p. 2; Aritake Shūji, *Shōwa keizai sokumenshi* (Tokyo: Kawade shobō, 1952), p. 180.

74. Kido Kōichi, *Kido Kōichi nikki,* 2 vols. (Tokyo: Tōkyō daigaku shuppankai, 1966), 1:21.

75. *Yomiuri shimbun,* 8 July 1930.

76. TAS, 29 July 1930, p. 2.

77. E.g., ibid., 19 June 1930, p. 2.

78. TAS, 18 Oct. 1930, p. 2.

79. TAS, 29 June 1930, p. 2; Matsuo, "Seiyūkai," p. 120.

80. TAS, 10, 25 June, 27 Oct. 1930, p. 2.

81. Yamanaka, pp. 154–63; *Shakai undō ōrai* 3 (Jan. 1931): 92.

82. Yamanaka, p. 167.

83. Baba, *Seikai jimbutsu fūkei,* p. 272.

84. Matsuo, "Seiyūkai," p. 125.

85. RGS, 1:1277.

86. Andō Masazumi, "Sojō ni tenkai subeki Hamaguchi naikaku no hisei, hyakushutsu," *Seiyū,* no. 364 (Jan. 1931): 8–9; Nakamura Takafusa, pp. 110–11, 132–33.

87. Itō, *Shōwa shoki,* pp. 276–79.

88. *Japan Chronicle,* 1 Jan. 1931, p. 4.

89. For supporters and opponents of the Social Bureau draft, see *Nihon shimbun,* 3 Dec. 1930, p. 2; *Shakai undō ōrai* 3 (Jan. 1931): 92.

90. TAS, 28 Jan. 1931, p. 2.

91. Matsuo, "Seiyūkai," pp. 123–25; Sassa, "Seikyoku," p. 84.

92. Baba, *Seikai jimbutsu fūkei,* pp. 217–18.

93. TAS, 19 Dec. 1930, p. 2; see also G. W. McDonald and H. F. Gospel, "The Mond-Turner Talks, 1927–33: A Study in Industrial Co-operation," *The Historical Journal* 16 (Dec. 1973): 807–29.

94. TAS, 20 Dec. 1930, p. 2.

95. *Nihon kōgyō kurabu nijūgonen shi,* 2:726.

96. Transcripts of the two conferences appear in Naimushō, *Rōdō rippō kondankai (dai 1, 2-kai) sokkiroku.*

97. Adachi Kenzō, *Adachi Kenzō jijoden* (Tokyo: Shinkōsha, 1960), p. 254.

98. *Chūgai shōgyō shimpō,* 2 Feb. 1931, p. 2.

99. TAS, 14 Feb. 1931, p. 2.

100. Draft appears in RGS, 1:454–58.

101. *Chūgai shōgyō shimpō,* 25 Feb. (evening) 1931, p. 1.

102. TAS, 21 Feb. 1931, p. 3.

103. RGS, 1:442.

104. Nishio, *Taishū,* pp. 274–75.

105. RGS, 1:469–72.

106. TAS, 14, 22 Feb. 1931, p. 2.

107. Baba, *Seikai jimbutsu fūkei,* p. 270.

108. *Chūgai shōgyō shimpō,* 23 Feb. 1931, p. 2.

109. "Zenkoku sangyō dantai rengōkai no seiritsu," *Rōdō,* no. 240 (June 1931), pp. 124–25.

110. TAS, 4, 21, 22, 24 Feb., p. 2; 22, 25 Feb. (evening) 1931, p. 1.

111. TGSGS, 59th sess., 24 Feb. 1931, pp. 452–53, 456.

112. *Chūgai shōgyō shimpō,* 16 Feb. 1931, p. 2; Itō, *Shōwa shoki,* pp. 257–63, n. 1.

113. Masumi, 5:253.

114. *Chūgai shōgyō shimpō,* 11 Jan. (evening) 1931, p. 1.

115. *Chūgai shōgyō shimpō,* 18 Feb. 1931, p. 4; 4 Mar. 1931, p. 3.

116. TAS, 20 Mar. 1931, p. 2; committee membership in Morita, pp. 185–86.

117. Furuya Tetsuo, "Dai 59-kai Teikoku gikai shūgiin kaisetsu," in *Teikoku gikai shi,* ed. Shakai mondai shiryō kenkyūkai, 9:153.

118. Baba, *Seikai jimbutsu fūkei,* pp. 271–72; see also TAS editorial, 27 Mar. 1931, p. 3; Itō, *Shōwa shoki,* pp. 279–80.

119. See Berger, pp. 39–43.

120. Yoshioka Shigeyoshi, "Rōdō kumiai kaigi no honshitsu to sono dōkō," SSJ, no. 146 (Nov. 1932), p. 353.

NOTES TO CHAPTER SIX

1. Document 5–32, Exhibit 284, "Kido, Marquis Koichi," International Prosecutorial Section, File 5, vol. 2, International Military Tribunal for the Far East, National Archives, Washington, D.C. I have corrected a few typographical errors.

2. Robert O. Paxton, *Vichy France: Old Guard and New Order, 1940–1944* (New York: W. W. Norton and Co., 1972), pp. 267–68.

3. Hozumi Shichirō, "Naikaku shingikai no shakaiteki naiyō," *Rōdō*, no. 287 (June 1935), p. 12.

4. Okōchi Kazuo, *Kurai tanima no rōdō undō* (Tokyo: Iwanami shoten, 1970).

5. Large, *Organized Workers*, pp. 167–68.

6. Nishinarita, "Manshū," p. 246.

7. Morita, pp. 186–88, 225–33.

8. *Minsei* 10 (Feb. 1936): 84, 86.

9. *Rōdō*, no. 273 (Apr. 1934), pp. 20–21.

10. Yoshida Shigeru, "Tokushūgō no hakkan ni atarite," *Shakai seisaku jihō*, no. 146 (Nov. 1932), p. 3.

11. "Kyōchōkai" kaiwakai (Machida Tatsujirō), ed., *Kyōchōkai shi—Kyōchōkai sanjūnen no ayumi* (Tokyo: "Kyōchōkai" kaiwakai, 1965), pp. 64, 70–73; Kurihara, pp. 26, 31.

12. Kimura Seishi, "Shōwa 9 nen shakai gyōsei no kaiko," SSJ, no. 185 (Feb. 1935), p. 4.

13. See Totten, *Social Democratic Movement*, pp. 71–79.

14. Ernest J. Notar, "Labor Unions and the *Sangyō Hōkoku* Movement 1930–1945: A Japanese Model for Industrial Relations" (Ph.D. diss., University of California, Berkeley, 1979), p. 131.

15. Gordon, *Evolution*, pp. 224–30; Notar, pp. 142–76.

16. Nishinarita, "Manshū," pp. 293–94, 299–302.

17. "Dai 20-kai taikai o mukau," *Rōdō*, no. 245 (Nov. 1931), pp. 2–3.

18. In the British case, see Bernard Semmel, *Imperialism and Social Reform: English Social-Imperial Thought, 1895–1914* (Cambridge: Harvard University Press, 1960).

19. "Hijō jidai ni okeru rōdō kumiai undō," *Rōdō*, no. 249 (Mar. 1932), pp. 2–3.

20. "Rōdō kumiai kaigi ni tsuite," *Rōdō*, no. 255 (Sept. 1932), p. 3.

21. *Rōdō*, no. 269 (Dec. 1933), p. 13.

22. Philippe C. Schmitter, "Still the Century of Corporatism?" *Review of Politics* 36 (Jan. 1974): 93–94.

23. *Industrial and Labour Information* 56 (11 Nov. 1935): 231; for an introduction to Italian corporatism, see Roland Sarti, *Fascism and the Industrial Leadership in Italy 1919–1940* (Berkeley: University of California Press, 1971), pp. 72–76.

24. See Gordon, "Business and the Corporate State."

25. SGS, 2:240–41.

26. RUN, 1933, p. 159; 1934, pp. 150–52.

27. *Rōdō*, no. 273 (Apr. 1934), p. 20.

28. Taira, *Economic Development*, p. 147; Large, *Organized Workers*, pp. 177–80.

29. RUN, 1934, pp. 286, 733–34; also William D. Wray, "Asō Hisashi and the Search for Renovation in the 1930s," in *Papers on Japan*, vol. 5 (Cambridge: East Asian Research Center, Harvard, 1970), pp. 62–64.

30. Spaulding, pp. 52–57; Weiner, pp. 88–90.

31. Hozumi, p. 12.

32. Berger, pp. 73–74.
33. *Shakai undō tsūshin,* 24 Feb. 1936, p. 2.
34. Masao Maruyama, p. 27.
35. *Shakai undō tsūshin,* 7 Oct. 1936.
36. TAS, 20 May 1936, p. 2; *Shakai undō tsūshin,* 22 May 1936, p. 1; RUN, 1936, pp. 97, 100–101, 166–67.
37. *Nihon rōdō nenkan,* 1937, p. 8.
38. RUN, 1937, pp. 146–47; Wray, pp. 72–73.
39. RUN, 1934, p. 285; *Rōdō,* no. 281 (Dec. 1934), p. 3.
40. RUN, 1934, p. 365.
41. "Wagakuni ni okeru rōdō iinkai no gaikyō," *Rōdō jihō* 11 (Jan. 1934): 7.
42. Miwa Yasushi, "1935 nen ni okeru Nihonshugi rōdō undō no hatten," *Nihon shi kenkyū,* no. 189 (May 1978), pp. 3–4.
43. Kumagai Ken'ichi, "Shōwa jūichi nen shakai undō gaikan," SSJ, no. 197 (Feb. 1937), pp. 4–5.
44. *Shakai undō tsūshin,* 24 Feb. 1936, p. 2.
45. Tomita Aijirō, "Sangyō heiwa e no michi," *Shimin* 26 (June 1931): 3–4.
46. See Yoshida Shigeru, "Rōdō kyōyaku tokushūgō," SSJ, no. 132 (Sept. 1931), p. 3; "Dantai kyōyaku to sangyō kyōroku," *Sangyō fukuri* (Mar. 1934), reprinted in *Rōdō,* no. 273 (Apr. 1934), p. 19; *Rōdō,* no. 276 (July 1934), p. 21.
47. Home Ministry's instructions to prefectural governors, 1934, quoted in SGS, 2:245.
48. Interview with Kitaoka, 13 Apr. 1979.
49. Cited by Itō Takashi, " 'Kyokoku itchi' naikaku-ki no seikai saihensei mondai—Shōwa sanjūnen Konoe shintō mondai kenkyū no tame ni," pt. 1, *Shakai kagaku kenkyū* 24 (Aug. 1972), p. 125.
50. Kurihara, pp. 24–30, 41; Itō, " 'Kyokoku itchi,' " p. 98.
51. *Yoshida Shigeru,* pp. 36, 41–45; Ōhashi Takeo, *Ōhashi Takeo shi danwa dai 1-kai sokkiroku,* Naiseishi kenkyū shiryō, no. 119 (Tokyo: Naiseishi kenkyūkai, 1972), pp. 32–33.
52. Spaulding, p. 54; Itō, " 'Kyokoku itchi,' " pp. 96–98.
53. *Tōkyō nichinichi* article, in Itō, p. 125.
54. *Yoshida Shigeru,* p. 70.
55. Kimura Seishi, pp. 3–4.
56. Nishinarita, "Manshū," p. 287; for patronage by local police in 1935, see Miwa Yasushi, pp. 11, 32–33.
57. *Shakai undō ōrai* 4 (Apr. 1932): 59.
58. Kyōchōkai, ed., *Rōdō nenkan,* 1936 (Tokyo: Kyōchōkai, 1936), p. 2.
59. "Chūshō kigyō ni okeru rōdō jōken no tekisei," *Rōdō jihō* 12 (Feb. 1935): 36–37.
60. Kyōchōkai, *Rōdō nenkan,* 1936, pp. 18–19.
61. *Industrial Labour Information,* 54 (6 May 1935): 202.
62. *Rōdō,* no. 285 (Apr. 1935), p. 3.
63. *Rōdō,* no. 289 (Aug. 1935), p. 3.
64. Kyōchōkai, *Rōdō nenkan,* 1936, p. 3.

65. Kitaoka, "Kyū-Shakaikyoku," p. 9; interview with Kitaoka, 13 Apr. 1979.

66. TAS, 20 May 1936, p. 2.

67. Gordon, *Evolution*, pp. 259–60.

68. RGS, 1:664–76; *Shakai undō tsūshin*, 27 Aug. 1936, p. 1.

69. Sugatani Akira, *Nihon shakai seisaku shi ron* (Tokyo: Nihon hyōron-sha, 1978), pp. 85–93.

70. *Nihon rōdō nenkan*, 1937, p. 6.

71. *Yoshida Shigeru*, p. 64.

72. "Rōdō sōgi chōteihō kaisei no naigi," TAS, 28 July 1934, p. 3; *Shakai undō tsūshin*, 15 June 1935, p. 1.

73. Saitō Ken'ichi, "Jiji kaisetsu: sōgi chōteihō no kaisei," *Rōdō*, no. 279 (Oct. 1934): 12–13.

74. *Nihon rōdō nenkan*, 1936, p. 629.

75. Nishinarita, "Manshū," p. 289.

76. Sakurabayashi Makoto, "Senji Nihon no rōshi kyōgisei: sangyō hōkoku-kai no kondankai o chūshin to shite," *Jōchi keizai ronshū* 18 (Mar. 1972): 41.

77. Nishinarita, "Manshū," p. 290.

78. Akagi Tomoharu to chiefs of Special Higher Police sections, *Rōdō jihō* 12 (May 1935): 162.

79. Nagano Wakamatsu, *Nagano Wakamatsu shi danwa dai 1-kai sokki-roku*, Naiseishi kenkyū shiryō, no. 86 (Tokyo: Naiseishi kenkyūkai, 1970), pp. 10–11; see also Miwa Yasushi, p. 11.

80. RUN, 1934, pp. 471–82.

81. See James B. Crowley, *Japan's Quest for Autonomy: National Security and Foreign Policy, 1930–1938* (Princeton: Princeton University Press, 1966), p. 299.

82. *Shakai undō tsūshin*, 6 Apr. 1936, p. 1.

83. TAS, 11 Sept. 1936, p. 11.

84. Notar, "Labor Unions," p. 189.

85. "Rikugun to rōdō kumiai," TAS, 13 Sept. 1936, p. 3.

86. Nishinarita, "Manshū," pp. 273–75.

87. Notar, "Labor Unions," pp. 296–300.

88. *Shakai undō tsūshin*, 26 Oct. 1936, p. 1.

89. Nishinarita, pp. 267–70.

90. Quoted in ibid., pp. 268–69.

91. TAS, 12, 13 Sept. 1936, p. 2.

92. Quoted in RGS, 1:506.

93. *Rōdō jihō* 15 (July 1938): 178.

94. Bank of Japan statistics, cited by Ujihara Shōjirō and Hagiwara Susumu, "Sangyō hōkoku undō no haikei," in *Fuashizumu-ki no kokka to shakai*, vol. 6: *Undō to teikō (pt. 1)*, ed. Tōkyō daigaku shakai kagaku kenkyūjo (Tokyo: Tōkyō daigaku shuppankai, 1979), p. 211.

95. Ibid., pp. 210–19.

96. *Shakai undō tsūshin*, 1 Sept. 1936, p. 1; also 22 Apr. 1936, p. 1.

97. Ibid., 3 Oct. 1936, p. 2.

98. Ibid., 1 Sept. 1936, p. 1; Sakurabayashi, p. 41.

99. With the notable exception of William Miles Fletcher, III, *The Search for a New Order: Intellectuals and Fascism in Prewar Japan* (Chapel Hill: University of North Carolina Press, 1982).

100. Studies by Kyōchōkai staff members include Isozaki Shunji, "Nachisu no shin-rōdō kenshō," SSJ, no. 163 (Apr. 1934): 39–52; section on German labor by Murayama Shigetada and Inaba Hidezō in Kyōchōkai, *Rōdō nenkan*, 1936, pp. 354–414; on the appeal of Nazi and Fascist policies to the intellectuals of the Shōwa Research Association, see Fletcher.

101. Kyōchōkai, *Rōdō nenkan*, 1938, p. 470.

102. T. W. Mason, "Labour in the Third Reich, 1933–1939," *Past and Present* 33 (Apr. 1966): 112–41; David Schoenbaum, *Hitler's Social Revolution* (Garden City, N.Y.: Doubleday and Co., 1966), pp. 86–90.

103. Yomiuri shimbunsha, ed., *Shōwa shi no tennō*, vol. 17 (Tokyo: Yomiuri shimbunsha, 1972), p. 200.

104. Ibid., pp. 43–46, 199–205.

105. Proposal appears in NRUS, 9 (1965): 590–93.

106. Ibid., p. 590.

107. Minami Iwao, "Wagakuni ni okeru shakai seisaku to rōdō kumiai no shōrai ni tsuite," SSJ, no. 200 (May 1937), pp. 159–60, 179.

108. Ujihara and Hagiwara, pp. 224–26.

109. Ibid., pp. 219–20; figures from *Rōdō jihō* 15 (July 1938): 178.

110. RGS, 1:867–77; for a detailed analysis of the formation of the Industrial Patriotic movement, see Ernest J. Notar, "Japan's Wartime Labor Policy: A Search for Method," *Journal of Asian Studies* 44 (Feb. 1985): 311–28.

111. Position paper of 1 June 1938, in Kanda Fuhito, ed., *Shiryō Nihon gendai shi*, vol. 7: *Sangyō hōkoku undō* (Tokyo: Ōtsuki shoten, 1981), p. 24.

112. Yoshii Yoshiko, "Sangyō hōkoku undō—sono seiritsu o megutte," *Hitotsubashi ronsō* 73 (Feb. 1975): 49.

113. Sakurabayashi, pp. 41–42.

114. See Morita, pp. 246, 274–280.

115. Document in Kanda, p. 65.

116. Ibid., pp. 595–96.

117. Nov. 1939, document in Kanda, p. 120.

118. Ibid., pp. 597–98; Ujihara and Hagiwara, p. 290.

119. Yoshii, p. 51.

120. Document in Kanda, p. 45.

121. Ujihara and Hagiwara, pp. 200–1.

122. Kanda, pp. 593–94; for the unions' responses to the Industrial Patriotic movement, see Notar, "Labor Unions," pp. 275–76, 357–58, 365–70.

123. Document in Kanda, p. 131.

124. See Berger, pp. 275–92; Fletcher, pp. 139–47.

125. Large, *Organized Workers*, pp. 208–20.

126. Italics mine. 5th subcommittee, budget committee, Lower House, in SGS, 2:716–17.

127. Kanda, pp. 593, 589–99.

128. Large, *Organized Workers*, pp. 220–21.

129. Quoted in Nishi Minoru, "Sangyō hōkoku undō no tenkai to rōdō kumiai no kaishō," SSJ, no. 239 (Aug. 1940), p. 162.

130. Matsuoka Komakichi denki kankōkai (Nakamura Kikuo), ed., *Matsuoka Komakichi den* (Tokyo: Keizai ōraisha, 1963), pp. 267–68.

131. Document in Kanda, p. 181.

132. RGS, 1:709–10.

133. See Fletcher, pp. 144–45.

134. *Yoshida Shigeru,* pp. 63, 67, 85.

135. Minami, "Wagakuni," p. 168.

136. "Senzen no rōdō gyōsei o kataru," RGS, supp., p. 25; Nishi, pp. 156, 162.

137. Kitaoka Juitsu, "Shakai gyōsei no kaiko," SSJ, no. 246 (Mar. 1941), p. 22.

138. Charles D. Sheldon, "The Politics of the Civil War of 1868," in *Modern Japan: Aspects of History, Literature and Society,* ed. W. G. Beasley (Berkeley: University of California Press, 1975), p. 48.

139. Schmitter, pp. 115–16.

140. Stanley G. Payne, *Fascism: Comparison and Definition* (Madison: University of Wisconsin Press, 1980), p. 72.

141. Morita, pp. 289–99, 302.

142. Johnson, pp. 153, 162–63.

143. Kōseishō nijūnen shi henshū iinkai, ed., *Kōseishō nijūnen shi* (Tokyo: Kōsei mondai kenkyūkai, 1960), pp. 77, 94–96.

144. Gordon, *Evolution,* pp. 287–94.

145. Nazi policy is described by Mason, pp. 130–36.

146. Gordon, *Evolution,* pp. 266–73, 275, 314–24.

147. For the Welfare Ministry's skepticism, see Notar, "Labor Unions," pp. 423, 427.

148. Monthly membership statistics appear in Kanda, pp. 554–55.

149. Especially Gordon, *Evolution,* pp. 303–8, 324.

150. Cited in ibid., pp. 302–3.

151. Cf. Notar, "Japan's Wartime Labor Policy," p. 325. According to the Welfare Ministry's *Kinrō jihō* (Nov. 1942), of the 396 "near disputes" in 1942, only 2 were initiated by industrial patriotic units. Cited by Sakurabayashi, p. 65.

152. Shōwa kenkyūkai, *Rōdō shintaisei kenkyū* (Tokyo: Tōyō keizai shuppanbu, 1941); Notar, "Japan's Wartime Labor Policy," p. 324.

153. Hattori Eitarō, "Seisan tōseika no rōmu kanri to sampō—tōseikai no kaidai," *Teikoku daigaku shimbun,* 29 June 1942, reprinted in Hattori Eitarō, *Hattori Eitarō chosakushū,* vol. 4 (Tokyo: Miraisha, 1969), p. 208.

154. Document in Kanda, pp. 488–89.

155. Professor Matsuoka Saburō, cited by Tezuka Kazuaki, "Senzen no rōdō kumiai hōan mondai to kyū-rōdō kumiaihō no keisei to tenkai," pt. 2, *Shakai kagaku kenkyū* 23 (Nov. 1971): 146; cf. Endō Kōushi, "1945 nen rōdō kumiaihō no keisei," pt. 1, *Nihon rōdō kyōkai zasshi,* no. 242 (May 1979), pp. 71–72.

156. Address at the ceremony marking the dissolution of the National Federation of Industrial Organizations, quoted in Sakurabayashi, p. 56.

NOTES TO EPILOGUE

1. Kitaoka, "Kyū-Shakaikyoku," p. 12.

2. Notably, John W. Dower, *Empire and Aftermath: Yoshida Shigeru and the Japanese Experience, 1878–1954* (Cambridge: Council on East Asian Studies, Harvard University, 1979); Johnson; Gordon, *Evolution.*

3. I wish to thank Richard Samuels for suggesting the original and productive theme of transwar continuity.

4. State-War-Navy Coordinating Committee 92/1, 4 Jan. 1946, quoted in Takemae Eiji, *Sengo rōdō kaikaku: GHQ rōdō seisaku shi* (Tokyo: Tōkyō daigaku shuppankai, 1982), p. 114.

5. Supreme Commander for the Allied Powers, Government Section, *Political Reorientation of Japan: September 1945 to September 1948,* vol. 1 (Washington: U.S. Government Printing Office, 1948), p. 29.

6. William Karpinsky (former Labor Division chief), in Lawrence H. Redford, ed., *The Occupation of Japan: Economic Policy and Reform* (Norfolk, Va.: MacArthur Memorial, 1980), p. 195.

7. Takemae, pp. 114–17; "Rōdōshō nijūnen no ayumi," *Rōdō jihō* 20 (Sept. 1967): 10.

8. Naisei mondai kenkyūkai, ed., *Kanryō no keifu* (Tokyo: Kōbunsha, 1954).

9. Matsumoto Seichō, *Gendai kanryō ron,* vol. 1 (Tokyo: Bungei shunjū shinsha, 1963), pp. 48–50.

10. In the case of the Ministry of International Trade and Industry, see Johnson.

11. Gordon, *Evolution,* pp. 262, 349.

12. Takemae, pp. 104–11.

13. Tezuka, pp. 146–47, 149.

14. Takemae, pp. 391–98.

15. Joe Moore, *Japanese Workers and the Struggle for Power, 1945–1947* (Madison: University of Wisconsin Press, 1983), pp. 14, 67–68.

16. Ibid., p. 234.

17. Cited in Matsuoka Saburō and Ishiguro Takuji, *Nihon rōdō gyōsei* (Tokyo: Keisō shobō, 1955), pp. 71–72.

18. *Shūkan rōdō,* 27 Oct. 1947, in ibid., pp. 78–79.

19. Ehud Harari, *The Politics of Labor Legislation in Japan* (Berkeley: University of California Press, 1973), pp. 65–67.

20. Solomon B. Levine, "Japan's Tripartite Labor Relations Commissions," *Labor Law Journal* 6 (July 1955): 466; Takemae, p. 273.

21. Instructions of 9 Oct. 1950, in Takemae, pp. 418–20; for details of Red Purge, see pp. 254–57.

22. Gordon, *Evolution,* pp. 369–72.

23. Dower, pp. 367–68.

24. Naisei, p. 8.

25. Harari, pp. 133–42; Benjamin C. Duke, *Japan's Militant Teachers* (Honolulu: University Press of Hawaii, 1973), p. 136.

26. T. J. Pempel and Keiichi Tsunekawa, "Corporatism Without Labor? The Japanese Anomaly," in *Trends Toward Corporatist Intermediation,* ed. Philippe C. Schmitter and Gerhard Lehmbruch (Beverly Hills: SAGE Publications, 1979), pp. 231–70.

27. I am also grateful to Mike Mochizuki for having shared his thoughts on postwar state-labor relations.

28. Hyōdō Tsutomu, "Rōdō kumiai undō no hatten," in *Iwanami kōza: Nihon rekishi,* vol. 23 (Tokyo: Iwanami shoten, 1977), pp. 114–15; for a similar agreement between Sōdōmei and the progressive business federation, Dōyūkai, in 1946, see Moore, pp. 226–28.

29. Hyōdō, p. 131; Shimizu Shinzō, "Sengo rōdō kumiai undō shi josetsu," in his *Sengo rōdō kumiai undō shi ron* (Tokyo: Nihon hyōronsha, 1982), pp. 21–24.

30. Shinkawa Toshimitsu, "1975 nen shuntō to keizai kiki kanri," in *Nihon seiji no sōten,* ed. Ōtake Hideo (Tokyo: San-ichi shobō, 1984), pp. 189–232; Kazutoshi Kōshiro, "Development of Collective Bargaining in Postwar Japan," in *Contemporary Industrial Relations in Japan,* ed. Taishiro Shirai (Madison: University of Wisconsin Press, 1983), pp. 215–20, 229, 248–49; T. J. Pempel, *Policy and Politics in Japan* (Philadelphia: Temple University Press, 1982), pp. 103–5.

31. Mike Masato Mochizuki, "Managing and Influencing the Japanese Legislative Process: The Role of Parties and the National Diet" (Ph.D. diss., Harvard University, 1982), pp. 348–53.

32. Takeshi Inagami, "Labor Front Unification and Zenmin Rokyo: The Emergence of Neo-corporatism," *Japan Labor Bulletin* 25 (May 1986): 5–8; also Koji Taira and Solomon B. Levine, "Japan's Industrial Relations: A Social Compact Emerges," in *Industrial Relations in a Decade of Economic Change,* ed. Hervey Juris, Mark Thompson, and Wilbur Daniels (Madison, Wis.: Industrial Relations Research Association, 1985), pp. 250, 283–92.

33. Nishio Suehiro, *Nishio Suehiro no seiji obegaki* (Tokyo: Mainichi shimbunsha, 1968), pp. 39–40.

34. Mike Tharp, "Getting Back in Touch," *Far Eastern Economic Review,* 1 Mar. 1984, p. 33.

35. Quoted in Inagami, p. 7.

Bibliography

UNPUBLISHED SOURCES

Tokyo. Kokuritsu kōbunshokan [National Archives]. Records of the Rinji sangyō chōsakai [Extraordinary Commission to Investigate Industry], 1920.

Tokyo. Ōhara shakai mondai kenkyūjo [Ōhara Institute for Social Research]. Kyōchōkai. "Rōdō kumiai hōan kankei shorui" [Papers relating to labor union legislation], 1921–24.

Tokyo. Ōhara shakai mondai kenkyūjo. Shakai seisaku shingikai. "Shakai seisaku shingikai ni okeru rōdō kumiaihō shingi keika" [Proceedings of the deliberations on labor union legislation in the Commission on Social Policy], 1929.

Tokyo. Tokyo University. Kobashi Ichita kankei monjo [Kobashi Ichita papers].

Washington, D.C. National Archives. International Military Tribunal for the Far East, 1945–46.

JOURNALS AND NEWSPAPERS

Chūgai shōgyō shimpō [Chūgai business news].

Chūō kōron [Central review].

Hochi shimbun [Hochi news].

Industrial and Labour Information (International Labour Office).

Japan Chronicle.

Japan Times.

Japan Weekly Chronicle.

Jiji shimpō [Jiji news].

Kaizō [Reconstruction].

Keisatsu kyōkai zasshi [Bulletin of the Police Association].

Kensei (Kenseikai).

Kensei kōron [Kenseikai review].

Kokka gakkai zasshi [Journal of the National Academy].

Minsei (Minseitō).

Nihon shimbun [Japan news].

Ōsaka mainichi shimbun [Osaka daily news].

Ōsaka asahi shimbun [Osaka asahi news].

Rōdō [Labor] (Sōdōmei).

Rōdō jihō [Labor times] (Naimushō shakaikyoku; Kōseishō rōdōkyoku; Rōdōshō).

Rōdō oyobi sangyō [Labor and industry] (Yūaikai).

Rōdō sekai [Labor world].

Rōdō undō [The labor movement].

Seiyū (Seiyūkai).

Shakai seisaku jihō [Social policy times] (Kyōchōkai).

Shakai undō ōrai [Comings and goings in the social movement].

Shakai undō tsūshin [Social movement report].

Shimin [The subject] (Chūō hōtokukai).

Taiyō [Sun].

Tōkyō asahi shimbun [Tokyo asahi news].

Trans-Pacific.

Yomiuri shimbun [Yomiuri news].

INTERVIEWS

Kageyama Shōzō. Tokyo. 19 Mar. 1979.

Kitaoka Juitsu. Zushi. 19 Dec. 1978, 13 Apr. 1979.

Kōri Yūichi. Tokyo. 17 Aug. 1978.

Kurokōchi Tōru. Tokyo. 20 July 1978.

Nakamura Takafusa. Tokyo. 2 Oct. 1978.

Nakarai Kiyoshi. Yokohama. 10 Aug. 1978.

Tokonami Tokuji. Tokyo. 25 Aug. 1978.

PUBLISHED SOURCES IN JAPANESE
Place of publication is Tokyo unless otherwise noted.

Abe Isoo. "Rikken Minseitō no seikō o hyōsu" [Judging the Minseitō's platform]. *Chūō kōron* 42 (July 1927): 88–91.

Adachi Kenzō. *Adachi Kenzō jijoden* [The autobiography of Adachi Kenzō]. Shinkōsha, 1960.

Akamatsu Katsumaro. *Nihon shakai undō shi* [The history of the Japanese socialist movement]. Tsūshin kyōiku shinkōkai, 1949.

Amanoya Keiji, "Ōshū ni okeru genka no rōdō undō" [Today's labor movements in Europe]. Part 2. *Keisatsu kyōkai zasshi,* no. 258 (December 1921), pp. 43–52.

Andō Masazumi. "Sojō ni tenkai subeki Hamaguchi naikaku no hisei hyakushutsu" [An exposé of the Hamaguchi cabinet's myriad cases of maladministration]. *Seiyū,* no. 364 (January 1931), pp. 8–13.

Andō Tarō. "Shokkō no torishimari oyobi hogo" [Regulating and protecting the workers]. *Taiyō* 2 (5 Dec. 1896): 55–59.

Aono Suekichi. "Saikin seikyoku no kansatsu" [A view of recent political developments]. *Kaizō* 9 (July 1927): 84–88.

Ariga Nagafumi. "Shokkō jōrei seitei no jiki ni tsuite" [When to enact the workers' ordinance]. *Kokka gakkai zasshi,* no. 129 (November 1897), pp. 917–39.

Aritake Shūji. *Shōwa keizai sokumenshi* [Sidelights in the history of the Shōwa economy]. Kawade shobō, 1952.

Asō Hisashi. "Minseitō, Kakushintō shutsugen ni taisuru hihan" [A judgment on the formation of the Minseitō and Kakushintō]. *Kaizō* 9 (July 1927): 89–92.

Baba Tsunego. *Gendai jimbutsu hyōron* [An evaluation of contemporary figures]. Chūō kōronsha, 1930.

———. *Seikai jimbutsu fūkei* [A view of personalities in politics]. Chūō kōronsha, 1931.

———. *Seikai jimbutsu ron* [Personalities in politics]. Chūō kōronsha, 1935.

"Chihō jichi to seitō ni tsuite" [Local autonomy and the political parties]. *Shimin* 24 (January 1929): 27–61.

"Chūshō kigyō ni okeru rōdō jōken no tekisei" [The amelioration of working conditions in small and medium enterprises]. *Rōdō jihō* 12 (February 1935): 36–38.

Dai Nihon teikoku gikai shi [Records of the Imperial Diet of Greater Japan]. 18 vols. Dai Nihon teikoku gikai shi kankōkai, 1926–30.

"Dai 20-kai taikai o mukau" [Welcoming the 20th annual convention]. *Rōdō,* no. 245 (November 1931), pp. 2–3.

Danshaku Dan Takuma denki hensan iinkai, ed. *Danshaku Dan Takuma den* [The biography of Baron Dan Takuma]. 2 vols. Danshaku Dan Takuma denki hensan iinkai, 1938.

Ebashi Takashi. "Shōwa shoki no tokkō keisatsu" [The Special Higher Police in the early Shōwa era]. *Kikan gendai shi,* no. 7 (June 1976), pp. 69–97.

Egi Tasuku. "Rōdō mondai" [The labor question]. *Kensei* 2 (October 1919): 20–28.

———. "Shippei hoken seido" [A scheme for sickness insurance]. *Kensei* 3 (January 1920): 8–12.

———. "Shisō mondai hihan" [Comments on the thought problem]. *Tōkyō asahi shimbun,* 17–18 Apr. 1928, p. 3.

Egi Tasuku kun denki hensankai, ed. *Egi Tasuku den* [The biography of Egi Tasuku]. Egi Tasuku kun denki hensankai, 1939.

————. *Egi Tasuku ronsō* [The writings of Egi Tasuku]. Egi Tasuku kun denki hensankai, 1938.

Endō Kōushi. "1945 nen rōdō kumiaihō no keisei" [The making of the 1945 Trade Union Law]. Pt. 1. *Nihon rōdō kyōkai zasshi*, no. 242 (May 1979), pp. 69–78.

Fujino Yutaka. "Kyōchō seisaku no suishin—Kyōchōkai ni yoru rōdōsha no tōgō" [The advance of harmonization policy—the Kyōchōkai's integration of workers]. *Kindai Nihon no tōgō to teikō*, 3:265–97. Edited by Kano Masanao and Yui Masaomi. Nihon hyōronsha, 1982.

Fujinuma Shōhei. *Watakushi no isshō* [My life]. Fujinuma Shōhei kankōkai, 1957.

Gotō Fumio. *Gotō Fumio shi danwa dai 1-kai sokkiroku* [Transcript, first interview with Mr. Gotō Fumio]. Naiseishi kenkyū shiryō, no. 4. Naiseishi kenkyūkai, 1963.

————. "Sengo Ōbei ni okeru jinshin no dōyō to kikō" [Trends in the convulsions in people's thought in postwar Europe and America]. *Keisatsu kyōkai zasshi*, no. 239 (April 1920), pp. 7–17.

"Gyakushi tōkō ni shōsenkyoku ron—musan kaikyū no kikensei zōka" [A backward-looking case for small electoral districts—dangers from the proletarian classes will increase]. *Minsei* 2 (October 1928): 2–3.

Hamaguchi Osachi. "Gendai naikaku no shissei to wagatō no taido" [Misrule by the present cabinet and our party's position]. *Minsei* 1 (December 1927): 2–11.

————. "Gōriteki keiki kaifuku no kichō" [The basis for a rationalized economic recovery]. *Minsei* 3 (September 1929): 2–5.

————. "Kokumin seikatsu no kiki" [The crisis in people's livelihoods]. *Kensei* 2 (August 1919): 26–32.

————. "Rikken Minseitō sōsai shūnin no ji" [Inaugural words from the Minseitō's president]. *Minsei* 1 (July 1927): 2–3.

————. "Sengo no keizai mondai" [Postwar economic problems]. *Kensei* 2 (January 1919): 40–47.

Hara Takashi. *Hara Takashi nikki* [The diary of Hara Takashi]. Edited by Hara Keiichirō. 5 vols. Fukumura shuppan kabushiki kaisha, 1965.

Hasegawa Kimiichi. "Chūshō kōgyō to rōdō mondai" [Small and medium industry and the labor question]. *Shakai seisaku jihō*, no. 129 (June 1931), pp. 195–214.

Hata Ikuhiko. *Kanryō no kenkyū* [A study of bureaucrats]. Kōdansha, 1983.

Hattori Eitarō. *Hattori Eitarō chosakushū* [Collected works of Hattori Eitarō]. Vol. 4. Miraisha, 1969.

Hayashi Hiroshi. "Naimushō shakaikyoku kanryō no rōdō seisaku kōsō" [The thinking behind the labor policy of bureaucrats of the Home Ministry's Social Bureau]. *Hitotsubashi kenkyū* 7 (April 1982): 84–99.

Hazama Hiroshi. *Nihon no shiyōsha dantai to rōshi kankei* [Japanese employers' associations and labor-management relations]. Nihon rōdō kyōkai, 1981.

Higuchi Hideo. "Demokurashii to nōson no jikaku" [Democracy and consciousness in the agricultural villages]. *Kensei kōron* 1 (August 1921): 2–7.

"Hijō jidai ni okeru rōdō kumiai undō" [The labor union movement during the emergency period]. *Rōdō*, no. 249 (March 1932), pp. 2–3.

Hiranuma Kiichirō. *Hiranuma Kiichirō kaikoroku* [The memoirs of Hiranuma Kiichirō]. Hiranuma Kiichirō kaikoroku hensan iinkai, 1955.

Horikiri Zenjirō. *Horikiri Zenjirō shi danwa (dai 2, 3-kai) sokkiroku* [Transcripts of the second and third interviews with Mr. Horikiri Zenjirō]. Naiseishi kenkyū shiryō, nos. 8, 10. Naiseishi kenkyūkai, 1963–64.

Hozumi Shichirō. "Naikaku shingikai no shakaiteki naiyō" [The social content of the Cabinet Deliberative Council]. *Rōdō*, no. 287 (June 1935), pp. 12–13.

Hyōdō Tsutomu. *Nihon ni okeru rōshi kankei no tenkai* [The development of labor-management relations in Japan]. Tōkyō daigaku shuppankai, 1971.

———. "Rōdō kumiai undō no hatten" [Development of the labor union movement]. *Iwanami kōza: Nihon rekishi*, 23:95–135. Iwanami shoten, 1977.

Iinuma Jirō. "Seitō seiji to Shōwa nōgyō kyōkō" [Party politics and the Shōwa agricultural depression]. *Shisō*, no. 624 (June 1976), pp. 155–73.

Ikeda Makoto. *Nihon shakai seisaku shisō shi ron* [A history of Japanese social policy thought]. Tōyō keizai shimpōsha, 1978.

Ikeda Seihin. *Kojin konjin* [Men of past and present]. Sekai no Nihonsha, 1949.

Imai Seiichi. *Nihon no rekishi*. Vol. 23: *Taishō demokurashii*. Chūō kōronsha, 1974.

Inoue Kiyoshi, ed. *Taishō-ki no kyūshinteki jiyūshugi* [Radical liberalism in the Taishō era]. Tōyō keizai shimpōsha, 1972.

——— and Watanabe Tōru, eds. *Kome sōdō no kenkyū* [Studies of the rice riots]. 5 vols. Kyoto: Yūhikaku, 1959–62.

Ishiwara Osamu. *Jokō to kekka* [Female workers and tuberculosis]. 1914; reprint ed., Kōseikan, 1970.

Isozaki Shunji. "Nachisu no shin-rōdō kenshō" [The Nazis' New Labor Charter]. *Shakai seisaku jihō*, no. 163 (April 1934), pp. 39–52.

Itō Masanori. *Katō Takaaki*. 2 vols. Katō haku denki hensan iinkai, 1969.

Itō Takashi. " 'Kyokoku itchi' naikaku-ki no seikai saihensei mondai—Shōwa sanjūnen Konoe shintō mondai kenkyū no tame ni" [The question of reconstituting politics during the era of "whole-nation" cabinets—investigating the issue of Konoe's new party in 1938]. Pt. 1. *Shakai kagaku kenkyū* 24 (August 1972), pp. 56–129.

———. *Shōwa shoki seiji shi kenkyū* [Studies in the political history of the early Shōwa era]. Tōkyō daigaku shuppankai, 1969.

———. *Taishō-ki "kakushin"-ha no seiritsu* [The formation of the Taishō era's "renovationist" clique]. Hanawa shobō, 1978.

Iwamura Toshio. "Musan seitō no seiritsu" [Formation of the proletarian parties]. *Iwanami kōza: Nihon rekishi*, 18:297–332. Iwanami shoten, 1975.

Izawa Takio denki hensan iinkai, ed. *Izawa Takio*. Haneda shoten, 1951.

Jinji kōshinroku [Who's who]. 1928, 1931 eds.

Kagoyama Takashi. "Kōjōhō no seiritsu to jisshi ni okeru kanryōgun" [The bureaucratic clique behind the enactment and operation of the Factory

Law]. *Nihon kindaika no kenkyū,* 2:65–87. Edited by Takahashi Kōhachirō. Tōkyō daigaku shuppankai, 1973.

Kaji Ryūichi, ed. *Meiji bunka shiryō* [Documents in Meiji culture]. Vol. 5. Fūkan shobō, 1960.

Kamei Kan'ichirō. *Kizoku, shihonka, rōdōsha* [Aristocrats, capitalists, and workers]. Chūseidō, 1931.

Kamii Yoshihiko. "Dai ichiji taisen chokugo no rōdō seisaku: chian keisatsuhō 17-jō no kaishaku tekiyo mondai o chūshin to shite" [Labor policy immediately following World War I: profiling the issue of interpreting and applying Article 17 of the Police Regulations]. *Rōdō undō shi kenkyū,* no. 62 (1979), pp. 150–81.

———. "Dai ichiji taisengo no rōdō seisaku—1926 nen rōshi kankeihō o megutte" [Labor policy following World War I—the labor-management relations legislation of 1926]. *Shakai seisaku gakkai nempō,* no. 23 (1979), pp. 123–52.

Kanda Fuhito, ed. *Shiryō Nihon gendai shi* [A documentary history of contemporary Japan]. Vol. 7: *Sangyō hōkoku undō* [The Industrial Patriotic movement]. Ōtsuki shoten, 1981.

Kano Masanao. *Nihon no rekishi.* Vol. 27: *Taishō demokurashii.* Shōgakkan, 1976.

Katō Takaaki. "Katō sōsai no enzetsu" [President Katō's address]. *Kensei* 2, no. 6 (26 July 1919), pp. 1–5.

———. "Rengō yokoku no senshō o shukushite" [In celebration of the victory of the Allied Powers]. *Kensei* 2 (January 1919): 3–8.

Katō Taiichi. "Rikken Minseitō no honryō" [The special character of the Minseitō]. *Minsei* 1 (September 1927): 32–38.

Kawai Eijirō. "Kan o jisuru ni saishite" [Upon resigning from government]. *Tōkyō asahi shimbun,* 17 Nov.–2 Dec. 1919, p. 3.

———. *Meiji shisōshi no ichidammen—Kanai Noboru o chūshin to shite* [One aspect of Meiji intellectual history—profiling Kanai Noboru]. 1941; reprint ed., Shakai shisōsha, 1969.

Kawamura Teishirō. *Kankai no hyōri* [The ins and outs of official life]. Yūsankaku shuppan, 1974.

Kawarada Kakichi. "Iwayuru rōdō kumiai no kōnin to chian keisatsuhō dai 17-jō ni tsuite" [The so-called official recognition of labor unions and Article 17 of the Police Regulations]. *Keisatsu kyōkai zasshi,* no. 247 (January 1921), pp. 30–39.

Kenseikai shi hensanjo (Yokoyama Katsutarō), ed. *Kenseikai shi* [The history of the Kenseikai]. Kenseikai shi hensanjo, 1926.

Kido Kōichi. *Kido Kōichi nikki* [The diary of Kido Kōichi]. 2 vols. Tōkyō daigaku shuppankai, 1966.

Kimbara Samon. "Seitō seiji no hatten" [The development of party politics]. *Iwanami kōza: Nihon rekishi,* 18:255–96. Iwanami shoten, 1975.

———. *Taishō-ki no seitō to kokumin—Hara Kei naikaku no seiji katei* [Parties and the people in the Taishō era—the course of politics under the Hara cabinet]. Hanawa shobō, 1975.

Kimura Seishi. "Shōwa 9 nen shakai gyōsei no kaiko" [Retrospective on social administration in 1934]. *Shakai seisaku jihō*, no. 185 (February 1935), pp. 1–33.

Kimura Teikichi. "Seikatsu to futsū senkyo" [Living conditions and universal suffrage]. *Rōdō oyobi sangyō* 8 (April 1919): 22–23.

Kisaka Jun'ichirō. "Chian ijihō hantai undō—1925 nen ichi-sangatsu ni okeru" [The campaign against the Peace Preservation Law, from January to March 1925]. *Taishō demokurashii*, pp. 299–335. Edited by Yui Masaomi. Yūseidō, 1977.

[Kitahara Yasue]. "Rōdō kumiaihō kara nukitotta hone" [The mutilated labor union bill]. *Jiji shimpō*, 27 Feb.–7 Mar. 1926.

Kitaoka Juitsu. "Kyū-Shakaikyoku no omoide" [Recollections of the old Social Bureau]. *Rōdō gyōsei shi yoroku*. Supplement to vol. 1 of *Rōdō gyōsei shi*. Edited by Rōdōshō. Rōdō hōrei kyōkai, 1961.

———. "Nagaoka Ryūichirō o omoide" [Recalling Nagaoka Ryūichirō]. *Taika*, no. 79 (Spring 1978), pp. 14–16.

———. "Shakai gyōsei no kaiko" [Retrospective on social administration]. *Shakai seisaku jihō*, no. 246 (March 1941), pp. 1–30.

———. "Shakaikyoku no setchi to rōdō gyōsei" [Labor administration and the creation of the Social Bureau]. *Naimushō gaishi*, pp. 140–48. Edited by Taikakai. Chihō zaimu kyōkai, 1977.

———. *Wagaomoide no ki* [My recollections]. Kamakura: Kamakura insatsu kabushiki kaisha, 1976.

Koizumi Matajirō. *Fusen undō hisshi* [The secret history of the universal suffrage movement]. Hirano shobō, 1928.

———. "Minshū seiji e no kaidan e" [Another step toward democratic politics]. *Kensei* 7 (March 1924): 13–15.

Komatsu Mitsuo, ed. *Nihon shimbun jūnen kinen—Nihon seishin hatsuyō shi* [The commemoration of ten years of the *Nihon shimbun*—an exaltation of the Japanese spirit]. Nihon shimbunsha, 1934.

Kōno Hironaka. "Futsū senkyo dankō no kyūmi" [The urgent need to enact universal suffrage]. *Kensei* 5 (March 1922): 1–4.

Kōno Mitsu, Akamatsu Katsumaro, and the Rōnōtō shokikan. *Nihon musan seitō shi* [The history of Japan's proletarian parties]. Hakuyōsha, 1931.

Kōseishō nijūnen shi henshū iinkai, ed. *Kōseishō nijūnen shi* [The 20-year history of the Welfare Ministry]. Kōsei mondai kenkyūkai, 1960.

Kuhara Fusanosuke ō denki hensankai, ed. *Kuhara Fusanosuke*. Nihon kōgyō kabushiki kaisha, 1970.

Kumagai Ken'ichi. "Shōwa jūichi nen shakai undō gaikan" [Surveying the social movement in 1936]. *Shakai seisaku jihō*, no. 197 (February 1937), pp. 1–67.

Kuribayashi Teiichi. *Chihō kankai no hensen* [Changes in prefectural bureaucratic personnel]. Sekaisha, 1930.

Kurihara Minoru. *Kurihara Minoru shi danwa dai 1-kai sokkiroku* [Transcript of the first interview with Mr. Kurihara Minoru]. Naiseishi kenkyū shiryō, no. 184. Naiseishi kenkyūkai, 1977.

Kuwata Kumazō. "Kōjōhō no seitei oyobi jisshi no yūrai" [Behind the enactment and operation of the Factory Law]. *Rōdō oyobi sangyō,* no. 58 (June 1916), pp. 35–39.

Kyōchōkai [Harmonization Society], ed. *Rōdō nenkan* [Labor yearbook]. Kyōchōkai, particularly 1936–38.

———, ed. *Saikin no shakai undō* [The social movement of late]. Kyōchōkai, 1929.

"Kyōchōkai" kaiwakai (Machida Tatsujirō), ed. *Kyōchōkai shi—kyōchōkai sanjūnen no ayumi* [The history of the Kyōchōkai—the 30-year course of the Kyōchōkai]. "Kyōchōkai" kaiwakai, 1965.

Maeda Renzan. *Tokonami Takejirō den* [The biography of Tokonami Takejirō]. Tokonami Takejirō denki kankōkai, 1939.

Maeda Tamon. "Ōbei shisatsu shokan" [Impressions of my tour of Europe and America]. *Keisatsu kyōkai zasshi,* no. 236 (January 1920), pp. 22–29.

Maruyama Masao and Fukuda Kan'ichi, eds. *Kaisō no Nambara Shigeru* [Remembering Nambara Shigeru]. Iwanami shoten, 1975.

Maruyama Tsurukichi. *Shichijūnen tokorodokoro* [Here and there for 70 years]. Shichijūnen tokorodokoro kankōkai, 1955.

Masumi Junnosuke. *Nihon seitō shi ron* [A historical study of Japanese political parties]. 7 vols. Tōkyō daigaku shuppankai, 1965–80.

Matsui Shigeru. "Kokumin to keisatsu" [The people and the police]. *Keisatsu kyōkai zasshi,* no. 236 (January 1920), pp. 11–21.

Matsumoto Seichō. *Gendai kanryō ron* [Contemporary bureaucrats]. Vol. 1. Bungei shunjū shinsha, 1963.

Matsuo Takayoshi. "Dai ichiji taisengo no fusen undō" [The universal suffrage movement after World War I]. *Taishō-ki no seiji to shakai,* pp. 159–204. Edited by Inoue Kiyoshi. Iwanami shoten, 1969.

———. "Dai ichiji taisengo no chian ijihō kōsō—Kageki shakai undō torishimari hōan" [The thinking behind the Peace Preservation Law after World War I—the bill to control radical social movements]. *Ronsō gendai shi,* pp. 131–67. Edited by Fujiwara Akira and Matsuo Takayoshi. Chikuma shobō, 1976.

———. "Seiyūkai to Minseitō" [The Seiyūkai and Minseitō]. *Iwanami kōza: Nihon rekishi,* 19:83–134. Iwanami shoten, 1976.

———. *Taishō demokurashii no kenkyū* [Studies in Taishō democracy]. Aoki shoten, 1966.

Matsuoka Komakichi denki kankōkai (Nakamura Kikuo), ed. *Matsuoka Komakichi den* [The biography of Matsuoka Komakichi]. Keizai ōraisha, 1963.

Matsuoka Saburō, and Ishiguro Takuji. *Nihon rōdō gyōsei* [Japanese labor administration]. Keisō shobō, 1955.

Minami Iwao. "Wagakuni ni okeru shakai seisaku to rōdō kumiai no shōrai ni tsuite" [Our nation's social policy and the future of labor unions]. *Shakai seisaku jihō,* no. 200 (May 1937), pp. 156–81.

Mitani Taichirō. "Seiyūkai no seiritsu" [Establishment of the Seiyūkai]. *Iwanami kōza: Nihon rekishi,* 16:137–78. Iwanami shoten, 1976.

———. *Taishō demokurashii ron* [A study of Taishō democracy]. Chūō kōronsha, 1974.

Mitsuchi Chūzō. "Rōdō kumiai no kenkyū ni tsuite" [A study of labor unions]. *Seiyū*, no. 236 (December 1919), pp. 1–6.

Miwa Ryōichi. "Rōdō kumiaihō seitei mondai no rekishiteki ichi" [The historical significance of the issue of enacting a labor union law], pp. 237–88. *Ryōtaisenkan no Nihon shihonshugi*. Edited by Andō Yoshio. Tōkyō daigaku shuppankai, 1979.

Miwa Yasushi. "1935 nen ni okeru Nihonshugi rōdō undō no hatten" [The emergence of the Japanist labor movement in 1935]. *Nihon shi kenkyū*, no. 189 (May 1978), pp. 1–35.

Miyachi Masato. *Nichirō sensōgo seiji shi no kenkyū* [Studies in the political history of the period following the Russo-Japanese War]. Tōkyō daigaku shuppankai, 1973.

———. "Nichirō zengo no shakai to minshū" [Society and the people following the Russo-Japanese War]. *Kōza Nihon shi*, 6:131–70. Edited by Rekishigaku kenkyūkai and Nihon shi kenkyūkai. Tōkyō daigaku shuppankai, 1970.

Mochizuki Keisuke den kankōkai, ed. *Mochizuki Keisuke den* [The biography of Mochizuki Keisuke]. Haneda shoten, 1945.

Mori Ariyoshi. *Seinen to ayumu: Gotō Fumio* [Advancing with the youth: Gotō Fumio]. Nihon seinenkan, 1979.

Morita Yoshio. *Nihon keieisha dantai hatten shi* [The history of the development of employers' associations]. Nikkan rōdō tsūshinsha, 1958.

Murakami Nobuhiko. *Meiji josei shi* [A history of Meiji-era women]. Vol. 3. Rironsha, 1971.

Myōga Fusakichi. *Nihon seitō no gensei* [The current state of Japanese political parties]. Nihon hyōronsha, 1929.

Nagai Ryūtarō. "Kokumin seikatsu saiken ni mukatte shingun seyo" [Onward toward reviving the people's livelihoods]. *Minsei* 6 (March 1932): 5–7.

"Nagai Ryūtarō" hensankai (Matsumura Kenzō), ed. *Nagai Ryūtarō*. "Nagai Ryūtarō" hensankai, 1959.

Nagai Tōru. "Rōdō undō to futsū senkyo" [The labor movement and universal suffrage]. *Shakai seisaku jihō*, no. 40 (January 1924), pp. 1–27.

Nagaoka Ryūichirō, *Kanryō nijūgonen* [25 years as a bureaucrat]. Chūō kōronsha, 1939.

Naimushō shakaikyoku dai ichibu [Home Ministry, Social Bureau, First Division]. *Rōdō undō gaikyō* [The state of the labor movement], 1922–24 (Secret). 3 vols. Meiji bunken, 1971.

Naimushō shakaikyoku rōdōbu [Home Ministry, Social Bureau, Labor Division]. *Rōdō kumiai hōan ni kansuru shiryō* [Materials relating to the labor union bill]. Naimushō shakaikyoku rōdōbu, 1930.

———. *Rōdō rippō kondankai (dai 1, 2-kai) sokkiroku* [Minutes of the (first and second) conference on labor legislation]. 2 vols. Naimushō shakaikyoku rōdōbu, 1930–31.

———. *Rōdō undō nempō* [Annual report on the labor movement], 1925–37 (Secret). 13 vols. Meiji bunken, 1971–72.

Naisei mondai kenkyūkai, ed. *Kanryō no keifu* [Bureaucratic lineages]. Kōbunsha, 1954.

Nakamura Masanori. *Nihon no rekishi*. Vol. 29: *Rōdōsha to nōmin* [Workers and farmers]. Shōgakkan, 1976.

Nakamura Takafusa. *Shōwa kyōkō: aru ōkura daijin no higeki* [The Shōwa depression: the tragedy of one finance minister]. Nihon keizai shimbunsha, 1978.

Nakano Seigō. "Futsū senkyo no ronjin" [The case for universal suffrage]. *Kensei kōron* 5 (April 1925): 10–15.

———. "Wagatō no kōchō suru kokka seichōshugi" [The philosophy of national regulation as proclaimed by our party]. *Minsei* 2 (February 1928): 26–31.

Nakano Yasuo. *Seijika Nakano Seigō* [Statesman, Nakano Seigō]. 2 vols. Shinkōkaku shoten, 1971.

Nambara Shigeru. "Rōdō kumiaihō o ronzu" [A discussion of labor union laws]. 2 pts. *Keisatsu kyōkai zasshi*, no. 244 (October 1920), pp. 1–8; no. 245 (November 1920), pp. 1–8.

Narusawa Akira. "Hara naikaku to dai ichiji sekai taisengo kokunai jōkyō" [The Hara cabinet and internal conditions following World War I]. 2 pts. *Hōrin shirin* (Hōsei daigaku) 66, no. 2 (February 1969), pp. 1–96; no. 3 (February 1969), pp. 54–108.

Nihon kin-gendai shi jiten [The encyclopedia of modern and contemporary Japanese history]. 1978 ed.

Nihon kōgyō kurabu gojūnen shi hensan iinkai, ed. *Zaikai kaisōroku* [Reminiscences of the business world]. 2 vols. Nihon kōgyō kurabu, 1967.

Nihon kōgyō kurabu nijūgonen shi hensan iinkai, ed. *Nihon kōgyō kurabu nijūgonen shi* [The 25-year history of the Japan Industrial Club]. 2 vols. Nihon kōgyō kurabu, 1943.

Nimura Kazuo. "Kameido jiken shōron" [A short treatise on the Kameido Incident]. *Rekishi hyōron*, no. 281 (October 1973), pp. 39–69.

———. "Rōdōsha kaikyū no jōtai to rōdō undō" [The condition of the working class and the labor movement]. *Iwanami kōza: Nihon rekishi* 18:93–140. Iwanami shoten, 1975.

Nishi Minoru. "Sangyō hōkoku undō no tenkai to rōdō kumiai no kaishō" [The emergence of the Industrial Patriotic movement and the dissolution of the labor unions]. *Shakai seisaku jihō*, no. 239 (August 1940), pp. 152–69.

Nishinarita Yutaka. "Manshū jihen-ki no rōshi kankei" [Labor-management relations during the era of the Manchurian Incident]. *Hitotsubashi daigaku kenkyū nempō: Keizaigaku kenkyū* 26 (January 1985): 241–311.

———. "1920 nendai Nihon shihonshugi no rōshi kankei—jūkōgyō rōshi kankei o chūshin ni" [Labor-management relations in Japanese capitalism in the 1920s, with emphasis on heavy industry]. *Rekishigaku kenkyū*, no. 512 (January 1983), pp. 1–20.

Nishio Suehiro. *Nishio Suehiro no seiji obegaki*. Mainichi shimbunsha, 1968.

———. *Taishū to tomo ni—watakushi no hansei no kiroku* [With the masses— a record of half my life]. Sekaisha, 1951.

Nishioka Takao. "Rōdō kumiai hōan o meguru jūnenkan" [Ten years of labor union legislation]. 2 pts. *Nihon rōdō kyōkai zasshi*, no. 59 (February 1964), pp. 22–31; no. 60 (March 1964), pp. 16–23.

Nōshōmushō shōkōkyoku. *Shokkō jijō* [The condition of factory workers]. 1903; reprint ed. Kōseikan, 1971.

Obama Ritoku, ed. *Meiji bunka shiryō soshō* [Documentary series on Meiji culture]. Vol. 1. Fūkan shobō, 1961.

Ogawa Heikichi. "Chian ijihō kinkyū chokurei happu made no keika" [The developments leading to the proclamation of the emergency imperial ordinance on the Peace Preservation Law]. *Nihon shimbun jūnen kinen—Nihon seishin hatsuyō shi*, pp. 271–80. Edited by Komatsu Mitsuo. Nihon shimbunsha, 1934.

[————]. "Seikai bōyūryokusha no iken" [Thoughts of one powerful political figure]. *Nihon shimbun*, 1 Dec. 1930, p. 1.

Ogura Takekazu. *Tochi rippō no shiteki kōsatsu* [A historical study of land legislation]. Nōrinshō nōgyō sōgō kenkyūjo, 1951.

Ōhara shakai mondai kenkyūjo [Ōhara Institute for Social Research), ed. *Nihon rōdō nenkan* [Japan labor yearbook]. Ōhara shakai mondai kenkyūjo shuppanbu, particularly 1920–39.

Oka Minoru. *Kōjōhō ron* [On the Factory Law]. Rev. ed. Yūhikaku, 1917.

Ōkōchi Kazuo. *Kurai tanima no rōdō undō* [The labor movement in the dark valley]. Iwanami shoten, 1970.

Okudaira Yasuhiro. *Chian ijihō shōshi* [A short history of the Peace Preservation Law]. Chikuma shobō, 1977.

Ōkuma Shigenobu. "Ōkuma haku no rōdō mondai dan" [An interview with Count Ōkuma on the labor question]. *Rōdō sekai* 6 (3 Apr. 1902): 7–8.

Ōno Rokuichirō. *Ōno Rokuichirō shi danwa dai 1-kai sokkiroku* [Transcript of the first interview with Mr. Ōno Rokuichirō]. Naiseishi kenkyū shiryō, no. 61. Naiseishi kenkyūkai, 1968.

Ōoka Ikuzō. "Kōjōhō jisshi hantai ron" [My opposition to implementing the Factory Law]. *Rōdō oyobi sangyō*, no. 61 (September 1916), pp. 32–33.

Ōsaka kōgyōkai gojūnen shi hensan iinkai, ed. *Ōsaka kōgyōkai gojūnen shi* [The 50-year history of the Osaka Industrial Association]. Osaka: Ōsaka kōgyōkai, 1964.

Ōtsuka Isei. "Okuyukashii Eikoku no kokuminsei" [The genteel national character of England]. *Keisatsu kyōkai zasshi*, no. 253 (July 1921), pp. 36–45.

"Rōdō kumiai kaigi ni tsuite" [Regarding the Congress of Labor Unions]. *Rōdō*, no. 255 (September 1932), pp. 2–3.

"Rōdō kumiaihō yōkyū no igi" [What's behind our demands for a labor union law]. *Rōdō*, no. 226 (April 1930), pp. 2–3.

"Rōdō kaikyū no hanseiji-netsu" [Antipolitics fever among the working class]. *Rōdō* 10 (April 1921): 2–3.

Rōdōshō [Labor Ministry]. *Rōdō gyōsei shi* [The history of labor administration]. 2 vols. Rōdō hōrei kyōkai, 1961–69.

"Rōdōshō nijūnen no ayumi" [The 20-year course of the Labor Ministry]. *Rōdō jihō* 20 (September 1967): 4–20.

Rōdō undō shiryō iinkai, ed. *Nihon rōdō undō shiryō* [Materials on the Japanese labor movement]. 11 vols. Chūō kōron jigyō shuppan, 1959–68.

Saitō Ken'ichi. "Jiji kaisetsu: sōgi chōteihō no kaisei" [Comment on the times:

the revision of the Disputes Conciliation Law]. *Rōdō,* no. 279 (October 1934), pp. 12–13.

Saitō Takao. "Kinkyū chokureian shingi ni saishi: Sūfu arawaretaru giron ni tsuite" [Deliberations on the emergency ordinance: The debate in the Privy Council]. *Minsei* 2 (August 1928): 37–41.

Sakurabayashi Makoto. "Senji Nihon no rōshi kyōgisei: sangyō hōkokukai no kondankai o chūshin to shite" [Labor-management councils in wartime Japan: profiling the Industrial Patriotic Society's discussion councils]. *Jōchi keizai ronshū* 18 (March 1972): 37–84.

Sassa Hiroo. "Jiyūshugi ka, fuashizumu ka" [What shall we have: liberalism or fascism?]. *Kaizō* 13 (January 1931): supp., 126–35.

————. "Seikyoku o shihai suru mono—kinkyū katō seiji no jissō" [Those who control politics—the real story on the financial oligarchy]. *Kaizō* 13 (May 1931): 77–86.

"1930 nen o mukau" [Welcoming 1930]. *Rōdō,* no. 223 (January 1930), pp. 2–3.

Senzenki kanryōsei kenkyūkai (Hata Ikuhiko), ed. *Senzenki Nihon kanryōsei no seido, soshiki, jinji* [The structure, organization, and personnel of the prewar Japanese bureaucratic system]. Tōkyō daigaku shuppankai, 1981.

Shakai keizai rōdō kenkyūjo, ed. *Kindai Nihon rōdōsha undō shi* [The history of the modern Japanese workers' movement]. Niigata: Hakurinsha, 1947.

Shakai mondai shiryō kenkyūkai, ed. *Dai 50-kai Teikoku gikai chian iji hōan giji sokkiroku narabi iinkai gijiroku* [Records of the proceedings and minutes of the committee on the peace preservation bill in the Fiftieth Imperial Diet]. Kyoto: Tōyō bunkasha, 1972.

Shakai mondai shiryō kenkyūkai, ed. *Teikoku gikai shi* [Records of the Imperial Diet]. 1st ser. 40 vols. Kyoto: Tōyō bunkasha, 1975–78.

Shakai seisaku gakkai [Social Policy Association], ed. *Rōdō sōgi* [Labor disputes]. Record of 7th Congress. 1914; reprint ed. Ochanomizu shobō, 1977.

Shiba Teikichi, ed. *Rikken Minseitō shi* [The history of the Minseitō]. 2 vols. Rikken Minseitō shi hensankyoku, 1935.

Shibusawa seien kinen zaidan ryūmonsha, ed. *Shibusawa Eiichi denki shiryō* [The biography and papers of Shibusawa Eiichi]. 58 vols. Shibusawa Eiichi denki shiryō kankōkai, 1955–65.

Shimada Saburō. "Jiyūshugi no shōri to senran no kyōkun" [The victory of liberalism and the lessons of the war]. *Kensei* 2 (January 1919): 11–25.

Shimizu Shinzō. *Sengo rōdō kumiai undō shi ron* [Studies on the history of the postwar labor union movement]. Nihon hyōronsha, 1982.

Shinkawa Toshimitsu. "1975 nen shuntō to keizai kiki kanri" [The 1975 spring offensive and economic-crisis management]. *Nihon seiji no sōten,* pp. 189–232. Edited by Ōtake Hideo. San-ichi shobō, 1984.

Shinobu Seizaburō. *Taishō demokurashii shi* [A history of Taishō democracy]. 3 vols. Nihon hyōronsha, 1954–58.

————. *Taishō seiji shi* [A history of Taishō-era politics]. 4 vols. Keisō shobō, 1951–52.

Shūgiin-Sangiin [The House of Representatives and the House of Councilors]. *Gikai seido shichijūnen shi* [The 70-year history of the parliamentary system]. 12 vols. Ōkurashō insatsukyoku, 1960–63.

Shōwa kenkyūkai [Shōwa Research Association]. *Rōdō shintaisei kenkyū* [Studies in the New Labor Order]. Tōyō keizai shuppanbu, 1941.

Sōdōmei gojūnen shi kankō iinkai, ed. *Sōdōmei gojūnen shi* [The 50-year history of the General Federation of Labor]. 3 vols. Kōyōsha, 1964–68.

"Sōsenkyo no kyōkun" [Lessons from the general election]. *Rōdō,* no. 225 (March 1930), pp. 2–3.

Suehiro Izutarō. "Rōdō kumiai torishimari hōan o hyōsu" [Critiquing the bill to control labor unions]. *Tōkyō asahi shimbun,* 10–14, 17, 19 Feb. 1926, p. 2.

Sugatani Akira. *Nihon shakai seisaku shi ron* [A history of Japanese social policy]. Nihon hyōronsha, 1978.

Sugihara Masami. *Atarashii Shōwa shi* [A new history of the Shōwa era]. Shinkigensha, 1958.

Sumiya Mikio. "Kōjōhō taisei to rōshi kankei" [The Factory Law system and labor-management relations]. *Nihon rōshi kankei shi ron,* pp. 1–40. Tōkyō daigaku shuppankai, 1977.

———. *Nihon chinrōdō shi ron* [A history of Japanese wage labor]. Tōkyō daigaku shuppankai, 1955.

———. *Nihon no rekishi.* Vol. 22: *Dai Nihon teikoku no shiren* [Trials of the Greater Japanese Empire]. Chūō kōron, 1966.

Suzuki Bunji. *Rōdō undō nijūnen* [20 years in the labor movement]. Ichigensha, 1931.

Tachibana Yūichi. *Hyōden: Yokoyama Gennosuke* [A critical biography of Yokoyama Gennosuke]. Sōjusha, 1979.

Taikakai (Gotō Fumio), ed. *Naimushō shi* [The history of the Home Ministry]. 4 vols. Chihō zaimu kyōkai, 1971–72.

Takahashi Kamekichi. *Nihon shihonshugi hattatsu shi* [A history of the development of Japanese capitalism]. Nihon hyōronsha, 1929.

Takahashi Yūsai. *Takahashi Yūsai shi dai 2-kai danwa sokkiroku* [Transcript of the second interview with Mr. Takahashi Yūsai]. Naiseishi kenkyū shiryō, no. 17. Naiseishi kenkyūkai, 1964.

Takemae Eiji. *Sengo rōdō kaikaku: GHQ rōdō seisaku shi* [Postwar labor reform: A history of GHQ's labor policies]. Tōkyō daigaku shuppankai, 1982.

Takemura Tamirō. "Jinushisei no dōyō to nōrin kanryō—Kosakuhō sōan mondai to Ishiguro Tadaatsu no shisō" [Instability in the landlord system and the Agriculture and Forestry bureaucrats—the issue of draft tenancy bills and the thought of Ishiguro Tadaatsu]. *Kindai Nihon shisō shi taikei.* Vol. 5: *Kindai Nihon keizai shisō shi,* pp. 323–56. Edited by Chō Yukio and Sumiya Kazuhiko. Yūhikaku, 1969.

Taketomi Tokitoshi. "Sengo no sūsei to taiōsaku" [Postwar trends and how to deal with them]. *Kensei* 2 (January 1919): 26–30.

Tanaka Giichi. "Seiyūkai naikaku no shisei" [The policies of the Seiyūkai cabinet]. *Seiyū,* no. 317 (July 1927), pp. 2–7.

Tazawa Yoshiharu. "Fusengo ni okeru seikai no bun'ya o ronjite, chihō gikai ni oyobu" [The political world after universal suffrage, with reference to the prefectural assemblies]. *Shimin* 22 (January 1927): 2–8.

———. *Seiji kyōiku kōwa* [Lectures on political education]. Shinseisha, 1926.

Tazawa Yoshiharu kinenkai, ed. *Tazawa Yoshiharu*. Tazawa Yoshiharu kinenkai, 1954.

Teikoku gikai kizokuin iinkai giji sokkiroku [Records of committee proceedings in the House of Peers of the Imperial Diet]. Kizokuin jimukyoku, particularly 1919–31.

Teikoku gikai shūgiin giji sokkiroku [Records of the proceedings of the Lower House of the Imperial Diet]. Naikaku insatsukyoku, particularly 1919–31.

Teikoku gikai shūgiin iinkai giroku [Records of committee proceedings in the Lower House of the Imperial Diet]. Shūgiin jimukyoku, particularly 1919–31.

Tezuka Kazuaki. "Senzen no rōdō kumiai hōan mondai to kyū-rōdō kumiaihō no keisei to tenkai" [The question of prewar labor union legislation and the making and evolution of the old Trade Union Law]. Pt. 2. *Shakai kagaku kenkyū* 23 (November 1971): 137–66.

Tomita Aijirō. "Sangyō heiwa e no michi" [The road to industrial peace]. *Shimin* 26 (June 1931): 2–4.

Tomita Kōjirō. "Sangyō teikoku no kempō to shite no kōjōhō" [The Factory Law: the constitution of our industrial empire]. *Rōdō oyobi sangyō*, no. 61 (September 1916), pp. 34–36.

Toriumi Yasushi. "Hara naikaku hōkaigo ni okeru 'kyokoku itchi naikaku' rosen no tenkai to zasetsu" [The rise and fall of the "whole-nation cabinet" idea following the collapse of the Hara cabinet]. *Tōkyō daigaku kyōyōgakubu jimbun kagaku kiō*, no. 54 (1972), pp. 65–122.

Tōyama Shigeki, and Adachi Yoshiko. *Kindai Nihon seiji shi hikkei* [A handbook of modern Japanese political history]. Iwanami shoten, 1961.

Tsurumi Yūsuke. *Gotō Shimpei*. 4 vols. Gotō Shimpei haku denki hensankai, 1937–38.

Uemura Kōsaku. "Rōdō hoken jisshi ni tsuite" [On the enactment of labor insurance]. *Kensei* 2 (February 1919): 10–12.

Ueno Terumasa. "Dai ichiji sekai taisengo no Nihon rōdō no tenkai—kaigun kōshō ni okeru rōdō undō to rōdō seisaku" [The development of the Japanese labor movement after World War I—the labor movement and labor policy in naval arsenals]. *Nihon shi kenkyū*, no. 163 (March 1976), pp. 170–88.

Ujihara Shōjirō and Hagiwara Susumu. "Sangyō hōkoku undō no haikei" [Background to the Industrial Patriotic movement]. *Fuashizumu-ki no kokka to shakai*. Vol. 6: *Undō to teikō (part 1)*, pp. 195–234. Edited by Tōkyō daigaku shakai kagaku kenkyūjo. Tōkyō daigaku shuppankai, 1979.

"Wagakuni ni okeru rōdō iinkai no gaikyō" [The state of works councils in our country]. *Rōdō jihō* 11 (January 1934): 5–9.

Wakatsuki Reijirō. *Kofūan kaikoroku* [The memoirs of Wakatsuki Reijirō]. Yomiuri shimbunsha, 1950.

————. "Sengo no saisei o ronzu" [A discussion of postwar public finance]. *Kensei* 2 (January 1919): 30–36.

Watanabe Haruo. *Omoide no kakumeikatachi* [Revolutionaries I have known]. Yoshiga shoten, 1968.

Watanabe Osamu. "1920 nendai ni okeru tennōsei kokka no chian hōsei saihensei o megutte" [The reconstitution of the public peace laws under the emperor-system state of the 1920s]. *Shakai kagaku kenkyū* 27, no. 5–6 (March 1976), pp. 153–237.

Watanabe Tōru. "Nihon ni okeru rōdō kumiai hōan no tōjō o megutte" [The advent of labor union legislation in Japan]. 2 parts. *Nihon rōdō kyōkai zasshi*, no. 87 (June 1966), pp. 2–10; no. 88 (July 1966), pp. 2–11.

XYZ. "Shakai minshūtō no seitai" [The true colors of the Social Democratic Party]. *Shakai undō ōrai* 2 (February 1930): 3–85.

Yamamoto Teijirō. "Seiyūkai no shin-seisaku" [The Seiyūkai's new policies]. *Seiyū*, no. 296 (November 1925), pp. 2–16.

Yamanaka Tokutarō. *Nihon rōdō kumiaihō kenkyū* [A study of Japan's labor union bill]. Moriyama shoten, 1931.

Yano Tatsuo. "Rōdō hōan o meguru gyōsei chōsakai gijiroku" [Minutes of the Investigative Commission on Administration, relating to labor legislation]. 2 parts. *Handai hōgaku*, no. 105 (January 1978), pp. 137–75; no. 106 (March 1978), pp. 171–204.

————. "Taishō-ki rōdō rippō no ichidammen—rōdō sōgi chōteihō no seiritsu katei" [One aspect of labor legislation during the Taishō era—the process behind the enactment of the Labor Disputes Conciliation Law]. *Hōseishi kenkyū*, no. 27 (1977), pp. 105–40.

Yasuda Hiroshi. "Seitō seiji taiseika no rōdō seisaku—Hara naikaku-ki ni okeru rōdō kumiai kōnin mondai" [Labor policy in the era of party politics—the question of officially recognizing labor unions during the Hara cabinet]. *Rekishigaku kenkyū*, no. 420 (May 1975), pp. 14–28.

Yasui Eiji. *Rōdō undō no kenkyū* [Studies of the labor movement]. Nihon daigaku, 1923.

————. "Wagakuni rōdō undō no sūsei" [Trends in our nation's labor movement]. Pt. 2. *Shimin* 17 (September 1922): 17–21.

————. *Yasui Eiji shi danwa dai 1-kai sokkiroku* [Transcript of the first interview with Mr. Yasui Eiji]. Naiseishi kenkyū shiryō, no. 14. Naiseishi kenkyūkai, 1964.

Yokoyama Gennosuke. *Nihon no kasō shakai* [Japan's lower strata of society]. 1899; reprinted in *Yokoyama Gennosuke zenshū*. Vol. 1. Meiji bunken, 1972.

Yomiuri shimbunsha, ed. *Shōwa shi no tennō* [The emperor in Shōwa history]. Vol. 17. Yomiuri shimbunsha, 1972.

Yonekawa Norinari. "Kyōchōkai no seiritsu katei—wagakuni ni okeru rōshi kankei antei no tame no minkan kikan no kōsō" [The formation of the Kyōchōkai—the thinking behind the private body that aimed to stabilize our nation's labor-management relations]. *Niigata daigaku keizaigaku nempō*, no. 3 (1979), pp. 55–77.

Yoshida Kyūichi. *Nihon shakai jigyō no rekishi* [A history of social work in Japan]. Keisō shobō, 1966.

Yoshida Shigeru. "Rōdō kyōyaku tokushūgō" [Special issue on labor agreements]. *Shakai seisaku jihō*, no. 132 (September 1931), pp. 1–4.

———. "Tokushūgō no hakkan ni atarite" [Preface to the special issue]. *Shakai seisaku jihō*, no. 146 (November 1932), pp. 1–4.

Yoshida Shigeru denki kankō henshū iinkai, ed. *Yoshida Shigeru*. Yoshida Shigeru denki kankō henshū iinkai, 1969.

Yoshii Ken'ichi. "Tazawa Yoshiharu ron" [A study of Tazawa Yoshiharu]. *Jimbun kagaku kenkyū* (Niigata daigaku), no. 53 (March 1978), pp. 1–27.

Yoshii Yoshiko. "Sangyō hōkoku undō—sono seiritsu o megutte" [The formation of the Industrial Patriotic movement]. *Hitotsubashi ronsō* 73 (February 1975): 35–52.

Yoshikawa Kan'ichi. "Fusen dai niji sōsenkyo to musan seitō" [The second general election under universal suffrage and the proletarian parties]. Pt. 2. *Shakai undō ōrai* 2 (April 1930): 20–40.

Yoshimi Yoshiaki. "Tanaka (Gi) naikakuka no chian ijihō kaisei mondai" [The controversial revision of the Peace Preservation Law under the Tanaka Giichi cabinet]. *Rekishigaku kenkyū*, no. 441 (February 1977), pp. 1–17.

Yoshino Kōichi, ed. *Zen Keinosuke tsuisōroku* [Recollections of Zen Keinosuke]. Nihon dantai seimei hoken kabushiki kaisha, 1959.

Yoshioka Shigeyoshi. "Rōdō kumiai kaigi no honshitsu to sono dōkō" [The nature of the Congress of Labor Unions and its future]. *Shakai seisaku jihō*, no. 146 (November 1932), pp. 352–63.

"Zenkoku sangyō dantai rengōkai no seiritsu" [The establishment of the National Federation of Industrial Organizations]. *Rōdō*, no. 240 (June 1931), pp. 124–25.

SOURCES IN ENGLISH

Abegglen, James. *The Japanese Factory: Aspects of its Social Organization.* Glencoe: The Free Press, 1958.

Ayusawa, Iwao F. *A History of Labor in Modern Japan.* Honolulu: East-West Center Press, 1946.

———. *Industrial Conditions and Labour Legislation in Japan.* Studies and Reports, ser. B (Economic Conditions), no. 16. Geneva: International Labour Office, 1926.

———. *International Labor Legislation.* Columbia University Studies in History, Economy and Public Law, vol. 91, no. 2. New York: Columbia University, 1920.

Beard, Charles A. *The Administration and Politics of Tokyo: A Survey and Opinions.* New York: Macmillan, 1923.

Beckmann, George M., and Okubo, Genji. *The Japanese Communist Party, 1922–1945.* Stanford: Stanford University Press, 1968.

Berger, Gordon Mark. *Parties Out of Power in Japan, 1931–1941.* Princeton: Princeton University Press, 1977.

Brody, David. "The Rise and Decline of Welfare Capitalism," in *Change and*

Continuity in Twentieth-Century America: The 1920's, pp. 147–78. Edited by John Braeman, Robert H. Bremner, and David Brody. Columbus: Ohio State University Press, 1968.

Cole, G. D. H. *The World of Labour*. 4th ed. London: G. Bell and Sons, 1919.

Conroy, Hilary. *The Japanese Seizure of Korea: 1868–1910*. Philadelphia: University of Pennsylvania Press, 1960.

Crowley, James B. *Japan's Quest for Autonomy: National Security and Foreign Policy, 1930–1938*. Princeton: Princeton University Press, 1966.

Dore, R. P. "The Modernizer as a Special Case: Japanese Factory Legislation, 1882–1911." *Comparative Studies in Society and History* 11 (October 1969): 433–50.

Dower, John W. *Empire and Aftermath: Yoshida Shigeru and the Japanese Experience, 1878–1954*. Cambridge: Council on East Asian Studies, Harvard University, 1979.

Dublin, Thomas. *Women at Work: Transformation of Work and Community in Lowell, Massachusetts, 1826–1860*. New York: Columbia University Press, 1979.

Duke, Benjamin C. *Japan's Militant Teachers*. Honolulu: University Press of Hawaii, 1973.

Duus, Peter. "Nagai Ryūtarō and the 'White Peril,' 1905–1944." *Journal of Asian Studies* 31 (November 1971): 41–48.

————. "Nagai Ryūtarō: The Tactical Dilemmas of Reform." *Personality in Japanese History*, pp. 399–424. Edited by Albert M. Craig and Donald H. Shively. Berkeley: University of California Press, 1970.

————. *Party Rivalry and Political Change in Taishō Japan*. Cambridge: Harvard University Press, 1968.

————, and Okimoto, Daniel I. "Fascism and the History of Pre-War Japan: The Failure of a Concept." *Journal of Asian Studies* 39 (November 1979): 65–76.

Emy, H. V. *Liberals, Radicals and Social Politics, 1892–1914*. Cambridge: Cambridge University Press, 1973.

Fletcher, William Miles, III. *The Search for a New Order: Intellectuals and Fascism in Prewar Japan*. Chapel Hill: University of North Carolina Press, 1982.

Garon, Sheldon M. "The Imperial Bureaucracy and Labor Policy in Postwar Japan." *Journal of Asian Studies* 43 (May 1984): 441–57.

Gordon, Andrew. "Business and the Corporate State: The Business Lobby and Bureaucrats on Labor." *Essays in Japanese Business History*. Edited by William D. Wray. Cambridge: Council on East Asian Studies, Harvard University, forthcoming.

————. *The Evolution of Labor Relations in Japan: Heavy Industry, 1853–1955*. Cambridge: Council on East Asian Studies, Harvard University, 1985.

————. "Workers, Managers, and Bureaucrats in Japan: Labor Relations in Heavy Industry, 1853–1945." Ph.D. diss., Harvard University, 1981.

Griffin, Edward Geary. "The Adoption of Universal Manhood Suffrage in Japan." Ph.D. diss., Columbia University, 1965.

Hamerow, Theodore S. *The Social Foundations of German Unification 1858–*

1871: Struggles and Accomplishments. Princeton: Princeton University Press, 1972.

Hamilton, Nora. *The Limits of State Autonomy: Post-Revolutionary Mexico.* Princeton: Princeton University Press, 1982.

Hane, Mikiso. *Peasants, Rebels, and Outcastes.* New York: Pantheon, 1982.

Harari, Ehud. *The Politics of Labor Legislation in Japan.* Berkeley: University of California Press, 1973.

Hastings, Sally Ann. "The Government, the Citizen, and the Creation of a New Sense of Community: Social Welfare, Local Organizations, and Dissent in Tokyo, 1905–1937." Ph.D. diss., University of Chicago, 1980.

Hay, J. Roy. *The Origins of the Liberal Welfare Reforms, 1906–1914.* London: Macmillan, 1975.

Heclo, Hugh. *Modern Social Politics in Britain and Sweden.* New Haven: Yale University Press, 1974.

Inagami, Takeshi. "Labor Front Unification and Zenmin Rokyo: The Emergence of Neo-corporatism." *Japan Labor Bulletin* 25 (May 1986): 5–8.

International Labour Office. *Industrial Labour in Japan.* Geneva: International Labour Office, 1933.

Johnson, Chalmers. *MITI and the Japanese Miracle.* Stanford: Stanford University Press, 1982.

Kidd, Yasue Aoki. *Women Workers in the Japanese Cotton Mills: 1880–1920.* Cornell University East Asia Papers, no. 20. Ithaca: Cornell China-Japan Program, 1978.

Kinzley, William Dean. "The Quest for Industrial Harmony in Modern Japan: The Kyochokai, 1919–1946." Ph.D. diss., University of Washington, 1984.

Kubota, Akira. *Higher Civil Servants in Postwar Japan.* Princeton: Princeton University Press, 1969.

Large, Stephen S. "Nishio Suehiro and the Japanese Social Democratic Movement, 1920–1940." *Journal of Asian Studies* 36 (November 1976): 37–56.

———. *Organized Workers and Socialist Politics in Interwar Japan.* Cambridge: Cambridge University Press, 1981.

———. *The Yūaikai, 1912–1919: The Rise of Labor in Japan.* Tokyo: Sophia University, 1972.

Levine, Solomon B. "Japan's Tripartite Labor Relations Commissions." *Labor Law Journal* 6 (July 1955): 462–82.

Lockwood, William W. *The Economic Development of Japan.* Princeton: Princeton University Press, 1968.

Maier, Charles S. "Between Taylorism and Technocracy: European Ideologies and the Vision of Industrial Productivity in the 1920s." *Journal of Contemporary History* 5, no. 2 (1970), pp. 27–61.

Marshall, Byron K. *Capitalism and Nationalism in Prewar Japan: The Ideology of the Business Elite, 1868–1941.* Stanford: Stanford University Press, 1967.

———. "Growth and Conflict in Japanese Higher Education, 1905–1930." *Conflict in Modern Japanese History,* pp. 276–94. Edited by Tetsuo Najita and J. Victor Koschmann. Princeton: Princeton University Press, 1982.

Maruyama, Masao. *Thought and Behavior in Modern Japanese Politics*. Edited by Ivan Morris. London: Oxford University Press, 1969.

Mason, T. W. "Labour in the Third Reich, 1933–1939." *Past and Present* 33 (April 1966): 112–41.

McDonald, G. W., and Gospel, H. F. "The Mond-Turner Talks, 1927–33: A Study in Industrial Co-operation." *The Historical Journal* 16 (December 1973): 807–29.

Mitchell, Richard H. *Thought Control in Prewar Japan*. Ithaca: Cornell University Press, 1976.

Mochizuki, Mike Masato. "Managing and Influencing the Japanese Legislative Process: The Role of Parties and the National Diet." Ph.D. diss., Harvard University, 1982.

Mommsen, W. J., ed. *The Emergence of the Welfare State in Britain and Germany, 1850–1950*. London: Croom Helm, 1981.

Moore, Joe. *Japanese Workers and the Struggle for Power, 1945–1947*. Madison: University of Wisconsin Press, 1983.

Najita, Tetsuo. *Hara Kei and the Politics of Compromise, 1905–1915*. Cambridge: Harvard University Press, 1967.

Notar, Ernest J. "Japan's Wartime Labor Policy: A Search for Method." *Journal of Asian Studies* 44 (February 1985): 311–28.

———. "Labor Unions and the *Sangyō Hōkoku* Movement 1930–1945: A Japanese Model for Industrial Relations." Ph.D. diss., University of California, Berkeley, 1979.

Notehelfer, F. G. "Japan's First Pollution Incident." *Journal of Japanese Studies* 1 (Spring 1975): 351–83.

———. *Kōtoku Shūsui, Portrait of a Japanese Radical*. Cambridge: Cambridge University Press, 1971.

Ogata, Kiyoshi. *The Co-operative Movement in Japan*. London: P. S. King and Son, 1923.

Okochi, Kazuo. *Labor in Modern Japan*. Tokyo: The Science Council of Japan, 1958.

Ouchi, William G. *Theory Z: How American Business Can Meet the Japanese Challenge*. Reading, Mass.: Addison-Wesley Publishing, 1981.

Pascale, Richard Tanner, and Athos, Anthony G. *The Art of Japanese Management: Applications for American Executives*. New York: Simon and Schuster, 1981.

Patrick, Hugh T. "The Economic Muddle of the 1920s." *Dilemmas of Growth in Prewar Japan*, pp. 211–66. Edited by James W. Morley. Princeton: Princeton University Press, 1971.

———, ed. *Japanese Industrialization and Its Social Consequences*. Berkeley: University of California Press, 1976.

Paxton, Robert O. *Vichy France: Old Guard and New Order, 1940–1944*. New York: W. W. Norton and Co., 1972.

Payne, Stanley G. *Fascism: Comparison and Definition*. Madison: University of Wisconsin Press, 1980.

Pempel, T. J. *Policy and Politics in Japan*. Philadelphia: Temple University Press, 1982.

————, and Tsunekawa, Keiichi, "Corporatism Without Labor? The Japanese Anomaly." *Trends Toward Corporatist Intermediation,* pp. 231–70. Edited by Philippe C. Schmitter and Gerhard Lehmbruch. Beverly Hills: SAGE Publications, 1979.

Pipkin, Charles Wooten. *Social Politics and Modern Democracies.* 2 vols. New York: Macmillan, 1931.

Poulantzas, Nicos. "The Problem of the Capitalist State." *Ideology in Social Science,* pp. 238–53. Edited by Robin Blackburn. New York: Vintage Books, 1972.

Pyle, Kenneth. "Advantages of Followership: German Economics and Japanese Bureaucrats, 1890–1925." *Journal of Japanese Studies* 1 (Autumn 1974): 127–64.

————. "The Technology of Japanese Nationalism: The Local Improvement Movement 1900–1918." *Journal of Asian Studies* 33 (November 1973): 51–65.

Redford, Lawrence H., ed. *The Occupation of Japan: Economic Policy and Reform.* Norfolk, Va.: MacArthur Memorial, 1980.

Roth, Guenther. *The Social Democrats in Imperial Germany: A Study in Working-Class Isolation and National Integration.* Totowa, N.J.: Bedminster Press, 1963.

Sarti, Roland. *Fascism and the Industrial Leadership in Italy 1919–1940.* Berkeley: University of California Press, 1971.

Scalapino, Robert. *Democracy and the Party Movement in Prewar Japan: The Failure of the First Attempt.* Berkeley: University of California Press, 1953.

————. *The Early Japanese Labor Movement: Labor and Politics in a Developing Society.* Berkeley: Institute of East Asian Studies/Center for Japanese Studies, University of California, 1984.

Schmitter, Philippe C. "Still the Century of Corporatism?" *Review of Politics* 36 (January 1974): 85–131.

Schneiderman, Jeremiah. *Sergei Zubatov and Revolutionary Marxism: The Struggle for the Working Class in Tsarist Russia.* Ithaca: Cornell University Press, 1976.

Schoenbaum, David. *Hitler's Social Revolution.* Garden City, N.Y.: Doubleday and Co., 1966.

Semmel, Bernard. *Imperialism and Social Reform: English Social-Imperial Thought, 1895–1914.* Cambridge: Harvard University Press, 1960.

Sheehan, James J. *The Career of Lujo Brentano.* Chicago: University of Chicago Press, 1966.

Sheldon, Charles D. "The Politics of the Civil War of 1868." *Modern Japan: Aspects of History, Literature and Society,* pp. 27–51. Edited by W. G. Beasley. Berkeley: University of California Press, 1975.

Shirai, Taishiro, ed. *Contemporary Industrial Relations in Japan.* Madison: University of Wisconsin Press, 1983.

Silberman, Bernard S. "Bureaucratic Decision-making in Japan: 1868–1925." *Journal of Asian Studies* 29 (February 1970): 347–62.

————, and Harootunian, H. D., eds. *Japan in Crisis: Essays on Taishō Democracy.* Princeton: Princeton University Press, 1974.

Skocpol, Theda. "Bringing the State Back In: Strategies of Analysis in Current Research." *Bringing the State Back In,* pp. 3–43. Edited by Peter B. Evans, Dietrich Rueschemeyer, and Theda Skocpol. Cambridge: Cambridge University Press, 1985.

Smethurst, Richard J. *A Social Basis for Prewar Japanese Militarism: The Army and the Rural Community.* Berkeley: University of California Press, 1974.

Smith, Thomas C. "The Right to Benevolence: Dignity and Japanese Workers, 1890–1920." *Comparative Studies in Society and History* 26 (October 1984): 587–613.

Spaulding, Robert M., Jr. "Japan's 'New Bureaucrats,' 1932–45." *Crisis Politics in Prewar Japan,* pp. 51–70. Edited by George M. Wilson. Tokyo: Sophia University, 1970.

Sumiya, Mikio. "The Emergence of Modern Japan." *Workers and Employers in Japan,* pp. 15–48. Edited by Kazuo Okochi, Bernard Karsh, and Solomon B. Levine. Tokyo: Tokyo University Press, 1973.

Supreme Commander for the Allied Powers. Government Section. *Political Reorientation of Japan: September 1945 to September 1948.* Vol. 1. Washington: U.S. Government Printing Office, 1948.

Taira, Koji. *Economic Development and the Labor Market in Japan.* New York: Columbia University Press, 1970.

———. "Factory Legislation and Management Modernization during Japan's Industrialization 1896–1916." *Business History Review* 44 (Spring 1970): 84–109.

———, and Levine, Solomon B. "Japan's Industrial Relations: A Social Compact Emerges." *Industrial Relations in a Decade of Economic Change,* pp. 247–300. Edited by Hervey Juris, Mark Thompson, and Wilbur Daniels. Madison, Wis.: Industrial Relations Research Association, 1985.

Tazawa, Yoshiharu. "Moral Significance of 'Harmonious Cooperation,'" *Shakai seisaku jihō,* no. 21 (May 1922), English section, pp. 1–7.

Tharp, Mike. "Getting Back in Touch." *Far Eastern Economic Review,* 1 March 1984, pp. 32–33.

Thompson, F. M. L. "Social Control in Victorian Britain." *Economic History Review* 34 (May 1981): 189–208.

Tiedemann, Arthur E. "The Hamaguchi Cabinet: First Phase, July 1929–February 1930: A Study in Japanese Parliamentary Government." Ph.D. diss., Columbia University, 1959.

Tipton, Elise Kurashige. "The Civil Police in the Suppression of the Prewar Japanese Left." Ph.D. diss., Indiana University, 1977.

Totten, George O. "Collective Bargaining and Works Councils as Innovations in Industrial Relations in Japan during the 1920s." *Aspects of Social Change in Modern Japan,* pp. 203–43. Edited by R. P. Dore. Princeton: Princeton University Press, 1970.

———. *The Social Democratic Movement in Prewar Japan.* New Haven: Yale University Press, 1966.

Turner, John Elliot. "The Origin and Development of the Kenseikai (Constitutional Political Association) of Japan, 1913–1927." M.A. thesis, University of Minnesota, 1949.

Vogel, Ezra F. *Japan as Number One: Lessons for America.* Cambridge: Harvard University Press, 1979.

Weiner, Susan Beth. "Bureaucracy and Politics in the 1930s: The Career of Gotō Fumio." Ph.D. diss., Harvard University, 1984.

Westney, D. Eleanor. "The Emulation of Western Organizations in Meiji Japan: The Case of the Paris Prefecture of Police and the Keishi-chō." *Journal of Japanese Studies* 8 (Summer 1982): 307–42.

Wray, Harry, and Conroy, Hilary, eds. *Japan Examined: Perspectives on Modern Japanese History.* Honolulu: University of Hawaii Press, 1983.

Wray, William D. "Asō Hisashi and the Search for Renovation in the 1930s." *Papers on Japan,* 5:55–97. Cambridge: East Asian Research Center, Harvard University, 1970.

Yasko, Richard Anthony. "Hiranuma Kiichirō and Conservative Politics in Prewar Japan." Ph.D. diss., University of Chicago, 1973.

Young, A. Morgan. *Japan Under Taisho Tenno, 1912–1926.* London: Allen and Unwin, 1928.

Yoshino, M. Y. *Japan's Managerial System: Tradition and Innovation.* Cambridge: M.I.T. Press, 1968.

Index

Compositor:	Huron Valley Graphics, Inc.
Text:	10/13 Sabon
Display:	Sabon
Printer:	Maple-Vail Book Mfg. Group
Binder:	Maple-Vail Book Mfg. Group